ML

KU-479-708

CURTAINS!!!

OR
A NEW LIFE FOR OLD THEATRES

05842634

ISBN 0 903931 42 7

published by

John Offord (Publications) Limited
in association with the Curtains!!! Committee
which operates under the auspices of SAVE Britain's Heritage

Printed by Eastbourne Printers Ltd.

D
725.82209'41
CUR

CURTAINS!!!

OR
A NEW LIFE FOR OLD THEATRES

being a complete Gazetteer of all the surviving
pre-1914 theatres, music halls of Great Britain
whether in theatrical use or not, whether complete
or fragmentary, together with maps, lists of demolitions,
notes on the most prolific architects, and with,
contributions from actors, engineers, architects,
historians and managers.

researched, compiled and written by the
Curtains!!! Committee: Christopher Brereton,
David F. Cheshire, John Earl, Victor Glasstone,
Iain Mackintosh and Michael Sell.

with additional contributions from Ken Dodd,
Clare Ferraby, Francis Reid, Derek Sugden,
Nick Thompson and David Wilmore

edited by Iain Mackintosh and Michael Sell
photographic editor Victor Glasstone

Contents

Foreword   Ken Dodd   7

Introduction   Iain Mackintosh   9

Sleeping Beauties   Christopher Brereton   19

Dressing the House   Nicholas Thompson and Clare Ferraby   41

The Preservation Game   John Earl   45

The Need to Know   Michael Sell   61

Restoring the Gaiety   Victor Glasstone   67

Mechanical Archaeology in the Theatre   David Wilmore   71

Engineering the Restoration   Derek Sugden   75

Restored Theatres Can be Viable   Francis Reid   79

The Gazetteer
   Key to the Gazetteer   82
   A to Z   83
   Historical Profile   197
   The Principal Architects   211
   List of Demolished Theatres   219
   Maps of existing buildings   225
   Statistical Summary   232

Acknowledgements   233

Biographical Notes on Contributors   234

Bibliography   235

Cover photograph
Douglas Isle of Man, Gaiety, one of Frank Matcham's finest theatres (1900), recently restored to its original lush magnificence (consultant Victor Glasstone).   *Victor Glasstone*

Facing page photograph
A success story: Nottingham Theatre Royal - renovated 1978   *John Donat*

Manchester Palace—renovated 1981

Victor Glasstone

Foreword

Ken Dodd OBE

The greatest moments of my life have been hearing laughter and seeing happy audiences in the famous theatres of this country. This has been my privilege at theatres as different as the 'Old Shakey' — The Shakespeare Theatre Liverpool and 'the posh one' — The Shakespeare Memorial Theatre Stratford, and it really is the most beautiful sound that I know. I have played a large number of our old and new theatres and had the delight of reopening the superb Theatre Royal Nottingham which contrasted with the sadness of working the last days of other great halls like the Glasgow Alhambra. I tell everyone that a visit to a live theatre show is the greatest entertainment experience they will ever have because when they are in a theatre they don't just watch the show, they take part in it.

This book is a celebration of buildings of a very particular nature — **Theatres** — temples of arts, emporiums of fun, forums of debate and argument. Whatever your favourite kind of theatrical performance it can only truly by brought to life in a real theatre. These great old theatres have tradition, . atmosphere, ghosts and memories of great actors, great entertainers and great shows. But as you know we have artistes and actors today who are just as great and skilled as the ghosts of the past and these beautiful theatres still provide audiences and performers alike with that most magical experience of our lives — a live show!

Looking at some of the entries in this book reminds me of the many fine buildings which exist but which we often overlook and this brings into question the manner in which we, as a nation, support the theatre.

The basis of our national policy is to provide grants and subsidies but this can become a two-edged sword. Ideally it should provide the life blood of the theatre but sometimes it seems to cushion ineffectual management and apathetic audiences from the realities of the present economic situation. It may be that the time for a new look at this philosophy is not far distant and perhaps with the exception of some larger opera companies and the big ballet productions maybe we should instead inject money into preserving the fabric of our many fine theatres so that we always have the buildings — it would then be up to impresarios and producers to provide the public with viable shows throughout the year. Ironically variety has had little or no help through grant aid and yet has often been called upon to make money to bail out theatres which have run into difficulties with a largely subsidised programme. The message seems to me to be clear — if some of those venues which appear on these pages are to survive then the theatre industry must come to terms with economic reality and particularly, be much more successful in its marketing policy.

Although I fought hard to save the more modern Royal Court in Liverpool and like to think that my show made a substantial contribution to the saving of the

Ken Dodd pictured in the No. 1 dressing room of Nottingham Theatre Royal prior to the gala reopening performance on 7th Feburary, 1978.

John Donat

Manchester Palace I will not subscribe to the view that all theatres must be saved — they must stand a chance of economic success. But no theatre can be a success unless it is a good working instrument with the right atmosphere. The **Curtains!!!** Gazetteer guides us to these theatres dark or alive which have that elusive atmosphere.

There is a continuity of live theatre certainly since Greek and Roman times and I would like to think that theatre will be with us 10,000 years from now for there is a basic human hunger for artistic communication; a natural desire for entertainment and intellectual stimulation and a fascination in watching human beings act out our comedies and tragedies. This sense of continuity can be very marked and I feel that revisiting a theatre is like renewing a relationship with a very precious member fo the family. Similarly it is like being bereaved when one hears of a theatre being closed whilst it is always a joy to be involved with the birth of a new or rebuilt theatre.

It is my pleasure to share the contents of this book with you and I hope it goes some way to make us all more aware of those theatres which are still in use as well as those which might be revitalised. I have had the pleasure of appearing in the majority of old theatres — my life time ambition is to play them all — and I am grateful for the experience which I would like to extend to you.

Introduction

Iain Mackintosh

Theatre Design Consultant and Chairman of Curtains!!!

The product of the **Curtains!!!** project is twofold: this book and a travelling exhibition. In presenting both to the British public the members of the committee are aware that they must first address two distinct specialised audiences and that only with the support of these two groups will the aim of the **Curtains!!!** project be achieved. This is to search out and identify Britain's finest old theatres and, whether or not they are in use at this moment (and many are not), to marshal evidence and argument that as many as possible should be retained for the pleasure of this and of future generations.

The two specialised audiences are the conservationist lobby and the theatrical profession.

The conservationist lobby

There is in Britain a long standing tradition of caring for our past. But until recently the conservationist image has been donnish if not eccentric, country town rather than city centre, upper middle class and hence elitest. In the seventies this changed and groups such as the parent body to **Curtains!!!**, **SAVE Britain's Heritage,** and museums such as the Victoria and Albert have captured the imagination of a wider public with well researched and highly polemical books and exhibitions on such themes as The Country House, The Parish Church and Railway Stations. Thus the **Curtains!!!** project can be seen first and foremost as a focus on yet another building type so long taken for granted, especially in the philistine fifties and sixties when so much was lost, The British Theatre.

To enlist the help of the conservationist lobby, which can encompass both civic societies and enlighted planners, is not going to be easy for four reasons. First is the problem that what really matters about a theatre, makes it excellent and of present and future worth as a setting for live performance rather than merely interesting or pleasant, is the quality of its interior. Not only are the auditoriums of much greater importance than facades but embellishments such as porticoes are exceptionally rare. Most late nineteenth century theatres are on infill sites and intrude so little on the High Street that their modestly decorated doors, windows and billboards have been hurried past by shoppers and Pevsner alike. Thus if the curtain was last rung down years ago, the interior boarded up, nobody notices when the demolition men finally move in.

Second, is the difficulty for the layman in assessing the total worth of a theatre interior without a show on the stage. Remove the incandescent glow from the stage which lights up capital, cornice and caryatid as well as the craning faces of the Sickertian gallery goers, and all the cultivated architectural connoisseur may see is an illogical, illiterate and apparently ill considered jumble from the plasterworker's catalogue. An empty theatre, in professional jargon a 'dark' theatre, is dead. An empty railway station has more glamour.

Third is unfamiliarity with the architects. Frank Matcham, Britain's most prolific theatre architect and responsible for 150 theatres, did not make the D.N.B. (of specialised theatre architects only one, C. J. Phipps, did). Architectural historians have simply avoided the subject altogether, both in their learned volumes and in otherwise excellent guide books.

A fourth difficulty for the eager conservationist is often the lack of enthusiasm shown by the theatre profession. Rather than welcoming the rediscovery of a potentially first class theatre the arts administrators retort that now is not a good time (is it ever?) to add to their problems. It is, they say, difficult enough to keep open the theatres they already have and therefore no sound economic reasons exist for even considering a new life for an old theatre.

The seasoned fighter, through disappointed by such a rebuff, should not be daunted. He will know that he is fighting for the next generation as much as for this. He did not have to prove instant economic viability for the parish church or the country house. Provided that he is convinced of the excellence of the building for which he is fighting then he will, it is to be hoped, take the long view. He will examine the possibility of moth balling or, better, an interim use such as bingo and remember that the sound economic equation alters each decade, that the ability of theatre fashion along with theatre finance to shift with the years is infinite and that only demolition, like death, is finite and final.

Conservation and the theatre profession

This has not been a hopeful introduction to the second specialised audience to whom the **Curtains!!!** project is addressed. And before casting around for rays of hope it is as well to realise that much of the theatre profession is going to be unenthusiastic for a variety of reasons.

First, as has been indicated, there are the fears and worries displayed by the administrators and arts organisations. Recession and government cuts have only exacerbated a dangerous trait in any bureaucracy organised around 'representative' committees, which is to protect the status quo and to resist any increase in the number of dependents when the gruel is getting thinner. The layman may wonder why dependent companies are allowed to struggle to make ends meet in the wrong theatre in the wrong part of the town when one of the sleeping beauties rediscovered by the **Curtains!!!** team needs only a kiss of life and a quick overhaul. But, 'now is not the time' and soldiering on in the wrong building continues to be the order of the day. It is ironic that the prolongation of an inadequate interim solution to a housing the arts problem can result in first the destruction of the more appropriate 'Royal' and second the slow death of the ill housed activity which could have made the 'Royal' work.

Even more sinister is the result when the Government appears to echo the apparently reasonable belief of many Artistic Directors that theatre is not a question of buildings but a question of people. It follows from this that capital works will receive the lowest priority. Indeed it was the announcement on 30th September, 1976 of the first and hardly noticed cut by Government, the reduction of the annual Housing the Arts allocation from £1.15 million to £0.5 million that led to the **Curtains!!!** project being set up after the traditional letter to **The Times**. This stressed the fact that what little was left of the dwindling stock of fine theatre was under threat through natural deterioration after 75 to 100 years service.

People before buildings is fine as an argument against imposing marble clad mausoleums on mid-west campuses or on third world capital cities. But as an argument that allows the destruction of marvellously human scaled theatres which bring actor and audience joyfully together in a close and powerful celebration of life, it is clearly ludicrous. But, alas, it is virtually impossible to underestimate the English intellectual's capacity to ignore and misunderstand the effect of environment upon creativity or performance. Nowhere has this been more apparent than in the theatre: in 1896 Edwin O. Sachs, author of the definitive and pan-European **Modern Opera Houses and Theatres,** described the British as "a people practically devoid of any feeling of architecture". Today directors and designers too often think of their work as taking place in a black box in which only the actor and the scenery is to register and into which people but not architecture are allowed to penetrate.

Another theatre lobby exists where support for breathing new life into old theatres may be sought. This is the grouping of theatre technicians, stage designers, architects and professional theatre consultants. There is no doubt that among all four can be found those who have worked hard to bring about the successes chronicled in these pages and in the travelling exhibition. On the other side of the coin are the times when the fine old theatres have received the thumbs down from those over anxious to have in their place the most modern buildings. This obsession for up-to-date equipment can extend even into listed theatres made safe from enemies without only to have their force diluted by friends within. Thus in one of our three working Georgian playhouses a raked stage complete with a set of working stage machinery has been replaced with an inappropriate flat stage for the sake of 'modern' scenic effect. Another unique set of mid Victorian steel machinery, which could easily have been used for the effects appropriate to nineteenth century opera or to pantomime, was junked to make a cheap orchestra room in one of Britain's greatest theatres. Edwardian West End theatres have been painted charcoal grey, while in a recently restored provincial opera house the control board has been placed in the crucial stage box, which produces a lop-sided one eyed effect in the proscenium zone, on the grounds that it was easier and marginally cheaper to put it there rather than centrally in the projection room at the back of the second tier. Almost everywhere the stage lighting obtrudes when a moment's thought could minimise the deleterious effect of the misplacing of necessary but often obtrusive equipment.

And yet the disastrous actions of these friends of the theatre should not surprise once it is realised that theatre people, both producers and technicians, generally live in the present. The current show is of greater concern than whether a theatre's architectural effectiveness is maintained rather than diluted. Fortunately the authorities have begun to realise the value of a good piece of theatre architecture and may, therefore, take greater care in future.

This is new. In the last decade those in charge of the dealing of what little is left of Britain's touring theatre had preferred the big barns, often ex movie palaces or theatres rebuilt in the late twenties for big name variety, to the smaller Victorian and Edwardian theatres on the grounds that only the former could provide the big grosses needed by the touring opera and ballet companies. Interestingly the economic argument is now increasingly reversed: the cost of finding 'product' suitable for the huge theatres for the greater part of the year when the lyric companies are not there creates more problems than the reverse situation of shoe horning the big companies into the medium sized theatres which are, for the remainder of the year, full of drama, variety, musicals (amateur or professional) that feels at home in the right size of theatre.

Of course almost any good performer could have told the authorities this home truth years ago. Indeed the best judge of how good a theatre is as a working instrument is often the actor. Occasionally he will be influenced by the state of the dressing rooms as a theatregoer will have his judgement effected by the queuing in tiny bars at the interval. The actor may not know how old the theatre is, who the architect was but he will know if the theatre enhances his performance, makes it easier or more difficult for the magic to happen. Yet, actors are also romantics and have been known to band together to try and save the second rate. This can cause great damage to the conservationist cause in the long term. No good will come of a protest which appears to be more than an indiscriminating attempt to save a theatre on the sole grounds that it provides employment for actors. Job preservation and theatre preservation must often be coupled together but should never be confused one for the other.

London, Hoxton Hall · an 1867 interior restored

Victor Glasstone

Leeds, Grand Theatre · now the home of Opera North   *Victor Glasstone*

The origins of the Curtains!!! project

The **Curtains!!!** project had started, like all good British protests, out of controlled frustration at the failure of authority to halt the steady erosion of the little that remains. A polemical exhibition and book was planned. But soon after the research had started it became apparent that the real enemy was not indifference but ignorance. Nobody knew what old theatres Britain still possessed let alone how good they were. There was simply no inventory whatsoever. Hardly any guide books even mention a town's theatres. Here was a building type which neither architect, historian nor environmental planner had studied let alone catalogued. Meanwhile a number of surveys had been started by various national bodies within the theatre but none had been finished let alone published. Ironically a Theatre Trust had been formed by Act of Parliament without anybody knowing what theatres there were to entrust.

So the **Curtains!!!** team sat quickly down to do the impossible: to take stock. Four questions 'What's gone?' What's left?' 'Is it any good?' 'What do we do with it?' were nailed to the masthead. It was a slow process for an ad-hoc, self-appointed un-paid team receiving small research grants for the reimbursement of a part of their expenses - four years in fact. Nothing was taken on trust: often the source books and periodicals of the period were wrong, chronicling intentions never realized as well as those achieved. One of the greatest enemies turned out to be the sentimental essayist more anxious to record irrelevant and often inaccurate show biz stories of a theatre long since replaced rather than establish the facts. But some 'stringers' turned out to be allies to the cause. Finally almost every report was checked by a member of the committee. The checking process will continue after publication, hence the tear off page at the rear on which we ask you, the reader, to add to the sum of knowledge. First and foremost this is to be a book of reference.

The need for qualitative judgements: vaut le detour

But, unless the stock was examined by those prepared to discriminate between the good and the bad in an authoritative manner, the book would be of interest only to the scholar. Accordingly the committee decided to introduce a system of stars in the time honoured Michelin pattern. The intention was to draw attention to what are the finest theatres whether or not they are in use. Hopefully this will lead to the rediscovery by communities of thought-to-be lost theatres and their eventual reopening even if this is delayed until after the long economic winter. If recession and decline continues (an unnecessary pessimistic view in the eyes of anybody who has studied the ups and downs of the English theatre), then at least this book will have served a purpose if it helps save a few already threatened theatres, the national importance of which had not been realised. The gazetteer and associated maps and charts are designed to draw attention to the best theatres wherever they are. Whether the best are saved should rightly be a matter of national as well as local concern.

On page 82 will be found further information on the classification system. Here perhaps it is worth adding an apology that some may find inconsistancies of judgement, notwithstanding the arguing within the committee as to whether to award ★, ★ ★, or ★ ★ ★. Some, for example, might find the ratings more stringent in London than outside London but they will have not have experienced the excitement on a wet winter's day of finding a good if not great forgotten Edwardian auditorium in a depressed northern mill town. But perhaps it is reassuring to say although there may be cavils between what is ★ ★ or what is ★ ★ ★ the cut off below ★ ★ is probably more certain and more consistent.

The results can be simply listed. It is thought that there were slightly over 1,000 theatres in use in Britain between 1900 and 1914 (always remembering that there is a grey area of music halls, cinemas, flat floor halls which have some but not all the accepted attributes of a theatre). Of these the state or fate of about 1100 have been established. 98 or so are in use, that is 9%, 85% have been demolished or irretrievably altered. This leaves approximately 6%, 69 in fact, that are not in use as theatres today but are restorable. Of these,54 rate ★ ★ or ★ ★ ★, 11 in London, 35 in the rest of England, and 4 each in Scotland

and Wales. Inevitably and properly interest will be focussed on some of these 54.

Arguments for conservation

Earlier in this introduction arguments for conservation were promised on top of evidence. The comparative arrangement of the evidence in itself provides one important argument: That this and that theatre is rare and/or good of its type or period. But more than this will be needed. Some arguments attractive at first may have to be discarded. Historical association is almost always insufficient — the 'Irving toured here' accolade soon becoming no more than a variation of where Queen Elizabeth slept. With effort one can link Sarah Siddons with the Theatre Royal Bristol but generally all the theatres in which our greatest actors or greatest playwrights worked have vanished. (The Lyceum, preservation of which is thoroughly recommended, is not Irving's theatre. It is also perhaps worth noting that after the 1969 Ministerial Inquiry, which did result in the saving of the Lyric Hammersmith auditorium for rebuilding elsewhere, the judgement was given that "the historic associations of the existing theatre although interesting were of insufficient weight" which left "the architectual merit of the building" in general and the "excellent Matcham plasterwork" in particular to save the day and the Lyric). Thus the reader must look elsewhere than in this book if he wants random theatrical anecdotes which are often fun but almost always irrelevant to the cause.

Nor will the cheaper-to-save-than-to-build-afresh proposition always turn out to be a reliable argument. Many fine old theatres were built of rubble at a time of speculative jerry building. The addition-to-the-townscape line is also limited, as has already been suggested most of the architectural pleasure being private and reserved only for those who penetrate their auditoriums.

While it must be hoped that other arguments present themselves to the proponents of individual cases there are generally only two arguments of decisive weight, the one environmental and the other theatrical.

Two decisive arguments

Although there are exceptions the environmental argument will hold in most cases. Theatres built in the boom years between 1880 and 1910 generally occupy prime down-town or city centre sites. In town after town across the western world city centres have become, during the day, sterile centres of business which attract shoppers and office workers but which, in the evening, lie empty windswept and open to muggers rather than merrymakers. The occasional pub, or restaurant, can not only by themselves change this. But a revived Royal, Empire, Grand or Alhambra can. Now theatre can repay its debt to the community by helping give back life to a city centre, repay a debt to society as well as provide opportunities for new small businesses or the extension of working hours for existing ones. The enthusiast urging the renovation of one city centre theatre can quote enough evidence from other cities to show that the social and economic return on the investment in the fabric will satisfy left and right alike.

The theatrical argument is as simple. Old theatres work. They are functional not so much in the mathematical matters of angle of sight or width of stage but in that they enable actors and audiences to come together, to enjoy each other. Sir John Gielgud summed it up when he wrote of the Old Vic: "It is warm, it is alive and it has a tattered magnificence about it. It smells and feels like a

Longton, Empire Theatre (1896), now a bingo hall.

Victor Glasstone

theatre, and is able to transform a collection of human beings into that curious vibrant instrument for an actor — an audience".

This brings one inevitably to the old versus the new. Ten years ago a case had to be made that old theatres are generally preferable to new ones but now, sadly to anyone as much concerned with building afresh as with restoring the old, the boot is probably on the other foot. Lack of cash and a general disenchantment with much of modern theatre architecture within the auditorium (bars and foyers being generally admired greatly) has led most of the theatre back to old buildings: the fringe in their found spaces within evocative old halls as much as opera companies making their homes in old touring theatres and thereby giving new life to the old. Here one further quotation may be allowed, this time from Somerset Maugham writing presciently a quarter of a century ago why he thought his collection of 18th and 19th century theatre paintings would brighten up the yet-to-be-conceived National Theatre. He wrote nostalgically of the old theatres, of "the glamour which put in a comfortable state of mind to enjoy the play you were about to witness. The theatres they build now are severely functional you can see from all parts of them what is happening on the stage; the seats are comfortable and there are abundant exits so you run small chance of being burnt to death. But they are cold. They are apt to make you feel you have come to the playhouse to undergo an ordeal rather than enjoy an entertainment".

Maugham was writing in 1955 at a time when he preferred the reassurance of red plush for his particular little brand of French window naturalism which was at home behind the Edwardian proscenium. Thirty years later the same theatres attract the modern director for different reasons. **Nicholas Nickleby** at the Aldwych or **Barnum** at the Palladium go where few performers (since the Crazy Gang) have dared to go: out into the auditorium. It is a paradox of which theatre designers of the eighties are belatedly aware. Such life enhancing shows as these work in the old theatres in a way much harder to realise effectively in the Olivier, Lyttleton, Barbican or Vivien Beaumont where the very functional efficiency of the design makes it much more difficult to break the mold.

The central theatrical argument for old theatres is, therefore, that the best of them are for all seasons and for all styles. They serve today's actors just as a Stradivarius serves succeding generations of violinists. Their effectiveness transcends the period in which they were built.

Thus the fashionable view of the 1950s and 1960s that categorised such theatres as picture frame theatres, out of the confines of which the actor had to break, turns out to be a reaction to how such theatres were used from the 1920s to the 1950s rather than to their true character and potential. In the last twenty five years those who have exchanged a good pre-1914 theatre for any of those larger (i.e. over 500 seats) new theatres which have been hailed as being ever more functionally efficient or providing greater freedom (or both) have generally found that they have lost more than they gained. The only newer theatres in which the intimacy has held, despite the use of simple architectural forms like those single slabs of seating which resemble a football stadium, have been those seating under 500. Our Victorian forefathers would have regarded such small theatres as wildly uneconomic — theirs was a more complex task to ensure that much larger audiences felt at one with the actor. This they did with a subtle combination of form and of decoration which cannot be passed over on the grounds that is hierarchical or merely old fashioned unless equally effective design proposals are put in their place.

In contrast most modern theatres whatever their size are, as Maugham feared, cold. It was a relief for the author of this introduction to discover at a conference in Munich held in 1977 that a Swedish behavioural scientist had put it all to the test. Wires had been connected to the heads of the 'audience'. After fifteen minutes preparation in a red and gold room you laugh easier, cry quicker than after fifteen minutes preparation for similar stimuli in a drab grey or black room. Any actor who has tried warming up an audience in a black box of a modern theatre will confirm this. (Interestingly this simple fact has been learnt by the current generation of architects and many of the very latest theatres are gaily decorated in complete contrast to those of the previous decade).

These then are the two principle arguments for giving new life to old theatres: they will help revive our dying city centres and they will attract audience and actors as much to the latest theatrical theatre event (play or musical) as to the English classics for which most of them, especially the older ones, are so well suited.

The contents of this book

The **Curtains!!!** book is designed first to be a reference and guide book, second to be a source book. The essays that precede the gazetteer are part analytic, part polemical, designed to provide ammunition for those actively engaged in saving our theatre heritage. Christopher Brereton, the chief investigator for England, Scotland and Wales, pinpoints those 'Sleeping

Beauties' which could most easily be awakened to serve communities which either lack a decent traditional theatre or which could well take an additional theatre slightly different in character to what they already have. John Earl, the editor of the London section, offers a guide to the Preservation Game as it is played throughout the country. Michael Sell explains how little research has been done in this field. There is a historic profile which sets out when the theatres were built and thereby shows how rare and valuable are the earlier, pre-1885, theatres. Architects, engineers and designers report on the problems of restoration from their own experience: Victor Glasstone on the Gaiety, Isle of Man; Derek Sugden, engineer of sound as well as of structure, comments on the Theatre Royal Glasgow and the Opera House Buxton; Nick Thompson and Clare Ferraby tell of their work in Nottingham and at the Duke of York's; Francis Reid, noted lighting man translated into manager of the Theatre Royal Bury St. Edmunds which he turned round from a low point to be a highly successful medium-scale country theatre, offers the encouragement that you don't need a thousand seats to succeed. David Wilmore, who with his own hands restored Britain's most complete set of nineteenth century stage machinery at the Tyne Theatre Newcastle, presents an introduction to the whole neglected subject of saving and using the old machinery.

There are also maps and appendices, one which picks out the work of the major theatre architects (information which can be found nowhere else) and another which makes a start in recording the date of demolition plus the architect's name for every demolished theatre which had been in use between 1900 and 1914. And throughout are the photographs arranged by the project's photographic editor, Victor Glasstone, who has contributed the majority from his own collection.

Finally this introduction cannot be concluded without a reference to the Acknowledgements on page 234. There will be found the thanks of the **Curtains!!!** team to all those who have helped on this long crusade. Now the project has materialised into book and exhibition, the **Curtains!!!** team turns the whole thing over to you, the reader.

In these pages will be found much background information which may be of assistance but which you may want to correct so that a second edition can be a better and more accurate book of reference. In the streets will be found the theatres themselves, the objects of our affection. These are a small remnant of the most extraordinary flowering of truly popular live theatre in the western world. If even only one or two of these are saved as a result of **Curtains!!!** it will all have been worthwhile.

18

Sleeping Beauties

Christopher Brereton

Architect and principal author of the Gazetteer excluding London

"A New Life For Old Theatres" is the optimistic part of this book's title, and perhaps the most important aim of its publication is to try to inspire interest in the rescue of some of Britain's magnificent old theatres from disuse. In skimming through the gazetteer it is the ★ ★ ★ and ★ ★ disused categories which matter most in this respect — the best old theatre buildings now either closed or languishing as bingo halls, warehouses, ballrooms etc. Taking it further the most obvious candidates for rescue are the highly rated theatres, not in use, situated in towns where, either there is no theatre at all, or at best some unsuitable public hall which has been pressed into service as a theatre.

In Barnsley the intact Theatre Royal (1899) is now used for bingo, whereas a hall, with about as much theatrical 'feel' as a supermarket, serves as the town's "Civic Theatre" — an illogical situation which could be reversed to advantage.

Doncaster, a town of similar size (82,000), at present has only a cinema with a stage in which to house touring productions, and yet the Grand Theatre (1899) stands waiting to be rescued from its present fate as a bingo hall. It is well situated in the town centre, although its fine and lively stuccoed facade is

Margate, Theatre Royal *Iain Mackintosh*   **Doncaster, Grand Theatre** *Ken Reeves*

Longton, Empire Theatre

Keith Gibson

Above: **Longton, Empire Theatre**   *Victor Glasstone*

Left: **Middlesbrough, Empire Theatre**   *Keith Gibson*

now squashed-up against the faceless flank of a vast 'superstore'.

Dunfermline now has no theatre where professional companies may perform and yet is currently in danger of losing its delightful Opera House (1900 and 1921) in an old fashioned 1960's style comprehensive redevelopment. Although it has been in use as a shop and store for many years it is restoreable and is just about right in size for the population of the town (54,000). It would be suitable either as a home for a drama company or as an addition to Perth, Aberdeen and Inverness on the Scottish touring grid.

The conurbation of towns which makes up Stoke-on-Trent ('The Potteries'), has, together with the contiguous town of Newcastle-under-Lyme, a population of over 330,000. At present occasional touring productions are put on in a great barn of a 'super cinema' in Hanley, or at a public hall with a makeshift stage in Burslem (a fine Edwardian Baroque hall, but not a theatre). Lurking quietly in Longton, another of the towns, however, is a little-known Matcham masterpiece, the Longton Empire (1896), now used for bingo after many years as a cinema. It has a large stage and a perfect auditorium, flexible enough in its multi-tiered design to be suitable either for intimate drama or for opera. As at Barnsley logic cries out that bingo be put on at the hall and theatre at the theatre!.

Margate, as a popular seaside resort, has two or three hall/theatres where seasonal shows are presented. Away from the sea front, however, in the old part of the town, is the Theatre Royal (1787 and 1874), now a bingo hall. The auditorium dates from 1874 — now a very rare period for theatre auditoria in Britain. Although the owner respects the building and keeps it in good repair, it is sad that one of the most beautiful little playhouses in the country should be put to this use. Attempts have been made in the fairly recent past to run it as a theatre, but it is really too small to be commercially viable. This could probably only be done with subsidy, but it is a deserving cause. It could perhaps share productions with an already established drama company in Kent — that at the

Middlesbrough, Empire Theatre

Keith Gibson

Marlowe Theatre, Canterbury, for example. It could also take tours by Kent Opera — the horseshoe auditorium would be a delightful setting for chamber opera.

Teeside, with Middlesborough at its centre, has a population of more than 300,000 but no theatre large enough to stage touring opera, ballet, musicals etc. And yet, with its twin-towered facade standing proudly alongside the town hall, there is a former theatre which, with minimal refurbishing, could perform this very function. The Empire (1899) is now a bingo hall; well maintained and very nearly intact. It will hopefully remain so as long as bingo is profitable, awaiting the day when the people of Teeside are ready to return it to the purpose for which it was built and is so eminently suited.

For the past twelve years, since the closure of the Lyceum Theatre (1897), the citizens of Sheffield have been unable to see lyric theatre without having to travel to Leeds, Manchester, or Nottingham. The Lyceum has a magnificent auditorium and is the last remaining theatre in Sheffield suitable for musical productions — the Crucible Theatre (1971), next door, has an open thrust stage. It is unlikely that the Lyceum could be run commercially as a theatre, and for it to reopen it would have to rely on public money. But this has not been forthcoming and the building has stood empty and decaying. In 1981 it was bought by a company as a venue for pop concerts. It is a sad reflection on the cultural values of one of Britain's largest cities that it could not be seen as a touring venue for English Opera North (the steel cities of the Ruhr have, not only theatres, but resident opera companies to perform in them!). But then, facing reality, at least the present function will keep the building watertight and leave open the vague possibility that it might, at some future date, revert to

Wakefield, Opera House   *Victor Glasstone*

Wakefield, Opera House

Victor Glasstone

Cardiff, Philharmonic Hall   *Brian Tarr*

theatre use — provided the acolytes of the pop groups don't tear off bits of the Rococo plasterwork in their enthusiasm, and the management don't start a process of desecration which could leave the Lyceum in a similar condition to that of London's Talk of the Town (the late Hippodrome).

In a rather different part of the country, at Tunbridge Wells, the Borough Council has its Assembly Hall, a large multi-purpose public hall with a stage — but decidedly a hall, not a theatre. Just around the corner, however, stands a real theatre, the Opera House (1902), now a bingo hall. It has an opulent Baroque frontage behind which lies an intimate auditorium. Tunbridge Wells may not be a particularly large town (97,000) but it is surely large enough to find room for both a public hall (used as such), and a medium-sized theatre. Evidently the local Civic Society thinks so — it is planning to convert a former church, opposite the Opera House, into a theatre!. Kent Opera at present visit the Assembly Hall; how much more appropriate if they performed at the Opera House — perhaps not grand enough to reverberate to the cry of "Ritorna vincitor!", but ideal for the softer cadences of "Il Ritorno D'Ulisse In Patria".

Another erstwhile opera house, yet even smaller than that at Tunbridge Wells, still exists in Wakefield (1894), and is again now a bingo hall. But even the trappings of bingo have failed to kill the inherent theatricality of its auditorium — one of the most delightful creations of Frank Matcham. Wakefield, which does not now have a theatre, is close enough to Leeds for demand for large scale musical productions to be satisfied at the Grand Theatre there. The Opera House would, however, be a highly suitable base for a resident drama company, with occasional chamber opera. Fortunately local people, including the City Council, appreciate the qualities and potential of the theatre and are trying to get it re-opened.

Sleeping Beauties can also be found in towns which already have a theatre

25

Aberdeen, Tivoli Theatre

Keith Gibson

Glasgow, Britannia Music Hall - auditorium exists at first floor level   *James Dunbar-Nasmith*

in operation, but would probably be capable of supporting another of a different kind.

Aberdeen (182,000) has, in His Majesty's Theatre, a large touring house, but there is no theatre with a resident drama company, which a city of its size deserves. A former theatre already exists that could fit such a role perfectly — the Tivoli, yet another bingo hall. It has an attractive facade (1872) and one of the finest smaller theatre auditoria (1909) in Scotland. Surely the oil-rich city could afford to take it on.

The Hippodrome in Brighton is at the opposite end of Britain and quite a different kind of theatre from the Tivoli, although designed by the same architect (Frank Matcham). it has a very large, very richly decorated, semi circular auditorium, and a big stage. It is far too large in fact for anything other than big-scale musical productions, but for this it is highly suitable. It would fulfil a need now unprovided for in Brighton and at the same time complement the role of the Theatre Royal, a fine medium-sized theatre, presenting drama and medium-scale lyric productions.

It has long been proposed that Cardiff, as the capital city in Wales, should have a National Theatre for Wales, housing a permanent drama company — possibly the already existing Welsh Theatre Company. At present this company has no proper base and performs, in Cardiff, at the New Theatre; the city's touring house. There already exists in Cardiff, however, a fine, intimate theatre which, if refurbished, would make a worthy National Theatre — The Prince of Wales (1878 and 1920), for many years a down-at-heel cinema. This is made more interesting as a proposition by the fact that the Prince of Wales is immediately next door to the Philharmonic Hall (1877), a rare surviving example of a music hall of the concert room type. They could form a most attractive and lively combination — larger scale drama at the Prince of Wales, and open-stage, experimental drama, and also concerts and recitals, at the Philharmonic; the two auditoria linked by common foyers.

In Glasgow there is another type of concert room type of music hall; the Britannia (1857) — now the only one to survive in Scotland. This fact alone makes it worthy of preservation but it deserves to be brought back to life as a theatre, either for performances of Scottish music hall entertainment, together with a museum, or as an open-stage theatre and theatre club, such as existed at the Close Theatre Club before it was gutted by fire in the late 1960's.

Cambridge could probably support only one professional theatre and this it already has in the Arts Theatre (1936). The A.D.C. Theatre is used for amateur productions by University groups, but it is a somewhat makeshift, not particularly attractive building. Far more distinguished, and indeed highly important, both architecturally and for its place in theatre history, is the former Festival Theatre in Newmarket Road, now a scenery workshop and store. It is unique in its combination of an early 19th century three tiered horsehoe auditorium, and the space-stage concept created by the removal of the proscenium wall by Terence Gray in 1926. It would be marvellous if the Unviersity groups could be persuaded to vacate the A.D.C. Theatre and take over the Festival Theatre — indeed a true festival theatre it could again become; staging summer seasons of specially mounted professional productions.

Aberystwyth is not a large town (10,600), but it has a university, on the campus of which is a small theatre, the Theatr y Werin, which offers a varied programme of productions. The town is also a popular seaside resort but does not now have a theatre for seasonal entertainment. The former Pier Theatre, in any case only ever a glass-roofed hall, is now used for bingo. Well situated in one of the main streets, however, is the former Coliseum Theatre (1905), now closed. Despite its late date it is a fine example of the earlier type of music hall, and its delightful horseshoe auditorium deserves to be fully refurbished and once more enlivened by performances of variety. Situated at first-floor level, with shops below, it would not be expensive to operate and could even make a profit.

Colchester is one of those towns which built itself a new theatre (the Mercury) despite the fact that a former theatre still exists; in this case a splendid one — the Hippodrome (1905), now inevitably given over to bingo. The Mercury seats 500 and has a resident drama company. The Hippodrome could seat approximately 900, but, due to its multi-tiered design, is no less intimate, and its larger capacity would have also allowed it to take occasional tours of opera, ballet etc. Given the situation as it is, however, Colchester is probably large enough (80,000) to support the Hippodrome's return to theatre use with a mixed programme of touring opera etc., amateur shows, concerts and films.

Swansea has its very fine Grand Theatre, offering a full and varied programme, which is most probably sufficient to meet the needs of the town. The disused Palace Theatre (1888) is, however, too good to be forgotten about. It has been for sale for some time but has recently been given some protection by listing. Fortunately the local Planning Authority are aware of its value and are hoping that a suitable use may be found. This might be as an all-purpose theatre, largely for amateurs, but also for use for films, recitals, meetings etc.

York is rather a similar case. Professional theatre is well provided for at the Theatre Royal, but there exists a fine former theatre, the Empire (1902), now a bingo hall. It is in the centre of the city, and, although unlikely to be viable as a professional theatre, could possibly be revived for use by amateurs, and for recitals, etc.

There are rather sad Sleeping Beauties which have little hope of being reawakened. These are the former theatres which, however splendid, are just in the wrong place — away from town centres and in areas where a theatre would be unlikely to thrive. If they have some other use, such as bingo, it is probably the only viable use that could be hoped for, and we can at least be grateful that the buildings are being kept heated and maintained. They seem to occur in the inner fringe areas of the large cities; formerly populous and lively communities, but now either a mix of decayed old housing and cleared sites, or 'estates' of flats surrounded by wasted acres of vandalised 'landscaped' open space.

In Liverpool, the Olympia (1905) and the Pavilion (1908) are in the former sort of area. Both are now bingo halls; their opulent auditoria well kept up.

In Manchester the Hulme Hippodrome (1901) and Playhouse (1902) stand side by side; their amazingly rich interiors incongruously in contrast with the bleakness of the surrounding blocks of flats. The Playhouse is now a B.B.C. studio theatre and the Hippodrome a bingo hall.

At Salford's Victoria Theatre even bingo failed, and the building is boarded-

London, Lyceum Theatre   *GLC*

Manchester, Playhouse Theatre, Hulme
Victor Glasstone

London, Lyceum Theatre

Victor Glasstone

up in the vain hope of protecting it from the vandals. For how long can the fine plasterwork of its auditorium survive?.

Even sadder than this is the fate of the Royal Hippodrome, Everton, Liverpool (1902), and the Theatre Royal, Blyth (1900). Their shattered interiors, illuminated by shafts of light through holed ceilings, have a melancholy beauty of their own, but a beauty no less transient than the scenes which once appeared on their stages.

But perhaps one should never be totally pessimistic — what is arguably the most beautiful of all the Sleeping Beauties, the Theatre Royal, Portsmouth (1884 and 1900) has, after a long and perilous sleep, been finally rescued and is now in the process of recovery.

London has its own Sleeping Beauties, some of which, at least, have a chance of rescue. It may soon again be possible to enjoy the exotic Franco-Venetian auditorium of the Playhouse (1907), now on its way back after several year's disuse. But, like the fine former theatres in the inner fringes of Liverpool and Manchester, what real hope is there for the Grand, Clapham Junction (1900), Tottenham Palace (1908), or that gloriously extravagant Matcham music hall, Hackney Empire (1901)? All, at least, are bingo halls and safe from immediate threat.

The Coronet, Notting Hill Gate (1898), and the Camden Theatre (1901), have more hope of reuse. Both are closer to the centre and in areas where a theatre could flourish. The Coronet has long been a cinema, but the Camden Theatre has recently closed after a period of use for pop concerts and a discotheque. The Round House is just up the road and doing well, and a fully restored Camden Theatre could compliment it; presenting the sort of show which cannot be done on an open stage — perhaps a home for visiting opera and dance companies (it is a far more attractive theatre than Sadler's Wells!)

The famous Wilton's Music Hall (1858 and 1878), as the property of the G.L.C., is safe from threat of demolition, and is currently undergoing a programme of repairs. The trust which hopes to re-open it is still attempting to raise funds.

The Lyceum (1834 and 1904), now a dance hall but with its splendid

London, Coronet

GLC

31

auditorium little altered, offers perhaps the most intriguing possibilities, in conjunction with three of London's other largest theatres — the Royal Opera House, Covent Garden, The London Coliseum, and the Theatre Royal, Drury Lane.

As the home of both the Royal Opera and the Royal Ballet, conditions at Covent Garden are cramped, and will remain so even when the new dressing rooms and rehearsal rooms, at present being built, are finished. Future planned phases of extensions would change that, but who can be sure they will get built?.

The volume of the auditorium of the Coliseum (2,358 seats) is very large — chiefly because of its great width. It is in fact too large and insufficiently intimate to be entirely suitable as a home for the English National Opera. It does, however, have excellent sight lines (especially from the well-raked stalls), and a very wide proscenium - 55 feet (which has to be considerably masked-down for the opera company). These two factors render the Coliseum ideally suited to be the home of a major ballet company, such as the Royal Ballet. Such a move, if it could be arranged, would relieve the pressure on Covent Garden; allowing it to function solely as an opera house.

The Theatre Royal, Drury Lane has all the attributes of an opera house, and yet has only on occasions been used as such during its history. It would make a perfect home for the English National Opera. Its noble foyers and staircases precede an auditorium which, although very nearly of the same seating capacity as the Coliseum, possess a far greater degree of intimacy — largely due to its narrower width. The proscenium, at 42 feet, is just about the right working size for E.N.O. The theatre also has the considerable added advantage of spacious workshops and scenery stores directly linked to the rear of the stage.

But what of the almost traditional use of Drury Lane as a home for musicals? This is where the Lyceum comes in. Its seating capacity when used as a theatre was 3,000. If reseated, by present stands, it would probably be nearer 2,500, which is greater than the capacity of Drury Lane (2,280), and more than adequate to be viable for expensive musicals. Its proscenium is 42 feet 8 inches and the stage 55 feet deep — again quite big enough.

If the owners of Drury Lane could be persuaded to sell or lease it to the E.N.O., and the E.N.O. to give up their lease on the Coliseum to the Royal Ballet, and if the G.L.C., on the expiry of the present short lease of the Lyceum to Mecca, could sell or long-lease it to the owners of Drury Lane, then a very happy result might be achieved; affecting four of London's largest and finest theatres, and, not least, reawakening one of them from a long slumber.

Manchester, Hulme Hippodrome: an unusually fine 1901 theatre of square form which is well maintained as a bingo hall and is unlikely to find an audience again for live entertainment.
Victor Glasstone

Tunbridge Wells, Opera House: a fine medium scale theatre at present used for bingo, but, being very well situated, could well be restored to serve both drama and opera.
Victor Glasstone

Derby, Hippodrome: a large variety theatre at present used for bingo but potentially a good touring theatre for the bigger companies.

Victor Glasstone

London, Hoxton Hall: recently restored 1867 auditorium, now part of a Quaker neighbourhood centre, which strongly evokes mid-Victorian music hall.

Victor Glasstone

Liverpool, Olympia: large and rare circus theatre in the oriental style, the site of which, outside the city centre, has prevented it becoming Merseyside's opera house.

Victor Glasstone

Edinburgh, King's Theatre: unusually opulent plasterwork of this 1906 theatre which has been generally underrated probably because it has had to serve as a grand rather than chamber opera house.

Victor Glasstone

Newcastle, Tyne Theatre: rare mid nineteenth century theatre (1867) with one of Britain's greatest auditoriums, here seen with walkdown installed for an amateur musical. *Darryl Williams*

40

Dressing the House

Nicholas Thompson and Clare Ferraby

Architect and Interior Designer responsible for renovations in Nottingham, London, Manchester and Watford.

Victorian and Edwardian theatres were a vivid reflection of the social aspirations and divisions of their age. Audiences were rigorously divided. The wealthy had fine entrances, leading into small but elegant foyers and approached their seats at the front of the circle by chandelier-lit staircases. The poor were herded into the pit or around the corner, past a pay box and up basic stairs into cramped galleries with the minimum of facilities. For half a century little was done by the theatre managers in the way of change except a reduction in numbers together with other minimal requirements to maintain their licences.

Our fine heritage of theatres can only survive by a hard commercial attitude to revenue. This requires matching the product to be seen on stage with the best facilities to attract large audiences often travelling considerable distances to the theatre and to ensure that they spend the maximum length of time in the public areas. Bottoms on seats is only part of the equation; the cash registers in the foyers are equally important to financial survial of the theatre. To achieve this it is often necessary to radically remodel the foyers to allow all to enter from the street through the main doors, congregate, eat and drink, purchase souvenirs, look at exhibitions and listen to foyer entertainment before entering the various parts of the auditorium. Thus the foyers need to be flexible and enjoyable spaces open throughout the day.

Likewise, refurbishment of auditoria needs to enhance the character and strengthen the inherent special audience/actor relationship whilst improving the comfort of the paying public. All this must be achieved whilst satisfying the varying but stringent demands of fire officers and somehow concealing, as best as possible, the increasing amount of technical equipment.

Backstage all must be planned to provide a temporary home for the best available companies where they can unload, store, prepare and arrive on stage to play their part without getting lost in the meantime. Thus the balance of foyers, auditoria and backstage is critical for the commercial success of the theatre.

Each theatre has a distinct spirit, character and flavour. Whether the mood is intimate, grandiose, flamboyant or classical, each one must be thoroughly understood before any design ideas are formulated. However much research is made into the original colouring, this is not necessarily appropriate for present day use. In the Victorian era lighting was low, sometimes virtually non-existent, so the use of light colours or sometimes garish colours were used which to our eyes, under modern lighting conditions, would be unacceptable. Today, with an increasing range of lighting techniques, we can conjure up an exciting atmosphere with the correct balance of tonal values, providing a neutral surround for the stage.

1865

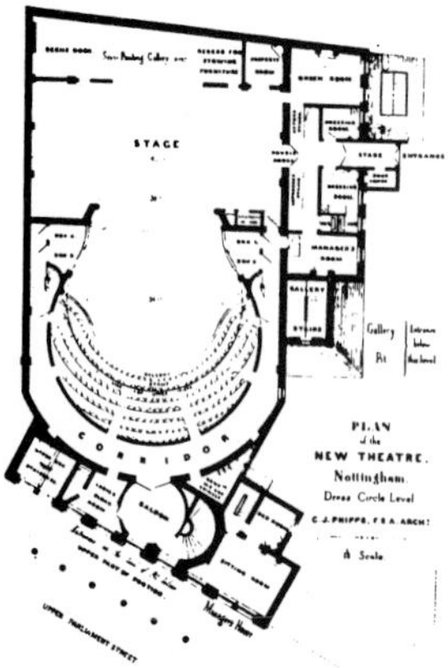

PLAN
of the
NEW THEATRE,
Nottingham.
Dress Circle Level
C. J. PHIPPS, F.R.I.B.A ARCH.T
& Scale

1982

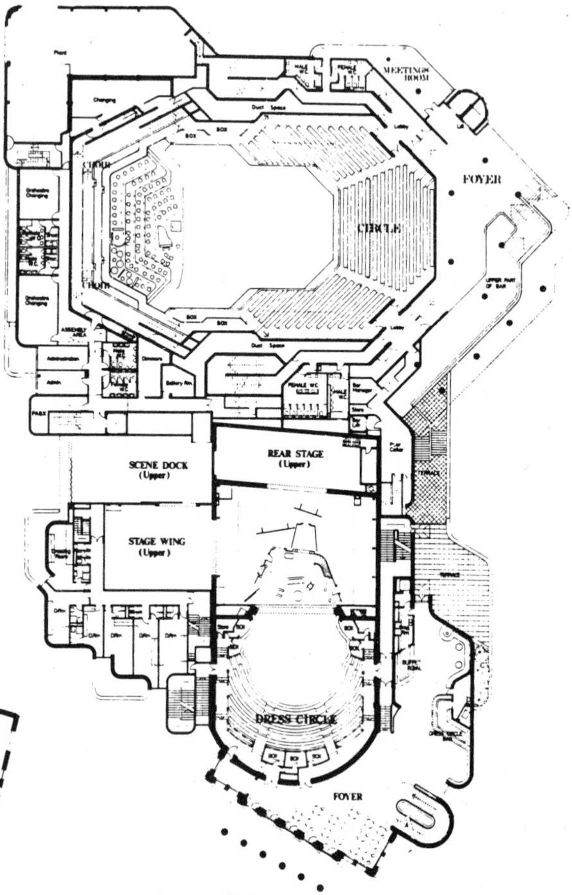

Concert Hall
Nottingham

Renton Howard Wood Levin
Partnership

1897

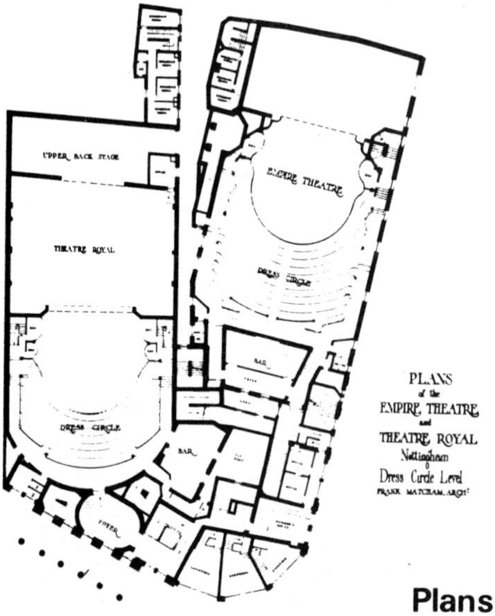

PLANS
of the
EMPIRE THEATRE
and
THEATRE ROYAL
Nottingham
Dress Circle Level
FRANK MATCHAM ARCH.T

Plans at Circle Level

The colour concept requires a unified approach, embodying the decoration additional plasterwork, upholstery, wallpapers, drapes, housetabs, carpets and decorative lighting. All these items are of paramount importance to the success of the final design. It is the subtlety of colour combinations, gilt highlights and different fabric textures that bring together the auditorium as a whole and should provide the palette for the rest of the building.

The Theatre Royal, Nottingham was built by C. J. Phipps in 1865 with major alterations in 1897 by Frank Matcham, who also built the Empire Palace of Varieties immediately adjacent to the Theatre.

The demands of the Empire left the Theatre Royal with smaller dressing rooms facing on to an alleyway, serving as a get-in and means of escape.

Matcham's layout and decoration managed to survive until 1967 when the Empire was demolished for a road widening scheme and a contemporary box office and foyer built on the site of the Theatre Royal.

By the mid-70's the Theatre Royal was dying fast. The Royal Ballet was no longer willing to persuade its dancers to run from temporary cabins across the car park onto the stage: the product was disappearing, audiences were low and the whole area was rundown with the adjoining hotel closing its doors. Our brief was to upgrade this theatre to be one of the best touring dates in the country, linking it with a major concert hall (due for completion in 1982) thus acting as a catalyst for the whole area. Having appraised the existing situation and opportunities, one had to balance the operational requirements essential to management against the emotional pleadings of the preservationists.

The initial task was to identify the essence of the existing building, which at Nottingham was the portico and the auditorium, and then prune, embellish and, where necessary, create anew. Detailed schemes were prepared for the conversion of the adjoining County Hotel into backstage accommodation alongside the second scheme for a new building before we were satisfied it was right to demolish the hotel. Once that decision was taken it allowed us to visually strengthen Phipps 1865 portico. This in turn permitted a concept of three levels of foyers linked by a grand staircase forming the focal point of the public areas and replacing the miniscule separate spaces and complex stairs shown in the earlier plans. These foyers and dressing rooms are expressed externally by undulating, inward-stepping solid forms as a foil to the projecting glass foyers of the new Concert Hall.

Nottingham, Theatre Royal - portico of 1865, renovated 1978   *Renton, Howard, Wood, Levin Partnership*

The approach to the renovation of the auditorium was one of enhancing the actor/audience relationship and attractive plasterwork. Unsympathetic details in design and colour had resulted in an auditorium that lacked any cohesion at the outset of the work in 1975. The subtle shades of green and gilt in the new interior have been used to pick out the balcony fronts and plasterwork, whilst the richer hues of the seats, ceiling and the special colourway of the William Morris wallpaper give the intimate atmosphere. A screen at the rear of the dress circle (based on Phipps' Edinburgh Lyceum Theatre of 1883) not only creates three delightful private boxes, which mask the down-stand beams, but also both increases the intimacy of the auditorium as well as allowing for light and sound lobbies between foyers and auditorium.

A similar approach was used for the refurbishment of the Duke of York's, one of London's most attractive West End theatres. The original 'renaissance' colour scheme of terracotta and cream wall, yellow and gold plasterwork and amber seats has been carried through into the foyers, bars and facade. Major structural work at the Theatre included the removal of the numerous columns which obstructed sightlines for much of the audience and the removal of a complete escape stair, thus providing more space for foyers, box office and bars.

The Palace Theatre, Manchester is another example where colour is used to modify an auditorium. The massive scale of the Theatre, combined with a conglomeration of Greek, Roman and Egyptian styles, bombastic decoration, rusticated walls and endless corridors gave the feeling of a mausoleum. With dark, rich depth of colour, the walls recede and other insignificant areas are toned down to give a background for the decoration to bring the auditorium down in scale with colour unifying the space and so creating an elegant atmosphere of the Edwardian era.

As with buildings, so it is necessary to retain and rebuild ones audiences. This leads to a minimal period of closure of the building. The Theatre Royal at Nottingham was dark for only 11 months and the Duke of York's for 6. This speed of construction, which was common in Victorian times, now has to be achieved by skilful project planning by architect, client and contractor to help ensure a viable commercial future for our old theatres.

London, Duke of York's 1892 - renovated 1979   *Steve Stephens*

The Preservation Game: Some Openings

John Earl

Principal author of the London section of the Gazetteer

Portsmouth Theatre Royal will be preserved.

Two or three years ago it would have seemed rash, even absurd, to make such an assertion. Now it will be accepted as a statement of fair probability, if not yet certainty.

Wilton's Music Hall will be preserved. Whatever struggles may still lie ahead, a dangerous corner has been turned.

The New Tyne Theatre, despite its present problems, will be preserved. Against all predictions it is alive and working — the only theatre in the land where a Victorian transformation scene can be mounted in true style.

Lost: The Granville, Walham Green. Its destruction triggered off an urgent reappraisal of the listing of theatres which gave new protection to 18 in London alone. *GLC*

Lost: St. James's Theatre

G.L.C.

Above: **Lost: Dublin, Queen's**   *Victor Glasstone*

Right: **Lost: Glasgow, Palace**   *Victor Glasstone*

Once a theatre whose preservation is at all practicable is in the hands of a competent, properly advised and energetic body, dedicated to securing its future, the chances of success are probably better today — even in an economic ice age — than they have been for many years. There is not much point, in fact, in addressing advice to theatre preservers who have already manoeuvred themselves into position from which the game can be won. The expert minds which have come together in Newcastle and Stepney and Portsmouth are well aware that they are in the business of finding particular solutions to particular, sometimes unique, problems. There are too many variables for a sure-fire success formula to be evolved to suit every case but there is, nevertheless, a certain amount of basic legal intelligence which needs to be acquired by anyone beginning to play the preservation game. What these notes attempt to do is to offer some pointers — not a comprehensive guide — to the earlier moves.

As with most serious games, the important thing is not to play with style but to win. We have seen too many excellent theatres smashed into the ground to regard further losses with equanimity. The Chelsea Palace, the Dublin Queen's, the Royal West London, the Queen's Poplar and scores of other thoroughly useful theatres were felled in the wasteful years of the fifties and sixties. Despite a vigorous campaign, the tide of destruction deprived Leicester of its only theatre in 1958. The rare and irreplaceable Theatre Royal could have been preserved for a fraction of the cost of the modern building that the city finally decided it should afford. Leeds Empire, a beautiful Matcham invention in a busy centre, well served by public transport, was destroyed for a development whose public benefits are now long forgotten. The Metropolitan Edgware Road fell to the progress goons in the sixties to accommodate a road which, in the event, did not pass through the site. The unique Bermondsey Star vanished without a thought being given to its value as a local resource. The St. James's Theatre had to go before official opinions were influenced by protest and official policies began to harden, but it was not until the gorgeous auditorium of the Granville was destroyed in 1971 that urgent thought was

Preservation triumphant: Hoxton Hall, an outstanding example of an old building sensitively restored and fully employed to serve modern needs.   *GLC*

given to the protection of theatres. Even so, buildings of the quality of the Glasgow Palace continue to be condemned and knocked down.

Despite the staggering scale of the losses, Britain still has a surprising number of old theatres and music halls. Many of those which are at present distressed by misuse or idle and rotting are beginning to attract the attention of would-be preservers and the appearance of the **Curtains!!!** gazetteer will doubtless bring others into the spotlight. It must be said at once that some of these dark temples are plainly unpreservable: poorly designed from the outset, structurally beyond redemption, unadaptable or (saddest of all) washed up on the farther shore of some devastating city 'improvement', scheme, their fate is sealed. Many others are worth fighting for: architecturally pleasing, well planned, repairable, improvable and capable of providing service and pleasure for years to come. Such buildings must not be thrown away unnecessarily and they should certainly not have to prove their right to survive. The onus should rest with intending destroyers to prove that amputation is necessary. And among all these disregarded assets there are some which, by any test, are of outstanding importance — brilliant theatrical wonders, architectural treasures, rare and fragile jewels. No matter what degradations they have suffered they must be preserved and given new life. It would be scandalous to do otherwise.

Whatever opposition a preservation campaign may run into, it is at least likely to gain a hearing today. The fifties and sixties were so obsessed with the idea of progress being synonymous with physical change, that the destruction of the recognizable attributes of an old city — the Georgian square, the corn exchange, the Victorian railway station, the grand hotel, the market hall, the jumbly shopping street, the tramway, the theatre and the music hall — was welcomed as a necessary preparation for a wonderful future. Now that the future has arrived we are inclined to be a little more careful about the past, but it is still necessary for the preserver to be vigilant and to act in good time.

First steps

If you have it in mind to labour for the preservation of a theatre, start now. By the time you are aware of a threat to a theatre, the chances are that a developer will have been investing time and money in preparing plans which envisage demolition. At no stage will your intervention be welcome, but if you wait until the iron ball is about to hit the masonry you will be faced with righteous anger and intransigence. Bloody confrontations make good copy and gather recruits to a cause but they are not the most efficient way of saving buildings — and this is particularly true when the developer is a local authority bent on destruction for the public good. (This is the situation now in Dunfermline where the local authority intends to sweep away an unique listed opera house to make room for the predictable and ubiquitous shopping mall). Most speculative developers are flexible by comparison. Their main objective is to achieve a predictable profit as quickly and as painlessly as possible. They will often accept constraints provided they are made known in good time.

It may be necessary at first to take risks and adopt a somewhat strident tone to attract attention, but a sober, professional approach must soon take over. Knowledgeable allies must be found, if progress is to be made. Theatres are extremely vulnerable buldings, often big and costly to maintain, with extensive roofs and gutters sheltering elaborately ornamented, relatively unadaptable volumes. They are frequently low earners or non-earners on prime sites and it is usually easier to make a case for demolition, or at least cessation of maintenance, than to argue for preservation.

A pressure group campaigning for the preservation of a theatre must have the knowledge and skill to enable it to argue from a position of strength on the structural, architectural and economic problems of such buildings. If the campaign becomes a theatre-owning project then properly paid professionals will have to be engaged, but at the outset enough volunteer talent can usually be attracted to the cause to ensure that a case can be made which is not hopelessly amateurish. In most cases it should be possible to recruit an architect, a building surveyor or an engineer, an accountant or a successful businessman, a solicitor and possibly a writer and a theatrical historian. If the theatre cannot find friends of this kind it is a loser. The attention of the national preservation societies (in many cases this will mean The Victorian Society and SAVE Britain's Heritage) should be engaged early. They will be able to give helpful advice, but they must not be expected to take an organizing role.

A campaign must keep itself in the public eye — publicity is important — but it must also be seen to be responsible, pressing for what is both desirable and possible. A business-like campaign will gather influential support (more about political support later) and will be taken seriously by the other players. It will also command local publicity and may hope thereby to influence local public opinion.

Lost: The Metropolitan, Edgware Road. Uselessly sacrificed, like the Coal Exchange and the Euston Arch. *GLC*

Protection of theatres

Some campaigners will have ownership as an objective and will be making soundings about concessions and calculating bar profits from the outset. Others will see themselves as catalysts, clearing the way for transactions to be concluded by others. In some cases it may be impossible to advance at all and then it may be necessary to consider whether it is possible simply to hold the status quo until the deadlock can be broken (Wilton's has waited eighteen years for the cavalry to arrive.)

Practically every campaign must start from a defensive position and almost the first questions asked by the supporters are: What special legal powers exist to protect theatres? Can demolition at least be prevented until preservation plans can be made?

It must be said at once that theatres as such have no special form of protection. A local authority which is criticized for failing to prevent the demolition or dereliction of a theatre may, in fact, have had no course of action open to it, short of acquisition. The protective measures urged by the Theatres Advisory Council and others have never reached the statute book. The Theatres Trust was, indeed, set up by Act of Parliament in 1976 but it was given onerous responsibilities without being endowed with the means to carry them out. Its most effective function is that of advising local authorities whether or not to accede to proposals to demolish or change of the use of theatres but, even here its advice need not be taken and its remit does not, for some reason, extend to Scotland or Northern Ireland.

Control of demolition

Having said that there are no unique safeguards for theatres it must next be observed that there is also in Britain no form of general control over the demolition of buildings. Despite growing opinion and a mass of evidence to suggest that such control is desirable, no government has seen fit to introduce it.

Notwithstanding contrary popular belief, it is still true to say that a building owner is free to destroy his own property. No permit of any kind is needed to hack through a painted ceiling, remove the slates from a roof or tear down an entire fabric.

There are exceptions to this general rule but they are clearly defined by statute. First, if the building is included in the Secretary of State's statutory list of buildings of special architectural or historic interest it may not be demolished or altered (inside or out) without a specific 'listed building consent.' Second, if it is in a designated conservation area it may not be demolished without consent. (What now follows relates to England and Wales, but similar measures apply to Scotland.)

Conservation areas

Of the two forms of protection, conservation area designation is the feebler, since it can deal only with demolition threats and does nothing in itself to prevent piecemeal mutilation. Designation of a conservation area rests entirely in the hands of a local planning authority. Properly used, it has prevented serious losses (the line was held in 1974 on the then unlisted Shaftesbury Theatre by this means) but nothing can be done in this way to protect an isolated building in undistinguished surroundings.

Lost: The Star, Bermondsey

Listing

The statutory lists provide a more effective form of defence. Here responsibility is split between central and local government. The Department of the Environment compiles and issues the lists, but the local planning authorities receive and determine most applications for listed building consent.

The grounds for and consequences of listing are not universally understood and should, perhaps, be paused over. The relevant Act of Parliament (now the Town and Country Planning Act 1971 S. 54 et seq) refers to 'buildings of special architectural or historic interest' and the words should be noted with care. Consistent practice, tested in disputed cases over many years, has shown that special interest can be defined with a fair degree of objectivity. Note, in any case, that buildings are **not** listed because they are fashionably admired, because they inspire local affection, because they are useful and capable of being preserved or because it would be a stupid waste to pull them down. These may be good reasons for working to save a building. They are not reasons for listing. The only test is that they should be of 'special architectural or historic interest.' Some theatrically unemployable remnants may pass this test, while thoroughly sound and useful buildings may fail it.

The circumstances of the building are not at issue at the time of listing. The law sensibly poses two separate questions, one of fact and one of practicality. The first: 'Is this building of special interest?' is for the Environment Secretary to answer. If the answer is 'yes', then he must list it without regard to other considerations. The second question: 'What steps should be taken to protect the special interest?' is asked only when there are specific proposals to be considered and, in this case, responsibility rests with the local planning authority dealing with the application for consent (unless it wishes to consent to demolition, in which case the Secretary of State has the opportunity to intervene). Listing, then, does not amount to a declaration that a building will be preserved against every buffet of fate, but it does mean that its claims for preservation cannot be set aside without public knowledge. Listing also opens up other avenues. Local authorities, for example, have powers to carry out emergency repairs to unoccupied and neglected listed buildings. (This is discussed later).

Despite the fact that important listed buildings are still occasionally lost, the protection afforded by listing is so important that it is necessary to inquire about any unlisted theatre under threat, 'Can it be listed?' A local authority may serve a building preservation notice to secure temporary protection until the Environment Secretary can make a decision on listing, but the process is not completely without risk for them. It is often quicker and as effective for anyone who is fairly sure of the building's merits to go straight to the Department of the Environment with a well argued case for listing, remembering the criteria, bearing in mind that facts and not passions will determine the matter and supporting the detailed documentation with the best available photographs.

The listing procedure and the lists themselves, which have been in existence for well over thirty years, should by now have come close to perfection but this is, sadly, far from being the case. The government's expert investigators who compile, revise and update the lists have been reduced to a disgracefully small team and many worthy buildings are still unlisted. A big push was made specifically on theatre listing after 1972, following the loss of the Granville, Walham Green, but the **Curtains!!!** Gazetteer shows that listing criteria have not been applied consistently and in certain parts of the country numbers of listable theatres remain unprotected. Because the official investigators cannot enter or research every building before making a judgement, they are forced to rely heavily on external appearances and readily available information. Theatres are losers on both counts. A perfunctory doorway squeezed between shops, often belies a magnificent auditorium built over backland, while behind the splendid nineteenth century facade of a Royal, Empire or Majestic there may be nothing more than an insipid cinema auditorium botched up in the thirties. Published information on the fabrics (rather than on the historical associations) of old theatres has, until recently, been non-existent for much of Britain. The barbaric splendour of the Granville was not lost because it had been judged unworthy. It was simply not known about.

In any consideration of the listing of a theatre it is to be hoped that it will be reviewed against its proper historical background. It is futile to criticize the design of an 1890's music hall for showing evidence of commercial demands having corrupted the 'purity' of its architecture. Theatre architecture in Britain, from beginning almost to end, has been an architecture of commerce rather than of national or municipal display. The Royal Opera House and the Paris Opéra have completely different ancestries. It is also, perhaps, worth underlining the fact that old theatres and music halls are now comparatively uncommon building types. A good late Victorian variety theatre auditorium is a very much rarer object than a good Victorian church and we cannot afford to make mistakes of omission in listing so small a population. Skilled advocacy is therefore important.

After listing

Given that a theatre is safely listed, what steps can be taken for its protection? All that can be done here is to summarize some of the main points. The serious inquirer must, at the very least, have digested Department of Environment Circulars 23/77 and 12/81, both entitled **Historic Buildings and Conservation Areas.** Despite their stodgy official appearance, they are easily the most lucid and useful guides to the subject. Most obviously, the controlling authority can refuse consent to works of demolition or harmful alteration. An aggrieved applicant can appeal against a refusal (or conditions attached to a consent) and the Secretary of State will then appoint an inspector to consider representations, commonly, but not always, at a public inquiry. In the longer run, the refused applicant who claims that refusal has made his building incapable of reasonably beneficial use can serve a purchase notice on the authority (but lack of beneficial use can be difficult to prove).

The proposal to demolish the Lyric, Hammersmith, led to an expertly argued public inquiry in 1967 and a decision the following year that, although the building could be demolished, the plaster interior should be reproduced if and when a new theatre was erected. This kind of compromise is not generally to be encouraged but in this case it was put forward and accepted and it worked brilliantly. Theatre preservers should note this decision for another reason. An historic building will stand or fall by what it is or might be, rather than by the memories surrounding it. Historical associations were not given much weight in the case of the Lyric. The Minister's decision spoke of the quality of the auditorium, its 'excellent Matcham plasterwork and its limited size and proportions, giving an intimate actor-audience relationship.'

Turning the tide of destruction · preservation must start somewhere: Portsmouth Theatre Royal has started the long climb back to useful life.   *Iain Mackintosh*

Control of alterations

The planning authority can use the consent apparatus to keep a tight control over alterations, preventing casual mutilation or erosion of the structural and architectural integrity of the building and governing the ways in which new works are to be detailed and executed. In some cases, of course, the local authority which wields the protective powers is itself the villain of the piece, having acquired a theatre almost accidentally, with land required for a road scheme or a housing development. This is almost the worst thing that can happen to an historic building, since few authorities make a good showing at settling inter-departmental conflicts and hardly any make provision for the care of buildings which were not acquired for retention. No authority can grant itself listed building consent to demolish or alter its own buildings - they have to apply to the Environment Secretary - but in the case of an unwanted building this all too often means that there will be a long period of neglect before a reluctant council can bring itself to accept the Secretary of State's almost inevitable decision and his insistence that they should set an example to other owners. Prolonged neglect and its ally, vandalism, can, in these circumstances, lead to such a state of disrepair that the building becomes a dangerous structure - and the need to remove danger is an effective defence against the charge of having carried out works of demolition without consent.

When the owner of the neglected building happens to be the authority with statutory power over dangerous structures, there may be murmurs of dissatisfaction from the interested public.

This special problem leads us to the next general point. The listed building consent control system can be highly effective in the hands of a determined authority with knowledgeable officers, but it is a system which responds to initiatives by others. It does not deal with the problems of disuse, disrepair and abuse.

Disuse and disrepair

Disuse and disrepair usually go hand in hand. Where an owner hopes to benefit from the redevelopment of a valuable site he is not likely to attend to the maintenance of buildings which he sees as encumbrances rather than assets. Where listed buildings are concerned the local authority has two possible courses of action. It can acquire a building compulsorily after serving a **repairs notice** specifying works necessary for the proper preservation of the building. If, after two months, the repairs have not been done, acquisition may proceed, but local authority preservation is such an underfunded activity that this kind of action is rarely contemplated until a building has become a thoroughgoing liability, which no authority in its right mind would acquire.

A more useful power is that provided by Section 101 of the 1971 Act. This enables an authority to enter an **unoccupied** listed building to carry out urgent repairs after giving seven days' notice of an intention to do so. The cost can then be recovered from the owner. Although the range of works which can be described as 'urgent' is not wide, this is a useful power which is more often seen to be employed and it is therefore a more potent negotiating weapon. The Secretary of State can also direct that the power to enter and repair is to apply to an unlisted building in a conservation area, if he is persuaded that its preservation is sufficiently important.

The Section 101 provisions can be specially useful in combating the deliberate neglect of a listed building. The execution of repairs, even temporary shoring, by the local authority can effectively block the defence that pre-emptive demolition has become necessary in the interests of safety or health.

Harmful use

Undesirable use of a building can be more difficult to deal with. The use of a theatre (listed or unlisted) as a warehouse, workshop, supermarket or for any other purpose remote from its established use can be controlled by the ordinary planning machinery. Certain changes, however, do not require permission. Uses within the same class, as defined by the Use Classes Order, are regarded as interchangeable. Class XVII comprises "theatre, cinema, music hall or concert hall." Whilst at first sight the grouping seems reasonable, a change from theatre to cinema may involve radical internal reconstruction (controllable only if the building is listed) of kinds which would make a return to live theatrical use expensive or improbable.

The amendment of this part of the Use Classes Order has been pressed for at least five years, but governments have so far failed to act.

Some apparently undesirable changes may, of course, be beneficial in certain circumstances, in that a building may thereby be maintained in repair until its preservation in a more appropriate use can be secured. Bingo has been the temporary salvation of many a surburban theatre which might otherwise have been demolished in the sixties. Wilton's Music Hall would probably have been lost in the fifties if it had not served a turn as a rag warehouse. The use was undesirable, even dangerous, but the hall remained in reasonable condition while it was so occupied and it deteriorated when the ragmen moved out.

Doing it yourself

We have already said that this essay cannot offer much useful advice to the preservation company in being, but before any company is formed, the 'say-couldn't-we-do-the-show-ourselves-right-here?' scene will have been acted out. At this stage excitement over possibilities is likely to have absorbed more time than discussion of formal organisation, but if theatre ownership is a real possibility, then the sooner the campaign shapes itself into a company the better.

It is neither difficult nor expensive to form a company for such a purpose but it will be necessary from the beginning to determine objectives as clearly as possible (but without undue rigidity: objectives are not the same thing as a programme of action) and to decide whether or not the company should attempt to obtain charitable status. The company can act before this latter point is settled but it may be wise not to start banking substantial sums of money until it can pay them into a charitable account (an existing charity with appropriate objectives may be able to help here, but be careful — the tax man is waiting to pounce).

The advantages of charitable status are considerable but the processes surrounding registration may involve lengthy negotiation with the Charity Commissioners and the Commissioners of Inland Revenue and registration will constrain the company's activities and the ways in which it can use its income.

A company which may not distribute its profits to its members and has charitable objects, such as the encouragement of the arts in order to advance education, provides the most useful machinery. It is not in law much different from a trust except in having the supreme advantage of relieving the directors or trustees of personal liability if they behave honestly and reasonably. Both a trust and a company will, when it is accepted as a charity, have an exemption from half its rates and from tax on any profit. The rating exemption is often valuable but the real advantage of a charity derives from its ability to receive money from other charities and by way of covenants. It can therefore raise and deal with donations in the most advantageous way.

Such a company is not particularly expensive to incorporate and register as a charity and although the whole process may with the intervention of authority take as long as six months there should be no difficulty with proper advice in achieving the result.

If the company trades in order to raise money the kind of trading will decide whether it can do so under its own aegis. Any consisting trading is unlikely to be within the main object of a charitable theatre company unless it is the presentation of plays. Otherwise it must be undertaken by a separate commercial company. That company by means of a covenant to the charity of its entire profit suffers no tax except VAT and the charity can recover tax on the profits paid to it. By this means it becomes legally the possessor of the gross profit of the trading company without itself trading.

The possibilities for trading profits may be reasonably valuable on some town sites. A music hall with a pub licence may do particularly well from lunch trade. But a much more significant gain may be within the charitable company's grasp if the site provides the possibility for a measure of extension or improvement or new building. The planning authority may be prepared to permit a profitable development if the profits provide an endowment for the preserved building. The 'air rights' deals which have worked to the advantage of 'landmark' buildings, in for example, New York and Montreal are not available under British law, but some conservation-minded authorities are prepared to negotiate 'Section 52 agreements' with developers on neighbouring sites to undertake (or pay for the carrying out of) restoration works to historic buildings not in the developer's direct ownership. Such 'planning gain' benefits drawn from profits generated by the issue of planning permissions have been questioned, but they work—and preservation companies and trusts should be alive to these possibilities.

Looking for grants

Most preservation companies will turn sooner or later to the Arts Council of Great Britain, the Historic Buildings Council, local athorities, local preservation trusts (where they exist) and the major charitable funds for grants. These will fall into two distinct categories: **Capital grants** which will assist them with the purchase, repair, restoration and equipping of their historic building and for their work in 'housing the arts' and **Revenue grants** to go toward meeting running costs in providing a cultural and education amenity for the Community.

Grant-making bodies of all kinds are inclined to be cool, if not impatient, with inquiries which take the form: 'We are thinking of preserving this building. How much will you give us?' The only approach which has the slightest chance of success is one which shows evidence of careful preparation and in the case of a theatre this must include realistic estimates of initial refurbishment costs, annual running expenses and income from ticket sales and other sources. No authority or organization is under a statutory or moral obligation to give money and the ones which are most likely to offer a significant amount are the ones which are most expert at spotting seductive non-starters.

This is not to say that there will be no sympathy for the problems of preservers who are having to inch forward, testing the ground at every step. It is sometimes sensible to spend a little money on a building to prevent deterioration while detailed plans are being discussed (as has been the case at the Theatre Royal, Portsmouth in 1980/81). An organisation which is clearly competent to grapple with the long term problems and is already well informed about such matters as means of escape requirements and local transport plans is the more likely to get help with its short term programme.

Political support

The preservation project which becomes a focus for party political conflict walks on broken legs, but preservation campaigns, whether or not they are directed toward ownership, accelerate from the moment they find broad political sympathy.

Theatre is still politically respectable. Politicians with no consuming interest in things theatrical recognise that, although stage entertainment is not the money-printing industry it once was, it is in fairly healthy demand and those who make provision for it are, by definition, civilized. Now that live theatres are uncommon, the town that has one is a cut above the town that has not.

The theatre preservation company which has among its trustees or directors two influential local politicians of opposing party colours should fly like a bird.

Proposals

We have so far considered what is rather than what might be. One of the most sweeping proposals made for the protection of theatres is that all of them, regardless of architectural or historic interest, should be subject to a form of special protection akin to that provided by listing. This would require legislation which, incidentally, would need to incorporate a very precise definition of the term 'theatre', but it would not be so drastic in its effect as the proposal put forward by the Federation of Theatre Unions in 1972. They pointed out that the greatest threat to theatres, especially in London, was high site values, leading to redevelopment proposals as leases fell in (in this connection note the disturbing picture painted by Lord Jenkins, Director of the Theatres Trust, in a talk to the London Society 19.3.80, published in The Society Journal). The Federation urged that all theatre sites (i.e. the freehold rather than the leasehold interest) should be acquired by the government or the appropriate local authority.

In the present harsh economic climate this solution is unlikely to commend itself and the record of official custodianship of theatres is, in any case, uneven. The Greater London Council's ownership of the Lyceum and the Garrick may have removed the risk of commercial re-development but it should be remembered that both were originally acquired for demolition and the Lyceum has not been used as a theatre for many years. Westminster City Council has recently disposed of the one theatre in its ownership on the open market.

The problem of theatres on valuable town centre sites must be solved urgently but, so far as public ownership is concerned, only a body which has nothing else to distract its attention is likely to give sufficient priority to the care and regeneration of theatres, and the only such body in sight at present is the Theatres Trust. For all its present weaknesses, the Trust is probably the best hope for the future.

The following steps might be considered:

(1) All theatres and music halls of special architectural or historic interest should be listed without delay. This is the simplest of precautions and the publication of the **Curtains!!!** Gazetteer should make this relatively easy. At the very least, the two and three star theatres in the gazetteer should be listed.

(2) The Theatres Trust should be endowed with sufficient income to enable it to exercise its most important power, that of owning theatres, and to carry out its other functions in a responsible and effective way. The Trust, we are told, has at present 'scarcely enough money to sustain itself in being' (Lord Jenkins, loc.cit).

(3) Local authorities in appropriate cases and after taking the advice of the Trust, should be prepared to serve repairs notices on listed theatres and accept purchase notices on any theatres with a view to re-selling freehold interests to the Trust.

(4) Similarly, they should be able to acquire compulsorily and re-sell to the Trust at existing use value, theatres which appear to be permanently disused (or are disused apparently prior to demolition) on sites which have no planning permissions for redevelopment.

There is nothing revolutionary in (1). So far as (2) is concerned, the Trust need not, as freeholder, be involved in the continuing expense of running the theatres. It would need professional support and this should be provided free or be funded from central government sources (to do less than this is to make nonsense of the continued existence of a body with statutory powers). The costs it would incur in acquiring and possibly repairing theatres might reasonably be provided from the National Heritage Memorial Fund. Given a properly funded Trust, (3) should present no difficulty. Only (4) would require legislation and it would be controversial legislation. Whatever is now done to give adequate protection to what remains of our inheritance of theatres is likely to be controversial, but the nettle must be grasped.

The Need to Know

Michael Sell

Historian and Secretary of Curtains!!!

'Theatre' means different things to different people. For the theatre owner it is the capital investment with which he plans to make a profit; for performers it is the building within which they hope not only to find good houses but also to have the facilities which mean that their skills can be given full rein; for the majority of local audiences it is the local temple of Thespeis to which they are attracted to see 'the drama', farce, comedy, variety, opera and ballet. Like any other economic activity in general 'you get what you pay for' and so it is with theatre and the quality of the building and the entertainment is as varied as in any other sphere of life.

After a period in the doldrums theatre building recommenced with a boom which stared in the 1860's and continued to gather pace until shortly before the First World War. It is now recognised that the 1870's mark the turning point in working class living standards brought about by a decline in the price of many essential goods. Particularly is this true of agricultural produce which was being imported from the Americas, Australasia and South Africa. Thus the working class had a rise in real income giving them the ability to widen their hitherto restricted range of purchases. One area which benefitted greatly from a new demand was the entertainment industry. Simultaneously with this new demand was the desire by investors to engage in enterprises which would bring a better return than they found in agriculture (where it was perhaps as low as 2%) and industry. Then, as now, the entertainment industry was full of pitfalls, but many investors seemed eager to support companies which were able to show that competitors at least made handsome profits.

How little we know

During the last decade writers on the theatre industry have tended to concentrate on the foremost theatres, architects and promoters to such an extent that the focus of attention seems firmly fixed on the grand and the spectacular rather than the ordinary.

Stoll and his great Coliseum, and the theatres of Frank Matcham, have all excited the imagination and been the subject of published works, but little has been written on the majority of theatre owners, architects or theatres. Biographical material has been forthcoming on the stars which shone brightly but little has been written on those artists whose names never appeared in lights but whose work, of whatever quality, was of great importance to those who lived in areas where only minor theatres existed, for the history of the theatre is often inextricably bound up with them.

The fact is that there are major areas of theatre research which require responsible scholarship dedicated to furthering our knowledge of theatre and of the entertainment of the period. A glance merely at the gazetteer

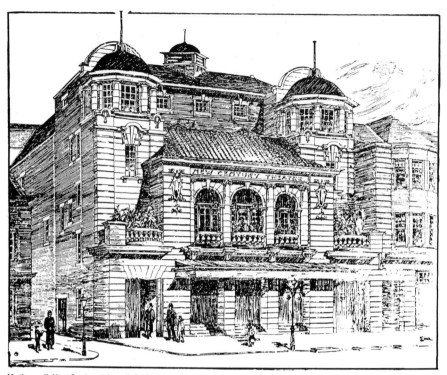

Motherwell, New Century · demolished 1934

will reveal that against some 190 theatres appears the comment 'architect unknown'. The situation is as bad when taken in the context of the demolished list where the architects of over 220 theatres have yet to be chronicled.

The major theatre architects are defined in this volume but the majority of the theatres cited were designed by less well known architects. The late eighteenth century saw a great expansion in the number of theatres and in the organisation of groups of players who travelled a known circuit. Perhaps the best known of these groups, and certainly the best chronicled, was the Fisher Circuit which was active in East Anglia, but most areas of the country were visited by one group or another. The theatres in which they played were either owned by the circuit or were built as speculative ventures by local builders or those involved with local commerce. The greatest number of these theatres were built to the designs of those involved in the construction or promotion and only rarely were architects used but the most important buildings of the period were designed by promoters who totally understood theatre and produced great playhouses — of this group William Wilkins is the most significant.

During the 1830's and 1840's many of these theatres closed their doors for the last time, to be taken over for other purposes.

The architects of the building boom

In the nineteenth century there was a complete reversal in the distribution of population which, in addition to increasing from almost 11m to 37m, changed from being 25% urban in 1801 to 25% rural at the end of the century with the mid-point coinciding with the middle of the century. This greatly increased population density throughout the country, and particularly in the swollen old and growing new urban centres differed considerably from earlier generations. The new urban population did not always have the family and village ties which controlled and disciplined society and thus the traditional pastimes gave way to new ones which were often initiated and organised by entrepreneurs who saw that there was a large scale demand for leisure entertainment.

The great boom in theatre building which has been described was therefore no accident but a response to a demand which substantially aided by developments in commercial organisation and, in particular, but the Company Acts of the 1860's which extended the concept of limited liability. In addition the gradual introduction of a system of urban transport after 1855 and the growth of street lighting in the same period made it safer to be abroad at night and travel to the theatre both cheap and convenient.

Thus a new group of theatrical entrepreneurs, architects, builders and showmen grew to dominate the scene, many of whom based themselves on London, but almost every town or city had imitators who varied in their expertise, their flair and their success.

The major architects accepted commissions from both the large orperator and the provincial promotor but the latter often looked more locally, perhaps in the hope of saving money. Indeed many of the provincial theatres were designed by architects who only ever attempted one theatre design. Some of the resulting temples were of the highest quality but some were poor and showed little comprehension of the needs of either the audiences or the players, with the consequence that within a short period they inevitably succumbed to competition and, by 1910, this often meant 'the amazing bioscope'.

There were however some extremely good theatres designed by architects whose work deserves greater investigation. For example Richard Horsfall and Sons of Halifax, who not only built the Theatre Royal in that town in 1905 but the following year altered the Palace Theatre there before moving across the Pennines to design the Burnley Palace in 1907 and returning to Yorkshire to produce the Huddersfield Palace two years later. In Scotland Alex Cullen of Hamilton appears to have undertaken commissions for theatre designs in Ayr, Motherwell, Falkirk and Kilmarnock between 1902 and 1904. Wimperis and Arber were responsible for the New Palace Theatres in Plymouth (1897) and Blackburn (1899) and, at the same time Henry Brunton was creating most interesting theatres in Cork and Dublin. It was to theatres designed by these and by many others that the theatre-going public took themselves at the height of the boom.

Competitions and cancellations

The late nineteenth century was a period of intense competition and, on occasion, theatre promotors instituted design competitions for new buildings which were entered by both the famous and the unknown. In 1865 Charles John Phipps, the doyen of theatre architects of the age, divided the premium put up for the design for the Theatre Royal, South Shields, with T. M. Clemence, the end product being a marriage between a Clemence facade and a Phipps interior. Clemence was the Borough Engineer and this is perhaps the first example of the holder of such an office designing a theatre. Similarly in 1894 the Blackpool Tower Company instituted a design competition for a 'new theatre, circus and market' which was entered by both Phipps and Matcham but which was won by Wylson and Long. (Promoters however, were not necessarily committed to commissioning the winner for the final design). At the present time such competitions are poorly documented.

Inevitably there were also a number of projects which did not come to fruition. A study of just one of the major theatre architects, Frank Matcham, shows that even before 1900 he had prepared abortive plans for theatres in Barrow-in-Furness, Birmingham, Chatham, Dewsbury, Huddersfield and Newcastle-upon-Tyne. The fact that the companies which promoted these projects engaged such an eminent architect indicates that their plans were substantial. Little is known of most of these projects, which include Fowler's National Opera House (1875) and the press of the period tended to eulogise over all new plans to such an extent that buildings are sometimes unrecognisable. Indeed, even the architect's own handouts are often extravagant in their phraseology and introduced rather meaningless descriptions which do not truly reflect the architectural features of the building.

Contemporary newspaper reports, for all their faults, often include details like the name of the builder and of the specialist sub-contractors while at the same time omitting that of the architect. The great boom in theatre building brought about a demand for specialist supplies which was met by a number of companies which have yet to be documented. Building contractors like Kingerlee's of Oxford worked in towns including London, Reading and Northampton and W. Wallis and Co. of Balham built many theatres in the capital. A. R. Dean & Co. of Birmingham became extremely important suppliers

Plymouth, New Palace

of seating and other fittings as well as acting as consultants in interior decor. For high quality decorative plasterwork de Jong and Co. were pre-eminent and Campbell Smith and Co. were the leading decorators. Other companies like E. Oldroyd & Co. of Leeds provided specialist fire protection apparatus and theatre heating.

The Moss-Stoll combine formed in 1899 gives some idea of the intricacies of theatre ownership for it was formed to acquire some ten existing companies and had an authorised capital of £1m. in £5 shares, half of which were 5% cumulative preference shares; power was also taken to enable the company to issue 4% perpetual debenture stock to the value of £.4m. This company controlled theatres in Scotland, Wales and England and formed the largest single chain of theatres which also had an association with Thornton's North East Circuit. The other regional circuits, with Broadhead's 'Bread and Butter' circuit in the North West and de Freece with the South of England Hippodromes are examples of the comparatively large scale organisation compared with the small family unit.

James Kiernan, the Liverpool theatre owner was very active in that city during the 'nineties and the incredible Dan Lowry guided the destinies of theatres in Ireland booking his Star Music Hall in Dublin in conjunction with the Malakoff Music Hall in Liverpool. Other theatres had links with other companies through membership of the board of directors. In 1907 the Burnley Palace Theatre Co. Ltd., was established with a capital of £15,000 in £1 shares with Frank MacNaghten as managing director which immediately linked the theatre with the North of England Theatre Corporation and his Vaudeville Circuit.

Families like the Curry's of Grimsby were locally important in the history of the theatre over a long period as were the Newsome's in Coventry while the Revill's were a major force in Lancashire. Milton Bode who in later life was described as a 'millionaire theatre owner' was lessee and owner of a number of theatres whereas Benjamin Sherwood, who opened the beautiful Wakefield Opera House in 1894 described himself in the deeds as a licensed victualler rather than a theatre owner. Wybert Rousby, famous principally as husband of 'the beautiful Mrs. Rousby', for whom Tom Taylor wrote many popular historical melodramas, at various times managed and owned theatres as far apart as Middlesborough, London and the Channel Islands. In a similar vein the architect W. G. R. Sprague built the Balham Hippodrome and held the licence himself for the first three years of its operation.

Robert Arthur, Tom Barrasford, The Livermore Brothers, Sefton Parry and numerous individuals, partnerships and private companies were all important in providing the theatre entertainment which is now a substantial part of our theatrical history and experience. There is still a need for much research to be done in the areas suggested here as well as in other specialist spheres of the theatre industry. Securing the future of some of our existing theatre buildings may be enhanced by a more detailed historical knowledge of their past and our social and civic heritage can only be the richer.

Douglas, Gaiety, before restoration

Victor Glasstone

Restoring the Gaiety

Victor Glasstone

Architect, Consultant for the restoration of the Gaiety Theatre, Douglas, Isle of Man and photographic editor of the book.

The Gaiety, Douglas, is one of Matcham's finest smaller theatres, and one of the best surviving from his mature period at the turn of the century. Fortunately, over the years it had not been wrecked by modernization, or by the addition of irrelevant excrescences. It was shabby, of course, and had lost much: the curtaining to its boxes, and the wallpapers; around the balcony front, the opaline lampshades had been replaced by celluloid horrors, but all the early bronzed and gilded sconces, and the ceiling chandeliers were intact, still with their frilly opaline shades. I doubt if the marvellous ceiling had been repainted since the building first opened in 1900. The roof was in need of extensive repair; but rain that had entered, had seeped, luckily, only down the side walls. The ceiling with its painted panels and garland of godesses in high relief had entirely escaped damage.

As a firm believer in historical accuracy, and having implicit trust in the intentions, and instinct, of a genius at theatrical atmosphere like Matcham, it was joy finding in the office of the theatre manager, Mr. Bob Wilkinson, two fine photograhs of the theatre taken soon after its opening. Contemporary descriptions, too, had enthused in 1900, and given a full description of colours and materials, and so on. The problem was one of re-creation and refurbishment (at the minimum cost), with the addition of a few tiresome details like extra fire doors with intermediate lobbies — the fire department of the Isle of Man being somewhat more sensitive to the fire hazard . . .

The job was spread over two years, as money became available. The roof was in the process of repair when I was called in, but the fire-break lobbies had already been installed, and a lot of money spent on a new sound and lighting system. The new switchboard sat incongruously in the Prompt stage box, and new spots had been attached to rails at gallery level. It would have been too costly to move all this, and the best that could be done was to drape off the switchboard more sympathetically (hiding its fire-proof panel), and paint out the spotlights. The ugly loudspeakers were tried below the new velvet orchestra valance, but the sound became muffled, and they were replaced on the sides of the proscenium, but painted out. An unsatisfactory compromise, but the Des O'Connors, and others who play the Gaiety in the summer, imagine they cannot function without amplification.

For the rest, it was a case of cleaning, restoring, and resurrecting lost atmosphere. The entire theatre was scaffolded, and the ceiling and paintwork washed down; at times, almost scrubbed. It came up good as new, with just the right muted tones of umber, cream, burnt yellows, touches of grey-blue, and that favourite of the period, "vieux rose". Even the panel paintings were washed down with a proprietory cleaner, without damage. The magnificent great painted drop-cloth, one of only two in Britain, was more tenderly cleaned. The only repainting done was a certain amount of touching up on the balcony

Douglas, Gaiety, after restoration *Victor Glasstone*

and box fronts, where generations of cleaning ladies had wiped off some of the colour and light gilding. An absolutely essential characteristic of turn of the century theatres is lush and fulsome drapery. Box curtains were always double, with inner and outer curtains at the openings, and the pelmets were heavily draped; smooth, material-covered pelmets did not become fashionable until much later. The problem was to find a velvet that would drape properly, yet be completely fireproof: nothing less would satisfy the fire authorities. In the end a material was used which felt horrible in the hand, but applied in large quantity had the desired effect. The inner walls of the boxes were painted with emulsion. Being in shadow they seem as though covered with a silk or flock wallpaper. Little drop-crystal chandeliers were hung in the centres of the pelmets to create chiaroscuro, as in the early photographs of the theatre.

The tabs and proscenium pelmet (smooth with braided decoration) were in reasonable condition, but the Isle of Man Government (owners of the Gaiety), was generous, and the original draped, flounced and roped extravaganza was copied — to great effect. As was the orchestra flounce, long since vanished, and hung on a new brass rail. Expensive details like these made all the difference.

The chairs, naturally, were in appalling condition, and the expense of shipping them off to Warrington crippling, but repadded and recovered these look far better than any modern equivalent. The voilent wallpaper of the early photographs was also a problem. Nothing carried by the normal suppliers was voilent enough, and a specially designed paper would have been too expensive. Eventually a gold paper with heavy brown flock sunflowers (or somesuch), was found in a newspaper advertisement. In the "ad", and in the piece, it was of stunning hideousness and vulgarity, but, once hung, it was completely right, and of just the correct scale. Matcham and his decorators **were** vulgar, but they knew perfectly well what they were doing.

The foyers of the Gaiety are not over-generous, but adequate. Happily, the theatre fronts onto the really broad pavement of the Harris Promenade, with its adjacent pubs and cafes: very lively in the summer when the theatre is used most. New extensive foyers were therefore not necessary (even if there had been the money), and the existing spaces were redecorated, with a new bar created from old offices at first balcony level: an area which had at one time been a refreshment room. The series of entrance doors along the main facade had been painted violet, something that Matcham would never have done. Cleaned down, they were found to be of mahogany, as described at the time.

In all, money was spent where it would produce the maximum effect. The total cost, inclusive of extensive roof repair, fire breaks, toilets, sound and lighting systems, worked out at just over £260,000; and the Manx Government were delighted to receive an award from the British Tourist Authority. Even more important, the theatre now plays to capacity audiences.

Douglas, Gaiety · detail of ceiling   *Victor Glasstone*

69

London, Palace - the grid

GLC

Mechanical Archaeology in the Theatre

David Wilmore

Restorer of 19th century stage machinery

An unlikely title for an essay on stage machinery you may say, but after visiting many theatres in London and the provinces I have often climbed over rubbish, delved through piles of newspapers and occasionally waded through water to look at excellent examples of stage carpenters' and stage machinists' art. This important, but small, band of craftsmen who filled in the stage area which was invariably left blank on the architect's plan, usually did so without writing anything down.

Yet today much stage machinery lies dusty, derelict or has been destroyed, simply because its importance has not been realised. On a number of occasions I have turned up at a stage door, wrangled with the stage door keeper to gain access only to be informed by the manager "No, nothing like that here" but having gained access to the extremities of the stage, grid and cellar have found a wealth of information to be recorded. Sadly, however, all too frequently the following up of clues as to the wherabouts of stage machinery only leads to disappointment.

Quite recently I visited a London theatre and was informed by the resident stage carpenter "That old stuff down in the cellar is really useful when I need a bit of timber in a hurry"; similarly the proud provincial manager "Doesn't it look nice since we got rid of all that clutter?", and there you are gazing at new walls, toilets and dressing rooms — a small return for a journey half the length of the country.

Nevertheless, stage machinery has not all been completely destroyed — in fact it can be restored. I have personally been in charge of a full scale renovation of Victorian stage machinery at the New Tyne Theatre in Newcastle-upon-Tyne for the past two and a half years. The theatre was built in 1867 and the machinery in question was installed at that time.

It is anyone's guess when last a Victorian wooden stage was used so we have been largely working in the dark. When we started I do not think it was realised how important the project was from an historical point of view, but today the theatre can boast what is believed to be the only working set of wooden Victorian stage machinery left in existence.

However there is still a significant amount of stage machinery left in London which could be restored, notably at Her Majesty's, The Playhouse (now closed) and the Alexandra Palace Theatre. Theatre managements probably do not realise that they might be sitting on a veritable goldmine. People would literally come from Outer Mongolia to visit a theatre in London with working Victorian stage machinery, and just think of the potential for a Christmas pantomime. No doubt you are saying "But what about the cost of employing the number necessary to run it?". Admittedly it is slightly more labour intensive than a 'normal' theatre but it really is astonishing what can be achieved with the correct rigging systems and good old mechanical advantage. At a recent pantomime in Newcastle we could raise two cut cloths and at the same time lower a backcloth using only two men, and it is quite feasible to do it with one man should the situation demand it! Why then do theatre managements fail to use the full potential of their theatre?

Almost every large theatre in Great Britain in the nineteenth century had wooden stage machinery of one kind or another. It was essential to guarantee a good box office. People came to the theatre not only to be entertained by the actor but to be astounded by the machinist and his transformation scenes.

If we could take a trip back in time to England 1870 and examine a typical opera house or large theatre we would probably find a wooden stage with all its 'trappings'. For instance, underneath the stage in the downstage area we would probably see 2, possibly 4 demon traps. These would of course be used particularly during the pantomime season when Aladdin rubbed his lamp, and as if from nowhere the genie appeared. The demon traps would be positioned symmetrically around the grave trap. This type of trap varied in construction, some were in effect small bridges employing a drum and shaft, while others were large demon traps employing only counterweights. Of course the classic use of this trap was in Hamlet during the Grave Scene — hence its name.

After this arrangement of small traps we would see a regular layout of bridges and cuts running the full width of the proscenium opening. This would probably start with 2 cuts followed by a bridge and so on in rotation, and we might expect to find 10 cuts and 5 bridges. The cuts are the narrow openings in the floor through which the tongue of the sloat passes carrying with it whatever the stage crew attach, be it a flat or a ground row. Of course the bridges were very versatile pieces of equipment which could simply be used as rostra on the stage, or as a means of transforming the scene from a glade to a Palace of a Thousand Jewels!

The understage area is only half the story; all kinds of scenery could be suspended from the grid and "flown in" at the appropriate time. By 1870 some of the theatres were beginning to use counterweighting, all-be-it on a small and simple scale by today's standards. However, most of the heavy scenery would have been attached to the drum and shaft system which would have been installed usually on the grid but sometimes on the upper fly galleries. This would allow one man to 'pull out' two cut cloths/back drops on his own — no mean achievement if you've ever tried to pull one out on a hemp line!

We would probably be able to see several sets of grooves suspended from the lower fly galleries. These were suspensions which guided flats and wings into position on the stage. It enabled one set of scenery to be prepared whilst a scene was going on. At the end of the scene the flats could be removed into the wing space, revealing anther set of flats behind the first pair. Of course there were many varying types of groove, and this is its operation in just a simplified form.

When all the machinery was co-ordinated together into a spectacular scene the effect could be staggering. In 1886 the Tyne Theatre and Opera House produced the pantomime Dick Whittington and his Cat, which had been written by E. L. Blanchard and had been performed at Drury Lane. On Monday December 27th 1886, the reporter for the Newcastle Daily Chronicle wrote:

"The realism of the shipwreck scene is extraordinary, and the difficulty in placing it on stage, may be guessed from the fact that the huge ship, which is seen to break up and sink weighs 3 tons! The set canvas of the picture was painted by the famous artist, W. R. Beverley, and it is one of the grandest representations of a raging sea that has been placed before an audience. The centre of the stage was seen filled by moving waves, worked by mechanism, and amongst them the great vessel pitched and rolled violently. Then the mast fell over the side, and the vessel collapsed and sank, whilst a ray of light, piercing through the gloom, showed Dick and his Cat clinging to a rock."

Oh! to have been there!

When Richard D'Oyly Carte built the Royal English Opera House in Cambridge Circus (now the Palace Theatre) he tried to improve the standard of stage machinery by employing Walter Dando, an engineer who had already had considerable experience in designing French stage machinery. In his initial design for D'Oyly Carte he proposed a stage built entirely of iron. However, this scheme was abandoned and a composite stage of iron and timber constructed. Nevertheless, the mechanism which he designed and installed within this framework was certainly innovative. Dando introduced (supposedly for the first time in England) a piece of stage machinery common to the European theatres known as "The Chariot and Pole". This allowed "flats" to be attached to poles, which were mounted on chariots, which ran on tram rails at mezzanine level. This meant that flats could be attached to the poles in the wing space and then pushed on stage, thus facilitating a smooth scene change.

The sloat system was retained, but it was modified by the introduction of counterweights, and coupling bars which enabled several sets of sloats to be operated simultaneously, and the overall effect was one of scenery changing in a smooth and co-ordinated manner.

The bridges were also retained, but were constructed entirely of iron and the old cumbersome drum and shaft was discarded and replaced with purchase pulleys and counterweights. Counterweights were also installed in the fly tower, but the drum and shaft system was still retained on the grid.

In 1896 Edwin Otho Sachs devoted a large portion of his treatise 'Modern Theatres and Opera Houses' to stage machinery, and in 1898 he brought out a patent based on the old bridge system used by the wooden stage machinery. This was in fact to be the preliminary design for the installation of stage machinery at the Theatre Royal, Drury Lane in 1899, and at the Royal Opera House, Covent Garden in 1901. The bridges were sophisticated structures of light steel lattice grider work of vast proportions. The Covent Garden bridges were in fact 40ft. long and 8ft. wide. The overall saving on expenses must have been considerable because each bridge was powered by electric motors. After the intial outlay of capital the machinery only required the attendance of a mechanic once a week, his wage being 30 shillings! As a result there was great unrest among the stage staff. Indeed several days after the completion of the installation and several days before the opening of a new opera season the entire stage staff, according to 'The Scientific American', were dismissed, "The British workman having apparently not taken to the modern appliances"!

Today the stage machinist is a technological wizard with a degree in hydraulics who usually installs machinery for a 'one off' production. When 'Jesus Christ Superstar' was in London at the Palace Theatre there was a special piece of modern machinery installed under the stage and when I visited the theatre I found the beginning and end of the story — a modern approach to machinery nestling among the old timber framework D'Oyly Carte had installed ninety years ago.

As the **Curtains!!!** survey has shown, many of our theatres have been saved from demolition by bingo and the cinema. In the case of the New Tyne Theatre the machinery lay hibernating for sixty years while the cinema projectors whirled on into the 1970's. Then at last they stopped and the machinery came back to life with the theatre. If it has been done once it can be done again and should be before all the relics pass beyond the point of return.

Glasgow, Theatre Royal - removing the television studio floor during the reconstruction of 1975   *Ove Arup & Partners*

Engineering the Restoration

Derek Sugden

Engineer and leader of the teams entrusted with the restoration of the Theatre Royal, Glasgow and the Opera House, Buxton.

The first view of the Hope Street elevation and entrance to the Theatre Royal, Glasgow in 1972 was depressing but penetrating inside the visitor would find, underneath the accumulated debris of sixteen years of Scottish Television's occupation, the achromatic remains of a once superb Victorian French Renaissance interior by that great master, Charles John Phipps.

When design started, feelings were very mixed and ranged from the euphoric to the most pessimistic about what could or could not be achieved. The difficulties experienced with applying the Building Regulations and GLC Bye-laws to Snape and Henry Wood Hall were already known but this time the Scottish Building Regulations had to be met and, at that time, they were administered by 'Masters' with many grand titles.

Very soon after the Building Contract started in October 1974 it was agreed that the structure of 'Theatre Royal' could only be described as a particular form of nineteenth century Glaswegian rubbish. A few weeks after work had started, any problems with the Scottish Building Regulations, the Fire Master, Master of Guilds, and all the other remnants of the medieval system of building control North of Hadrian's Wall, paled into insignificance compared with keeping the structure in position and tolerably stable. After gutting the fly tower, any new fixings for fly galleries, fly floors and new theatre engineering installations presented great problems. When the inner skin of stonework was drilled or cut away the internal rubble fill ran out as if the life blood of the building was running away. When an optimistic client asked for an investigation into the removal of the props, added at some time to the front of the dress circle balcony to control vibration and resonance, the structure caused further anxieties. The removal of the flooring to examine the structure they had propped revealed a system of timber cantilevers which, particularly in the slips, could only be described as "having been left to the carpenter to work something out". The exposed timber cantilevers were reinforced with new structural steel beams fixed to the existing timbers with coach bolts. New steel cantilevers were used to reinforce the slips and techniques were developed to fix these with long bolts and connectors through the full thickness of the masonry walls in a similar way to the fixings developed for the fly tower. These fixings also used modern grouting methods incorporating epoxy materials.

The Opera House, Buxton, designed by Frank Matcham and built in 1903 was, in contrast to Glasgow, very well put together with well constructed stone walls and a timber structure for the stage tower. There were no structural problems as at Glasgow and no heartaches about the integrity of the structure but, like Glasgow, orchestra pits were needed of much greater size and depth, requiring cantilever stage construction and deep excavations which always seem to coincide with streams, rivers and natural springs!

The essential tasks were: to create an orchestra pit as large as the geometry and acoustic of the auditorium would allow, and to restore the Opera House as near as possible to Matcham's original design.

A new orchestra pit for eighty players was achieved by introducing cantilever steel beams without any disturbances to the original stage structure. The electrical installation was renewed. In the auditorium, new positions for modern stage lighting were introduced, while throughout appropriate decorative light fittings were reinstated. On stage there is a choice of stage lighting controls: either the reconditioned 'grand master' of the 1930's or the opportunity to connect any portable modern memory system. There is a new heating system using the old radiators. The original ventilation system was reinstated, and a unique piece of restoration was the gas fired 'sunburner' in the centre of the dome which was dismantled, cleaned and modified for North Sea gas. It is now controlled by modern electronics and the burner was fired on the first night for everyone to see.

In finalising the colour scheme Arups were guided not only by descriptions in the Press of 1903 but by the discovery of an old carpet, about three layers down, in one of the boxes. This proved to have been made by a firm in Brighouse, who wove the carpet on an old loom of 1907 in the original pattern and colours. This carpet and the wall tiling in the stalls provided the palette for the colour scheme of blue, brown, cream, white and gold.

Matcham was no purist where architectural style was concerned, and juxtaposed classical and art nouveau forms. This can be seen in the Upper

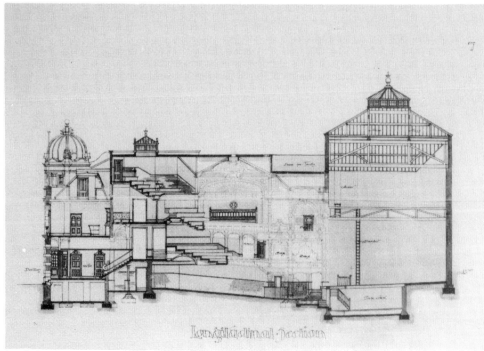

Longitudinal Section by Frank Matcham

Circle and Dress Circle bar where the Edwardian stained glass windows, renewed by matching old glass, appear in a classical setting.

Acoustic measurements taken in October 1977 indicated a powerful sound with a very good distribution throughout the house. The evening of July 30th 1979 confirmed that the elusive balance between voice and orchestra had been achieved. The refurbishment had been completed in six months at a total cost, exclusive only of external works to the stonework, of only £303,000.

Common to all these conversions and restorations are the technical and aesthetic problems of incorporating modern mechanical and electrical systems in buildings with woefully inadequate spaces for the distribution of services. The aim has always been to incorporate them in a sensitive and unobtrusive way and is part of the whole approach of not wishing anybody to know that another architect has been there. Sustaining this idea through the design of the reconstruction and restoration of our old theatres makes everything else seem easy.

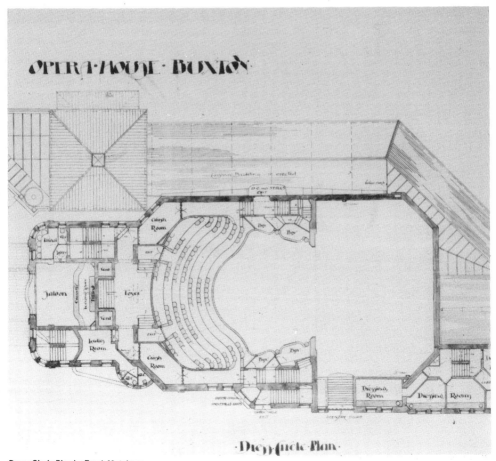

Dress Circle Plan by Frank Matcham

Bury St. Edmunds, Theatre Royal - there is an exit today where once there was a stage box

Steve Stephens

Restored theatres can be viable

Francis Reid

General Administrator Theatre Royal, Bury St Edmunds 1979/81

There are two basic categories of theatres: producing theatres which manufacture their own shows, and touring theatres which buy ready made product.

Old theatres in general and small old theatres in particular are not really suitable for use as producing theatres since they lack the necessary rehearsal, workshop, storage and administrative spaces. Moreover, production theatres are expensive to run and in the present economic climate it is difficult to envisage a time when funds will become available for new theatre-based companies.

On the other hand, touring theatres need less funding and have a much more flexible budget. Because they can range across the entire spectrum of drama, dance and music, they have become known as Mixed Programme Theatres (hereafter MPTs). This very title indicates the way in which the MPT not only survives but fulfills a true **community** role-the width of the programme appeals to several overlapping audiences.

A true MPT will, in the course of a three month season present mainstream drama, fringe drama, opera, ballet, contemporary dance, traditional jazz, progressive jazz, folk, rock, country & western, classical concerts, childrens shows of all kinds plus, of course, the local operatic societies.

Such a programme is just as feasible in 350 seat Bury St. Edmunds as in 1200 seat Nottingham. The larger theatre has the stage size and auditorium capacity for the big stuff and is strategically located so as to make an ideal regional centre for visits by the major national lyric and drama companies; and it can house the expensive musicals, the expensive solo entertainers, and the commercial plays loaded with expensive television names.

The major national companies cannot look at 350 seat Bury but smaller units such as Opera 80 and The Singers Company are geared to produce high quality work of the right scale, while modern dance companies like Extemporary positively benefit from the intimacy. The experimental (fringe or alternative if you like these rather unsatisfactory terms) companies attract young audiences who would not be seen dead at an Agatha Christie — yet the thriller or comedy with telly names will often reduce its guarantee to play in a nice old cosy actor's theatre if the alternative is a long journey to a concrete barn. Remember that lovely old variety act whose notepaper carried the tongue in cheek billing **Cheaper than an Interval?** Well, Bury has often sold itself to producing managers as **Cheaper than a week out!**

Jazz musicians will often look upon a small theatre as a jazz club and accordingly price themselves downwards: they put intimacy before commerce. And audiences show willingness to pay an extra pound or so to see bands and folk singers in the atmospheric intimacy of their local theatre, rather than burn that money in driving to a cheaper seat in a bigger, newer, bleaker hall.

The crunch question must be: if we rescue a theatre, can we afford to run it as a MPT?

Well, the rule of thumb is to look to the local authority to fund the overhead. The programme can then be balanced so that box office income plus Regional Arts Association project funding pays for the productions.

Industrial sponsorship? Don't count on it. Industry wants to be associated with success and glamour. This costs money: so it can be chicken and egg time. Sponsorship to improve the quality of the programme is fine, but as a potential contributor to overhead it is very risky.

It is possible to take a contribution out of box office to help with the overhead — Bury has been forced to do this, and it can, of course, be done. But only at the expense of the programme quality.

However the overhead of a small theatre need not be large, and it can be budgeted rather accurately: rent, rates, heating, lighting, cleaning, basic advertising and staff. Staff for such a theatre can be small. Bury runs on six full-time professionals: Administrator, House Manager, Box Office Manager, Box Office Assistant, Resident Stage Manager/Electrician and Assistant Stage Manager. Two part-time cleaners (12 hours a week each) and a part-time secretary (9 hours weekly). The bar is let on concession and the sweets, ices and programmes are sold by volunteers. In the tradition of touring theatre, the stage management is augmented by hourly casuals as required.

A restored 350 seater can work in a town of 27,000 people set in a rural area — and the cost pales into insignificance when compared with the cost of providing sports facilities. Provided that we think positively of the advantages in scale of small MPTs with containable budgets, then surely we should restore some of the beautiful 400-800 seat temples that the great god Bingo, in its infinite wisdom, has preserved.

Bury St. Edmunds, Theatre Royal - a near full house   *Steve Stephens*

Gazetteer

of all pre-1914 Theatres and Music Halls

Contents of the Gazetteer   81

Key to the Gazetteer   82

Gazetteer A-Z
Information for the provinces compiled by
Christopher Brereton and for the London Area
by John Earl   83

Historical Profile prepared by Iain Mackintosh based on
the work of Christopher Brereton and John Earl   197

The Principal Architects   211
Biographical notes by Victor Glasstone and
based on a list of their work collated by
David F. Cheshire with John Earl and
Michael Sell.

List of Demolished Theatres
Compiled by David F. Cheshire with John Earl
and Michael Sell   219

Maps showing the major existing theatres   225

Statistical Summary collated by Iain Mackintosh   232

Key

Information

The information here contained was gathered and checked in three stages: first by examining contemporary sources (in particular **The Stage Guide of 1912**); second by enquiries to and reports from contacts in various towns (librarians, record offices and volunteer researchers); and third, by detailed inspection of almost every theatre by a member of the Curtains!!! Committee (the initials of the author appear under every entry but usually both theatre and entry have been double checked by another member).

Classification system

The system of classification arose naturally out of the indexing and checking of entries. Both the categories and the rating of individual entries were the subject of continous debate at meetings of the Committee held from 1978 to 1981. In so far as classification is ever possible the Committee is now confident that they have devised a system that separates the unusual from the conventional, that establishes both present and potential use and that rates the used and usable theatres in appropriate categories of interest and of importance.

Sequence

The order is alphabetical by town, and within each town alphabetical by the present or last used name of the theatre. In England, Scotland and Wales the county or region is shown after the name of the town; Irish towns are shown simply as being in either Eire or Northern Ireland. The Greater London theatres are grouped together under London in a single alphabetical sequence, although the London Borough in which the theatre is located is indicated in the heading of these theatres.

Roman or *Italic*

The name of each theatre is printed in either Roman or *Italic*. Thus in Harrogate, North Yorkshire, one finds **Opera House** and *Royal Hall*. Those theatres, the names of which are printed in the first, Roman, style have the attributes of a conventional theatre appropriate to the age in which they were built e.g. proscenium arch, flytower, raked stalls plus one or more balconies. These were generally known as theatres or grand variety theatres. It is hoped that the Gazetteer, taken together with the Demolished list, provides a complete record of the state or fate of every conventional theatre flourishing in Britain between 1900 and 1914.

Buildings with their names printed in the second, *Italic*, style are more heterogeneous and their inclusion has been the result of a more subjective approach. Such theatrical buildings, both those which have long been demolished and those which do survive and now command attention, were never listed so thoroughly in contemporary reference books and hence the Gazetteer's claim of comprehensiveness cannot be advanced for the *Italic* entries. These include 19th century music halls, private theatres used by professionals, hippodromes, circus theatres, pier theatres, Kursaals and other significant flat floor theatres or halls. Generally vanished theatres of this second sort have not been included in the Demolished List. Lastly, in both groups wholly amateur theatres and open air theatres have been excluded.

In the London descriptions 'D.H.' refers to an entry in Diana Howerd's 'London Theatres & Music Halls .

★★★, ★★, ★ and other ratings

On the line below the name of the theatre and above the general heading will be found the rating of the theatre. These ratings are quite independent of whether or not the theatre is currently in use as a theatre although it should be noted that every starred theatre if not now in use is undoubtedly restorable.

★★★	A very fine theatre or music hall etc. of the highest theatrical quality.
★★	A fine theatre or music hall etc. which is an excellent example of its type.
★	A theatre or music hall of some interest and quality.
★ facade only	Of what remains only the Facade, and occasionally the shell, dates from pre-1914 and is of merit and of interest.
pre-1914 fragment only	These entries include both archaeological fragments which may, for example, throw light on the design of smaller Georgian playhouses and also whole sections of superceded theatres such as the 1879 Shakespeare Memorial Theatre, parts of which were incorporated in the back stage areas of the present theatre which dates from 1932. (This category is not comprehensive and also overlaps with both the 'facade only' list and those theatres in the Demolished List such as the New Theatre, Oxford, and Royal Court, Liverpool, the entries of which conclude with the word 'replaced').
no rating	Of lesser interest — sometimes a half complete third rate theatre or merely enough of a remnant to prevent the theatre appearing in the Demolished List.
disused	This is applied to all starred entries, including " ★ " Facade only, to signify that a starred theatre is not in current use as a theatre.

Address, name, architects and present use

The headings in bold type underneath the rating follow a standard pattern: street or area in town (plus London Borough in the case of Greater London entries); the names by which the theatre has been known (generally within brackets); the names of architects involved in the present building (plus in exceptional theatres the architects of previous buildings on the same site); and lastly the current use of the theatre building.

Key to authors of Gazetteer

C.B.	Christopher Brereton	M.G.	Mervyn Gould
D.F.C.	David Cheshire	V.G.	Victor Glasstone
J.D.-N	James Dunbar-Nasmith	I.M.	Iain Mackintosh
J.E.	John Earl	M.S.	Michael Sell
E.G.	Elizabeth Grice	D.W.	David Wilmore

82

Gazetteer A to Z

Aberaman,
Mid Glamorgan

Grand Theatre
★ disused
Cardiff Road.
(Formerly: Poole's Palace)
1908, architect unknown.
Bingo.
Built as a Miners' Public Hall and Institute - a type common in South Wales (New Theatre, Mountain Ash, q.v.) Institute on ground floor with auditorium above. Fully equipped stage - 21ft. proscenium, 28ft. depth and 39ft. grid. Shallow balcony on three sides. Altered on conversion to cinema in 1930's. Impressive, five-storeyed, red brick façade surmounted by Flemish gable above a big mullioned and transomed arched window. The ground floor has three large, arched and predimeted entrance doors. Small fly tower projecting above main roof.   C.B.

Aberavon,
Mid Glamorgan

New Theatre
Talbot Road.
(Formerly: Empire Theatre)
1912, architect unknown.
Now shops and offices.
Only the shell and much altered facade now survive.   C.B.

Aberdare,
Mid Glamorgan

Hippodrome
Cannon Street.
1858, architect unknown.
Bingo.
Built as a Temperance Hall for concerts, meetings, etc. Renamed Hippodrome in early 20th c. when music hall performances given.
Converted to a cinema called the Palladium in the late 1920's when the originally pedimented facade was completely altered and stuccoed over, and the auditorium reconstructed.   C.B.

Aberdeen,
Grampian

Alhambra Music Hall
Guild Street.
1875 (converted from Church built in 1794), architect unknown.
Shop.

Aberaman, Grand Theatre   *Bill Slinn*

Theatrical use ceased c.1907. Interior gutted and subdivided. All that now remains is the plain, stone, gabled and pitched-roofed shell, broken into by shop display windows.   C.B.

Empire Palace Theatre
Bridge Place.
1898, John Rust.
Dance Hall.
The interior was completely reconstructed as a cinema with one large balcony in 1929. The three-storeyed symmetrical, granite facade survives largely intact - plain with a pediment over the three central bays and three large doorways with thin broken segmental pediments.   C.B.

His Majesty's Theatre
★ ★ ★
Rosemount Viaduct.
1906, Frank Matcham.
Theatre.
A well-preserved example of Matcham's later style. Auditorium remarkably intimate for its 1,800 seats -achieved by three closely stacked balconies (including a rather cramped top balcony). These curve around to meet an elaborate composition of superimposed boxes flanking each side of the proscenium. The plasterwork is uncharacteristically restrained for Matcham and shows the influence of the Georgian style revival - especially in the design of the ceiling which is flat and divided into panels by egg and dart moulded beams. Deep plaster freize of figures in relief above the proscenium. Proscenium width 30ft., stage depth 40ft., grid 57ft.
The silver-grey granite facade again shows Georgian influence in the rusticated quoins and keystones of the windows but is also typically Matcham in the free Baroque of the central bay which breaks forward on two attached Ionic columns and has a curved gable above the parapet.
Asymmetrically placed pavilion to the right surmounted by a large dome, carried on a drum of columns - reflecting the dome of the church to the left of the theatre.

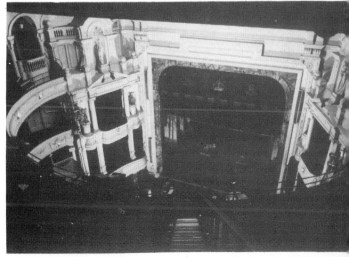

Aberdeen, His Majesty's Theatre   *James Dunbar-Nasʹ ʹth*

Now owned by the Local Authority and run as a touring theatre. Closed in October 1980 for two years for restoration and modernisation. Auditorium to be redecorated in original colours and counterweighted flying to be installed on the stage.
Listed Grade B. C.B.

Theatre
pre 1914 fragment only.
Queen Street.
1780, architect unknown.
Became a chapel in 1789 and later hotel stables. All that now survies is a much altered brick front onto Shoe Lane. C.B.

Tivoli Theatre
★ ★ ★ disused.
Guild Street.
1872, C. J. Phipps and James Matthews.
1897, auditorium altered by Frank Matcham.
1909, auditorium reconstructed by Frank Matcham.
Bingo.
Opened as Her Majesty's Theatre.
The delightful Italian Gothic polychromatic stone facade dates from 1872. The intimate auditorium, however, owes its present character to Matcham's reconstruction of 1909. Two balconies - the first of nine rows and a gallery above of ten padded benches. Two superimposed boxes on each side of the proscenium, stepped-down in level from the balcony fronts and flanked by tall Ionic columns. The upper boxes have canopies surmounted by cartouches set in front of characteristic shell hoods.
The rectangular proscenium is framed by slender, garlanded colonnettes

Aberdeen, Tivoli Theatre
James Dunbar-Nasmith

which carry scrolled brackets. Above is a tympanum with rounded corners framing a cartouche. The most splendid feature of the auditorium is the opulently decorated circular ceiling, incorporating four painted panels. The proscenium is 28ft. 6in., stage depth 27ft., and grid height approximately 45ft. By present standards the auditorium would seat approximately 800 and, although used for bingo, has suffered very few alterations.
The Tivoli would make an excellent second theatre for Aberdeen, being smaller in scale than the much larger His Majesty's and thus more appropriate for drama or chamber lyric theatre.
Listed Grade B. C.B.

Aberystwyth, Dyfed

Bridge End Theatre
pre 1914 fragment only.
1818, converted from a storehouse, architect unknown.
Warehouse/shop.
In use as a theatre only until 1826. Later turned into a malthouse. Interior completely gutted and the plain, altered exterior shows no signs of its theatrical use. C.B.

Coliseum
★ ★ ★ disused.
Terrace Road.
1905, Arthur Jones.
Closed.
Remarkable for its auditorium which has the character of a mid 19th century music hall, although built much later. This is at first floor level with shops below and could now seat approximately 800. Slightly raked main floor with iron columns supporting two shallow balconies - semi-circular at the rear and extending with straight arms of three rows along the side walls to meet a simply-framed, elliptically-arched proscenium. The balconies have elaborately fretted cast-iron balustrades with *Art Nouveau*-inspired decoration. Plain, flat ceiling subdivided by thin plaster ribs running between cast iron roses. Small music hall stage and low grid. Exuberant facade to Terrace Road which, although vulgar, is stylistically more of its time than the auditorium. Three-bay, gabled centre with two unequal levels of windows above the altered ground floor, divided by debased Ionic pilasters. Symmetrical flanking bays

Aberdeen, Tivoli Theatre
James Dunbar-Nasmith

Aberystwyth, Coliseum Theatre
Crown Copyright, RCAHM, Wales

with semi-circular oriels boldly projecting at first floor level and surmounted, above the cornice, by cupolas. At present closed after a period of use as a cinema but could be readily restored and used for variety, music hall, recitals, concerts, meetings, simply staged drama, etc.
Listed Grade II. C.B.

Royal Pier Pavilion

1896, Marks.
Bingo.
At the shore end of the pier. A long, narrow, iron and glass hall with a flat floor and no balcony. Central 'nave' with an arched roof, divided by widely spaced iron columns from narrower 'aisles'. Proscenium approximately 22 ft. (within width of central 'nave'). Stage depth approximately 26ft. No fly tower. Foyer destroyed by fire in 1960. C.B.

Altrincham,
Gtr. Manchester

Hippodrome

Stamford Street.
1912, Butterworth and Duncan.
Bingo and Cinema.
Built as a cine-variety house. Simple brick facade with flanking cupolas. Originally a typical early cinema auditorium with one balcony, panelled side walls and segmentally-arched ceiling. Now completely altered and subdivided with cinema above and bingo on ground floor.

Arundel,
West Sussex

Theatre

pre 1914 fragment only.
18 Maltravers Street.
1807, architect unknown.
Part of Henry Thornton's circuit. Although the theatre was demolished in 1836, a house on the site may incorporate part of the side walls. D.F.C.

Ashby-
De-La-Zouch
Leicestershire

Lyric Theatre

Lower Church Street.
c.1798, architect unknown.
Disused.
Plain, brick exterior with pitched tiled roof, situated behind the 2½ storeyed, three-bay Georgian facade of a former public house. Entrance through ground floor of pub; the applied timber pilasters and steep pediment date from c.1912 when the theatre was converted

Aberystwyth, Coliseum Theatre   *Crown Copyright, RCAHM, Wales*

to a cinema. The present state of the interior also dates from this time and is a plain room with a flat floor, simply panelled walls and open platform stage. C.B.

Ashton-
Under-Lyne
Gtr. Manchester

Booth's Theatre

Stamford Street/Booth Street.
1860's converted from Oddfellow's Hall and renamed People's New Concert Hall.
Later renamed Booth's Theatre.
Pub and Store.
Exterior much altered and interior completely gutted. C.B.

Ayr, Gaiety Theatre
James Dunbar-Nasmith

Tameside Theatre

Oldham Road.
1905, J. J. Alley.
Theatre.
Plain brick exterior typical of Alley, although the facade was remodelled on conversion to cinema use in 1933. Auditorium completely reconstructed at same time - now with one balcony and typical '30's decor. Stage retained; proscenium 35ft., stage depth 45ft. Leased by Local Authority and name changed in 1976 from Empire to Tameside Theatre. C.B.

Ayr,
Strathclyde

Gaiety Theatre
★

Carrick Street.
1902, J. McHardy Young.
1904, reconstructed after fire, Alexander Cullen.
Theatre.
Intimate auditorium with two balconies - the first of six rows and the second, now of only three rows, after reconstruction rollowing a fire in 1955 when the seating capacity was reduced from approximately 1,000 to 570. Single boxes at the level of each balcony on either side, framed by pilasters and surmounted by a broken segmental pediment with a cartouche. The proscenium is very low in relation to the height of the auditorium - the top of the frame being only level with the underside of the upper boxes. Above is an almost equal height of wall up to the ceiling, decorated with a heavy, segmentally-arched panel. Saucer-domed ceiling, undecorated apart from a moulded frame with cartouches at intervals. Plasterwork on balcony and box fronts

Ayr, Pavilion Theatre   *James Dunbar-Nasmith*

in a rather coarse Edwardian Baroque style. Proscenium 23ft., stage depth 30ft., grid 42 ft. Theatre now owned by local authority and used for summer shows, amateurs and occasional touring productions.
Dull exterior, largely post 1955.   C.B.

Pavilion Theatre
★ disused.
The Green.
1911, J. K. Hunter.
Dance Hall.
Built near seafront promenade for music hall entertainment and dancing. A long, narrow auditorium, with approximately 600 seats. Flat main floor and one horseshoe balcony, returning along side walls. Barrel-vault ceiling. Apart from acanthus leaf decoration on the proscenium there is no decorative plasterwork. Proscenium 23 ft., stage 30 ft. (to curved back wall), grid height approximately 35ft. Plain exterior, apart from a tall slender Italianate tower at each of the four corners of the long, low auditorium roof.   C.B.

Bacup,
Lancashire

Empire Theatre
Rochdale Road.
1893, Walters and Love (also proprietors).
Amateur theatre.
Reconstructed from a former iron-founder's premises and opened as Royal Court Theatre. Name changed to Empire in 1918. Auditorium now much altered, with one balcony and a capacity of approximately 520. Proscenium 26 ft., stage depth 33 ft. Situated away from town centre on the side of a steep slope with entrance at upper level through a completely plain and featureless exterior.   C.B.

Bangor, County Theatre
Victor Glasstone

Balmoral,
Aberdeenshire

Balmoral Castle
Aberdeenshire.
Temporary private theatre and ballroom on the Royal Estate.
1851, Edward T. Bellhouse.
? present use.
A free-standing single storey structure in the grounds of the Royal Estate, claimed to be the 'earliest surviving example of Victorian architecture constructed of iron'. Designed and prefabricated by Bellhouse of the Eagle Foundry, Manchester, for the Prince Consort. 'The structure comprises 16 cast iron structural pilasters, with foliated capitals, which support the wrought iron roof trusses. The pilasters are bolted to base plates, fixed to a timber foundation. The wall panels of horizontal, galvanized corrugated iron

are secured to corrugated profiles on the pilasters. The gables of the building are decorated by a cast iron barge board, and the roof ridge is made up of iron castings of the fleur-de-lis design. The roof incorporates a ventilator - a wooden valve which was formerly operated by a rope and pulley. No design provision was required for a fire, or artificial lighting in the building'.
V.G. from an article by Edwin Johnston in **Domus** 614/1981.

Bangor,
Gwynedd
County Theatre
★ disused.
1912, architect unknown.
Bingo.
Former Tabernacle chapel of c.1850, converted to a theatre in 1912. This was done by adding a brick fly-tower to one side of the square-shaped stone chapel and a small, stuccoed foyer etc., on another side. The auditorium (approximately 800 seats) is square on plan and has an unusual five-sided balcony, which may survive from the chapel, with six steeply-raked rows. A short central section facing the stage is linked by canted sections to side arms at right-angles to the proscenium. Straight, panelled parapet. The impression is reminiscent of contemporary theatre architecutre, e.g. Haymarket Theatre, Leicester. Elliptically-arched proscenium with a cartouche above the centre. Original flat, panelled ceiling of the chapel. Could be restored to use although it should be noted that Bangor now has a new theatre on the University campus.   C.B.

Barnsley,
South Yorkshire
Alhambra Theatre
★ disused.
Doncaster Road.
1915, P.A. Hinchcliffe.
Closed.
Built as a large variety theatre with three balconies and stage boxes,

Barnsley, Alhambra Theatre
Victor Glasstone

Barnsley, Theatre Royal

Victor Glasstone

decorated with Baroque plasterwork. Now internally mutilated with the boxes removed, a rectangular platform built out in front of the first balcony and a false ceiling put in below the level of the upper balcony front. Very shallow stage, approximately 20 ft. Exterior intact - tall and impressive, heavily detailed Baroque facade in faience (now painted) sited on a bleak round-about at the entrance to the town-centre from the south. Rusticated ground floor and mezzanine with the two storeys above articulated by seven bays of giant Ionic demi-columns. Heavy, dominant attic storey with a raised centre and two *oeil-de-boeuf* windows on either side.   C.B.

Theatre Royal

★ ★ ★ disused.
Wellington Street.
1899, Walter Emden, with Herbert Crawshaw as executant.
Bingo.
Privately owned and, although operated as a bingo club, is completely intact inside and out.
Delightfully intimate auditorium (approximately 900 seats if re-seated to present standards) with two well-curved balconies of six rows each, terminating in boxes linked vertically by superimposed columns. Rectangular proscenium with a curved sounding-board above and a domed ceiling. Richly modelled Baroque plasterwork. Proscenium 24 ft., stage depth 30 ft. Although very successful theatrically the auditorium lacks the sophistication of Emden's metropolitan interiors at the Duke of York's and the Garrick (q.v.) to a degree that cannot entirely be put down to comparative lack of funds. It may be that the local architect, Crawshaw, was rather free in his interpretation of Emden's intentions. Good three-storeyed, five-bay stone facade. Rusticated, arched entrance doors and pedimented first floor windows. Triangular pediment over the three central bays with "Theatre Royal" carved on a scroll in the tympanum.
One of Britain's most important surviving medium-sized theatres which are no longer in use as such. Restoration highly feasible and would give back to Barnsley and its neighbourhood a real theatre in place of the present grim civic hall/'theatre'. Not listed - should be.   C.B.

Barrow-In-Furness,
Cumbria
Palace Theatre

Duke Street.
1873, architect unknown.
Bingo.
Opened as Salvation Army Hall. Later called New Amphitheatre, and in 1920 renamed the Palace. Plain pitched-roofed exterior with no fly tower and rendered facade dating from the 1920's. Large auditorium also reconstructed in 1920's with one straight-fronted balcony.   C.B.

Tivoli Theatre

★ Facade only/disused.
Forshaw Street.
1868, architect unknown.
Warehouse.
Opened as Alexander Music Hall. In 1886 renamed Star Palace of Varieties. In 1902 renamed the Tivoli and in 1934 the Regal Cinema.

Barrow-in-Furness, Tivoli Theatre
James Dunbar-Nasmith

Originally a small music hall behind, and linked internally to a pub, but also with a separate access next to the pub. This front still survives; stuccoed of two storeys and one wide bay. Segmental pediment above entrance and a Venetian window at first floor level, framed between pilasters and surmounted by a triangular pediment. The music hall was later enlarged and the interior survived until relatively recently, but has now been stripped out for storage purposes.
Listed Grade II   C.B.

Barry Dock,
South Glamorgan
Theatre Royal
Broad Street.
1910, W. E. Knapman.
Cinema.
Severely plain red brick facade. Converted into a cinema in the 1930's when the stage was removed and absorbed into the auditorium which was completely reconstructed with one balcony.
C.B.

Bath,
Avon

Palace Theatre
★ Facade only/disused.
Saw Close.
1886, architect unknown.
1895, rebuilt, Wylson & Long.
Bingo.
Opened as Pavilion Music Hall. Renamed Lyric in 1895 and Palace in 1903. Auditorium competely altered with one straight-fronted balcony in 1930's. Stage removed and opened up into volume of auditorium on conversion to a ballroom in 1955.
Facade of 1895 survives intact - a handsome music hall front of one wide bay only, recessed at first floor level behind

a balustraded balcony, flanked on each side by single giant Corinthian pilasters carrying a bracketted cornice. Pyramid roof. Grade II.   C.B.

Theatre Royal
★ Facade only/disused.
Orchard Street.
1750, Thomas Jelly.
1767, reconstructed, architect unknown.
1775, reconstructed, John Palmer.
Masonic Hall.
The interior has been completely rebuilt for its present purpose, but the shell and front to Orchard Street are basically intact. The axis of the auditorium and stage lay parallel to the street and were contained within a coursed rubble, pitched-roofed structure which still exists. Between this and the street is a shallow range, formerly containing lobbies, staircases, etc. The ashlar facade has three storeys and seven bays of plain sash windows - hardly distinguishable from adjacent houses. Former doorways to pit, boxes and galleries now removed and replaced by windows. Present pedimented entrance dates from conversion to Freemason's hall.
Called Theatre Royal from 1767 - first provincial theatre to be given patent. Closed in 1805 after the owners had built the present Theatre Royal in Beauford Square. Grade II.   C.B.

Theatre Royal
★ ★ ★
Beauford Square.
1805, George Dance the Younger and John Palmer.
1863, reconstructed, after fire, C. J. Phipps.
1902, altered, Verity.
Theatre.
The principal facade of Dance's theatre is to Beauford Square, on the long axis

of the auditorium/stage. Fine restrained Neo-Classical design in ashlar with a three storeyed, five-bay centrepiece. Panelled pilasters above ground floor, with masks carved in relief in the frieze over the tops of each pilaster, and linked by swags. Large Royal Arms with two lyres each side, set on parapet above cornice (now seriously eroded). As one of the most important surviving examples of Georgian theatre architecture this facade deserves to be rescued from its present neglected state. Entrance moved to Saw Close when theatre reconstructed in 1863. Phipps added an Italianate three-bay arcaded entrance in front of the ground floor of a fine early 18th century house.
The auditorium was Phipps' first theatre commission, and survives largely intact (865 seats), with two lyre-shaped balconies, delicate plasterwork and a stalls circle with a panelled front. Balconies carried along front edge by iron columns. Unfortunately the continuity of the line of the tiers has been broken by the removal of the gallery slips, the restoration of which is highly desirable. Superimposed stage boxes framed between slender colonnettes with foliated capitals supporting a flared elliptical arch, repeated on either side above what were formerly the gallery slips. Saucer-domed ceiling, now lacking its original painted decoration.
Proscenium 28 ft., Stage depth 40 ft., Grid 40 ft. The stage, although in a somewhat rickety condition, is an almost intact mid-Victorian stage complete with contemporary machinery. This includes traps and also barrels and drums above the fly floor which are the most important over-stage machinery, not on a grid, to remain in Britain.
In October 1980 it was announced that the National Theatre would become a regular visitor to the Theatre, and that a major scheme of renovation was planned.
Listed Grade II*   C.B.

Bath, Theatre Royal

Beccles,
Suffolk

Theatre
pre-1914 fragment only.
Sheepgate Street.
1814, David Fisher (owner and designer).
Part of a bank.
The brick shell of the auditorium/stage remains to the rear of Lloyds Bank, of which it has formed a part since 1945. The interior has been stripped out but one fascinating remnant survives -wooden pilasters, probably part of the boxes, now fixed against a wall.   E. G.

Bedford,
Bedfordshire

Royal County Theatre
Midland Road.
1899, Henry Young.
1930's, auditorium reconstructed.
Bingo.
Auditorium totally reconstructed in 1930's with one balcony. Stage, with brick fly tower, still remains. Exterior completely altered.   C. B.

Belfast,
Northern Ireland

Grand Opera House
★ ★ ★
1895, Frank Matcham.
1980, restoration by Robert McKinstry.
Theatre.
Used as a cinema for many years then closed after bomb damage. Re-opened as a theatre in 1980 after undergoing a splendid scheme of renovation and restoration (architect Robert McKinstry, theatre consultant John Wyckham). The magnificent auditorium is probably the best surviving example in the U.K. of the Oriental style applied to theatre architecture - largely Indian in character with intricate detail on the sinuously curved fronts of the two balconies and an elaborate composition of superimposed boxes surmounted by onion-domed canopies. The ceiling, which is divided into several richly-framed painted panels that have been exquisitely recreated by artist Cherith McKinstry, is supported on arches above the gallery slips, with large elephant heads at springing level. Proscenium 39 ft. 8 in., stage depth 45 ft., grid now increased to 60 ft. from 52 ft. Large new orchestra pit, the sharp single radius curve of the orchestra rail providing the only slightly jarring note in this superb auditorium.
The exterior, of brick and cast stone, is in a free mixture of Baroque, Flemish, and Oriental styles - typical of Matcham's earlier work. He made good use of the open corner site by building up the composition of his design in stages, linked by strapwork scrolls, to the triangular-pedimented central gable which is flanked by domed minarets. The new projecting glass extension to the first floor bar is a welcome addition, quite in the spirit of Matcham's architecture (c.f. Theatre Royal, Portsmouth) the only reservation being the lack of supporting columns which are visually, if not structurally, necessary. Now a touring theatre and Ulster's only venue for major opera and dance companies. Capacity now 1,050.
Listed Grade II.   C. B./I. M.

Royal Hippodrome
Great Victoria Street.
1907, Bertie Crewe.
Cinema.
Facade completely redone. Interior smoothed over with 30's decor on conversion to cinema.   C. B.

Beverley,
Humberside

Theatre
90, Walkersgate.
1754, architect unknown.
House.
Used by 18th c. circuit companies for 20 years. Now entirely domestic in appearance - a two-storeyed, five-bay brick house with pantile roof. Theatre interior completely destroyed.
Listed Grade II.   C. B.

Belfast, Grand Opera House   *Anderson and McKeekin*

Bexhill-On-Sea,
East Sussex

Gaiety Theatre
(Formerly: York Hall).
1895, architect unknown.
Bombed. Shell rebuilt as garage 1959.
D. F. C.

Bilston,
West Midlands

Hippodrome
c. 1914.
Bingo.
A cine-variety theatre - although with an unusually tall fly-tower.
C. B.

Birkenhead,
Merseyside

Music Hall
★ ★ disused.
Claughton Road.
1862, architect unknown.
Closed (until recently a bingo hall called the Astor).
Later renamed the Queen's Hall.
Important survival of early music hall. Impressive, Italianate stuccoed exterior like a big Non-Conformist chapel - on corner site with two show fronts. Entrance for a narrower side, three bays and two storeys projecting one bay in front of higher, triangular-pedimented auditorium block. Three rusticated arches on ground floor in wide central bay. Large, arched window above with triangular pediment over, flanked by smaller arched windows in side bays. Long-side elevation with tall blank-arcades above rusticated ground floor. Panels below the arches frame projecting busts of composers - Beethoven, Weber, Haydn, etc.
Auditorium at first floor level. It would be usual for a music hall/concert room of this period to have a flat main floor and a shallow balcony around three sides. Here considerable alterations appear to have taken place - the balcony, if there ever was one, has been removed and the floor is raked. Very shallow stage.
(Not listed but should be). C. B.

Birmingham,
West Midlands

Alexandra Theatre
pre-1914 fragment only.
John Bright Street.
1901, Owen and Ward.
1935, Largely rebuilt, Roland Satchnell.
Theatre.
Opened as Lyceum, name changed to Alexandra in 1902. Most of Owen &

Ward's building was demolished and rebuilt in 1935—except for plain brick dressing room wing flanking one side of auditorium and stage. The present theatre is administered by a trust and is run as a touring theatre with occasional seasons of repertory.
C.B.

Hippodrome
Hurst Street.
1899, F. W. Lloyd.
1924, auditorium reconstructed, Burdwood and Mitchell.
1963, facade rebuilt and foyers remodelled.
Theatre.
Opened as Tower of Varieties—both music hall and circus. A tall Moorish tower survived until demolished in 1963. Internally reconstructed as a large music hall with a fine auditorium called the Tivoli in 1900. Auditorium entirely reconstructed in a neo-classical style with one very deep balcony in 1924. Foyers and facade completely and badly redone in 1963. Side elevation to Inge Street exhibits original moulded brickwork, arched windows etc., of the 1899 buildings.
Refurbished 1980/81—new dressing rooms, grid raised from 50ft. to 70ft., and auditorium re-seated and redecorated to fine effect. Unfortunately the opportunity was not taken to deepen the stage.
Now Birmingham's major touring theatre. C.B.

London Museum Music Hall
Park Street.
1863, architect unknown.
Restaurant and Karate Club.
Music hall at rear of Royal George Public house. Renamed Canterbury in

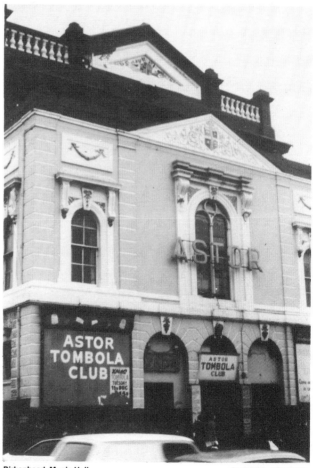

Birkenhead, Music Hall

Christopher Brereton

1880, then Pavilion, then Museum again, and Coutt's Theatre in 1895. Bullring Cinema from 1912. The interior has been gutted and subdivided, and has lost all original features. Exterior survives almost intact in form of a plain rectangular brick structure with pitched roof. Street elevation on one long-side—rendered and relieved by series of blank arches.
C.B.

Newtown Palace

1912, architect unknown.
Bingo.

Of interest as an unusually large and basically intact cine-variety house. Large, wide and deep auditorium with one deep balcony with slips along side walls to meet splays flanking proscenium. Elaborate plasterwork on balcony front, panelled ceiling and proscenium arch. Plain facade—wide, low, and white painted. Long low side elevation with brick fly tower.
C.B.

Old Rep Theatre

★ ★

Station Street.
1913, S. N. Cooke.
Amateur Theatre.
Formerly Birmingham Repertory Theatre.

Historically important as first purpose-built repertory theatre in Britain. Design influenced by Munich Kunstlertheater of 1908. Built on narrow site with steeply raked stalls, one straight-fronted balcony, (Barry Jackson would have chosen a bigger single tier had it not been for the small site) and plain panelled side walls. Flat, coffered ceiling. 468 seats, proscenium 22ft., stage depth 24ft., grid 50ft. Good classical facade in brick and stone with Ionic pilasters through first and second floors in centre.
C.B.

Prince of Wales Theatre

pre-1914 fragment only.
Broad Street.
1856, architect unknown.
1866, interior reconstructed.
1876, new facade, architect unknown.
1881, interior reconstructed.
1911, Frank Matcham, auditorium reconstructed.
Shops.

Part of facade only remains, incorporated into shops. Opened in 1856 as Royal Music Hall and Operetta House. Became Prince of Wales Theatre in 1865. Reconstructed 1866. The auditorium of this date was large and very fine with three horseshoe balconies. New facade built 1876 -curiously reticent for so important a theatre. Interior reconstructed again in 1881 and finally in 1911 - architect Frank Matcham. Bombed in 1941 and subsequently demolished except for the lower part of the 1876 facade.
C.B.

Palace Theatre

Summerhill Road.
1905, architect unknown.
Factory.

Built as a small variety theatre on the fringe of the city centre. All that now remains is the altered corner entrance facade in faience, the interior having been completely gutted.
C.B.

Bishop Auckland, Durham

Hippodrome

★ disused.
Railway Street.
1908, architect unknown.
Bingo.

Intact inside and out. Auditorium (approximately 800 seats if reseated to pre-

Bishop Auckland, Hippodrome
James Dunbar-Nasmith

sent standards) has two, almost straight, balconies, each with long slips parallel to side walls. Consoles forming panels on front of first balcony, but no other enrichment, and no plasterwork on second balcony. A single box at first balcony level flanking either side of the rectangular framed proscenium (24ft. square). Flat ceiling panelled with simple geometrical design. Stage floor lowered to stalls level. Plain facade in brick with cast stone dressings. Arched windows in upper storey with the word "Hippodrome" on panel. Brick side elevations with fly tower.
In good condition,—restoration to theatre use feasible.
J.D.-N/C.B.

Theatre Royal

Newgate.
c.1870, architect unknown.
Supermarket.

Later became the King's Hall, Interior gutted. Facade of no merit—completely reconstructed in early 1900's; ground floor later removed for present purpose.
C.B.

Blackburn, Lancashire

Palace Theatre

The Boulevard.
1899, Wimperis and Arber.
Bingo/Cinema.

Interior completely gutted and subdivided, with bingo below and cinema above. 1960's concrete frontispiece above entrance, but side elevations of

Birmingham, Old Rep Theatre   *Photos circa 1924, Victor Glasstone Collection*

some interest—arched and circular windows in bays, articulated by polygonal projecting ribs. Small fly tower. C.B.

Blackpool, Lancashire

Grand Theatre

★ ★ ★

Church Street.
1894, Frank Matcham.
Theatre.

The auditorium of this theatre is one of Matcham's finest creations, combining intimacy with a sense of imposing spaciousness. He achieved this by stacking the audience vertically in three closely-spaced, relatively shallow, balconies which curve well around the sides, separated from the proscenium by only one box on either side at dress circle level. These boxes are each surmounted by an elaborate arched-and-pedimented canopy rising above the level of the gallery front. Splendid high round-arched proscenium frame with open plaster-work decoration on the inside of the arch, and large oval painted panels in the spandrels, by Binns of Halifax. Magnificent oval ceiling incorporating six painted panels of composers. Opulent plasterwork (by the

Plastic Decoration Co.) on balcony fronts, boxes, proscenium and ceiling. Proscenium 30ft., stage depth 30ft., grid 50ft. Seating capacity, if the present benched gallery was reseated, approximately 1,300 (now 1,500).
Exterior in plain brickwork, apart from the Baroque-corner entrance in stone, surmounted by a jolly, copper fish-scale dome, rising behind scrolled gables with finials.
The theatre survived a threat of demolition in 1973. Funds were subsequently raised by the Grand Theatre Trust to purchase the building. It was reopened as a touring theatre in 1981. Listed Grade II.

C.B.

Hippodrome

pre-1914 fragment only.

Church Street.
1895, J. D. Harker.
Theatre/Cinema.

Built as a large ballroom/music hall called the Empire with a flat floor and gallery around three sides, and shallow stage. Converted to circus in 1900 and renamed Hippodrome. In 1910 arena removed, main floor raked for cinema use, with seasonal variety. Various subsequent alterations made until 1962 when the building was almost totally rebuilt with a new auditorium and facade—only the basic side walls remaining of the old structure.

C.B.

Regal/Royal Pavilion

1909, architect unknown.
Bingo/Amusements.

Altered auditorium of no merit. Facade plastered over, and devoid of original features. C.B.

Theatre Royal

1868, architect unknown.
Bingo.

Opened as the Assembly Rooms—a hall with a gallery on three sides and small stage, above an arcade with shops, bar, etc. Later called the Theatre Royal. In 1907 called Tivoli cinema. Interior completely reconstructed in 1930's. Exterior basically intact on a triangular site at the junction of two streets. Undistinguished design in brick with stone dressings. Low octagonal 'tower' at corner, and plain side elevations. C.B.

Tower Ballroom

★ ★ ★

1899, Frank Matcham.
Dance Hall.

Although not a theatre, the Tower Ballroom makes use of much of the repertoire of theatre architecture, and is one of Matcham's most important works. The Tower Buildings were designed in 1894 by Maxwell & Tuke—Matcham was called upon to redesign the original ballroom in 1899.

Blackburn, Grand Theatre   Elsam, Mann and Casper

Blackpool, Tower Ballroom   *Photo circa 1905, Victor Glasstone Collection*

The interior conveys an impression of quite staggering opulence. Two tiers of shallow balconies around three sides of the rectangular hall—the upper one in the form of bow-fronted boxes. Proscenium frame to the orchestra platform is flanked by onion-domed boxes in Matcham's characteristic style. Segmentally-arched ceiling divided into richly-framed painted panels. and supported along the sides by winged caryatids. Badly damaged by fire in 1956 and restored by Andrew Mazzei.
Listed Grade II. ★   C.B.

Tower Circus
★ ★ ★
1894, Maxwell and Tuke architects of Tower complex.
Circus.
The circus interior is possibly by Frank Matcham. Fitted in between the four giant legs of the Tower itself, this gorgeous interior and the Great Yarmouth Hippodrome (q.v.) are the only surviving examples in Britain still in use of the once popular circus/hippodrome building, a type common throughout Europe in the 19th century. Seating on two levels with the upper level in the form of four balconies, each spanning between the legs of the Tower with great arches above. Wonderfully fanciful Alhambresque plasterwork enrichment on balcony fronts, arches, ceiling, and orchestra box.   V.G./C.B.

Blackpool, Tower Circus
Photo circa 1910
Victor Glasstone Collection

Winter Gardens Theatre
★ ★ ★ disused.
1878, built as a glass-roofed winter garden, architect unknown.
1889, converted to theatre by Thomas Mitchell.
1897, auditorium reconstructed by Wylson and Long.
Part of the huge once magnificent, now slightly seedy, Winter Gardens complex, to which it is linked by a wide, encircling arched-roofed ambulatory. Splendidly opulent apsidal-ended music hall interior. First balcony with nine rows in the centre; the second being of 12 rows, set back to the line of the sixth row of the first balcony. The

sides curve around to meet superimposed stage boxes framed between giant enriched composite columns, surmounted by segmental pediments. Richly decorated ceiling over the whole space—caryatids rising through perimeter cove to support a centre subdivided into deeply coved panels ornamented by garlands. Seating capacity approximately 1,700. Proscenium 31ft. 6in., Stage depth 39ft.
The future of this unusual but distinguished theatre is uncertain; all exit routes terminate in the ambulatory which throws into question the theatrical future of yet another magnificent auditorium in a town already well served with theatres. An unusual theatre may require unusual solutions but its retention is strongly recommended.
Listed Grade II.   C.B./I.M.

Blyth,
Northumberland
Theatre Royal
★ ★ ★ disused.
Trotter Street.
1900, William Hope & J. C. Maxwell.
Warehouse.
Excellent auditorium although now in a sadly dilapidated condition. Seating capacity if reseated to present standards would be approximately 1,200.
Two curved balconies supported by iron columns. The front of the lower balcony (with ten rows) is divided by consoles into panels, each decorated by a cartouche supported by cherubs; these in turn are flanked by cherubs

Blackpool, Winter Gardens Theatre

riding chariots drawn by winged horses. Upper balcony front decorated with repeated festoons. Proscenium flanked on each side by superimposed boxes at the level of the balconies. The lower box, framed by pilasters, is made tripartite by two slender colonnettes supporting delicate arches. The upper box is under a semi-circular arch; the front repeats the decoration of the first balcony. Proscenium framed by slender Corinthian pilasters supporting a straight-headed arch with rounded corners and elaborate scrolled brackets. Large central cartouche flanked by trumpeting cupids. Saucer-domed ceiling in overall rectangular frame. Proscenium width 28 ft., stage depth 40 ft., grid 50 ft.

Undistinguished and partly altered exterior. Entrance pavilion at the right end of one long-side elevation. Stuccoed panel in upper storey with "Theatre Royal" in raised lettering, with small triangular pediment over, and slated mansard roof.

Not listed, but should be. Threatened with demolition by Local Authority, to provide a car park! C.B.

Bognor Regis
West Sussex

Pier Theatre
1912, G. C. Smith.
Discotheque.
The theatre is situated at the shore end of the pier, which itself dates from 1865. Although only a modest example of its genre, the stuccoed exterior goes some way to relieve the bleakness of the promenade. The small fly tower was removed in 1977. Interior much altered from original form, but balcony still remains. C.B.

Bolton,
Lancashire

Mawdsley Street Theatre
pre-1914 fragment only.
1859, architect unknown.
Theatre itself was demolished in 1869, bu the cellars were incorporated in the still existing County Court. D.F.C.

Boston,
Lincolnshire

Theatre
Market Place.
1777, architect unknown.
Warehouse.
In use as a seed warehouse since c.1820. Interior completely gutted. Restrained pedimented facade, displaying a roundel inscribed "Theatre", basically intact, although ground floor much altered. M.G./C.B.

Blyth, Theatre Royal   *James Dunbar-Nasmith*

Bournemouth,
Dorset

Boscombe Hippodrome
★ ★ ★ disused.
Christchurch Road.
1895, Lawson & Donkin.
Dance Hall.
Opened as Grand Pavilion Theatre. Renamed Hippodrome in c.1910. Built as part of a development including the spacious Boscombe Arcade (intact) and Salisbury Hotel. The theatre front, in brick with stone dressings, is subservient to that of the arcade, and difficult to identify separately from the shops and former hotel on either side. It consists basically of three, very tall, mullioned and transomed windows each surmounted by a Flemish gable. The auditorium is most unusual and interesting, with the character of an early music hall. Above the flat main floor is a shallow balcony carried on iron columns with a semicircular end and straight side arms and an openwork iron balustrade incorporating acanthus leaf decoration. Tall, slender iron columns rise from the front edge of the balcony to support a curved ceiling and a lateral arcade, with florid openwork spandrel decoration. A wide promenade runs around the rear of the balcony, above which, carried on a further ring of columns, is a second, shallower balcony set back behind the arcade. The galleries originally ran straight up to the proscenium wall, but in c.1910 a range of paired boxes was put in on either side, flanked by giant composite columns and decorated with Baroque

Bournemouth, Theatre Royal
Christopher Brereton

faience exterior. Entrance at the apex, under a dome carried on a drum of giant Corinthian columns. Set further back, two domed square towers rising above the rear wall of the auditorium. Large, though intimate auditorium (1,600 seats) with two deep, slighly-curved balconies. Rectangular proscenium frame with elliptically-arched painted tympanum over, flanked on either side by paired superimposed boxes, framed by composite columns. These are surmounted, above second balcony level, by a broad semicircular arch between terms. Centre of ceiling rises up into a high, octagonal dome. Richly modelled, well detailed plasterwork. Proscenium 36 ft. 6 in., stage depth 32 ft., grid 50 ft. Now owned by the Local Authority and run as a touring theatre.
Listed Grade II.   C.B.

Empire Theatre
pre-1914 fragment only.
Great Horton Road.
1899, W. G. R. Sprague.
Hostel.
Entrance front only remains. The theatre, which was situated behind the large Alexandra Hotel, was demolished following a fire in 1952. The hotel building, now used by Bradford College, still exists. Access to the theatre was through the central five bays of the ground floor, articulated by paired attached columns set between arched openings and reached by a broad flight of steps from the street.   C.B.

Theatre Royal
Manningham Lane.
1864, Andrews and Pepper.
Closed.
Opened as the Royal Alexandra - name changed to Theatre Royal in 1867. Interior completely rebuilt as a cinema in 1921. At the same time a projecting, stuccoed entrance foyer was built out

Bradford, Alhambra Theatre
Keith Gibson

from the original stone facade, the pedimented upper part of which rises behind. Plain stone side elevation with pitched-roofed fly tower.
                                      C.B.

Brecon,
Powys.

Royal Theatre
pre-1914 fragment only.
Danygaer Road.
1784, architect unknown.
Warehouse.
In use as a theatre until 1870. Only the much altered, completely gutted shell remains.   D.F.C.

plasterwork. At the same time the proscenium was reconstructed - a tall plaster frame, straight-headed with rounded corners. Proscenium 26 ft., stage depth 37 ft., grid approximately 50 ft.
Apart from some fittings used in connection with the present purpose, the auditorium and stage are intact and could be restored to theatrical use. By present standards it would seat approximately 800.
Listed Grade II.   C.B.

Theatre Royal
★ Facade only/disused.
Albert Road.
1882, Kemp, Welch & Pindar.
Cinema and Bingo.
Auditorium and stage completely remodelled - bingo below with cinema over. Good facade, however, remains -stuccoed, of four bays and four storeys with giant Corinthian pilasters embracing first, second and third storeys. Straight entablature over.
Listed Grade II (for facade).   C.B.

Bradford,
West Yorkshire

Alhambra Theatre
★ ★ ★
Great Horton Road/Morley Street.
1914, Chadwick and Watson.
Theatre.
Maximum advantage taken of triangular corner site in the dramatic if rather coarsely handled composition of the

Bradford, Alhambra Theatre   *Keith Gibson*

Brighton, Hippodrome

Victor Glasstone

Bridlington,
Humberside

People's Palace
pre-1914 fragment only.
Prospect Street.
1896, architect unknown.
Bombed in 1942 but the rusticated entrance remains surmounted by a segmental pediment. The remainder of the site is a car park. C.B.

Rope-Walk Theatre
pre-1914 fragment only
1789, architect unknown.
Shop.
In use as a theatre until 1833. Original interior gone and only the basic shell, much altered, remains. C.B.

Brighouse,
West Yorkshire

Albert Theatre
Huddersfield Road.
1899, Sharp & Waller.
Bingo.
Interior completely reconstructed as a cinema in 1930's with one large balcony, though original stage remains. Stone exterior largely intact but of little interest - a broad, gabled facade with ranges of closely-spaced window openings. C.B.

Brighton, Palace Pier Theatre
Victor Glasstone

Brighton,
East Sussex

Gaiety/Royal Hippodrome
pre-1914 fragment only.
Lewes Road.
1876, Messrs, Stanning.
Portions of ornamental wall and cellars are still visible below the block of flats which now stands on the site. D.F.C.

Hippodrome
★ ★ ★ disused.
Middle Street.
1900, Frank Matcham.
Bingo.
Long, low and very restrained stuccoed facade to Middle Street. Central entrance flanked by square Italianate towers with pyramid tiled roofs. The reticent exterior is scant preparation for the huge, opulently decorated, semi-circular auditorium. Originally a dual purpose circus/variety theatre, and now possibly the finest surviving example of its type in Britain. The arena was soon given over to permanent seating facing the proscenium. There is only one balcony (with seven rows) curving with the walls to meet the single, large onion-domed boxes which flank each side of the wide, low proscenium.
The most spectacular feature of the auditorium is the vast ceiling in the form of a panelled 'dome' which covers the whole space and is richly decorated with boldly modelled Baroque plasterwork. It is supported, above the level of the promenade which surrounds the rear of the balcony, by square, tapered columns. In the centre of the ceiling is a small open cupola with a balustraded gallery around the inside.

Palace Pier Theatre
★ ★ ★ disused
1901.
Closed (after being hit by a barge in 1973).
It is sad to see this, one of Britain's finest surviving pier theatres, slowly mouldering away. Surrounded on the outside by Moorish arcading with an onion-domed pavilion at each of the four corners. The auditorium was also originally Moorish but was later redone with delicate 18th French style plasterwork. The theatre is intact, with only superficial alterations. It could be readily restored to use. However, owing to the great size of the auditorium it would only be suitable for dance, opera, musicals, etc., and possible orchestral concerts. Seating capacity approximately 1,800. Proscenium 39 ft., stage depth 38 ft., grid 50 ft.
Listed Grade II. C.B.

Theatre Royal
★ ★
New Road.
1807, architect unknown.
1866, auditorium and stage rebuilt and facade altered by C. J. Phipps.
1894, exterior reconstructed by C. E. Clayton.
1927, auditorium redecorated by Sprague and Barton.
Theatre.
When the first building was extended and reconstructed by C. J. Phipps in 1866 the original structural walls and colonnade were retained. The height was, however, increased, and a glazed extension added at first floor level. Internally the stage area was updated and a typically intimate 'Phippsian' auditorium was constructed, shaped like a squeezed horseshoe, with three closely-spaced, steeply-raked balconies supported by iron columns. The 1866 colour scheme was purple, cream and buff. The boxes at 1st and 2nd balcony levels are framed by twinned, fluted pilasters above extremely attentuated consoles flanking omnibus boxes. Flat, circular ceiling over the well of the balconies. Unfortunately in 1927 most of the auditorium plasterwork was redone in French neo-classical style by Sprague and Barton. All that survives of Phipps' scheme of decoration is a deep freize of 'Jacobean' strapwork above the proscenium. In 1894 C. E. Clayton replaced the original facade with a new design in red brick with stone dressings. It is very reticent; distinguished only by small octagonal flanking turrets with ogee domes. This provided entrances only to the pit and upper levels of the auditorium; the main entrance being to the left, in the end pavilion of a terrace of 1807, giving access to pleasant foyers and staircases decorated with pilasters above a mahogany dado. Con-

Brighton, Theatre Royal
Victor Glasstone

foyers and staircases decorated with pilasters above a mahogany dado. Contemporary with the 1894 front is a colonnade of small coupled columns with bulbous bases, which extends, on a slightly larger scale, in front of the main entrance. The theatre is privately owned and run as a touring theatre for drama (a reopened Hippodrome would certainly be complementary to the Royal, being on a entirely different scale). It is immaculately maintained in the auditorium front-of-house areas. The present seating capacity is 1,000, proscenium 29 ft., stage dpeth 31 ft., grid 50 ft.
Listed Grade II.   C.B./D.F.C.

West Pier Theatre

★ disused.

1893.
Closed.
Like the Palace Pier Theatre a fine example of its type and, again like the Palace, sadly delapidated. Music hall interior with cast iron galleries on three sides. Capacity approximately 1,000, proscenium 27 ft., stage depth 23 ft.
Listed Grade II.   C.B.

Bristol,
Avon

Hippodrome

★ ★

St. Austine's Parade.
1912, Frank Matcham.
Theatre
This is Matcham's last major work and is typical in scale of the largest variety theatres built in the decade before the first World War. Well designed auditorium (capacity 1,975) - wide, though not too deep, and successfully related to the 48ft. proscenium (stage depth 60 ft., grid 60 ft.). The stalls have an unusually good rake, and the two big cantilevered balconies do not have the oppressive overhangs from which some theatres of this date suffer. The elliptically-arched proscenium is set in a deep, panelled reveal with niches at the sides. At the ends of the balconies are ranges of six boxes, three on each level, divided by giant Tuscan columns which carry the second balcony slips. The ceiling is in the form of a large saucer dome, the 'eye' of which is capable of being slid open for summertime ventilation. The Baroque plasterwork is sparsley applied, producing a slightly barren appearance, further accentuated by the loss of the original painted decoration on the pendentives below the dome, on the dome itself, and at the sides of the proscenium.
The theatre would benefit greatly from a thorough restoration, including a more tasteful colour scheme with draperies to the boxes as near as possible to the original (photographs exist). The narrow entrance front was in the form of a square tower with a tall pavilion roof surmounted by a metal sculptural group - deliberately so designed by Matcham in order to make

Bristol, Hippodrome   *Keith Gibson*

maximum impact. The upper levels of the tower are now removed and most of the decorative detail obliterated. The Hippodrome is now a touring theatre, excellent for opera, ballet and large musicals, though too large for drama.
Listed Grade II.   C.B.

Theatre Royal

★ ★ ★

King Street.
1766, Thomas Patey.
1800, Alteration to auditorium by James Saunders.
1903, new facade and front-of-house by W. Skinner.
1973, stage rebuilt and new front-of-house by Peter Moro.
Theatre.
The auditorium is a remarkable survival of an 18th century city theatre, with similar dimensions to the contemporary Theatre Royal, Drury Lane. Whereas it is thought that Drury Lane may have had a slightly fan-shaped auditorium with the tiers facing the stage on a shallow curve, the balconies at Bristol are fully semi-circular in the centre, and very nearly parallel at the sides. Stage-boxes framed between giant Corinthian pilasters. The stage originally projected as far as the outer pilasters, but has long been cut back to

the inner pair, and the crucial Georgian proscenium doors removed.
As first built the theatre had a stalls circle of boxes and one tier above. In c. 1800 a further tier was added with a deep gallery in the centre. The ceiling slopes steeply upwards from the line of the outer pair of giant pilasters to the back of the gallery. The tier fronts are supported by slender, fluted Tuscan columns at 9 ft. centres. Most of the delicate, gilded, filigree decoration on tier fronts, pilasters and ceiling dates from the early and mid 19th century, a fact often ignored by those who erroneously believe the Theatre Royal to have retained a mid-Georgian atmosphere.
In 1972 the whole structure of the 18th century stage house with its splendid Victorian machinery was demolished and rebuilt with an inappropriately flat stage instead of the raked stage the form and sightlines of the auditorium demand.
Surprisingly the opportunity to restore the original apron and proscenium arch doors was not taken. The machinery was taken out and may be put on display, but this is scant compensation for such an incredibly destructive act. A model of the stage machinery was put on display in the theatre foyer in 1981. In 1972 W. Skinner's mediocre 1903 en-

Bristol, Theatre Royal *Derek Balmer*

trance front was also demolished and replaced by a new studio theatre, the New Vic. A new entrance was made through the adjacent imposing mid 18th c. facade of the former Cooper's Hall.

An opportunity was lost to make use of the fine 65 ft. x 30 ft. hall at first floor level as a main saloon for the theatre. It now forms the well and landing of a staircase leading from ground floor to first balcony level.

Seating capacity 660. Proscenium 25 ft., stage depth 45 ft., grid 48 ft. The theatre has been the home of the Bristol Old Vic Company since its formation in 1946.
Listed Grade I. C. B./I. M.

Broadstairs,
Kent

Bohemia Theatre
pre-1914 fragment only.
High Street.
c. 1895, architect unknown.
Only the box office (now a shop) and the entrance canopy columns now remain following a fire in 1962. D. F. C.

Bungay,
Suffolk

New Theatre
★ facade only/disused
Broad Street.
1828, David Fisher (owner and designer).
Factory.
Excellent facade - stuccoed, of three bays and two storeys. The bays are defined by giant Tuscan pilasters under a deep entablature. Pedimental tablet over the central bay, which is further emphasized by a tall, arched entrance opening. Interior stripped for post-1846 use as public hall, but the gallery (and the staircases to it) survives. Dressing room intact under ex-stage area. Now houses Bungay Textiles.
Listed Grade II. D. F. C./E. G./C. B.

Bungay, New Theatre
Christopher Brereton

Bristol, Theatre Royal *Derek Balmer*

Burnley,
Lancashire
Empire
★ ★ disused
St. James Street.
1894, G. B. Rawcliffe.
1911, auditorium reconstructed,
architect unknown.
Bingo.
The auditorium, as reconstructed in
1911, has two slightly-curved, wide,
deep balconies, terminating in superimposed stage boxes framed between
Corinthian columns. Segmentally-
arched proscenium (38 ft.) now with a
false ceiling inserted half-way over
stage. Flat, panelled ceiling with circular centre panel. Restrained plasterwork on balcony and box fronts.
Capacity approximately 1,200, by present standards. Stage level raised to
give access to basement from
auditorium for present purposes. Narrow facade completely altered.
The theatre could be readily restored to
use, although the shallow stage (25 ft.
deep, and backed by a river) would be a
drawback.   C. B.

Burton-Upon-Trent,
Staffordshire
Hippodrome
pre-1914 fragment only
George Street.
1867, opened as St. George's Hall,
by Essex, Nicholl & Goodwin.
1902, rebuilt as New Theatre & Opera
House, by E. Forshaw.

1910, renamed Hippodrome.
1934, reconstructed as Odeon Cinema.
Cinemas.
All that now remains of the 1902 theatre
is the former front, to the rear of the present building and of little interest - two
storeys, brick and terracotta, with three
main bays, each of three small arched
windows at first floor level.   C. B.

Bury,
Lancashire
Theatre Royal
Market Street.
1889, Frank Matcham.
Reconstructed in 1919, 1937, 1971
and 1972.
Twin Cinemas.
Interior completely altered. Exterior
swathed in metal sheeting.   C. B.

Bury St. Edmunds,
Suffolk
Theatre
★ facade only/disused
1734, Architect unknown.
1775, Robert Adam reconstructed
exterior.
Art Gallery.
In 1774 Robert Adam proposed new
elevations for the old Market Cross
Theatre which had been in use as a
theatre since 1734 by both the Duke of
Grafton's Comedians (The Norwich
Company) and the Grammar School. In
1819 William Wilkins converted the first
floor into a public or concert room and
transferred all the fittings to his new

theatre in Westgate Street (q.v.)
No trace of theatrical activity or
evidence as to the layout of this small
playhouse remains. The public room
was recently restored as an Art Gallery.
Fine exterior with piano nobile, complete with Venetian arches under
pediments on all four sides flanked
with niches and windows, over a heavily
rusticated ground floor. It is in excellent condition and conforms to the
original drawing by Adam of an end
elevation which is still in the possession of the Corporation.   I.M.

Theatre Royal
★ ★ ★
Westgate Street.
1819, William Wilkins.
1906, some alterations by Bertie
Crewe.
1965, restored by Ernest Scott.
1974, further improvements by Norman
Westwater.
The Bury theatre is unusual in that it is
one of the few existing 19th century
theatres built by major but non-
specialist architects - others being The
Royal Opera House, Covent Garden
(q.v), the Grand, Leeds (q.v), and the
Theatre Royal, Drury Lane (q.v).
William Wilkins was, for all his distinction as a leader of the Neo-Classical
movement (his work includes Downing
College, Cambridge and the National
Gallery, London) a man of the theatre.
He was proprietor of the East Anglian
circuit, which includes the Festival
(formerly Barnwell) Theatre in Cambridge (q.v) and had rebuilt all his
theatres before he decided to erect
what he decided would be "a theatre of
ample dimensions and elegance" in
Westgate Street, Bury St. Edmunds.
The auditorium is on four levels and
originally held 800 (building regulations
and greater comfort result in the present day capacity of 352 plus 20 standing). The pit is surrounded by a double
horseshoe of boxes, the lower tier having four rows of tip-up seats in the centre where once were boxes. The upper
tier which is supported by 16 slender
cast iron pillars on the forward edge of
the tier below, consists of an unbroken
sweep of 15 boxes with no pillars to
obstruct the view. This is achieved by
the setting back of the gallery above
behind a canopy, an effect that gives
the whole a grace and an elegance
which one might associate more with a
European court theatre than an English
country playhouse. The auditorium
walls are a deep salmon pink which
allows the eye to dwell on the upper tier
front with its sphinxes and winged grif-
fins in gold on ochre and the lower tier
with its crimson screen panels, also in
flat painting, on a grey ground.
The proscenium is rectangular in
shape, 24 ft. wide and 18 ft. high, and is
flanked by pairs of marbled Tuscan
pilasters between which are curved and
panelled proscenium arch doors. The
line of the present fore-stage, which is
also convertible into an orchestra pit,
dates not from 1819 but from 1906 when
the theatre was redecorated by Bertie

Burnley, Empire Theatre   *Victor Glasstone*

Crewe. Other twentieth century solecisms that jar include the plush velour seats in the pit, the centre gangway inserted in 1965 and the removal of the stage boxes which linked the lower tier to the outer proscenium pilasters. A 1906 improvement which pleases is the breaking open of the screen wall behind the upper tier of boxes.

The exceptionally large stage, 40 ft. wide, 40 ft. deep, had been removed between 1925 when the theatre closed and 1962 when it ceased to be a barrel store for the neighbouring brewery, and the theatre was restored by a specially formed Trust who employed Ernest Scott as architect assisted by Iain Mackintosh as consultant. The modern stage surface is unfortunately flat where once it was raked. Although the walls and main roof trusses are original, the scenic suspension system is modern and depends on a tubular structure introduced in 1965 to take the load down on to concrete pads in the basement below.

The theatre is built of red brick and presents an attractive small scale classical facade to Westgate Street. Above the porte-cochere, now glazed, is the windowless circle bar, introduced in 1906 and extended in 1974 to include additional escape stairs from the gallery. The theatre is free standing save for an uneasy connection with the adjoining house, reputedly modelled by Wilkins himself on land he sold off to pay for the theatre.

The theatre is now used as a medium scale touring and amateur theatre by a charitable company, while the freehold has, since 1975, been in the hands of the National Trust whose sole theatre it is.

Listed Grade I.   I. M.

Bury St. Edmunds, Theatre Royal   *Victor Glasstone*

Buxton, Opera House   *Martin Charles/Arup Associates*

Buxton,
Derbyshire

Opera House
★ ★ ★
The Square.
1903, Frank Matcham.
1979, renovated by Arup Associates.
Theatre

A masterpiece of Edwardian theatre architecture, completely intact and repaired and redecorated in 1979 to re-open as a theatre after many years' use as a cinema. (architects led by Derek Sugden with assistance from Theatre Projects Consultants). Stone exterior with entrance façade flanked by twin, leaded domes on low, columned drums. Superbly intimate auditorium of 960 seats with opulent Baroque plasterwork by De Jong. Two balconies with a gallery as a continuation of the second balcony, but divided from it by a parapet. Small box at each end of first balcony framed between columns supporting a little plaster canopy. Superimposed stage boxes, stepped-down in level, with upper box backed by characteristic niche flanked by terms. Curved head of proscenium carried on heavy scrolled consoles. Splendid oval,

Buxton, Opera House
Martin Charles/Arup Associates

saucer-domed ceiling set with six richly-framed, oval painted panels. The sunburner has been restored and is probably the only working theatre lighting fitting from the age of gas in the whole of Britain. Proscenium 30 ft., stage depth 40ft., grid 50ft.
Festival Theatre (July/August) run by locally supported Trust which is run both as an amateur and a touring theatre for the remainder of the year.
Listed Grade II.   C.B.

Playhouse
St. Johns Road.
1889, W. R. Brydon.
Nightclub
Part of Winter Gardens, Pavilion, Opera House complex. Formerly called Palace Theatre and Hippodrome. Low stone facade, on long axis of auditorium/stage, flanked at either end by elaborately carved gables. Pitched roof overall auditorium and stage-no fly tower. Auditorium much altered, with suspended ceiling at level of front of the single balcony. Main floor built up as flat terraces for tables and chairs.   C.B.

Cambridge,
Cambridgeshire
Festival Theatre
★ ★ ★ disused
Newmarket Road.
(formerly Theatre Barnwell or Theatre Royal, Barnwell).
1808 or 1816, William Wilkins.
1926 reconstructed by Terence Gray and Harold Ridge.
This theatre survives today almost intact as a workshop and wardrobe administered by the Cambridge Arts

Theatre Trust (founded in 1936 to run Cambridge's only remaining professional theatre, the Arts Theatre built in 1936). The Festival, as it has been known since 1926, provides remarkable evidence of two periods of theatre architecture: the late Georgian playhouse in that its three level horseshoe auditorium is intact, and the open staging techniques of the 1920's. In 1926 Terence Gray assisted by Harold Ridge and Norman Marshall totally removed the old proscenium and created a space stage complete with revolve, fixed cyclorama and Schwabe lighting according to the ideas that had been propounded by Gordon Craig for the preceding 25 years but had not been put into practice elsewhere in the U.K. The date of the actual building is uncertain. William Wilkins, architect of the surviving Theatre Royal, Bury St. Edmunds (q.v) is known to have demolished the old eighteenth century Barnwell theatre in 1807 and replaced it with a new theatre in 1808. But this was on the opposite side of the Newmarket Road on a site next to the Sun Inn. The present building is either a new construction of 1816 or else, if the story of switch of site is incorrect, a major rebuild of the same date. In either event it is unlikely that there ever was an imposing entrance, the theatre being originally reached down an alley where the 1926 foyer now stands alongside a still surviving house by William Wilkins. The theatre is rectangular in shape and of solid brick construction. The horseshoe of the three levels, two tiers of boxes with gallery over, stands within the square end of the auditorium of the building. The upper levels are supported by slender iron pillars on the

leading edge of the circles which continue up to the ceiling except in the centre of the gallery. The rear walls of the boxes remain intact and the original box doors remain. On the face of the tiers the 1926 decoration has been partially removed and Biblical texts can be seen which date from the period between 1878 and 1920 when the theatre was a mission hall.
The removal in 1926 of the proscenium and proscenium arch doors was neatly achieved; the already curved ends of the tiers being simply returned to the side walls. On the face of the vast overstage lighting bridge the original pediment remains as reminder of the width of the original 24 ft. proscenium. The stage itself was completely reconstructed in 1926 and is now an important and unique relic of the development of the open stage.
The Festival theatre, originally built outside of the City boundary because of virulent opposition in a University City to theatres in general, has for a century been in the 'wrong' part of the now larger city of Cambridge. However, the pattern of urban revival in the Kite area suggests that before long the theatre might find itself in more congenial surroundings. In this event the opportunity might present itself for an unusual rejuvenation of this unique theatre: it should be possible to restore the theatre in such a way as to make it possible to set it up either as Wilkins' Georgian Theatre Royal or as Gray's space stage Festival of 1926, a flexible arrangement highly appropriate to University use. Reconstructed in this way the theatre's capacity would be approximately 450.
Listed Grade II.   I.M.

Cambridge, Festival Theatre   *Victor Glasstone*

Canterbury, New Theatre
David F. Cheshire

Cannock,
Staffordshire

Forum Theatre
Market Hall Street.
(Formerly, Hippodrome).
1912, architect unknown.
Amateur theatre.
Rendered entrance front. Tall pitched roofed fly tower rising behind the auditorium. Small music hall auditorium (capacity 450) with a flat main floor and one balcony at the rear with straight rows, extending into narrow slips running parallel to the side walls to meet the elliptically arched proscenium. All very plain, with no decorative plaster work.   C.B.

Canterbury,
Kent

Alexandra Music Hall
Northgate.
(Formerly, Princess Alexandra Theatre, Canterbury Music Hall).
c. 1750, architect unknown.
Shop.
Front to Northgate entirely domestic in appearance - an altered 16th or 17th c. house with shop windows inserted at ground floor level. Former auditorium to rear, now in use as hardware showroom. Its present appearance is probably of mid-19th century date. A very simple, very small, music hall - the overall dimensions being only 18ft. wide x 35 ft. long. Flat main floor and balcony around 3 sides, straight across the rear and wide enough for only one row of seats. The ballustrade is now covered over with hardboard. Flat ceiling with exposed timber beams. Miniature proscenium with a plain elliptical arch. Tiny lean-to stage now altered. Theatrical use ceased in 1898. Listed Grade II.   C.B.

New Theatre
★ facade only/disused
1790, architect unknown.
Offices.
Good facade to Orange Street of c.1820 - stuccoed, of three bays and three storeys. Tall windows in piano nobile with inward-sloping jambs of 'Egyptian' character, fashionable at the time - e.g. Egyptian Hall, Piccadilly and Egyptian House, Penzance. The entrance of the theatre was earlier to the rear of the building, from Dancing School Yard. This is now a completely plain brick wall with modern windows. Theatrical use ceased in 1859 when the structure was condemned as unsafe.
A warehouse until 1960 when the interior was completely gutted and subdivided for office use.   C.B.

Cardiff,
South Glamorgan

Palace & Hippodrome
★ facade only/disused
Westgate Street.
1887, Waring and Son, and Jones.
Warehouse/shop incorporating altered facade.
Opened as Grand Theatre. Renamed Palace & Hippodrome in 1907. Lively stuccoed front of three storeys with

Cardiff, Palace & Hippodrome
Bill Slinn

three central bays slightly recessed between flanking, one-bay pilastered pavilions. Ground and first floors altered. Tall windows in upper storey with Corinthian pilasters and steep pediments. Balustraded parapet. Interior completely gutted.   C.B.

New Theatre
★ ★
Park Place.
1906, Runtz & Ford.
Theatre.
Brick exterior of little merit apart from curved, corner entrance under a high-level stuccoed colonnade flanked by small, domed, octagonal turrets. Intimate but theatrically rather cool auditorium (1,168 seats) with two

Cardiff, New Theatre   *Victor Glasstone*

Cardiff

balconies on slight curve. Rectangular proscenium frame flanked on either side by two boxes at the level of each balcony, subdivided with giant, fluted, Ionic columns with a straight entablature over. The second balcony front, set well back from the line of the first, abuts the side walls directly, with a stretch of blank wall separating it from the boxes. Very restrained plasterwork decoration on balcony fronts and flat ceiling. Proscenium 30ft., stage depth 50ft. (to rear wall), grid 55ft. Now owned by Local Authority, run as a touring theatre also staging regular seasons of the Welsh National Opera Company. Listed Grade II.   C.B.

Philharmonic Hall

★ ★ ★ disused
St. Mary Street.
1877, Jackson & Son (builder?).
Subsequent names: 1886, Philharmonic Theatre.
1892, Stoll's Panopticon.
1918, Pavilion Picture Theatre.
Bingo.

Important and rare surviving example of a music hall of the earlier concert-room type (Wilton's of 1859, q.v., Britannia, Glasgow of 1859, q.v., City Varieties, Leeds of 1865, q.v.). Characteristic and little altered auditorium - a rectangular

hall with slightly-raked main floor and one balcony around three sides (the centre section later increased in depth to the rear). The balcony sides, supported on slender iron columns, have a serpentine configuration and were probably originally divided by low partitions to form boxes. Balcony fronts of *bombé* section enriched with foliated plasterwork. Narrow proscenium framed by well-modelled, coupled Corinthian demi-columns on pedestals. Original apron stage in front of proscenium now cut back, and a very shallow stage behind. The side walls of the auditorium, above balcony level, are articulated by Corinthian pilasters. Deep ceiling originally divided into panels, now obscured by modern tiles. Deep cove at the sides pierced by lunette windows now boarded over.

Foyer with elaborate plasterwork of c.1918. Facade of some merit, but more important as part of the group from the corner of Wood Street to the end of St. Mary Street. Symmetrical debased classical design of seven bays and three storeys in moulded brickwork. Ground floor altered but the two upper storeys have segmentally-arched windows between pilasters. Triangular pediment over the three central bays with the name "Philharmonic Hall" painted in faded lettering in the tympanum.

Music-halls of the concert-room type are now extremely rare and very few are comparable with the Philharmonic in degree of ambition and extent of preservation. The capacity, seated to modern standards, would be approximately 800. Restored this theatre would be a significant addition to the range of auditoriums available to the performing arts in Wales' capital city and would undoubtedly be complementary to all other existing and proposed theatres and concert halls. It is well situated in the city centre. Listed Grade II.   CB.

Prince of Wales Theatre

★ ★ disused
Wood Street and St. Mary Street.
1878, Waring & Sons and W. D. Blesslay.
1920, auditorium reconstructed by Willmott & Smith.
Cinema.

Opened as New Theatre Royal. Good three-storeyed, Gothic, painted stone facade to Wood Street - traceried windows, canopied niches, etc. The entrance, however, is now around the corner in St. Mary Street (adjacent to the Philharmonic Hall) where one bay of the shop buildings, reflecting the Gothic style of the theatre, was rebuilt in a

Cardiff, Philharmonic Hall (left), and Prince of Wales Theatre (right)   *Victor Glasstone*

104

Cardiff, Prince of Wales Theatre
Victor Glasstone

Greek Revival style in 1930 - giant columns *in-antis* above the ground floor linked by a triangular pediment; open below and framing a square-headed niche containing a statue.
The auditorium was also reconstructed in 1920 in the same distinctive Grecian style. Three straight balconies with slips, imposing proscenium flanked by giant fluted Ionic columns carrying a big triangular pediment (open below as at entrance) with a large bas-relief Grecian freize above. Flat panelled and coffered ceiling.
An unusual and interesting auditorium which deserves to be restored to theatre use. Capacity approximately 1,000. Proscenium 26ft., stage depth approximately 30ft., grid 48ft.
Listed Grade II.   C.B.

Victoria Music Hall
pre-1914 fragment only
St. Mary Street.
1880's, architect unknown.
Offices.
Originally a small music hall at first floor level. Interior gutted and subdivided. All that now remains is the entrance, to one side of the ground floor of a plain, painted brick facade - double doors in a tall frame with arched fanlight. Remains of paybox on staircase.   C.B.

Carlisle,
Cumbria

Palace Theatre
Botchergate.
1906, Owen & Ward.
Triple Cinema
Interior completely gutted. Plain, brick, gabled front with arched windows - of no merit, and hidden from street behind a row of shops with passageway through.   C.B.

Royal Theatre
1851, architect unknown.
Facade only.

The Theatre
pre-1914 fragment only
Blackfiars Street.
1813, William Macready (also the owner).
Shop.
William Macready was the father of William Charles Macready who played at the theatre several times. It closed in 1848 and was converted into tenements. Part of the facade, facing onto St. Cuthbert's graveyard, is now incorporated into Binns Department Store.   D.W.

Castleford,
West Yorkshire

Queen's Theatre
Commercial Street.
1899, built as Queen's Hall, by R. McDowell.
1904, renamed Hippodrome.
1909, reconstructed as Queen's Theatre by A. Winstanley.
Shop.
Interior gutted but brick exterior intact apart from altered ground floor. Corner site with two elevations. Main front has three principal storeys with bays articulated by plain pilasters and blank arches at upper level in two middle bays, surmounted by a pedimental gable. Projecting three-sided oriel at second and third storeys on corner. Shallow fly tower.   C.B.

Chatham,
Kent

Theatre Royal
★ disused
102 High Street.
1899, G. E. Bond, rebuilt 1900 after fire.
Shop.
About half of this fine brick built theatre, which closed in 1955, still remains. A furniture show room occupies most of the foyer areas as well as the stage itself which was gutted after a fire in 1960's.
At street level no trace of the main entrance can be seen, but at first floor level the Italianate loggia plus stained glass windows and small towers which were originally capped with onion domes, remain. On the Manor Road side the large high-level name sign is clearly visible.
The stalls floor of the auditorium has been levelled off with new concrete work and is used for storage. After the fire the proscenium was bricked in and the damaged range of flanking boxes completely removed, although the splay can be traced on the ceiling

Chatham, Theatre Royal
David F. Cheshire

which survives. All three tier fronts, which are richly decorated with plasterwork, are intact. There is interesting timberwork and tiling in the side passages and to the rear of the circles. The theatre if restored would hold between 1600 and 1800 and would provide a much better theatre for the Medway Towns than the Central Hall, Chatham, which is nevertheless doing well under Civic management. However, the Theatre Royal is probably too far gone to make restoration economically feasible.
Not listed.   I.M.

Chatsworth House,
Derbyshire

Private Theatre of Duke of Devonshire
★ ★
1830, Wyattville.
A rare example of a private theatre, in this case on the first floor of a tower at the north end of a long wing added by Wyattville to the ducal palace of Chatsworth from 1820-1827. It is really a multi-purpose, flat-floored ballroom/theatre of modest dimensions with windows along the side walls, a central doorway at one end flanked by two large, slightly-raised boxes, and a small gallery for servants above. Fine ceiling, panelled to form frames for late 17th century paintings by Cheron and Thornhill. The most notable feature, theatrically, however, is the proscenium, which, although painted in the flat, gives the illusion of florid plasterwork frame with a richly draped and tasselled inner frame. There is also

Chatsworth House, private theatre of the Duke of Devonshire   *Trustees of Chatsworth Settlement*

a splendid contemporary act-drop depicting a view of the Elizabethan Chatsworth. Shallow stage without a flying grid but with original pulleys, wings and borders, etc. Listed Grade I.   C.B.

Chelmsford,
Essex

Regent Theatre
Moulsham Street.
C.1912, architect unknown.
Bingo.

An excellent example of its type and date - an early cine-variety house. Stuccoed facade with a wide, recessed, balustraded balcony at first floor level above the entrance, surmounted by stepped pediment ornamented by a cartouche. End bays with Ionic pilasters framing arched windows. Shallow brick fly tower rising behind the auditorium roof. Typical early cinema auditorium with one balcony.   C.B.

Cheltenham,
Gloucestershire

Coliseum
Albion Street.
1913, H. T. Rainger.
Bingo.

Opened as Hippodrome. Called Coliseum from 1920. Interior reconstructed in 1930's as a cinema when the stage was removed and incorporated within the auditorium. Stuccoed, gabled facade basically of 1913.   C.B.

Everyman Theatre
★ ★ ★
Regent Street.
1891, Frank Matcham.
Theatre.

Opened as the New Theatre and Opera House: renamed The Everyman Theatre in 1960. Painted brick facade of little merit - not helped by the insertion, in 1960, of a big rectangular bay window at first floor level and an ugly canopy. Excellent intimate auditorium (679 seats), similar in scale and character to the Lyric, Hammersmith. Two slightly-curved balconies of seven rows each; the upper one sub-divided by a raised parapet. Straight slips to one large box on each side of the proscenium, with splendid Rococo canopies carried on a slender, shaped colonnettes. Round-arched proscenium as at Hammersmith, but without open-work plaster frills. Very fine, saucer-domed ceiling incorporating painted panels in rich Rococo frames. Proscenium 24ft. 6in., stage depth 35ft., grid 45ft. Owned by Local Authority. Home of a repertory theatre company.
Listed Grade II.   C.B.

Cheltenham, Everyman Theatre   *Keith Gibson*

New Clarence Theatre
(Formerly Sadlers Wells Theatre).
C.1795, architect unknown.
Garage.

Chester,
Cheshire

Royalty Theatre
City Road.
1879, opened as Prince of Wales, architect unknown.
1882, rebuilt as Royalty by B. E. Entwhistle.
1958, auditorium remodelled.
Disused.

Restaurant in front of house, auditorium disused. Plain, painted, brick front and shallow fly tower. Apart from its basic structural form, the present sad appearance of the auditorium is due to the 1958 reconstruction; boarded fronts to the two balconies, plain side walls without boxes, plain ceiling and proscenium.   C.B.

Chesterfield,
Derbyshire

Civic Theatre
1879, built as Stephenson Memorial Hall, by Smith & Woodhouse.
1898, reconstructed by W. H. Wagstaff.
1948, reconstructed as Civic Theatre, by C. Bond.
Theatre.

Gothic exterior, in brick and stone, of the 1878 Hall. Present auditorium dates from 1948 reconstruction. Plain, with straight balcony. 549 seats. Proscenium 26ft., stage depth 35ft. The home of a repertory company.   C.B.

Chichester,
West Sussex

Theatre
★ facade only/disused.
South Street/Theatre Street.
1791, Thomas Andrews (builder).
Shop.

Chichester, Theatre   *David F. Cheshire*

Colchester, Hippodrome

Victor Glasstone

A corner site on a main street. Although only the brick facade and basic structural shell now remains this is an important example of a small, late 18th century town theatre. The facade has been marred by the insertion of a shop window across the full width at ground level, but above that everything is authentic. The three middle bays have a blank, square central panel flanked by tall sash windows and are emphasized by a triangular pediment. End bays again with blank panels, Brick cornice with parapet above, concealing the pitched roof.   C.B.

Clacton-on-Sea,
Essex

Operetta House
Rosemary Road.
1894, J. W. Chapman.
1930's reconstruction.
Bingo.
Theatre on first floor of the old town hall buildings - stalls and one balcony, stage depth 23ft., proscenium 22ft. 6ins. Renamed Tivoli in 1936. Reconstructed in late 1930's and renamed Savoy, with new frontage and remodelled auditorium.   C.B.

Cleethorpes,
Lincolnshire
Empire Theatre
Alexandra Parade.
1896, architect unknown.
Bingo.
Opened as Alexandra Theatre.

Pier Pavilion
1875, architect unknown.
1907, rebuilt after 1903 fire, architect unknown.
Seasonal theatre, seats 575 on a flat floor. Prosenium 30ft. wide, stage depth 18ft.

Colchester,
Essex

Hippodrome
★ ★ ★ disused
High Street.
? Original Building.
1889, reconstructed by Frank Matcham (after a fire).
1905, major reconstruction, architect unknown.
Bingo.
The original building was severely damaged by fire in 1889 and the reconstruction, including a new stage and a virtually new auditorium, was carried out by Frank Matcham. In 1905 a further major rebuilding took place. In the auditorium the structural forms of the two balconies were probably retained but the boxes, proscenium, ceiling and all the plasterwork were redesigned. A new entrance front was also provided. Only very minor alterations have been carried out since 1905 and the building survives as an exceptionally fine example of a medium-sized Edwardian Theatre.
The intimate auditorium has two well curved balconies of nine and ten rows each, partly supported on slender cast iron columns. Each balcony terminates in two bow-fronted boxes on either side. The boxes are divided by squat columns linked by arches - ogee at the lower level and elliptical above. The rectangular proscenium has a moulded frame richly decorated with foliated plasterwork. Over the top of the proscenium is a big cartouche supported by reclining female figures. This forms the focal point of the remarkable ceiling which is in the shape of a huge shell, its ribs radiating outwards and upwards from the cartouche. Raked stage now occupied by bingo machinery, but the flies are intact above a false ceiling. Proscenium 25ft. 6ins., stage depth 36ft. grid 50ft. The busy Edwardian Baroque facade makes a good contribution to the varied frontages of the fine High Street. It is in the brick with ample stone dressings and of an oddly asymmetrical design - three main bays and three storeys, with a 'centrepiece' surmounted by a curved pediment with the name "Grand Theatre" in the tympanum, above three blind *oeil-de-boeuf* openings. Three windows to each of the first and second floors, divided by pilasters. But the bays flanking this 'centre', although of broadly similar design, are of unequal width - the bay to

Colchester, Hippodrome   *Victor Glasstone*

the right is a squashed-up version of that to the left. Altered ground floor, and modern canopy. Although a new repertory theatre called the Mercury Theatre has been built in Colchester, the Hippodrome could nevertheless still be restored and used to house medium scale touring productions, concerts, amateur groups, etc. If reseated to modern standards of comfort the capacity would be approximately 900. C.B.

Colne,
Lancashire
Hippodrome
Newmarket Street.
1914, R. S. Pilling.
Amateur theatre.
Built as a cine-variety house. Long, narrow auditorium (approximately 500 seats) and small stage with low flies. Simple ashlar, gabled facade with two round-arched, rusticated entrance doorways. C.B.

Consett,
Durham
Empire Theatre
Front Street.
c.1900, architect unknown.
Theatre/cinema.
Pleasant, rendered facade with a pedimented three-bay centrepiece of 2 storeys, articulated by slender superimposed demi-columns.
Intimate auditorium with one balcony, capacity 589. Proscenium 32ft., stage depth 22ft., no flying grid. Owned by Local Authority since 1976. D.W./C.B.

Globe Theatre
★ ★ disused
Front Street.
1896, W. Aynsley.
1915, auditorium remodelled, architect unknown.
1956, partly gutted.
Ballroom.
Opened as The New Theatre. The facade survives largely intact apart from the altered ground floor. It is rather plain of ashlar, three stories under a straight parapet, and three main bays divided by pilaster strips. Three

Cork, Palace Theatre
photo circa 1925, R. W. Hammond

big, arched windows at *piano nobile* level. The auditorium originally had two balconies - the upper one a benched gallery. In 1915 it was remodelled, the gallery removed and one balcony constructed, extending into a raised-up, narrower rear section. The name was changed to Theatre Royal, but a few months later changed again to Globe Theatre. It closed as a theatre in 1926. In 1956 the adjacent Freemasons Hotel took over the building, inserted a ceiling at the level of the balcony front and converted the stalls area and stage into a ballroom. Above this ceiling, however, virtually all is intact. The upper half of the elliptically-arched proscenium (21ft. 6in) can be seen, surmounted by a pediment. The side walls are decorated with elongated plasterwork panels and the flat ceiling by a pattern of linked circular panels with an elaborate central rose. C.B./R.B.

Cork,
Eire
Apollo Theatre
pre-1914 fragment only
86 Patrick Street.
c.1798, Michael Shaunahaul (?).
Offices.
Most of the original shell is incorporated in premises now used by 'The Cork Examiner'.

Dun Theatre
19 Father Matthew (ex-Queen) Street.
1909, architect unknown.
Offices.
Important in terms of theatrical rather than architectural history, this little theatre operated on the upper floor of the building. In use as a theatre only until 1916.

King's Theatre
pre-1914 fragment only
Tuckey Street.
1799. Michael Shannahan.
Shell still exists and now contains a public hall.

Palace Theatre of Varieties ★ ★
1897, H. Brunton.
Cinema (occasional theatre use).
Unusual and interesting auditorium -one balcony only, partly supported on cast iron columns with rich capitals. 2 boxes on either side - but at stalls level, and surmounted by domed canopies with elaborate strapwork cresting above. On the side walls over the boxes are large painted panels. The rectangular proscenium is also enriched by strapwork.

Royal Victoria Theatre
pre-1914 fragment only
26 Cook Street.
1838, architect unknown.
Auction mart.
Converted from Diorama. Some indications of theatrical use (e.g. part of old gallery) are still evident.

Consett, Globe Theatre, detail of proscenium *Ron Berryman*

Theatre Royal
Oliver Plunkett Street,
(formerly George's Street/Princes' Street).
1736, Sir Edward Lovett Pearce.
Cork Farm House - a confectionary shop.
Plain exterior with shop front. All theatre fittings removed. Based on Pearce's plans for Augies Street Theatre, Dublin (q.v.). In use as theatre until 1791. D.F.C.

Theatre Royal
29 Oliver Plunkett Street,
(formerly George's Street).
1853, Hargrave.
General Post Office.
Interior converted completely, but facade largely intact.

Cradley Heath,
West Midlands
Royal Theatre
c.1912, architect unknown.
Cinema/Bingo.
A cine-variety theatre. Interior rebuilt in 1930 but the exterior is original - a simple gabled facade in brick with terra cotta dressings and small pinnacles at ends and apex of gable. A row of four blocked circular windows surrounded by pedimented frames at first floor level, above a large terracotta panel with "Royal Theatre" in raised lettering. Brick fly tower approximately 30ft. deep. C.B.

Craig-y-nos Castle,
West Glamorgan
Adelina Patti's Private Theatre
★ ★ ★
1891, Bucknall & Jennings.
Theatre (occasionally used).
Added by Dame Adelina Patti and her husband, the tenor Nicolini to the existing neo-Gothic house. The most ambitious of the few private theatres in

Britain, and still intact. Like Chatsworth, it also functioned as a ballroom but has a proper stage with fly tower, and also original machinery and scenery. The small, rectangular auditorium has a coved and panelled ceiling and the walls are richly articulated by giant, fluted Corinthian columns. The proscenium flanked by columns, has a central pedimented tablet with the names of Verdi, Rossini and Mozart. The flat floor can be tilted downwards towards the stage to form a raked auditorium and a sunken orchestra pit opened up. The main house is now used as a hospital.
Listed Grade II.   C.B.

Crewe,
Cheshire
Lyceum Theatre
★ ★
Heath Street.
1911, Albert Winstanley.
Theatre.
A rebuilding of a theatre built in 1889, designed by Alfred Darbyshire and destroyed by fire in 1911. Very plain, gabled, brick facade. Good intimate auditorium of 850 seats (this includes the present benched gallery). Two balconies with slips to superimposed stage boxes surmounted by onion-domed canopies. High relief plasterwork on fronts - cartouches supported by reclining female figures. Elliptically-arched proscenium (28ft.) and circular, coved centre to ceiling, decorated with heavy scrolled brackets and garlands. Owned by Local Authority, used both for repertory and medium scale tours.
Listed Grade II.   C.B.

Craig-y-nos Castle, Adelina Patti's private theatre   *Victor Glasstone*

Cromer,
Norfolk
Pier Pavilion
1906, architect unknown.
1953, reconstructed.
Theatre.
Listed Grade II.

Town Hall Theatre
1890, Edward Skipper.
Wine Store.
Listed Grade II.

Darlington,
Durham
Civic Theatre
★ ★ ★
Park Gate.
(Formerly Hippodrome).
1907, G. F. Ward.
Theatre.
The auditorium has two balconies and one pedimented box either side, at first balcony level. Rectangular proscenium 28ft. 6ins. with a heavy cartouche

Crewe, Lyceum Theatre   *Keith Gibson*

Darlington, Civic Theatre   *Christopher Brereton*

Derby, Grand Theatre   *Victor Glasstone*

above. Ceiling plasterwork 'painted out'. Capacity reduced from 1,100 to 600 by installation of a bar in rear stalls area, and disuse of upper balcony. Auditorium could be made considerably more attractive by a well considered colour scheme designed to emphasise the decorative plasterwork. Exterior of red brick with terra-cotta enrichments - pilasters, serpentine pediments etc. Main front on one longside with entrance emphasized by a high, pyramid-roofed pavilion. Acquired by Local Authority in 1958 and renamed Civic Theatre.   C.B.

Deal,
Kent

Globe Theatre
Marine Barracks.
c.1796, architect unknown.
Theatre.
Basic structural shell probably of original date. Completely plain exterior with unadorned window openings, pitched roof over auditorium and glazing in stage roof. Existing auditorium (383 seats) has a utilitarian 20th c. appearance. Small, traditionally equipped stage. The theatre is currently used by the Royal Marines for concerts and musicals.   D.F.C./I.M.

Theatre Royal
King Street.
1890, architect unknown.
Cinema.
Originally built as an Oddfellows Hall. A large, plain rectangular building on one of the main access roads to the sea. It was the principal centre for concerts and theatrical entertainment until c.1910, since when it has been mainly used as a cinema. Long, narrow auditorium, shallow stage with low grid.   D.F.C..

Derby,
Derbyshire

Grand Theatre
★ facade only/disused
Babbington Lane.
1886, Oliver Essex.
1900, interior reconstructed by Frank Matcham.
Dance Hall.

Only the 1886 facade survives - remainder completely reconstructed as a dance hall in 1959. A symmetrical design, stuccoed and of nine bays and three storeys with an attic storey above the entablature. Wider end bays with giant Corinthian pilasters to first and second storeys framing tripartite windows. Three central bays also articulated by pilasters with *oeil-de-boeuf* windows above in the attic.   C.B.

Hippodrome
★ ★ disused
1914, Marshall & Tweedy.
Bingo.
A large variety theatre approximately 1,800 seats, and still intact. Stalls below street level with two, deep, slightly-curved balconies above. Small single

Derby, Hippodrome   *Victor Glasstone*

Derby, Theatre Royal   *Victor Glasstone*

boxes either side at first balcony level, framed by giant pilasters carrying a serpentine pediment. Rectangular proscenium surmounted by a big segment-headed panel framing a garland. Flat ceiling with concentric circular moulded panels in rectangular frame. Rich Baroque plasterwork on balcony fronts, proscenium, ceiling, etc., rather coarse in detail. Proscenium 35ft., stage depth approximately 40ft. Dull exterior in brick with terracotta dressings.
Well situated in the City Centre, the theatre could be readily restored to provide Derby with a touring theatre.   C.B.

Theatre Royal
★ disused
Bold Lane.
1773, architect unknown.
Magistrates Court.
Converted from a former malthouse in 1773. Closed by 1864 and converted into a mission hall with an intermediate floor put in. The basic brick shell and pitched roof remain largely intact. The stuccoed facade of three wide bays and two storeys has been altered - the three arched entrances removed and replaced by a strip of plate glass windows, and the arched windows above have been lengthened downwards. Straight cornice and parapet. Although now much pulled about this is nevertheless a valuable surviving example of an 18th c. playhouse.
Listed Grade II.   C.B.

Dinnington,
South Yorkshire

Lyric Theatre
1911.
Theatre
Originally presented melodrama, then became the Picturedome, then a dance hall in the 1920's, and latterly a storeroom. In 1980 the local Council revived it as a theatre for amateur and occasional professional performances

and other uses including dancing etc. The auditorium is long and narrow with a flat floor - capacity 400. Fully equipped stage with flies. Plain, 2 storey, 3 bay front in brick with a central entrance flanked by shops.   C.B.

Doncaster,
South Yorkshire

Grand Theatre
★ ★ disused
Station Road.
1899, J. P. Briggs.
Bingo.
Still intact, although used for bingo since 1961. Intimate auditorium of approximately 1,000 seats. (If reseated to present standards). Two well curved balconies with good plasterwork on fronts - the upper one a benched gallery. Single, pedimented boxes in otherwise blank side walls flanking rectangular-framed proscenium 26ft., stage depth irregular, 32ft. on centreline. Plain ceiling. Excellent three-storeyed, stuccoed, Baroque facade on one long-side of the theatre. Complex rhythm of bays articulated by coupled and single pilasters and groupings of arched windows and doorways. Broken serpentine pediment over three central bays. This facade is now almost impossible to appreciate, having been hemmed in by a 1970's 'super-store'. The theatre could be readily restored, and is of a size suitable for both drama and musical productions.
Listed Grade II.   C.B.

Douglas,
Isle of Man

Empire Theatre
Regent Street.
1893.
2 shops on ground floor, with amusement arcade above.
Structural walls remain with interior completely altered. The large space of the amusement arcade at first floor level must have been part of the auditorium. This space is on two levels. Date of alterations unknown.   V.C.

Gaiety Theatre
★ ★ ★
Promenade.
1893, W. J. Rennison (opened as Pavilion).
1900, reconstructed by Frank Matcham.
Theatre.
One of the best of Matcham's surviving theatres. Excellent stuccoed facade -busy and festive. Three-storeyed towers with low pyramid roofs and dormer pediments on each face, flanking a two-storeyed centre section with a columned loggia at first floor level, surmounted by a curved gable. Higher curved gable to rear wall of auditorium rising behind, with a small pediment on top. Splendidly opulent auditorium, fitted by Matcham into the narrow shell of the old Pavilion. Two balconies, set well back from the stage, the lower one running into a range of three boxes either side with half-domed plaster canopies over, projecting beyond the face of the straight slips of the upper balcony. Rectangular proscenium opening set within

Douglas, Gaiety Theatre   *Victor Glasstone*

an overall segment-headed frame. Painted tympanum with figures of putti. Magnificent ceiling with painted panels of the four seasons. The whole thickly encrusted with richly modelled Baroque plasterwork. Rare and well preserved painted act drop depicting an exotic oriental scene. Usual seating capacity 960, (1,300 with rarely used gallery) proscenium 28ft. 6ins., stage depth 50ft., grid 48ft. Owned by the Manx Government and run as a touring and seasonal theatre. Recently sympathetically refurbished (Victor Glasstone, consultant). Unlike most other recent renovations, a proper attempt was made to get back to the exact effect which Matcham intended, with colours and really full box hangings and curtains faithfully reproduced. Even the wall paper is as close to the original as it was possible to find.

Listed Grade II. C.B.

Grand Theatre

★ facade only/disused

Victoria Street.
1882, built by Thomas Lightfoot.
1888, reconstructed: Matcham called in when building already under construction.
Cinema behind original facade.

The early history of the building is confused. Matcham took over once the building was already in construction. His plans for the theatre are extant and, if the fine facade is by him, must be one of his earliest still standing. The interior was completely gutted in 1935 when the theatre became the Regal Cinema. Externally the building is an important feature of Victoria Street. V.G.

Theatre Royal

Wellington Street.
1858, architect unknown.
Café, flats and store (?) behind.

Low gabled facade to street. Ground floor a café with residential use above. Rising up behind is the pitched roofed stone shell of the auditorium/stage block. Diagonally across the street is a pub called "The Theatre Royal". V.G.

Victoria Hall

Prospect Hill.
1862, architect unknown.
1882, name changed to Gaiety.
1888, rebuilt, architect John Taylor.
South Douglas Old Friends' Association Hall.

Two flat floored halls with stages. Open truss roofs. No decoration. Entrance down narrow passage. V.G.

Wellington/ Waterloo Theatre

Strand Street.
1820, architect unknown.
Disco and Bar.

Lower floor of Wellington Buildings erected as a public market. Upper floor, was intended for assemblies. Used by 'Gentlemen Actors' in 1820. For a time called Waterloo Theatre and from 1820

Theatre Royal; subsequently Wellington Hall. The building is externally quite intact with the large barn-like structure of the hall rising above surrounding buildings. Interesting pedimental end to Strand Street, fronting a large pitched roof. Ground floor currently an ice-cream parlour, with a disco and bar at upper level. V.G.

Douglas, Grand Theatre
Victor Glasstone

Downham Market, Norfolk

Theatre Royal

Playhouse Yard.
1829, architect unknown.
Betting Shop.

Interior completely altered. Small, rectangular, brick shell remains, but the original pitched roof has been replaced by a flat one. Original wide entrance doorway, flanked by Tuscan pilasters, facing the entrance arch to playhouse yard from the Market Square. C.B.

Dublin, Eire

Crow Street Theatre

pre-1914 fragment only

1758, architect unknown.

Partly demolished 1836, some walls incorporated in replacement building -now a clothing factory. D.F.C.

Fishamble Street Theatre

pre-1914 fragment only

(Formerly, Gentlemen's Theatre, Fishamble Street Music Hall).
1741, Richard Castle.

Demolished but parts incorporated in replacement building. D.F.C.

Gaiety Theatre

★ ★ ★

South King Street.
1871, C. J. Phipps.
Theatre.

Little altered early Phipps theatre. Very fine auditorium in which Phipps successfully achieved both intimacy and a sense of space - qualities in common with, for example, his Lyceum, Edinburgh, Theatre Royal, Glasgow and Lyric, London (q.v.).

Originally three horseshoe balconies supported by iron columns along their front edge, curving around to a stack of superimposed stage boxes with 'omnibus' boxes at stalls level. The boxes are flanked by tall, slender coupled colonnettes, their shafts entwined with foliage decoration. The fronts of the boxes and the first and second balconies are richly decorated with strapwork, scrolls, etc. In 1955 the top balcony (gallery) was removed and the second balcony extended to the rear. The arms of the first balcony have four boxes on each side, raised above the seating behind parapets. Characteristic circular ceiling, divided into wedge-shaped panels with delicate plasterwork decoration.

Restrained facade forming part of the street frontage - four storeys and five bays, in banded brickwork with stone dressings. Ground floor with an Italian Romanesque style ten-bay arcade of round arches on short columns with foliated capitals. Plain modern canopy, then five bays of coupled arched windows to *piano nobile*. Plain rectangular openings in third and fourth storeys and straight parapet above the cornice. Seating capacity 1,185, proscenium 27ft. 6ins., stage depth 38ft., grid 50ft. One of Dublin's major theatres. C.B.

Olympia

★ ★ ★

Crampton Street.
(Formerly Empire Palace, Star of Erin Music Hall, Monster Saloon Music Hall).
1855, architect unknown.
1879, rebuilt, by J. J. Callaghan.
1892, reconstructed, by J. J. Farrall.
1897, rebuilt, by R. H. Brunton.
Theatre.

Dublin, Gaiety Theatre *Eric Hart*

Important large touring theatre (1,450 seats). Plain, four-storeyed, stuccoed facade of domestic appearance but distinguished from flanking buildings by a delightful enriched iron and glass porch with a curved roof. Fine auditorium with two large balconies. Imposing, wide and high, elliptically-arched proscenium 34ft. wide, flanked by a stack of six boxes on each side, subdivided by slender colonnettes with bulbous bases. Second balcony slips

Dublin, Olympia   *Eric Hart*

above. Balcony and box fronts, proscenium and ceiling richly decorated with delicate Rococo plasterwork. The proscenium arch collapsed in 1974 causing much damage to the auditorium. After a successful fundraising campaign, however, all was carefully restored.   C.B.

Smock Alley Theatre
pre-1914 fragment only.
1662, architect unknown.
1735, rebuilt, architect unknown.
Demolished 1815, but Church of St. Michael & John incorporates some of the theatre's foundations.   D.F.C.

Tivoli Theatre
pre-1914 fragment only.
(Formerly, Lyric Theatre, Grand Lyric Music Hall).
1897, W. H. Bryne.
Partly demolished in 1928, the remains incorporated in Irish Press Offices.   D.F.C.

Dumfries,
Dumfries and Galloway

Theatre Royal
★ facade only
Shakespeare Street.
1792, architect Thomas Boyd.

1876, auditorium reconstructed and new f.o.h. and facade by C. J. Phipps.
1909, auditorium reconstructed as cinema.
1959, reconverted to a theatre.
Amateur theatre.
The basic, pitched-roofed shell of 1792 survives. Restrained but dignified two-storeyed stuccoed facade by Phipps, with central arched doorway flanked by two blank-arched openings. A series of small rectangular windows, subdivided by pilasters, under the eaves.
In 1909 Phipps' delightful auditorium was completely rebuilt as a cinema with one straight-fronted balcony (re-using only the foliated iron balustrade of Phipps' dress-circle) and blank side walls. On reconversion to a theatre in 1959 this auditorium was modified in a thin neo-Georgian manner which bears no relation either to Boyd's interior or to Phipps'.
Listed Grade B.   C.B.

Dundee,
Tayside

Gaiety Theatre
★ facade only/disused
Victoria Road.
1875, McCulloch & Fairley.
1903, alterations, W. Alexander.
Cinema.
Now called the Victoria Cinema. Auditorium much altered for cinema use and the shallow stage incorporated within its volume. Good painted stone facade survives intact - three main storeys and three bays with pedimented windows at first floor level and, above the cornice, an attic storey with a large Venetian style, semicircular-arched and traceried window. A small triangular pediment above, linked to the lower side bays by scrolls.   C.B.

Dundee, Gaiety Theatre
James Dunbar-Nasmith

Theatre Royal
★ facade only/disused
Castle Street.
1809, Samuel Bell.
Good, restrained, ashlar facade only remains (after 1888 fire), the remainder having been rebuilt as offices.
Listed Grade B.   C.B.

Dundee, Theatre Royal
James Dunbar-Nasmith

Dumfries, Theatre Royal   *David Hope*

Dunfermline,
Fife

Hippodrome and Opera House

★ ★ disused.
Reform Street.
1900, Roy Jackson.
1921, reconstructed by Swanston.
Shop and Store.

"Hippodrome" was added to the original title in 1921. Although the exterior is not exciting - a plain, 2 storey frontage to Reform Street, flanked by little pavilions - the auditorium is very successful. It is of particular interest in that it is still wholly a theatre, showing very little sign of the influence of the contemporary boom in cinema building. It is a reconstruction, within the old outside walls, of Jackson's auditorium of 1900. This had 2 balconies supported on iron columns, stage boxes and a domed ceiling. The new scheme substituted cantilevered balconies and completely changed the form of the ceiling, boxes, proscenium and the style of the decorative plasterwork. This is now in a Louis XV manner; reminiscent of some of Sprague's work. The proscenium frame, with its little, scrolly broken pediment over the top, is set within a deep arched reveal. This

takes in boxes at dress circle level. Swanston also raised the fly tower and increased the wing space of the stage. The proscenium is 24ft. and the stage depth 31ft. If reseated, by present standards, the capacity would be approximately 650.

The building is generally sound, although in a run-down condition, and would make an excellent all-purpose theatre for Dunfermline and the surrounding area. Communications are now very good since the opening of the Forth road bridge. A comprehensive redevelopment scheme, including all the usual ingredients of supermarket, car park etc., threatens the building (1981). As one of the most attractive medium-sized theatres in Scotland its retention and return to its original purpose is highly recommended.
Listed Grade B.   C. B.

Durham,
County Durham

Theatre Royal
Saddler Street.
1771, architect unknown.
Fire 1869 - Facade only remains.

Closed as a theatre in 1791. Now only the front remains - a plain three-bay, three-storeyed stuccoed facade of

Georgian domestic appearance. Plain sash windows in first and second floors. The ground floor has a recessed porch with two Tuscan columns in the centre, behind which are three doorways which may have been entrances to the theatre. There is, however, a continuous wooden cornice over, which also embraces two large, small-paned shop windows to the left and right, apparently part of the same design - which could, therefore, date from post 1791.
     C.B.

Eastbourne,
East Sussex

Devonshire Park Theatre

★ ★ ★
Compton Street.
1884, H. Currey.
1903, proscenium and boxes reconstructed by Frank Matcham.
Theatre.

Built on a sloping site with the stalls below entrance level - hence the low facade, which, in keeping with its seaside location, is flanked by white stuccoed Italianate towers with pyramid roofs (1884). Spacious en-

Dunfermline, Hippodrome and Opera House

James Dunbar-Nasmith

trance foyer covered by a richly decorated dome (1884). Intimate auditorium (955 seats) with two balconies supported by iron columns and delicate plasterwork to their fronts. These, and the saucer-domed ceiling, which covers the whole of the auditorium to the rear of the upper balcony, are by Currey. (Recent experiment has shown that if funds were available it would be possible to strip the top coats of paint on the ceiling panels and reveal the original flat painting.) In 1903 Frank Matcham designed a new proscenium arch and stage boxes - one at each side at first balcony level, with an 'omnibus' box below and an enriched plasterwork panel above. The proscenium is rectangular with heavy corner brackets and a tympanum over, with pendentives at the sides under the dome. Proscenium 26ft., stage depth 25ft. The theatre is owned by the Local Authority and is well maintained following its recent lease to a private management who also own the Theatre Royal, Haymarket, Theatre Royal, Brighton and the Richmond Theatre, and who now run the theatre as a touring theatre. Listed Grade II. C.B.

Pier Theatre

1899, architect unknown.
Only the original exterior remains. After a fire in 1970 the interior was completely gutted and converted into the Dixieland Showbar. D.F.C.

Royal Hippodrome

★ ★

Seaside Road.
1883, C. J. Phipps.
Theatre.
Originally called the Theatre Royal. Restrained but good symmetrical stuccoed facade with shops flanking the entrance and eleven bays of rectangular windows at first floor level, subdivided by small Corinthian pilasters. A seven-bay upper storey with Tuscan pilasters and a shallow hipped roof above the cornice.
The breadth of this facade (88ft.) gives the impression of a large theatre. In fact the auditorium is small (644 seats) and intimate. Two horseshoe balconies, supported by slender iron columns, curve around to meet stage boxes

Eastbourne, Devonshire Park Theatre *Victor Glasstone*

originally framed between giant Corinthian columns carrying a deep, flared, elliptical arch. 'Omnibus' boxes at stalls level. Flat circular ceiling with characteristic deep, panelled coves at the sides. There is an arcade at the rear of the first balcony, smaller in scale but similar to that of the Lyceum, Edinburgh. In general shape the theatre has much in common with the Theatre Royal, Northampton (q.v.). The balcony fronts were originally enriched with delicate scrolled plasterwork, but, about five years ago, this was removed together with the Corinthian columns flanking the boxes. What we see now is the rather sad, unadorned basic form of a Phipps auditorium. The plasterwork could, and should, be restored. Proscenium 24ft. 6ins., stage depth 23ft. 6ins., grid 43ft. Owned by the Local Authority who stage summer shows. C.B.

Eastbourne, Royal Hippodrome
Victor Glasstone

Eccles, Greater Manchester

Crown Theatre

Church Street.
1899, Campbell & Horsley.
Bingo.
Opened as the Lyceum. Later renamed the Grand and called the Crown Theatre from 1907. Auditorium completely altered for cinema use in 1932. Facade largely intact - tall, of moulded red brickwork with asymmetrically placed corner tower. Stage demolished. C.B.

Edinburgh,
Lothian

Garrick Theatre
Grove Street.
1897, architect unknown.
1906, opened as New Pavilion, renamed Prince of Wales. 1906, Alhambra. 1909, Pringles Picture Palace. 1917, Garrick. Facade part of a bakery.

Only the dull two-storeyed sandstone facade survived a fire in 1921. The ground floor has arched openings to left and right of its altered centre with three big mullioned and transomed windows at first floor level under a straight parapet.   C.B.

King's Theatre
★ ★ ★
Leven Street.
1905, Swanston & Davidson.
Theatre.

Opulent Rococo auditorium remarkable for its ranges of superimposed boxes flanking the proscenium - nine on each side with three at each level; the lower ones subdivided by large freely-modelled terms. The boxes are not, however, well related to the balconies,

which abut them arbitrarily. There were originally three balconies but the topmost was removed in 1951, and the middle one extended back, unfortunately to the detriment of the theatrical atmosphere at this level, resulting in large areas of blank side wall with rear seating which feels a long way from the stage. The proscenium is rather low in relation to the height of the auditorium with a deep panel, decorated by pilasters and a cartouche, between the structural head of the opening and the surmounting serpentine broken pediment. Shallow saucer-domed ceiling. Present capacity of theatre 1,530 (without the orchestra pit in use), proscenium 32ft., stage depth 56ft.

Richly decorated entrance lobby and first floor foyer reached by a broad marble staircase. Four-storeyed symmetrical ashlar sandstone facade - two side bays of superimposed windows flanking a broad central bay with a big rusticated arch above the entrance. Coupled Ionic columns through third and fourth storeys, framing a two-storeyed oriel and surmounted by a semicircular pediment. From time to time plans are prepared for this theatre to be completely refurbished, but so far no-one has got beyond drawing board stage. This is a pity because it is potentially a first class chamber opera or

drama house which could serve Edinburgh well.
Owned by the Local Authority and run as a touring theatre except during the annual Edinburgh Festival when it is pressed into service as an opera house.
Listed Grade B.   C.B.

Edinburgh, Royal Lyceum Theatre
Victor Glasstone

Royal Lyceum Theatre
★ ★ ★
Grindlay Street.
1883, C. J. Phipps.
Theatre.

One of the finest and least altered of the ten surviving interiors by Phipps. An unfortunate scheme of redecoration was carried out in 1978 but hopefully this will, in time, be remedied. Intimate yet spacious auditorium of approximately 1,200 seats (including top balcony, not now normally used) with three horseshoe balconies supported by iron columns, curving around to meet the proscenium - straight parapets, decorated with rich and delicate plasterwork scrolls, lozenge and circular panels etc. Three proscenium boxes each side at first balcony level, subdivided by small composite columns with bulbous bases. Imposing proscenium, 28ft. wide × 33ft. high with a facetted rectangular frame decorated with filigree plasterwork of Italian Renaissance character.
Elliptical tympanum over with painted panel of the muses. Characteristic deep coves above the gallery slips supporting a beautiful circular ceiling subdivided into richly decorated radiating panels. Backstage the arrangements are antiquated without being interesting historically. The flying is still operated by hemp lines without the benefit of any counterweight system. Stage depth 42ft., grid 54ft.
Excellent stuccoed facade - French classical with steep mansard roof, curved corners and three central bays at first and second floor levels articulated by giant attached Corinthian columns with triangular pediment over. Side elevation (recently well restored) with giant Corinthian pilasters.
Owned by the Local Authority, which leases the theatre to one of Scotland's leading repertory companies founded in 1964, the Royal Lyceum Company.
Listed Grade B.   C.B.

Edinburgh, King's Theatre   *Victor Glasstone*

Eye,
Suffolk

Theatre Royal
1815, David Fisher (owner and designer)
Garage.
The red and white brick facade is largely unaltered - except for a display window at ground floor level. The interior has been completely gutted. In use until 1850.   D.F.C/E.G.

Farnworth,
Greater Manchester

Queen's Theatre
Peel Street.
1899, Bradshaw & Gass.
Club.
Interior completely altered and exterior rendered over, obliterating all original features.   C.B.

Felixstowe,
Suffolk

Pier Pavilion Theatre
1911, Rogers.
Theatre.
Utilitarian pier theatre.   D.F.C./E.G.

Folkestone,
Kent

Leas Pavilion
★
The Leas.
1910, architect unknown.
Theatre.

Folkestone, Leas Pavilion
David F. Cheshire

Converted from a restaurant (1902) into a concert party venue in 1910: further slight conversion carried out in 1929 (since when it has been in continual use for repertory seasons). The 'restaurant' atmosphere continued into the 1960's -as the balcony held tables and chairs; teas could be taken there, and at one's seat in the stalls during matineé performances. This facility has now been withdrawn.
Other than a false proscenium which hides a very nice plasterwork frame this subterranean theatre is basically intact and is one of the more unusual in the U.K.   D.F.C.

Gainsborough,
Lincolnshire

King's Theatre
1904, converted from hall, architect unknown.
Bingo.
The former Albert Hall (1885) was converted into a theatre in 1904, a new facade being added at the same time. It became a cinema in 1911.   D.F.C.

Gillingham,
Kent

Gem Music Hall
13/17 King Street.
1912, architect unknown.
Garage.
Free-standing music hall in quiet residential back street. The exterior (including canopy over entrance) is intact, although somewhat delapidated. In use until 1917.   D.F.C.

Glasgow,
Strathclyde

Atheneum Theatre
★
Royal Scottish Academy of Music & Drama
Buchanan Street.
1892, J. J. Burnet.
Theatre.
Small theatre (600 seats) for performances by students of the Academy. Shallow-raked stalls and one balcony with semi-circular centre and straight slips to the proscenium (22ft.). Flat ceiling with moulded panels and circular centre. Present colour scheme is a very dark blue. Fine ashlar facade - a tall and narrow, two-part, asymmetrical composition. Stair tower with a cupola to the left of a five-storeyed section. This has superimposed bay windows framed within an arch surmounted by a steep gable, broken into by an aedicule.
Listed Grade A.   C.B.

Glasgow, Atheneum Theatre
James Dunbar-Nasmith

Bridgeton Cross Olympia
★ facade only/disused
1910, George Arthur & Sons.
Closed.
Only the imposing ashlar Edwardian Baroque facade survives, the remainder having been rebuilt as a cinema in the 1930's. The principal feature is the curved corner entrance with giant attached Ionic columns above the ground floor and a low dome rising from the parapet above the entablature. To the right five bays of giant pilasters, flanked by two-bay rusticated ends. This facade brings a measure of dignity to an otherwise derelict and devastated area.
Listed Grade B.   C.B.

Glasgow, Bridgeton Cross Olympia
James Dunbar-Nasmith

Britannia Music Hall

★ ★ ★ disused

Trongate.
1857, Gildard & Macfarlane.
Storeroom above shop.

Important as the only surviving early music hall in Scotland; substantially intact, although now in a sadly neglected state. The auditorium is at first floor level; the former entrance now occupied by a shop. Overall dimensions of auditorium 46ft. wide × 50ft. deep. One balcony of three rows on three sides. Flat, panelled ceiling with coved sides above an elaborate cornice. Typical small music hall stage, 12 ft. deep, without flying space, behind a simple proscenium painted on canvas - 20 ft. wide.

The well of the auditorium, between the balcony fronts, is now filled with the wooden pitched-roof of a storeroom occupying the main floor. The roof-space above the ceiling of the auditorium appears to have housed the dressing rooms. The roof itself is now in a near-derelict condition.

Good Italianate facade to Trongate in painted ashlar stone. The two storeys above the shop have nine bays of closely-set arched windows. The top floor has 16 bays of small arched windows in the form of an arcade, with a small triangular pediment over the middle four bays. Music halls of this type and date are now extremely rare anywhere in Britain and as such the Britannia fully deserves a careful and sympathetic restoration.

Listed Grade B.   C.B.

Citizen's Theatre

★ ★ ★

Gorbals Street.
(Formerly, Her Majesty's Theatre, Royal Princess's Theatre).
1878, Campbell Douglas & Sellars.
Theatre

The theatre formerly had an imposing facade with a giant order of Tuscan columns. This was sadly demolished in 1977, together with the adjacent Palace Theatre. Very fine auditorium (793 seats) with two lyre-shaped balconies with rich plasterwork, supported by iron columns with large ornamented capitals. Superimposed stage boxes with caryatids above. There are no actual sides to the proscenium arch - the opening being framed by the inner pilasters of the boxes which are capped with caryatids. Flat, plain ceiling with deep, panelled coves at the sides. Dramatic new colour scheme in 1979. Proscenium 30ft., stage depth 42ft., grid 52ft. Well preserved stage machinery. The proposed southern flank of the so-called "inner-ring road" (which in fact involved the destruction of large tracts of the central area) originally threatened the theatre, but this has now been indefinitely postponed.

The theatre is the home of the distinctive Glasgow Citizens Theatre Company whose flamboyant style of production and of décor has given it a special place in contemporary European theatre.   C.B.

Glasgow, Citizen's Theatre   *Keith Gibson*

Coliseum

Eglinton Street.
1905, Frank Matcham.
Cinema.

Built as a large variety theatre in the Gorbals. Auditorium gutted for cinema use - the two large balconies replaced by one. Exterior basically intact - brick with stone dressings. Narrow entrance facade projecting forward from one end of the rear wall of the auditorium -asymmetrical design with a big octagonal tower on the corner, with a top stage of coupled arched windows and a pointed roof surmounted by a cupola. Main entrance to the left, originally through a high arch with an open arcaded loggia above and a steeply-pitched pavilion roof. Now only the top of the roof is visible behind a tacked-on modern frontage.   C.B.

King's Theatre

★ ★ ★

Bath Street.
1904, Frank Matcham.
Theatre.

One of the best examples of Matcham's later manner. An important theatre which cost the large sum of £50,000 to build. Free-Baroque ashlar exterior on a corner site with two show fronts. Entrance on one long-side, through one of two matching pavilions projecting forward from the main bulk of the auditorium/stage block. Very large ball-finials on the corners of the parapets. Splendidly opulent auditorium (1,840 seats) in a mixture of Baroque and Rococo. Three cantilevered balconies curving around to a complex arrangement of three boxes on each side, sur-

Glasgow, King's Theatre   *Victor Glasstone*

119

mounted by elaborate half-domed canopies. Above the second balcony slips is an arcade of conches supported by fluted columns. Twelve-sided ceiling with richly decorated radiating panels. The proscenium has an outer rectangular frame enclosing a heavily emphasized inner frame, surmounted by a serpentine pediment broken by a large cartouche. Proscenium 30ft., stage depth 50ft. (to rear wall), grid 55ft.

The theatre is now owned and administered by the Local Authority who stage tours, musicals, pantomime, summer shows and amateur productions, a 'popular' policy which balances that of the Theatre Royal.

Listed Grade B   C.B.

New Metropole Theatre

★ ★ disused
St. George's Cross.
(Formerly, West End Playhouse).
1910, W. B. Whitie.
Closed.

Located away from the city centre. Good sandstone ashlar facade in Louis XV style - five bays with canted corners and giant fluted coupled Ionic pilasters flanking central bay through second and third storeys. Continuous entablature with deep parapet above. Intimate auditorium (approximately 1,300 seats) with two balconies and superimposed stage boxes. Restrained Baroque plasterwork. Ceiling altered. Shallow stage. Used intermittently as a variety theatre until recent closure. Threatened with redevelopment in 1981.

Listed Grade B.   C.B.

Pavilion Theatre

★ ★ ★
Renfield Street.
1904, Bertie Crewe.
Theatre.

A large variety theatre (1,445 seats) still in use as such. Two wide and deep, serpentine-fronted, cantilevered balconies. One box each side at first balcony level framed between columns carrying a deep-soffited elliptical arch above the proscenium. The proscenium itself has been altered. The side walls at second balcony level are articulated by blank arches carried by terms and rising into coves under the main ceiling. This is divided into panels with a square centre, raised-up into a deep cove, with a sliding roof for ventilation. Good Rococo plasterwork on ceiling, balcony and box fronts, etc. Proscenium 36ft., stage depth 24ft., grid 50ft.

Prominent corner site. Main facade, in terra cotta, on one long-side, to Renfield Street - three main bays with segmental pediments, each bay subdivided into three subordinate bays with circular windows below the pediments. Facade to Renfrew Street (the rear wall of the auditorium) flanked by square staircase towers with pointed roofs.

Listed Grade B.   C.B.

Theatre Royal

★ ★ ★
Hope Street.
1867, opened as Bayliss' Coliseum, architect G. Bell.
1869, renamed Theatre Royal.
1880, rebuilt after fire by C. J. Phipps.
1895, rebuilt after fire, again by Phipps.
1975, major refurbishment, architect Arup Associates.
Theatre and Opera House.

Glasgow, Pavilion Theatre
James Dunbar-Nasmith

Rescued from use as a T.V. studio in 1975 and magnificently restored, by a team led by Derek Sugden, as a home for Scottish Opera at a cost of £3m. including £300,000 for purchase (Theatre Consultant: John Wyckham). This is the largest, and possibly the finest theatre by Phipps to survive. Prior to closing in 1956 the capacity was 1,950. It is now

Glasgow, New Metropole Theatre
Christopher Brereton

Glasgow, Theatre Royal

Arup Associates

1,560. Three balconies - the first with a serpentine front, and the upper two horseshoe. Originally fully supported by iron columns, some of which have now been removed and cantilevers inserted - a very difficult operation. The balcony slips meet superimposed stage boxes set between pairs of giant Corinthian columns with enriched shafts. The entablature continues the line of the third balcony front and has a richly decorated frieze which returns above the rectangular-framed proscenium (34ft.). Spanning between the columns is a deep elliptical arch which forms a tympanum above the proscenium. Characteristic coves above the gallery slips carrying a splendidly decorated circular ceiling. The balconies are relatively deep - 11 rows each, and their rather excessive overhangs tend to mar the otherwise fine spatial qualities of the auditorium. The plasterwork decoration on balcony fronts, ceilings, etc., is in a delicate combination of Renaissance strapwork and Rococo and is of excellent quality. The refurbishment work included a successful Victorian pastiche in the new entrance foyer and main staircase. The painted stone exterior is of little merit -an immensely long front of 19 bays of rectangular windows, part two storey, part three. The entrance, lacking its original canopy, is emphasized by three arched windows under a segmental pediment, surmounted by a small square tower - yet to receive its restored dome.
Listed Grade B.   C.B.

Gloucester,
Gloucestershire

Palace Theatre
pre-1914 fragment only
(Formerly, New Theatre & Opera House; Theatre; New Theatre).
1791, architect unknown.
1857, rebuilt, architect unknown.
1897, reconstructed by J. P. Briggs.
Dismantled 1922 - doorway surmounted by bust of Shakespeare remains.

Goole,
Humberside

Theatre Royal
Adam Street.
1841, architect unknown.
Store.
A small theatre with a capacity of 850 in 1896 and an 18ft. proscenium. Bombed by a Zeppelin 1915; now only the simple brick exterior survives - one elevation with five bays of blank semi-circular arches through two storeys. Some original arched doorways and sash windows. New openings made to store.
                                              C.B.

Tower Theatre
Carlisle Street.
1912, architect unknown.
Bingo.

Later renamed Coliseum. Undistinguished brick facade on axis of auditorium/stage. Auditorium completely altered as a cinema in 1938 with one large balcony. Stage survives. C.B.

Gosport,
Hampshire

Theatre
High Street.
1796, architect unknown.
Shops and store.
Built as part of Henry Thornton's circuit of theatres. Others were at: Henley (q.v.), Newbury (demolished 1976), Andover (demolished), Farnham (demolished), Reading (demolished), Guildford (demolished), Windsor (demolished), Arundel (q.v.), Chelmsford (demolished), Croydon (demolished), Weybridge (demolished), Ryde (demolished) and Oxford, where he used (1799-1809) the real tennis court at Merton College, which still stands.
At Gosport the manager's house, theatre tavern and coffee house have been converted into shops. An arch (blocked in) led to the theatre itself which is at right angles to the High Street facade. This still stands and is used as a store.   C.B.

Grassington,
North Yorkshire

Theatre
1790.
House.

Gravesend,
Kent

Theatre
New Road/Garrick Street.
1808, architect unknown.
Shop.

Single-storey building on corner site on main shopping street.
At the front a new facade has been constructed and a new roof put on. The side walls (including those of the manager's house at rear) have been repaired by the present occupiers. The building had previously been derelict for some years following long use (since 1883) by the Salvation Army. It was one of Trotter's theatres. D.F.C.

Tulley's Bazaar
Milton's Hall, Windmill Street/ South Street.
1835, architect unknown.
Probably altered in 1850's/60's.
Shop and store.
Free-standing early Victorian concert room with plain exterior decorated with classical features, virtually unaltered, except for insertion of shop frontage in main entrance. One-third of the building in use by Unwin's Wineshop, and the remainder as a store for Lancaster's Removers. The stage has been removed.

Great Yarmouth,
Norfolk

Gorleston Pavilion
1898, J. W. Cockrill.
Theatre.
Impressive domed red-brick building with decorative terra-cotta panels, balustrades and stained-glass windows in an exuberant Art Nouveau manner. The entrance is currently spoiled by modern advertisement boards. Inside the layout is typical of a Victorian seaside music hall with a small gallery supported by decorative iron girders, and a flat main floor (capacity 750). Painted panels of theatregoers in boxes on the side walls - not original. Sliding roof for use in hot weather. The present proscenium dates from 1919. The theatre is now used for summer shows.
                                        E.G./D.F.C.

Great Yarmouth, Hippodrome   *Elizabeth Grice*

Great Yarmouth, Hippodrome

Hippodrome

★ facade only

Golden Mile.
1903, R. S. Cockrill.
Circus.

Impressive exterior with twin, domed towers, large lunette windows and Art Nouveau terra-cotta panels. Unadorned circus auditorium with an arena, 42ft. in diameter, still capable of being lowered and flooded for acquatic performances - original equipment restored in 1981. Excellent acoustics for orchestral concerts (1,500 seats).   E.G./D.F.C./C.B.

Royal Aquarium Theatre

Seafront.
1876, architect unknown.
1883, converted to theatre by Bottle & Olley.
Cinemas.

A large red brick structure with arcading and panels on the main south front. Lower half of facade disfigured by modern advertisement boards. Originally used (as its name suggests) as an aquarium, but in 1883 was rebuilt as a theatre. Completely redone as a three-in-one cinema in 1970. The complex also includes the Little Theatre (1925).   E.G./D.F.C.

Wellington Pier Theatre

1903.
Seasonal theatre.

Original design with octagonal turrets at the four corners and a big cupola on top. Auditorium seated 1,500. Reconstructed 1960 when 1,600 seats were installed together with one balcony. Proscenium 26ft. Stage depth 26ft.

Windmill Theatre

1908.

Guernsey, Channel Islands

Hippodrome

St. Julien's Avenue, St. Peter Port.
c.1880, architect unknown (as a skating rink).
c.1900, converted to theatre.
Closed.

In use as a cinema from 1912-1929 and a repertory theatre from 1929-1939. All theatre fittings now removed.   D.F.C.

St. Julien's Theatre

St. Julien's Avenue, St. Peter Port.
1876, William Robillard.
Cinema.

Completely altered on conversion to a cinema in 1930.   D.F.C.

Halifax, Civic Theatre

Guildford, Surrey

Theatre Royal

North Street.
1861, opened as Country & Borough Halls. Thomas Goodchild.
1912, rebuilt as Theatre Royal.
Cooperative Society store.

Originally built as the huge County & Borough Halls with frontages on both North Street and Leapale Road. The large hall was converted to a full theatre in 1912 and continued in operation until 1933 when it was closed because of inadequate safety precautions. The two facades, of local Bargate stone, clearly indicate the buildings use with the scene dock doors being particularly prominent.   M.S.

Halesworth, Suffolk

Halesworth Theatre

pre-1914 fragment only

London Road.
1785, architect unknown.
1809, rebuilt, architect unknown.

The Rifle/Drill Hall opened on this site in 1892 may incorporate parts of the old theatre.   D.F.C

Halifax, West Yorkshire

Civic Theatre

★ ★

Commercial Street.
(Formerly, Victoria Hall.)
1901, Clement Williams.
Theatre & Concert Hall.

Built as a concert hall called the Victoria Hall (present seating capacity

1,600). The platform was set behind a permanent proscenium frame (width 45ft.) and was, from the beginning, intended for occasional theatrical use. Following the purchase of the hall by the Local Authority a fully equipped flytower was built in 1964 (stage depth 29ft.) and the name changed to Civic Theatre; though still used for concerts, etc. The fine auditorium has a European opera house look about it, with a semi-circular rear wall and two semicircular balconies extending along the sides to the wide proscenium. Panelled ceiling with deep, enriched cove. Flat main floor. Spacious and elaborately decorated entrance foyer and main staircase with stained-glass dome. Good, free-classical, ashlar exterior on an important site at the junction of two roads. Imposing curved entrance facade with first floor windows divided by coupled columns and square flanking towers surmounted by tall cupolas. Listed Grade II. C.B.

Theatre Royal

★ facade only/disused

Southgate.
1905, Richard Horsfall & Son.
Bingo.
Only the exterior survives, the interior having been completely gutted for bingo. Excellent Edwardian Baroque ashlar facade, unusually formal for an English theatre. Three main storeys with an attic. Flanking bays surmounted by open segmental pediments enclosing enriched circular windows. Three central bays above the arched entrances emphasized by giant Ionic pilasters, and a triangular pediment set against the attic storey. C.B.

Halifax, Theatre Royal   *Victor Glasstone*

Hamilton,
Strathclyde

Playhouse

★ facade only/disused

Quarry Street,
(Formerly, Victoria Hall).
1887, A. Downie.
Shop.
Interior completely altered - originally a small music hall at first floor level with one balcony on three sides and a shallow stage without flies. Renamed the Playhouse in 1928. Symmetrical painted ashlar facade to Quarry Street survives unaltered above ground floor. An odd amalgam of styles - two-storeyed bay windows with corbelled gables flanking a five-bay central section with big mullioned and transomed windows at first floor level. Smaller windows above, divided by coupled pilasters and a large tripartite arched window in the centre surmounted by a small gable. C.B.

Hanley,
Staffordshire

Theatre Royal

Pall Mall.
1841, opened as Royal Pottery Theatre.
1871, rebuilt by R. Twemlow.
1888, reconstructed by Phipps and Matcham.
1894, reconstructed by Matcham.
1951, rebuilt after fire. Architect J. Wild of Forshaw & Greaves.
Bingo.

Hamilton, Playhouse
Christopher Brereton

The rear wall of the stage of the 1894 building survives - brick with stone dressings and articulated by seven bays of tall blank arcades between pilasters with foliated capitals.
The rebuilding of the theatre in 1951 was rather remarkable considering the generally perilous state of provincial commercial theatre at the time. In the event it only survived 10 years before succumbing to bingo. The auditorium is intimate for its large capacity (1,800) and has 2 big balconies facing a 40ft. proscenium flanked by boxes. Stage depth 32ft., grid 52ft. It could be restored to use relatively easily but Matcham's Empire Theatre, Longton (q.v.) in the same conurbation is a better theatre. C.B.

Victoria Music Hall

Glass Street.
(also known as People's Music Hall)
1861, architect unknown.
Warehouse.
Later used as a skating rink, a cinema and then a nightclub. Interior gutted. The basic plain rectangular structure with a hipped roof survives. Original entrance completely altered. C.B.

Harrogate,
North Yorkshire

Opera House

★ ★

Oxford Street.
1900, J. P. Briggs.
1972, refurbishment by Roderick Ham & Partners.
Theatre.
A delightfully intimate theatre, very well suited to its present role as a repertory playhouse in this attractive Victorian spa town. The site is wedge-shaped at the junction of two streets. The stage is at the wide end, with an irregularly shaped rear wall, and the side walls of the auditorium converge towards the back. There are two serpentine-fronted balconies and two boxes either side at each level, divided by delicate pilasters and surmounted by broken scrolled pediments. Balcony and box fronts richly decorated by cartouches supported by *putti*, garlands, etc. Regtangular framed proscenium with a

Harrogate

large cartouche above. Central part of ceiling carried up into a dome. Intimate foyer with richly modelled Arts and Crafts frieze with prancing figures. In 1972 a major scheme of refurbishment was carried out by Roderick Ham & Partners, including reseating and the reduction of the gallery to two rows. The total capacity was reduced from 797 to 475. At the same time the front of house dressing rooms, etc., were reorganized and up-dated. The exterior has a four-storeyed octagonal tower at the apex of the site, with a steeply pitched roof and cupola.
Listed Grade II.   C.B.

Royal Hall
★ ★ ★

Ripon Road.
1903, Frank Matcham.
Hall (concerts, musicals, conferences, etc.)

Opened as the Kursaal; renamed Royal Hall in 1914. Although a multi-purpose hall rather than a theatre its inclusion is justified by its use of many of the elements of theatre architecture, as an excellent example of its type and as an important and well preserved example of Frank Matcham's work. The richly decorated rectangular auditorium (1,336 seats) has a balcony of 12 rows at the rear, continued with two rows along the side walls where it is divided into three bow-fronted sections. Below these, raised slightly above the main floor, are six boxes on each side. The

Harrogate, Opera House   *Keith Gibson*

Harrogate, Royal Hall

proscenium (30ft.) is flanked at balcony level by two painted panels. Along the side walls are large, arched, stained-glass clerestory windows with caryatids between, supporting a continuous bracketted cornice below the splendid coved ceiling. The stone exterior expresses the bulk of the main hall with its pitched roof and central, domed lantern. There are glass roofed terraces outside the promenades encircling the auditorium. Owned by the Local Authority.
Listed Grade II.   C.B.

St. James's Hall
Cambridge Street.
1882, architect unknown.
Supermarket.
In use as a cinema from 1910 to 1959. The upper part of the original facade is still intact but all else has been remodelled.   D.F.C.

Theatre Royal
pre-1914 fragment only
Church Square.
1788, architect unknown.
House.
Exterior basically intact. Stone facade with prominent gable and central doorway with Tuscan columns. All theatre fittings removed, but manager's lodgings etc. may remain. In use until 1830.
D.F.C.

Hastings,
Sussex

Gaiety Theatre
Queen's Road.
1882, C. J. Phipps.
Cinemas.
With a local history of extreme antipathy to the theatre from both the Church and the magistrats, the developers responsible for the Gaiety asked Phipps to design something as little like a theatre as possible. This he did by making the building look like insurance offices. At ground level a restaurant was incorporated to the left of the inconspicuous main entrance, and an arcade to the right. The theatre became a cinema in 1932. Conversion into multi-cinemas in 1972 completely removed all trace of the original interior.   D.F.C.

Hippodrome
★ facade only/disused.
Pelham Place.
(Formerly Empire Theatre, Royal Marine Palace of Varieties).
1899, Ernest Runtz.
Bingo and Amusements.
Prominent sea-front site, wedged-up against the side of the cliff on which stands Hastings Castle. Apart from the insertion of a floor at the level of the first balcony front, the essential features of the auditorium survived until 1978 when it was finally wrecked. The enriched terra cotta exterior is basically til 1978 when it was finally wrecked. The

Hastings, Hippodrome
David F. Cheshire

enriched terracotta exterior is basically intact, however, although marred by a crude modern canopy. The facade lies along the axis of the auditorium/stage and is flanked at each end by imposing domed pavilions with Arts and Crafts octagonal turrets at their front corners. The pavilions are linked by four large, semicircular-arched windows at first floor level and a loggia (now glazed) of squat coupled columns below the eaves of the pantiled roof. Here the style is vaguely Spanish Renaissance (Empire Middlesborough, q.v.).   C.B.

Heanor,
Derbyshire

Empire Palace
1911, architect unknown.
Cinema.
A cine-variety theatre. Small auditorium with one balcony with a panelled front and plain side walls. Proscenium removed and stage taken into volume of auditorium. Altered facade with a flat modern frontispiece but retaining some decorative painted stonework over a side doorway.   C.B.

Henley-on-Thames,
Oxfordshire

Kenton Theatre
New Street.
(Formerly Theatre and Playhouse).
c.1805, shell of present building.
c.1880, reconverted to theatre use.
1967, re-modelled Maurice R. Day & Associates.
Amateur Theatre.
The shell is probably that of the theatre identified by James Winston when compiling The Theatric Tourist in 1805. The theatre was converted into a chapel or meeting hall in the middle of the nineteenth century, from when the fine pair of round-headed windows on each side of the auditorium most probably date. The existing double curved single balcony dates either from then or from the time later in the century when it was reconverted into a theatre. After the se-

cond World War it was still in use as a theatre being patched up from time to time by local volunteers including, it is said, the artist John Piper, who reputedly rebuilt the proscenium with his own hands. The old theatre was closed on safety grounds in 1963.
The present proscenium dates from the 1967 remodelling which left only the earlier windows, the balcony front and the central ceiling mounting for a sunburner. The decorative style of the auditorium is domestic neo-Georgian with little theatrical atmosphere. Proscenium arch is 25ft. wide ana the stage only 17ft. deep with a small fly tower over. Capacity is 280.   I.M.

Hexham,
Northumberland

Theatre
1823, architect unknown.
This simple building has been gutted almost completely. Part of it is now used by a monumental mason. The remainder is derelict.   D.F.C.

Horsham,
Sussex

New Theatre
Pirces Place,
(Formerly, Theatre Royal).
c.1800, architect unknown.
W.I. Hall/Dancing School.
Used as a theatre until 1830. Obscurely situated up an alley behind the Stout House on the town's main square. The building now contains a Women's Institute market on the partitioned-off stage area and a dancing school in the completely altered former auditorium.
D.F.C.

Hoylake,
Merseyside

Lighthouse Pavilion
Alderley Road.
1911, L. H. Clegg.   Theatre.

Hoyland,
South Yorkshire

Empire-Hippodrome
West Street.
(Formerly, Princess' Theatre).
1893, architect unknown.
c.1920, reconstructed as cinema.
Bingo.
In c.1920 original stage removed and auditorium expanded and completely rebuilt as a cinema - one straight balcony, plain side walls and plain, flat ceiling. At the same time the brick facade was also completely redone.
C.B.

Huddersfield,
West Yorkshire
Hippodrome
Queensgate.
1905, converted to theatre by W. Cooper from a riding school of 1846.
1960's, rebuilt as cinema.
Only the fly tower and the lower part of the side walls of the auditorium remain following rebuilding in the 1960's.
C.B.

Hull,
Humberside
Grand Theatre & Opera House
George Street.
1893, Frank Matcham.
1935, reconstructed as cinema.
Closed.
Auditorium and stage completely reconstructed in 1935 as the Dorchester Cinema, with one large balcony. At the same time Matcham's facade was extensively altered, plastered over and extended at the sides. All that is now recognizable from the original design are the windows in the central bay and some vestiges of detail in the end bays.
C.B.

Hyde,
Greater Manchester
Theatre Royal
★ ★ disused
Corporation Street.
1902, Campbell.
Cinemas.
Good, intimate auditorium (approximately 1,000 seats) with two balconies curving around to meet the proscenium (29ft.) which has been altered. Restrained plasterwork on balcony fronts and ceiling. The stage (40ft. deep) has been adapted to use as small cinema. Red brick facade, nine bays wide and three storeys high with a triangular pediment over the three central bays, decorated with moulded brickwork. Although partially altered, the theatre could be restored to use and is well situated in the town centre.
C.B.

Ilkeston,
Derbyshire
Hippodrome
Lower Granby Street.
1909, converted from a temperance hall of 1870.
Store.

Hyde, Theatre Royal   Christopher Brereton

A very small music hall at first floor level which originally had a tiny stage, flat main floor and small gallery. In use only until c.1917. Interior completely altered. Exterior survives - a plain rectangular, two-storeyed brick structure.
C.B.

New Theatre
Lord Haddon Road.
(Formerly, Theatre Royal, Coliseum).
1895, architect unknown.
1929, rebuilt as cinema.
Bingo.
Only the fly tower and dressing rooms survive from 1895; the present auditorium, front of house and facade date from the rebuilding of 1929.
C.B.

Ipswich,
Suffolk
Hippodrome
St. Nicholas Street.
1905, Frank Matcham.
Bingo.
The auditorium was unusual for Matcham in that it had only one deep balcony which met widely-splayed side walls (no slips or boxes). In 1964 these were removed together with the plasterwork on the proscenium and the balcony was reconstructed. All that now remains of the original interior is the ceiling, which covers the whole space of the auditorium. It has a flat centre with radiating panels. Dull painted brick exterior, much altered in the 1920's when two storeys were added above the previously single storey curved corner entrance.
C.B.

Jersey,
The Channel Islands
Opera House
★
Gloucester Road, St. Helier.
1900, Adolph Curry.
1921, reconstructed after fire by Jesty & Baker.
Theatre.
The Opera House was built on the site of the previous Theatre Royal, and opened with Lillie Langtry in **The Degenerates.** Only the impressive stucco facade (a charming provincial interpretation of a Parisian commercial theatre of the 1880s) survives from

Jersey, Opera House   *Victor Glasstone*

1900. The interior was completely rebuilt in 1921 after a fire, and is in the ciné-variety manner of the day: two simple balconies, surmounted by a fine panelled ceiling radiating out from a semi-circular dome. The slips of the dress-circle dip down towards the proscenium, while the gallery is nearly straight-fronted. Both have somewhat sparse gilded plaster festoons. In c.1960, when the building returned to theatrical use after post-war years as a cinema, six badly designed boxes on two levels were added to the side walls. If reshaped and redecorated, these boxes would be a definite gain to the bleakness which must have prevailed earlier. The simple proscenium frame, topped by a curious stepping-up to the ceiling, has a 'thirties flavour, but was in fact built when the opening was widened to 27'0" in 1976. For a building of the period there are quite spacious foyers and bars at various levels. Seating capacity 709.   V.G.

Kendal,
Cumbria
New Playhouse
Market Place.
1758, architect unknown.
Working Men's Institute.
Closed as a theatre in 1789. Interior completely altered. Rendered facade of domestic appearance. Three storeys

Kendal, Shakespeare Theatre
James Dunbar-Nasmith

and four bays of plain sash windows in first and second floors, above an altered ground floor. Pitched roof above a straight eaves.
Listed Grade II.   C.B.

Shakespeare Theatre
★ disused
Highgate.
1789, architect unknown.
Store.
Closed as a theatre in 1834 and converted into a ballroom. Sited at the far end of the long, narrow yard of the Shakespeare Hotel. Interior gutted, but the exterior intact. A simple, rectangular building of stone with a pitch-

ed roof. Three-bay, gabled front with a central, arched doorway reached by a flight of steps and flanked by plain sash windows. A single, square window in the centre of the gable.   C.B.

Kilkenny,
Eire
Theatre
1902, architect unknown.
Exists as a lighting emporium.   D.F.C.

Kilmarnock,
Strathclyde
King's Theatre
★ facade only/disused
King Street.
1904, Cullen.
Cinema and Bingo.
Interior completely rebuilt following a fire in 1975, with a cinema above a bingo hall. Exterior survives basically intact. Good, French Renaissance ashlar facade of three storeys. Altered ground floor. The three central bays at first floor level have large, round-arched windows, and above, at high level under the deeply projecting cornice, three squared-headed windows subdivided by small attached columns on brackets.

Lancaster Grand   *Alan Betjemann*

The flanking bays, containing staircases, have lunette windows in the upper storey, framed between elongated composite pilasters. Polygonal turrets, above, with steeply pitched roofs. C.B.

Palace Theatre
Green Street.
1903, Steel.
Theatre.
Formerly a public hall in the Corn Exchange (1862, with a robust Victorian classical exterior).
Converted to a music hall with a fully equipped stage in 1903. Unfortunately as a theatre it suffers from a defect common to most hall conversions - it is long and narrow in proportion, with a balcony isolated from the stage by blank side walls. Seating capacity 625. Proscenium 24ft., stage depth 30ft., grid 35ft. Run by Kilmarnock Arts Guild for professional and amateur drama, opera, ballet, etc. C.B.

Kings Lynn,
Norfolk
Guildhall
pre-1914 fragment only
King Street.
15th century guildhall converted into theatre 1766.
Occasional theatre and concert room.
In 1948 sufficient remained of the 1766 playhouse interior to enable Richard Southern to make a complete reconstruction in model form which is now kept in the theatre. At the time, the theatre had not been in use for a very long time, the Norwich circuit of playhouses having started to decline as early as the 1840's.
In 1951 the Guildhall re-opened as a theatre, its principal use being for the annual Kings Lynn Festival. The present auditorium bears no resemblance whatsoever to the Georgian auditorium, being simply a single shallow rake of seating under the exposed rafters of the medieval roof. The historical value of this fine building is totally unconnected with its short theatrical life.
Listed Grade I. I.M.

Kirkaldy,
Fife
King's Theatre
High Street.
(Formerly, Hippodrome, Opera House).
1904, Swanston & Syme.
Cinemas.
Auditorium and stage rebuilt as a cinema in 1937 and recently subdivided into three small cinemas. Ashlar sandstone street front survives with the entrance through the ground floor of the end-part of a block of shops, with two floors of flats above. Projecting polygonal turret on corner with ogival dome. C.B.

Lancaster,
Lancashire
Grand Theatre
★ ★
St. Leonard's Gate.
1782, opened as The Theatre, architect unknown.
1843, altered by E. Sharpe and renamed The Music Hall.
1884, altered.
1897, altered by Frank Matcham.
1908, burnt out and rebuilt inside original shell by Albert Winstanley and renamed Grand Theatre.
Amateur Theatre.
Of the 1782 building only the basic stone shell survives. The 2½ storey, four-bay, stuccoed front was redone in 1908 - simple, rectangular windows with moulded frames, arched central doorway, quoins and straight cornice with later attic addition above. The 1908 auditorium (570 seats) has one balcony of 9 rows with rich plasterwork on its front, curving around to stage boxes flanking an elliptically arched proscenium (22ft.) which survives from 1843. Flat ceiling with raised moulded frame and restrained plasterwork. Wedge-shaped stage approximately 28ft. deep on the centre line. The theatre is owned and used by Lancaster Footlights Club.
Listed Grade II. C.B.

Hippodrome
Dalton Square.
1902, converted from a temperance hall of 1859: itself a conversion of an R.C. Chapel of 1799.
Local Authority offices.
The interior was completely reconstructed in 1931 as a cinema with one balcony and the small stage incorporated within the auditorium. Ashlar front to Dalton Square, which forms the end of a handsome terrace of houses. The side walls show the arched windows of the former chapel/temperance hall. In 1980/81 the interior was gutted for offices, the facade restored and the arches in the side elevation unblocked and windows inserted. C.B.

Leamington Spa,
Warwickshire
Bath Street Theatre
pre-1914 fragment only
Bath Street.
1813, J. Simms.
Shop.
Theatre use stopped in 1833. Only the outline of street front remains. Originally a pretty, three-bay facade with a rusticated ground floor, arched first floor windows, lunette windows above, and giant Corinthian pilasters with a small pediment over the central bay. This is now completely altered - shop front on ground floor, two rectangular

windows above, and a plain brick parapet. C.B.

Theatre
Clemens Street.
1848, converted from a chapel in 1816.
Factory.
Closed as a theatre in 1866. The much altered two-storeyed stuccoed facade and pitched roofed brick shell survive but the interior has gone. The ground floor has lost its five arched entrance doors and three-bay, square-columned porch. Of the three tall windows in the first floor the one to the right retains only its triangular pediment and a crude, oblong window has been inserted below. C.B.

Theatre Royal
Holly Walk.
(Formerly, Opera House).
1883, Osbourne & Reeding with C. J. Phipps.
Garage.
Auditorium completely reconstructed as a cinema with one balcony in 1934, and now used as part of a garage with a wide opening in the rear wall of the stage. Symmetrical red brick facade survives, but of little merit. C.B.

Leeds,
West Yorkshire
City Varieties
★ ★ ★
The Headrow.
(Formerly, Thornton's Varieties, Stansfield Varieties).
1865, G. Smith (?).
Variety theatre.
Opened as Thornton's Varieties - Thornton himself may have been partly responsible for its design. The most famous of the few surviving early music halls, and a classic of its type. Rectangular auditorium (713 seats) with two balconies, straight at the rear with slips along the side walls, sub-divided into boxes at the lower level by slender colonnettes. Shallow stage with apron and low flies behind an elliptically-arched proscenium (17ft.). Flat ceiling over the whole space. Good plasterwork on balcony fronts, with festoons etc. No facade - entrance along a passage from street.
Listed Grade II. ★ C.B.

Coliseum
★ facade only/disused
Cookridge Street.
1885, W. Bakewell.
Scenery Workshop.
Interior completely reconstructed as a cinema in 1930's. Brick and stone exterior original. A big, gabled, Gothic facade with traceried windows, central rose window, pinnacles, etc. George Corson's Grand Theatre of 1878 had already set a precedent for a Gothic theatre in Leeds. C.B.

Leeds, Coliseum   *Leeds City Council*

Empire Palace

Briggate.
1898, Frank Matcham.

The splendid theatre was completely demolished in 1961, but remainder of block (containing an arcade and shops) of which it formed an integral part, remains.   C.B.

Leeds Grand Theatre & Opera House

★ ★ ★

New Briggate.
1878, George Corson.
Theatre and Opera House.

A one-off theatre for the architect, but probably the finest of its size in Britain. An unusually ambitious project, originated in Leeds by local industrialists, occupying a ¾ acre site and costing the large sum of £62,000 to build. The scheme also included a concert hall - now a cinema. This lies parallel to New Brigggate above a row of six shops, to the right of the entrance front of the theatre itself, thus producing a facade 162ft. long, executed in brick with stone dressings, in an extraordinary mixture of styles of which Gothic and Romanesque predominate. The shops were originally set within a segmentally-arched arcade, now obliterated by modern fronts. Likewise the concert hall has lost its original round-arched traceried entrance, which had reflected that of the theatre. The sky-line of the theatre facade bristles with Gothic turrets and the central gable is pierced by a rose window. Unusually spacious main stair, rising in one flight and branching into two. Magnificent auditorium (1,550 seats) with three sweeping horseshoe balconies supported by iron columns. The first and second balconies have six rows and their arms are divided into six boxes on each side. The third balcony is divided by a parapet into a gallery of nine rows rising behind an amphitheatre of four rows which extends into slips at each side. Above these is a

Leeds City Varieties   *Leeds City Council*

fourth level consisting of upper slips. The balcony fronts are very richly decorated with deeply-undercut plasterwork, incorporating imaginatively designed foliated scrolls, bosses, etc. Splendid ceiling in the form of a saucer-dome carried on four flattened arches with fretted Gothic fan-vault pendentives. The proscenium, flanked by two superimposed boxes at first and second balcony levels, has an outer frame of clustered Gothic shafts, carrying a moulded flattened arch, and a grandiose semi-circular-arched inner frame with rich scalloped decoration (32ft. 6in. wide and 40ft. high). The upper stage boxes were originally flanked by caryatids which still survive in store and ought to be put back.

The installation of a new orchestra pit elevator in 1975 unfortunately resulted in the removal of the original front edge of the stage which now appears too abruptly cut off. Stage depth 48ft., grid height 60ft. Rear-stage 17ft. deep beyond an arch 28ft. 6in. wide. Allied to the stage are, by the standards of most other touring theatres, lavish scene docks, workshops, rehearsal rooms, etc. The theatre was purchased by Leeds Corporation in 1974 and since 1978 has been the base of the English National Opera North. Adaptations to the theatre for this purpose included the removal of the unique, wonderfully complex stage machinery below stage level; an early iron stage in full working order complete with bridges, traps, cuts, sloats, etc., in the traditional early/mid 19th c. style - a tragic and irreplaceable loss which was unnecessary as the required accommodation could have been created in adjoining buildings.
Listed Grade II ★　　　　C.B.

Leeds Grand

Leek,
Staffordshire
Grand Theatre
1900, architect unknown.
Cinema.
Auditorium redone in 1930's with one straight balcony. Proscenium 26ft. Shallow stage with low grid. Undistinguished brick exterior.　　C.B.

Leigh,
Greater Manchester
Grand Theatre & Hippodrome
Leigh Road.
1908, Prescott & Bold.
Cinemas.
Auditorium completely rebuilt as two cinemas. Facade basically intact apart from altered ground floor - a symmetrical composition in red brick with terracotta dressings. The style is a mixture of Arts and Crafts and Edwardian Baroque. The end bays rise up into small square towers surmounted by low domes behind shaped parapets. *Oeil-de-boeuf* windows in the upper stage. Three-storeyed centre with a pitched roof and cupola.　　C.B.

Theatre Royal & Opera House
Lord Street.
1885, architect unknown.
Casino/Nightclub.
Interior completely reconstructed with one deep balcony. Brick facade, although altered, is basically intact.

Lichfield,
Staffordshire
David Garrick Memorial Theatre
Bore Street.
1872, architect unknown.
Shop.
Opened as the St. James's Hall; renamed Palladium in 1912; Lido in 1936 and David Garrick Theatre in 1949. Auditorium rebuilt in 1949 with one, straight-fronted balcony and blank side walls - now above false ceiling of shop. Stuccoed facade also altered in 1949 -three arched windows at first floor level original; upper floor with square windows and straight paparpet is 1940's. Shop front on ground floor. C.B.

Lincoln, Theatre Royal　　*Roderick Ham*

Lincoln,
Lincolnshire
Theatre Royal
★ ★
Clasketgate.
(Formerly, County Theatre, New Theatre).
1893, Bertie Crewe & W. G. R. Sprague.
1907, reconstructed by W. Hancock.
1945, entrance front rebuilt.
Theatre.
Delightful and very intimate auditorium (485 seats). Two slightly curved balconies with short slips to superimposed boxes flanking proscenium. Good Rococo plasterwork on balcony and box fronts and proscenium. Plain ceiling. Proscenium 21ft. 6ins., stage depth 25ft. 6ins. The dull exterior of 1934 presents an unappealing outward image and the theatre would greatly benefit from a similar scheme to that carried out at York Theatre Royal. Owned by Local Authority. Formerly a resident repertory theatre who planned first a new theatre and second a renovation of the existing building before going bankrupt in the mid 1970's. Now an occasional touring theatre.
Listed Grade II.　　C.B.

Liverpool,
Merseyside
Olympia
★ ★ ★disused
West Derby Road, Everton.
1905, Frank Matcham.
Bingo.
Rare surviving example of a circus/variety theatre (q.v. Brighton Hip-

podrome), and basically intact apart from the raising of the stalls floor to stage level and the insertion of staircases from the ends of the first balcony down to the stalls. The auditorium is vast (approximately 2,300 seats), fanning outwards from the 48ft. proscenium to very wide balconies at the rear. The first balcony is of 12 rows, with ten boxes underneath at the back of the stalls. Above is a balcony of six rows with a further six rows raised above, behind a parapet. The balcony fronts, which are intricately decorated with oriental motifs, are set out on a shallow curve to meet the side walls. These are enriched by three bays of oriental panelling divided by pilasters topped by large plaster elephants. The rectangular proscenium which has open scrollwork in the corners and interlaced blank arches above, is flanked by two large boxes on each side, at lower balcony level. One of these is facing away from the stage and is surmounted by an opulent onion-domed canopy. It can only have been of use for circus performances. The ceiling, which is canted upwards from the proscenium towards the gallery, is divided into rectangular panels but is otherwise strangely plain. The stage is 41ft. deep and the grid 68ft. Originally there was an arena of 42ft. diameter projecting half-way into the auditorium and capable of being hydraulically sunk and flooded with water for acquatic performances. Although the pit below still remains, the elaborate machinery has gone. Apart from a small foyer with a deeply-coved ceiling, the front-of-house spaces are very cramped for so large a theatre. The facade is of enormous width, reflecting the rear wall of the auditorium. The entrance is through a central pavilion with a columned loggia at second floor level, and surmounted by a steep pyramid roof above a lunette window. The side wings are canted away from the centre and terminate in two-bay pavilions.

The theatre could be fairly readily restored to use, although located outside the City Centre, in an unpromising area.

Listed Grade II ★   C.B.

Park Palace
disused
Mill Street, Toxteth.
1894, architect unknown.
Factory.

A small music hall in a suburb approximately 1½ miles from the City Centre. Simple rectangular auditorium, originally with one balcony around three sides, now removed. The delightful proscenium arch and small stage with low grid still survive, although the stage floor has been reduced to main floor level. The proscenium is flanked by fluted Corinthian columns with bulbous acanthus leaf bases and surmounted by a straight entablature and broken triangular pediment. The coat of arms which formerly decorated its centre has been preserved by the present owner. The exterior is very plain and has been much altered.   C.B.

Liverpool, Pavilion Theatre
Victor Glasstone

Pavilion Theatre
★ ★ disused.
Lodge Lane.
1908, J. J. Alley.
Bingo.

A large variety theatre in a suburb approximately two miles from the City Centre. The auditorium (1,700 seats) is intact and in good condition. There are two very wide, slightly curved balconies of eleven rows each, partly supported on iron columns. These terminate in a composition of four boxes on either side, two at each level, stepped-down from the balcony fronts. Dividing the boxes are giant pilasters, carried on big scrolled brackets projecting from the side walls of the stalls.

The box fronts and lower balcony front are decorated by large cartouches, and the upper balcony front by repeated festoons between cartouches. The boxes are widely angled away from the richly

framed rectangular proscenium, which, although in fact 36ft. wide, appears narrow in relation to the great width of the auditorium. Polygonal ceiling carried on very deep coves above the boxes and the proscenium and divided into panels by terms. Unaltered stage, 38ft. deep. Plain gabled facade, largely rebuilt and of no merit.   C.B.

Playhouse
★ ★ ★
Williamson Square.
1866, Opened as Star Music Hall, architect unknown.
1898, reconstructed, architect unknown.
1912, auditorium altered by S. D. Adshead and name changed to Playhouse.
1968, New Foyers, back stage facilities etc., architects Hall, O'Donahue and Wilson (project architect Ken Martin). Theatre.

The excellent, stuccoed exterior of the old Star Music Hall survives largely unaltered. Seven bays wide and two main storeys with an attic. First floor articulated by Corinthian pilasters, with a straight entablature over. The attic storey, again with pilasters, has oval windows in the two flanking bays and circular windows in the three central bays which are further emphasized by a broken triangular pediment. Small cupolas near the corners. Intimate auditorium (760 seats) with two slightly curved balconies of six rows each, supported by iron columns with foliated capitals. The balconies probably date from the 1898 reconstruction. The delicate trellis work decoration on their fronts together with the single,

Liverpool, Playhouse   *Keith Gibson*

Liverpool, Playhouse   *Victor Glasstone*

predimented side boxes and Greek Revival style pilastered panels above, date from 1912. Plain, flat ceiling. Proscenium 30ft. wide. Stage 32ft. deep. In 1968 a new entrance with bars and restaurant above, was added to the left of the old facade, with workshops etc., behind. The new work takes the form of a big cantilevered glazed drum, higher than the old building, with a smaller, largely solid drum intersecting half-way up on the left. This can hardly be said to be a successful addition, even accepting that a contrast was clearly aimed for. The theatre is the home of one of Britain's senior repertory companies, founded in 1912.
Listed Grade II.   C.B.

Royal Hippodrome

★ ★ disused

West Derby Road.
1876, J. T. Robinson and opened as Hengler's Grand Cirque.
1902, reconstructed by Bertie Crewe and renamed Royal Hippodrome.
Derelict.
A big variety house situated close to the Olympia. The restrained stuccoed front of the 1876 building was largely retained in the reconstruction of 1902. Narrow entrance between single-storey shop fronts projecting forward from the higher rear wall of the theatre. This is seven bays wide and relieved by plain pilasters linked at the top by segmental arches below an attic storey. Crewe's auditorium (approximately 2,000 seats) has two slighly curved, deep balconies and a 40ft. proscenium with an enriched concave frame, straight headed with rounded corners. Flanking boxes grouped under large serpentine broken pediments. Stage depth 40ft. This was potentially the best big theatre remaining in Liverpool, but is now a shattered wreck after years of neglect and vandalism, sadly situated in a bleak and devastated environment.
Not Listed.   C.B.

Liverpool, Royal Hippodrome
Victor Glasstone

Llandudno, Gwynedd

Arcadia Theatre

Promenade.
(Formerly, Riviere's New Opera House).
1900, architect unknown.
Seasonal theatre.
A long, low, narrow hall (1,137 seats) with shallow stage. Dull, featureless exterior with small fly tower at the end of a long pitched roof.   C.B.

Llandudno, Grand Theatre   *Victor Glasstone*

Grand Theatre

★ ★ ★

Mostyn Broadway.
1899, G. A. Humphreys with Edwin Sachs as consultant.
Seasonal theatre.
A large, free-standing building, sited just outside the town centre near the south end of the promenade. Gaunt, red brick facade surmounted by a wide gable and flanked by low, semi-octagonal towers. Very fine, intimate auditorium of 1,000 seats with two well curved balconies of eight rows each, terminating in two boxes either side at first balcony level and one above. The boxes are divided by slender colonnettes with enriched shafts. Spanning the auditorium above the boxes is a segmental arch with lattice decoration, which has richly decorated panelled reveals. Saucer-domed ceiling with a plaster sunburst around a central rose. The plasterwork generally on balcony fronts, boxes, proscenium and ceiling is of excellent quality with delicately modelled foliated scrolls, festoons, *putti*, musical intruments, etc. Proscenium 27ft. 6ins., stage depth 38ft., grid 50ft. Although completely intact inside and out, the theatre, which is privately owned, would benefit greatly from being fully refurbished and re-equipped. It is potentially the best theatre in North Wales, and would be well suited for use by Welsh National Opera and other drama, dance and opera companies.

132

Llandudno, Palladium
Victor Glasstone

Llandudno is a very attractive resort which has so far contrived to escape largely unscathed from many of the environmental horrors commonplace today. It would make an excellent setting for an annual festival of music and drama, in which a restored Grand Theatre could play a major role.
Listed Grade II. C.B.

Palladium

★ facade only/disused
Gloddaeth Street.
1920, A. Hewitt.
Cinema above Bingo.
Probably designed prior to the 1914-18 war. Originally with two balconies and boxes (approximately 1,400 seats), the interior has now been sub-divided, but not completely gutted - lower box fronts, and part of proscenium etc., still visible in bingo hall. Splendidly robust Edwardian Baroque stuccoed facade. The central bay, above the entrance, has giant Ionic demi-columns supporting a triangular pediment which encloses a semicircular rusticated arch and a large oriel window. Symmetrical square flanking towers, with angle pilasters carrying segmental pediments, and surmounted by octagonal domes.
Listed Grade II. C.B.

Pier Pavilion

★
1883, B. Nelson.
Theatre (seasonal shows).
At the landward end of the pier. A large pitched-roofed iron and glass structure with gabled transepts and aspidal-ended towards the promenade. Encircled by a veranda supported by slender iron columns. Auditorium on upper level with a balcony on three sides. Some Rococo plasterwork on balcony front and proscenium, but ceiling obscured by modern tiles. (2000 seats). Proscenium 28ft., stage depth 29ft. No fly tower - grid 36ft.
Listed Grade II. C.B.

Prince's Theatre

Mostyn Street.
1880's, Humphreys & Bradley.
Supermarket.
Only the vaguely Gothic facade survives above an altered ground floor. A slightly recessed centre with four tall segment-headed windows is flanked by end bays with coupled windows under a segmental arch. Above is an attic storey with a series of small closely-spaced windows under a steeply pitched roof. This is an interesting if not particularly distinguished, facade and makes a distinctive contribution to the streetscape. C.B.

Lochgelly, Fife

Opera House

Main Street.
c.1912, architect unknown.
Bingo.
A cine-variety theatre. Dull auditorium -one straight balcony with slips along side walls; undecorated front. Plain ceiling. Shallow stage with low flies. Undistinguished brick facade with narrow windows. C.B.

GREATER LONDON

Adelphi

pre-1914 fragment only.
Strand W.C.2.
City of Westminster.
(Formerly Sans Pareil, Theatre Royal Adelphi, New Adelphi 1858 Century Theatre 1901 and Royal Adelphi 1902.)
1930 Ernest Shaufelberg with a facade altered by T. P. Bennett in 1937 but with parts of 1869, 1882 and 1887.
Theatre.
The Shaufelberg building incorporates rear elevation and flank wall of earlier theatres on site. Nothing now remains of the Sans Pareil of 1806, the Samuel Beazley facade of 1840, or the auditoria of 1848 (by M. D. Wyatt), 1858 (by T. H. Wyatt and Stephen Salter) or 1900 (Runtz and Ford). The Royal Entrance in Maiden Lane is probably of 1868-69 (a surviving alteration to the 1858 building) by Joseph Lavender. The rest of the Maiden Lane elevation is of 1882, by Spencer Chadwick. Part of Chadwick's facade of 1887 survives alongside the modern Strand facade as Queensland House (no longer part of the theatre).
In the present state of the building, only the many-windowed, somewhat domestic elevation to Maiden Lane is of more than common interest. The Royal Entrance, near which William Terris was murdered in 1897, adjoins the now vacant site of the notorious Cyder Cellars concert room (later a rehearsal room used by Diaghilev and others). The aggressively plain terra-cotta Strand facade with integral letters and sign frame, by T. P. Bennett, makes an interesting contrast with Chadwick's classical front alongside.
The Shaufelberg interiors are now of some interest as good and complete examples of their kind and date.
Proscenium 37ft. Stage 36ft. deep with big revolve. Capacity is 1510. For a full account of the complex building history of this site, see **Survey of London** vol. XXXVI p. 245 et seq. J.E.

Albery

★ ★ ★
St. Martin's Lane, W1.
City of Westminster.
(Formerly the New Theatre).
1903, W. G. R. Sprague; the interior and auditorium decoration by Claude Ponsonby.
Theatre.
Built by Charles Wyndham on land he had to acquire before building Wyndham's Theatre, with which it stands back-to-back, divided only by St. Martin's Court.
Stone free classical facade to St. Martin's Lane in three major bays, the centre slightly advanced and pedimented over an Ionic pilastered order. Flank and rear elevations in yellow and glazed brick.

Llandudno, Pier Pavilion *Victor Glasstone*

The interior has suffered little alteration of any consequence. Entrance foyer rectangular with Corinthian pilasters. Pleasing auditorium with three variously curving 'cantilever' balconies. The Ponsonby design, with its delicate plaster ornament, was described in 1903 as 'exquisite . . . of the period of Louis XVI . . . adhered to even down to the minutest details throughout'. Despite changes to the painted decorations and hangings, much remains of its original opulence, and it is lovingly maintained.

Proscenium 31ft. 6in. wide. Stage about 42ft. 6in. deep with slightly raking back wall. Capacity 835.

Listed Grade II.   J.E.

Aldwych

★ ★ ★

Aldwych, W.C.2.
City of Westminster.
1905, W. G. R. Sprague.
Theatre.

Built as part of the Aldwych/Kingsway development and designed as a pair to the Strand (Waldorf) Theatre q.v., the two theatres standing at either end of Marshall Mackenzie's slightly later Waldorf Hotel. Important in the Aldwych streetscape and a fine stone-faced, classical corner building in its own right. In three major bays each of four storeys plus a sheer attic over the main entablature, the two outer bays, facing Aldwych and Drury Lane respectively, matching, with giant order of engaged columns through second and third floors, carrying pediments with enriched tympana pierced by lunettes at attic level, the centre bay recessed and turning the corner as a bold, pilastered bow.

An excellent Sprague auditorium with a good theatrical atmosphere, but in mutilated condition, alterations since c.1960 having been almost entirely to its architectural disadvantage. Proscenium altered and lower stage boxes

Albery   *Victor Glasstone*

removed to accommodate forestage. Lights slung about everywhere, with little sympathy for Sprague's design and eighteenth century style ornament. Two balconies, the former gallery seating now forming the rearward extension of the upper circle. Boxes framed by fluted Ionic piers on tall pedestals, carrying entablature blocks and semi-circular arches. Proscenium was originally a square enriched frame above which was a deep panelled frieze with centre cartouche and a cove sounding board.

The present colour scheme is drab, being almost entirely charcoal grey in the now dated late sixties style relieved only by partial touching in with gold paint on the plaster decoration.

The Aldwych has been the home of the Royal Shakespeare Company since 1960, pending completion (in 1982) of their new London home at the Barbican. The Aldwych is a fine theatre which will benefit in every way from a more sympathetic refitting and redecoration. As it stands today it is an instructive example of the way in which theatrical quality can be ruthlessly sacrificed to transitory production styles.

Proscenium 31ft. wide. Stage 40ft. 6ins. deep. Remains at cellar level of formerly elaborate Edwardian stage machinery. Capacity is 994.

Listed Grade II.   J.E.

Alexandra Palace Theatre

★ disused

Muswell Hill and Wood Green.
Haringey.
1875 by J. Johnson, with alterations, principally in 1922. (Johnson's partner, Alfred Meeson, designed the first Palace which burnt down in 1873, soon after it was built, and was immediately replaced by the present building).

It is not known whether Johnson had assistance with the design of the theatre, but the evidence of the building itself suggests that it was the work of someone with no previous experience of theatre design. Its history has been depressing. It was an abject commercial failure in the decades when theatre business generally was at its most profitable.

The theatre is completely embedded in the Palace complex. Although it has one external wall, its separate identity is not discernible in the long north elevation of the Palace. The auditorium is extraordinary - more like a big music hall or concert hall than a theatre; a large rectangular room with raked floor, the long sides now occupied by low enclosed corridors (presumably inserted to improve means of escape) which give the impression of side balconies. There is a single balcony, facing and far distant from the stage and there was originally a second, upper balcony, now removed. The present appearance of the room probably owes more to Macqueen Pope, who ordered the 1922 alterations, than to Johnson.

Aldwych   *GLC*

Alexandra Palace Theatre   *GLC*

Coarse plaster ornament of two periods, the earlier (e.g. the ceiling) bolder and not unpleasing. Figure sculpture, probably original, in niches either side of proscenium.

The existing, faded 'toy theatre' colour scheme, although not original, is highly evocative.

The most interesting survival is the stage (proscenium 36ft. wide) which has a fine complex of wooden machinery both below stage and in the fly tower in restorable condition. A primitive set of scene grooves from this theatre is now in the possession of the Museum of London.

The auditorium is one of the oldest now surviving in London, archaeologically of rare interest but intractable as a theatre. Following the recent Palace fire (which left it undamaged) the owners, Haringey Council, are considering uses for the theatre. It would make a splendid concert room or cabaret restaurant for spectacular productions (if there is ever a call for such an enterprise in N.22). Its future must lie with music, variety and amazing tricks rather than serious drama. The capacity with modern spacing would be between 1,100 and 1,500 depending on arrangement of balconies.   J.E.

Ambassadors
★ ★ ★
West Street, W.C.2.
Camden.
1913, W. G. R. Sprague.
Theatre.

Next door to the St. Martin's Theatre q.v. Low, three storey ashlar faced elevation, curving into Tower Court. Restrained classical style with channelled pilasters carrying segmental pediments. Crowning parapet and balustrade with ball ornaments.

Elegant auditorium, described in contemporary reports as being in Louis XVI style with ambassadorial crests and a colour scheme of Parma violet, ivory and gold. Apart from redecoration the auditorium remains virtually intact. Circular ceiling with central chandelier; panelled border and deep cove penetrated by arches springing from fluted Ionic pilasters. Richly framed and festooned roundels with armorial decorations in arch tympana. Flat basket-arched proscenium flanked by single tall boxes. Horseshoe-curved single balcony with raised tier at rear.

An architecturally pleasing auditorium with an intimate atmosphere.

Proscenium 24ft. 6ins. wide. Stage depth 20ft. 6ins. Capacity is 453.

Listed Grade II.   J.E.

Apollo
★ ★ ★
Shaftesbury Avenue, W.1.
City of Westminster.
1901, Lewen Sharp; the auditorium decoration by H. van Hooydonk.
1932, alterations by Shaufelberg.
Theatre.

This was Sharp's only complete theatre (he made major alterations to

Apollo   GLC

Camberwell Palace in 1908) and it is externally unlike any other theatre of its time in London.

With the Lyric, the Globe and the Queens, all grouped on the north side of Shaftesbury Avenue, the Apollo forms part of one of London's most important theatre streetscapes. The main facade is in a free Renaissance style with a distinct Art Nouveau flavour. Stone, in three main storeys with a tall attic above the cornice; three major bays, the outer two treated as pavilions with flat canted fronts around which the main cornice breaks. Prettily framed *oeil-de-boeuf* windows to the attic; the pavilion attics treated as short, flat domed towers with spectacular figure sculpture (pairs of winged figures with

Ambassadors   GLC

Apollo   GLC

flowing drapery) by T. Simpson. Well restored iron and glass canopy over entrance. Flank and rear facades in red brick.

Lively auditorium with splendid plaster enrichment in Louis XIV manner (somewhat interfered with by Shaufelberg in 1932). Three 'cantilever' balconies terminating in elaborately modelled serpentine fronted boxes. The angle of view from the upper balcony is said to be the steepest in London. Proscenium arch with bold architrave moulding, lyre-buckled at intervals. Relief in tympanum over proscenium. Finely enriched oval ceiling on pendentives. Good foyer and anteroom to Royal box. Modern stalls bar. Proscenium 30ft. wide. Stage 28ft. 6ins. deep. Capacity is 627 without the gallery on the fourth level which would hold about 120 with modern spacing. See Survey of London Vols. XXXI and XXXII.

Listed Grade II.   J.E.

Banqueting House

Whitehall.
City of Westminster.
1619-22.

Inigo Jones, subsequently completely refaced externally, but in accordance with Jones's design. Interior magnificently restored in recent years.

Built to replace Smythson's Banqueting House of 1609, which was destroyed by fire in 1619. A key building in the history of art and architecture in Britain and revered as one of our most precious monuments. Not a theatre, but its importance in theatrical history makes it impossible to ignore. Jones had been designing prosceniums, stage machines, etc., for court masques since the early years of the seventeenth century and the new building continued to be used for masques until 1640. Jones's design certainly provided for the requirements of the masque (e.g. in avoidance of internal columns) and his most sophisticated machines and single-point perspectives were designed for this room.

In 1649 the Banqueting House served as ante-room to the execution scaffold of Charles 1.

Well documented, and the subject of many published works dealing with its architectural, historical and theatrical significance, e.g. **History of King's Works III; Survey of London** (St. Margaret, Westminster; Whitehall); Orgel and Strong: **Inigo Jones; Theatre of the Stuart Court;** Per Palme; **Triumph of Peace.**

Listed Grade I - Also a scheduled Ancient Monument.   J.E.

Bohemia

Ballards Lane, Finchley.
Barnet.
(Also known as Old Bohemia and Alcazar Hall or Cinema).
c.1900/1914.
Architect unknown.
Factory.

The precise status and building history of the Bohemia require considerable further research before a proper assessment can be made of what now remains. It is a complex of buildings behind the shops in Ballards Lane, filling the backland between two side streets. It is easily missed and even when found, its external fair-faced fletton brick walls make no architectural statement.

The building consists of a galleried hall connected at the rear to an auditorium. It appears to be the successor of a theatre built in a little pleasure garden, a late Victorian or Edwardian resort which is said to have had a mill and a Chinese garden. The 'theatre' was probably rebuilt as 'ciné-variety' before World War I. It had both cinematograph and music and dancing licences in 1913 (probably earlier) the latter licence apparently covering the 'summer and winter gardens'. In that year there were complaints that stages for 'al fresco entertainments' had been built at either end of the theatre without consent. The building was reputedly used in World War I for the manufacture of observation balloons. Was a cinema again until at least 1920 but became a blacking works and had other industrial uses before the present one.

The auditorium is now the main factory workshop, full of machinery and partly divided, but its form is easily discernible. Segmental barrel-vaulted ceiling of nine bays with relief (Anaglypta or similar) decoration to the panels. Plaster moulded proscenium. Flat auditorium floor. Stage area subdivided. No flying space. Proscenium about 38ft. wide. Auditorium about 95ft. × 60ft. No balcony. Projection box. The linked dance hall is much altered but has the substantial remains of a grand staircase.   J.E.

Borough Theatre

pre-1914 fragment only

Stratford Broadway, Stratford E.
Newham.
1895, Frank Matcham.
1906, alterations by H. Pyke.
1933, completely reconstructed internally as cinema, architect unknown.
Disused.

Brick and stone facade to the Broadway in Jacobean style. Shops on ground floor. Tower. Name of theatre in large letters at high level. The corner entrance composition was massively altered in the cinema conversion and now presents an almost featureless rendered face. Deprived of its major emphasis, what is left of Matcham's work seems lacking in coherence. Nothing of Matcham remains in the auditorium which has one balcony and a shallow stage.   J.E.

Broadway

pre-1914 fragment only.

Kilburn High Road, N.W.6.
Camden.
(Formerly Kilburn Empire and, from 1928, Essoldo).
1908, W. G. R. Sprague (superseding a 1906 design by Hingston).
1928, altered.
1970, front and interior reconstructed.
Cinema.

Opened 1908 as a variety house and circus with a reputed capacity in excess of 1,900. Converted to a cinema in 1928, then bingo, then back to cinema. Originally a theatre of some modest architectural interest but devastated by the 1971 works which totally disguised the facade and placed an isolated cinema 'pod' within the auditorium, fortunately leaving some major parts of the plasterwork in situ but concealed. Two balconies, the upper one above the modern false ceiling. It is difficult to determine how far this theatre might be architecturally restorable.

Archaeologically interesting stage with animal traps and elephant pits in the cellar. Proscenium was originally 38'4" wide. See also D.H. 414.

Byfeld Hall

117 Church Road, Barnes S.W.13.
Richmond upon Thames.
(Also known as Barnes Theatre and Van Dyke Cinema. Now Olympic Studio).
1906, architect unknown.
Recording studio.

Status uncertain. Was licensed for both stage plays and music and dancing 'with a proper stage'. Capacity in 1910 was 500.

Red brick and stone in a mildly flamboyant Dutch baroque style. At ground floor the facade is divided into two main elements; the entrance and three separate shop fronts. The three-doored entrance to the hall is given a rather grand treatment with heavy stone arches. Above the entrance is a stone panel with the date, 1906. At first floor level there is a bay window (now bricked in) which must have served a public room, probably a restaurant. On the side elevation, above an arched window, is the name Byfeld Hall.

The interior retains most of the original staircases serving the various public rooms at the front of the building. Entrance hall altered. The hall on the first floor is now the main recording studio and may be only half the original size as the result of the insertion of a floor at balcony level (if there ever was a balcony).   C.S./J.E.

Camden Theatre

★ ★ disused

Camden High Street.
Camden.
(Formerly: Camden Hippodrome, Royal Camden and Music Machine).
1901, W. G. R. Sprague.
(recently Dance Hall/Pop Music Centre).

Symmetrical stone facade in free classical manner. Large copper dome now robbed of its lantern. Despite some mutilation, still an imposing corner building viewed across a busy road junction.

Radical internal alterations were carried out when the theatre was converted to disco use. Despite this, it remains a beautiful auditorium with two partly cantilevered balconies (gallery now closed). Modelled plasterwork by Waring and Gillow. Marble proscenium arch with segmental pediment and, on either side, marble columns rising from caryatids, defining four bays, three of

Camden Theatre GLC

name Sam Collins's Music Hall. The site, which backed on to an old burial ground, was so restricted that no major replanning or improvement was possible after the 1897 reconstruction and the pub remained embedded in the front of the building until a destructive fire in 1958, following which the hall itself was demolished. The facade in its late nineteenth century form survives (a little altered), but there is now no relic of the theatre itself. The facade bears a G.L.C. blue plaque commemorating 'Collins' Music Hall' DH.168.   J.E.

Comedy
★ ★

Panton Street, S.W.1.
City of Westminster.
(Proposed as the Lyric or Alexandra but opened as Royal Comedy, 'Royal' dropped in 1884).
1881, Thomas Verity.
1911, reconstruction vestibule and bars, by Whiting and Peto.
1933, altered.
1955, altered by Cecil Masey and A Macdonald.
1980, canopy by Sir John Burnet Tait & Partners.
Theatre.
The exterior is virtually the same as when it was built. A good, painted stone, pedimented classical facade to Panton Street, fronted now by a modern, slightly anaemic wrought iron canopy. This theatre has one of the few pre-1890s auditoria in London and despite alteration, it is still essentially Verity's design. Three tiers with pretty plaster ornament. The 1954-5 works altered the form of the lower balcony fronts.
There appears to be no authoritative architectural account of the building. Although not quite in the same class as the Criterion, a theatre of its date and quality merits the kind of detailed study that the other Verity theatre has had. Proscenium 24ft. 6in. wide. Stage 21ft. 6in. deep. The capacity is 786.
Listed Grade II.   J.E.

which contain boxes in two tiers. Shallow domed ceiling. The latest alterations include the laying of a dance floor covering a large part of the stalls area and penetrating the deeply cut-away stage. A balcony has been formed over the stage, surrounding the dance floor. The floor level at the front of the dress circle has been raised, necessitating a guard rail above the original circle front.
Small, elaborate foyer (bronze plaque of Ellen Terry), above which was originally a 'promenade and winter garden'.
Proscenium 32ft. wide. Capacity if reseated to modern standards likely to be approximately 1,400.
Despite the seemingly extensive conversion works, the essential character of the building is undamaged and it would be perfectly capable of restoration to theatrical use. DH. 127.
Listed Grade II.   J.E.

Castle Theatre
pre-1914 fragment only
Whitaker Avenue, off Hill Street, Richmond.
Richmond upon Thames.
(Formerly: Theatre Royal, New Theatre, Castle Assembly Rooms).
1889, architect unknown.
'Bier Keller'.

The large assembly room attached to the mid-nineteenth century Castle Hotel was converted to a theatre by F. C. Mouflet in 1889. Mouflet later employed Matcham to build the Richmond Theatre on another site (1899). The assembly room still shows signs externally of the theatre conversion but has been much altered internally and is now a 'Bier Keller' attached to the hotel.   J.E.

Collins's Music Hall
Islington Green.
Islington.
(also known as the Lansdown Arms and Islington Hippodrome).
Probably 1862 (as the hall at the rear of the pub) architect unknown.
1885, adjoining house taken to provide new entrance and hall largely rebuilt, Edward Clark.
1897, partly reconstructed and improved, Drew, Bear, Perks and Co. (? with E. A. E. Woodrow).
1908, repairs after fire; subsequent minor alterations.
Frontage only remains.
The music hall attached to the pub was licensed to Sam Collins (Vagg) from 1863 until his death in 1865, after which it was run by his widow Anna Vagg and then Herbert Sprake, retaining the

Comedy GLC

Coronet

★ ★ disused

**103-111 High Street, Notting Hill W.11.
Royal Borough of Kensington and
Chelsea.
1898, W. G. R. Sprague.
Cinema.**

Exterior of painted stone and despite
some architectural losses, important in
the local townscape. Classical with
giant pilasters above ground floor; alter-
nate major bays emphasized by
pediments breaking the crowning
balustrade. Over the corner entrance a
short, round tower is crowned by a
dome.

The auditorium was perhaps never in
the same class as Sprague's West End
theatres, and it now looks sad and un-
cared for, but it is remarkably complete
and well worth preserving and restoring. Plaster ornament in Louis XVI manner. Two elliptically curved balconies.
Square enriched architrave to proscenium flanked by blank bays where
the boxes should be. The box bays are
framed by attenuated Corinthian columns with enriched lower shafts, set on
lofty pedestals and carrying an entablature with a segmental broken pediment. A flat arched ceiling spans between the 'box' fronts. Domed ceiling
over auditorium. The Coronet is one of
London's most important unlisted
theatres. It should be returned to
theatrical use.

Stage (1910) 32ft. deep. Capacity with
modern spacing likely to be approximately 800. J.E.

Criterion Theatre

★ ★ ★

**Piccadilly.
City of Westminster.
Built as a restaurant and theatre for
Messrs. Spiers and Pond, on the sites
of Nos. 219-221 Piccadilly and 8 and 9
Jermyn Street.
1874, Thomas Verity.
1878, complex extended to east.
1883-4, theatre altered, also by Thomas
Verity.
Theatre.**

The theatre and restaurant building has
a fine classical facade in Second Empire manner which 'despite alterations
and disfigurements . . . may still be
regarded as the best surviving work of
Thomas Verity, a leading theatre architect of his day'. **(Survey of London**
vol. XXIX). The facade facing Piccadilly
Circus is stone, now painted.

Apart form redecoration the auditorium
is still in its 1884 form, which was a
modification, rather than a reconstruction, of the 1873 design. It is one of the
oldest and most completely preserved
auditoria in London, most others having
been built, rebuilt or much altered after
the London County Council came into
existence in 1889. It has two balconies;
the dress-circle is serpentine-fronted,
terminating at the curved box fronts,
which are at a slightly higher level; the
upper circle is in a continuous lyre-
shaped curve terminating on the proscenium wall and incorporating boxes.
The tiers are supported on slender iron
columns. Flat circular ceiling. Splendid

coloured tile and mirror decorations to
vestibule, stair etc. The (independent)
restaurant suites were unsympatheti-
cally altered in the 1960's, but the old
Long Bar with 'glistering' ceiling exists
as a shop.

Proscenium 25ft. wide. Stage 21ft. 9ins
deep. The entire theatre is below
ground level (in this respect, unique
when built but regarded as beneficial
from the safety point of view) the stage
having a flat ceiling with minimal flying
space. The 'get-in' of new scenes is ac-
complished by the use of one of the
prompt side boxes, which has a raked
front from which a staging or ramp is
built to reach the stage. Storage space
is cramped. Two-piece safety curtain.

The theatre was used by the BBC as a
sound studio for the duration of World
War II but has otherwise been in practically continuous theatrical use. One
of the most important surviving mid
Victorian theatres in Britain, rivalled only by the Old Vic, Royal Opera House,
Theatre Royal Margate and New Tyne
Theatre. Capacity 645.

Listed Grade II. J.E.

Crouch End Hippodrome

pre-1914 fragment only

**Tottenham Lane, N.8.
Haringey.
Known as Crouch End Public Hall or
Queens Hall (1896); Crouch End Opera
House (1897) and Hippodrome (by
1912).**

Criterion Theatre

Victor Glasstone

1896, by E. Edmondson and Son of Highbury as a public hall with an orchestra at one end and a proscenium stage at opposite end, the whole open on one side to a huge supper room. Converted (perhaps before completion) to opera house with theatrical auditorium, balcony and boxes by Frank Matcham. Adapted to cinema use about 1915, suffering a series of later alterations (by John Tarver with Norfolk and Prior, 1913; E. A. Stone 1920; W. C. Thomerson, 1926; W. E. Trent 1929 and Gaumont British 1933).

Severely war damaged in World War II and never reopened. The Matcham facade has been replaced by a plain commercial infill building. All that remains is part of the back stage structure, a brick building of no visual interest, now used for storage. D.A./J.E.

Dalston Theatre

★ disused

12 Dalston Lane.
Hackney.
(Also known as Dalston Circus 1886, North London Colosseum 1887 (and many variants on this name), Dalston Theatre of Varieties and, lately, the Gaumont cinema).

1886, architect unknown.
1898, reconstructed by Wylson and Long and later altered.
Car Auction Room.

Opened as a circus, quickly became a variety theatre, converted to cinema in 1920's, closed by c.1962 and in present use as a car auction room since c.1964. Modest exterior but interesting as a theatrical survival in a changing inner suburb. Narrow single bay entrance front with Corinthian pilasters; single storey on line of shops in Dalston Lane and taller, to align with older terrace, behind. This section, containing old front offices (now sub-let as a club) probably belongs to the first period of building. Flank elevation to Rosebery Place with low relief stucco arcading is probably by Wylson and Long. Upper parts of external walls of auditorium obviously later than lower parts. Asbestos roof.

The auditorium is an astonishing sight, with up to 80 cars parked on the raked floor where the audience should be, and auctioneer's offices and rostrum on the stage. The auditorium as it is now seen must date in part from the adaptation to cinema use c.1920-5.

Large and near-rectangular, with sharply raked wood-boarded concrete floor. Very wide and deep, fully can-tilevered balcony with serpentine front between long side slips, broken on either side by a big, pedimented box and terminating with false stage boxes turned to face obliquely into the auditorium. A formerly existing (pre-cinema) upper balcony has been removed. Ceiling with flat-domed centre. Wide proscenium. The plaster ornament looks thin in relation to the large volume and the extensive flat wall surfaces.

Rather knocked about, but still suprisingly complete, considering its use for the last 16 years. It would be possible to restore this theatre if there was ever a need for a large auditorium in this area, but it would be difficult to justify solely on architectural grounds. D.H. 208. J.E.

Drury Lane Theatre Royal
★ ★ ★

Drury Lane (the entrance is actually in Catherine Street, formerly Brydges Street).
City of Westminster.
1636, a temporary playhouse existed.
1663, first permanent building by Wren or Webb, or possibly Richard Ryder.
1674, rebuilt after fire by Wren.
1696-1762, various alterations.
1775, auditorium altered and reconstructed by Robert Adam.
1974, entirely rebuilt by Henry Holland.
1812, entirely rebuilt by Benjamin Dean Wyatt following fire.
1814, proscenium altered.
1820, alterations, probably by J. Spiller.
1822, auditorium remodelled by Samuel Beazley.
1831, altered by Beazley & colonnade added.
1837, redecorated by Crace.
1841, 1847, 1851 & 1870, various minor alterations.
1901, auditorium remodelled by Philip Pilditch.
1922, auditorium entirely rebuilt by Emblin Walker, Jones and Cromie.

As now seen, the main structural shell, the staircase, rotunda, saloon etc. are by B. D. Wyatt, 1811-12 with portico probably by J. Spiller, 1820, and side colonmade by S. Beazley. 1831. The present auditorium is that of 1922.

Drury Lane shares with Haymarket and Lyceum the distinction of being entirely pre-Victorian in external appearance, and its entrance facade is the earliest now surviving in London on a working theatre. It is a pity that the portico of 1820 is so obvious an addition to Wyatt's restrained but elegant Neo-Classical design.

The Russell Street colonnade added by Beazley 1831 is a valuable townscape feature in the Covent Garden area. The staircase, rotunda and saloon are un-paralleled in any London theatre for historical importance, theatrical atmosphere and splendour. Inevitably the comparatively modern auditorium disappoints after all this promise, but it is of considerable architectural quality in its own right and from a theatrical point of view remarkably successful and intimate, the more suprising when it is remembered that in the

Dalston Theatre   GLC

1920's theatre architecture reached bottom. The style is Empire with a rectangular proscenium with modelled elliptical typmanum over. The proscenium is separated from three tiers of curving balcony fronts by a frame with deep canted side walls containing three bays of boxes at three levels, framed by pilasters and columns of imitation lapis lazuli with gilt capitals carrying an entablature from which a flared and coffered elliptical-arched ceiling springs across to form a deep sounding board. Present capacity is 2,283.

Proscenium 42ft. wide. Raking stage (flat at back) 80ft. deep. Elaborate metal sub-stage machinery with six bridges (two tilting); see **Stage Year Book** 1910 for description. Extensive counterweight system. Vast backstage area with extensive scene stores, workshops etc.

Historically one of the most important theatres in the world. Its right to present theatrical entertainments derives from the Royal Patent (still in the possesion of the theatre) granted by Charles II to Killigrew in 1662. No site in the country has a longer continuous theatrical tradition.

For a complete and authoritative architectural account, see **Survey of London** vol. XXXV. See also: Leacroft, **Development of the English Playhouse.** Listed Grade I. J.E.

Duke of York's   *GLC*

Duke of Connaught Coffee Tavern

33 Woolwich New Road, Woolwich S.E.18.
Greenwich.
(Also known as Royal Assembly Rooms (from 1891), Smith's Empire (1906) and Woolwich Picture Palace).
1881, W. Rickwood.
Shops, etc.

One of London's few coffee taverns with a performance hall. Professional status uncertain, but described as 'Variety Theatre' c.1906. It became one

Theatre Royal Drury Lane   *N.M.R.*

of the first picture houses in Woolwich district. Now in fragmented occupation, shops, restaurant, etc.

Stock brick, Gothic, with a rather bare chapel-like appearance, as befits a temperance establishment. Of some townscape value but will be demolished in connection with town centre improvements. J.E.

Duke of York's
★ ★
St. Martin's Lane, W.C.2.
City of Westminster.
(Formerly Trafalgar Square 1892-4 and Trafalgar 1894-5).
1892, Walter Emden.
1950s, altered by Cecil Beaton.

1979, internal alterations, Renton, Howard, Wood, Levin Theatre.

Painted brick and stone elevation, four storeys in height in three major bays, the centre one being three windows wide on the top two storeys, with a pretty open loggia at first floor level, guarded by a balustrade between Ionic columns. Ornamental iron and glass canopy over the entrances. The theatre is detached, with narrow passageways to left and right, each with iron gate, overthrow and lantern. The dressing rooms are in a separate building at the rear.

Narrow auditorium with the proscenium arch completely filling the end wall. Three balconies with single boxes at each level and double boxes flanking at dress and upper circle levels. Good plaster ornament. Emden's design did not overcome the difficult sighting problems. The narrowness of the house and the depth of the balconies, which were of early concrete construction, led to an unfortunate number and placing of columns, making many seats almost unusable. The cut-off at higher levels is also severe. In 1979 most of the columns were removed. The loss of the columns is not as damaging as it would be in some cases, but the introduction of a very large visually prominent beam over the gallery, which as a result is permantly out of use, must be criticized. (There is little doubt that this beam, necessary only for the suspension of the upper balconies after removal of the columns, could have been placed above the roof as first intended had funds been available). The box office removed from the foyer at the same time was a 1950's addition designed by Cecil Beaton. The gallery bar area is now a broadcasting studio for the theatre's new owners, Capital Radio.

Proscenium 26ft. 2ins. wide. Stage 34ft. deep. Capacity 661.
Listed Grade II. I.M./J.E.

Empire
pre-1914 fragment only
Leicester Square.
City of Westminster.
Proposed as Phoenix and Queen's but opened as Empire; Empire Theatre of Varieties from 1887; Empire Theatre again from 1898; cinema from 1928.
1884, Thomas Verity.
1887, internal refurbishment by Romaine Walker.
1893, additions by Frank Verity.
1904, radical remodelling by F. Verity.
1927, converted to cinema by F. G. M. Chancellor (assoc. of Matcham & Co) and T. W. Lamb of New York.
1963, major reconstruction by George Cole.

In its present state the theatrical interest of the building is slight and there is nothing left to recall the extraordinary history of the Empire and its notorious promenade. Parts of the external structure, however (especially on the west side) predate the 1927 rebuilding and are remnants of the Frank Verity works. Behind the illuminated sign to Leicester Square is the 1927 facade; a loggia in the form of a Venetian window.
See **Survey of London** vol. XXXIV for a full account of the site and buildings.
J.E.

Empress Theatre of Varieties
pre-1914 fragment only
Brighton Terrace, Brixton.
Lambeth.
(Also known as Empress Music Hall; lately the Granada Cinema and now Granada Bingo and Social Club).
1898, Wylson & Long.
1931, radically reconstructed.
c.1958, converted to cinema.
Bingo.
The Wylson & Long building can be detected externally in the carcase of the main auditorium and stage, all faced with red machine-made bricks. The rest dates from the major reconstruction of 1931 and is of little architectural interest, although the rendered corner tower, in its hard Art Déco manner, has some townscape interest.
The interior is entirely of the 1930's (with some later adaptations) but of little distinction. The auditorium, with one balcony, is large, with the character of a cinema rather than a theatre, but it retains its old stage. The proscenium has recently been cut away and the stage area is now incorporated into the auditorium for its present use. Front of house accommodation seems to have been generous, but the four-storey frontage building has been virtually abandoned. D.H. 267.
J.E.

Evans's Music & Supper Rooms
pre-1914 fragment only.
King Street, Covent Garden.
City of Westminster.
Built behind No. 43 King Street, an early eighteenth century house attributed to

Garrick Theatre

Victor Glasstone

Thomas Archer, converted to an hotel, which by the 1830's had a thriving supper room. The music hall, built over the garden in 1856, was by William Finch Hill; altered by J. H. Earley in 1871 and later reconstructed internally by Mewes and Davis.
Demolished, but the altered house front remains and provides telling evidence of continuing disregard for theatre history. In the course of a recent (and imperfect) reinstatement of Archer's design, the iron-arched cellar entrance to the historically important first supper room was destroyed. The broken bits were salvaged by the museum of London, which also has fragments of Finch Hill's Islington Empire facade (dem. 1981) to gain inches for an improbable road scheme).
See **Survey of London** vol. XXXVI.
Listed Grade II.
J.E.

Garrick Theatre
★ ★ ★

Charing Cross Road, W.C.2.
City of Westminster.
1889, Walter Emden in association with C. J. Phipps.
Theatre.

Built while Phipps was still under a cloud as a result of the Exeter fire but the auditorium probably owes more to Phipps than to Emden.
The long facade occupies a key position at the curved southern end of Charing Cross Road, where it widens into an approximately triangular space enclosed on the south side by the classical stone flank elevation of the National Portrait Gallery. The corresponding enclosure on the east side is formed by

the 140ft. long Portland and Bath stone facade of the theatre. This is divided into three related but independent elements. On the left, the main entrance is classical, with a loggia colonnade at first floor level and with all the stone now painted. On the right, two less elaborately articulated classical compostions relieve the long flank of the auditorium.

Excellent interior in a free Italianate manner with three balconies including disused gallery. Like the Duke of York's there is no proscenium arch as such, the stage being framed by the flat box fronts. Nearly all the plaster ornament is intact and there are some slight traces of the original decoration scheme. Good atmosphere, but the auditorium cries out for opulent redecoration and hangings. The front-of-house accommodation is curiously planned so that the best space (giving on to the loggia) cannot be effectively used and is demoted to the role of a waiting room, never seen by the public. Proscenium 28ft. 9ins. wide. Stage 34ft. deep. Capacity is 663 without the gallery.

Listed Grade II.   J.E.

Globe
★ ★ ★

Shaftesbury Avenue, W1.
City of Westminster.
(Formerly: Hicks Theatre 1906-1909).
1906, W. G. R. Sprague.
Theatre.

Designed with the Queen's as part of a single composition with closely similar architectural treatment to the two corners of the block (the symmetry now lost by the reconstruction of the Queen's q.v.). Forms part of an important group of theatres on the north side of Shaftesbury Avenue.

Portland stone in free classical manner. Two bays to Shaftesbury Avenue, three to slightly recessed corner quadrant and three to Rupert Street. Four storeys with an iron canopy on ornamental brackets over the entrances. Above this, Italianate treatment with cornice hoods to windows, *oeil-de-boeuf* at third floor and crowning cornice and balustrade. The corner is more boldy modelled, with giant Ionic order of attached columns rising through second and third floors and with short tower crowned by a stone dome.

Auditorium in Louis XVI style; the plan contained by a circle with the proscenium forming a tangent to the curve. Two 'cantilevered' balconies, the lower elliptically curved, the walls at each level enriched with pairs of Ionic columns carrying entablatures, a theme repeated in the Grand Saloon. The balconies terminate at the boxes (altered in 1930's), framed between square-shafted giant Corinthian columns supporting the returns of the entablature above the square proscenium. Circular panelled ceiling. Later boxes have been removed from the back of the dress circle. Fine dress circle bar and main foyer. A most impressive interior. Proscenium 30ft. wide. Stage 36ft. 4ins. deep. Some machinery, sliders and paddles, etc. date from original construction. Grave trape and 2 × 4-post traps. Six drums above grid. Partly hemp-worked. Capacity is 885.

Listed Grade II.   J.E.

Golders Green Hippodrome
★ ★

North End Road, N.W.11.
Barnet.
1913, Bertie Crewe.
1969, altered as a TV studio.
1972, altered as BBC sound studio.
BBC Concert Hall.

On a prominent corner site with a symmetrical stone or stucco main facade. Above the entrances a 7-bay centre with debased giant Ionic order with urns above the entablature; channelled and quoined pavilions flush with the facade at either end, rising as short pedimented towers to frame the prominent roof, which has a central cupola. The auditorium aims at decadent Roman splendour but misses the mark; interesting in its parts, but not a satisfying, totality. Square proscenium opening, the lintol supported by console brackets. Above this, a huge (and bare) sounding board sheltering flanking pavilions which contain two levels of boxes with an extra, impractical box facing directly toward the audience at the upper level. The pavilions have an uncomfortable pendant corner, but the boxes themselves are framed by 'correct' Roman Doric columns supporting a full entablature which continues over the proscenium, the whole composition

Globe Theatre   *National Monuments Record*

Golders Green Hippodrome   G.L.C.

Grand, Clapham Junction   *GLC*

being crowned by lion-drawn chariots, reminiscent of the Coliseum, but too small to astonish. The Doric theme is continued in a triglyph frieze on the upper of the two hesitantly serpentine balcony fronts, but the plaster decoration, taken as a whole, is nonetheless eclectic.

The sound broadcasting use has resulted in a partial restoration of the auditorium decoration, but the upper balcony is blocked off. The stage now extends forward into stalls area. Lighting frame suspended from proscenium cove.

Capacity when last used as a theatre 2200. Proscenium 37ft 6in wide, stage originally 29ft deep.

Listed Grade II.   J.E.

Grand
★ ★ disused
St. John's Hill, Clapham
Junction.
Wandsworth.
(Formerly: (New) Grand Theatre or
Palace of Varieties).
1900, E. A. Woodrow.
Bingo.

Replaced the Grand Hall on an adjoining site. Opened by Dan Leno who, with Herbert Campbell and others, was involved in the building of this hall.

The massive street facade, with large areas of machine-made red brick relieved by terracotta ornament has recently been cleaned and re-pointed. The total effect may not be architecturally particularly distinguished but is important to the street scene and expresses the character of the area at the time it was built - vulgar and confident, rather than prim and elegant.

An extraordinary auditorium, again not of outstanding architectural quality, but pleasingly theatrical with its lavish display of plaster ornament in Chinese taste, e.g. shallow domed ceiling in the form of an inverted willow pattern plate, tented box fronts, dragon heads, etc. Two balconies with serpentine-curved front to lower (grand circle). The effect of the auditorium has been severely damaged by the insertion of a false ceiling concealing the upper balcony front, upper walls and domed ceiling. The removal of stalls seats by the present users (Mecca Bingo) has produced a curiously archaic effect, like a very early palace of varieties. The foyer decorations have been stripped.

Proscenium opening (1912) 30ft. Original stage depth 30ft. Grid but no machinery. Good access from side street.

A thoroughly restorable theatre but big (2,500 seated in 1912; 900 for bingo after closure of gallery, probably 1,500 if completely reseated to modern standards). Affected by a redevelopment scheme which seems to be hanging fire. D.H. 330.   J.E.

Grand Palais
133 Commercial Road, Stepney.
Tower Hamlets.
c.1911, architect unknown.
Cinema/offices.

Built as New Kings Hall. Original use uncertain but probably designed with future cinema use in mind and known as Cohen Moses Cinematograph Hall from 1914/15. Subsequently a dance hall and then c.1926 became a Yiddish theatre, remaining in this principal use until 1961, with occasional benefit performances after this date. Retained music and dancing licence until at least 1963. Described as 'public hall' throughout its period of theatrical use. Now a thriving little Indian cinema.

Behind buildings and easily missed. At centre of a uniform early 20th century row of shops with facade in machine-made bricks with stone dressings. Entrance differentiated only by a glass canopy (name on pelmet) and a pedimental hump in the parapet and cornice crowning the facade. Short corridor with box office leads to centre of one side of auditorium. Tiny; rectangular, with pilasters and some plaster ornament. Recent alterations (e.g. balcony now forms part of first floor commercial letting) has obscured original form, but it would not be too difficult to ascertain the shape and appearance of the Yiddish theatre from what now remains. Basement hall not seen.   J.E.

Greenwich Theatre
pre-1914 fragment only.
Stockwell Street, S.E.10.
Greenwich.
(entrance in Crooms Hill).
(Known as Crowder's Music Hall and
Picture Gallery, Parthenon Palace of
Varieties Greenwich Hippodrome,
Barnard's, etc.)
Pre-1869 and rebuilt 1871, architects
unknown.
1885, reconstructed by J.G. Buckle.
1895, rebuilt by Mr Hancock.
1969, remodelled B. Meeking.
Theatre.

The narrow entrance facade to Croom's Hill is modern, by Meeking. The flank wall to Nevada Street seems to be part of the old Crowder's Music Hall and is probably seen in its 1885 dress. A stucco lettered panel, 'Parthenon Palace of Varieties' is still just legible. The corner pub, the 'Rose & Crown', rebuilt in 1888, perhaps by Frank Matcham, is contained in the angle of the site but is now separate from the theatre.

Although contained within an old shell, the auditorium is for all practical purposes a new building by Meeking, in a single steep rake with open stage and forestage.

This theatre is D.H. 346. It is sometimes confused with the demolished Greenwich Theatre (Morton's, D.H. 347).   J.E.

Hackney Empire
★ ★ ★ disused
Mare Street, E.8.
Hackney.
1901, Frank Matcham.
Bingo.

A magnificent example of a turn-of-the-century variety palace. Matcham at his most imaginative. Built for Oswald Stoll, the fourth of his big suburban variety houses and now the only survivor in Greater London. Opened December 1901 with 'two shows a night' policy. Equipped from the outset with a small cine-projection box.

Excellent site with street frontages on three sides. Great townscape value. Splendidly exuberant terracotta facade to Mare Street, described at the time as being 'carried out in Victorian design'. Three bays, the wide centre one having a curiously framed and arched first floor opening, the narrow outer bays treated as short towers, very slightly advanced and topped by finely modelled domes (removed 1979); all very eclectic and uninhibited.

Entrance vestibule and double staircase with white marble and alabaster finishes. Opulent auditorium, again highly mannered and eclectic in its details, with three balconies (top one disused). Dress circle with boxes at back. Square, deeply coved and ornamented ceiling. Marble proscenium, the opening flanked by splayed buttresses with elaborate niches (originally containing electric number panels) crowned by Indian domes. The arch itself and its pierced tympanum form a serpentine pediment.

One of the most perfect examples of Matcham's work in London. The Mecca Bingo house style has, however, led to an unfortunate interior decoration. This has removed practically all trace of the old painting and gilding which had survived, soiled, but surprisingly complete, until early 1978. Now only the marble and alabaster surfaces and the allegorical paintings, richly framed in rococo plasterwork, remain untouched. Stage 60ft. wide and over 40ft. deep. Proscenium approx. 34ft. wide. D.H. 359.

Listed Grade II.   J.E.

Hackney Empire

Haymarket Theatre Royal

★ ★ ★

Haymarket, S.W.1.
City of Westminster.
1821, John Nash.
1880, C. J. Phipps (rebuilt auditorium).
1905, C. Stanley Peach (rebuilt auditorium).
Theatre.

Present facade, rear elevation and much of the structural shell are by Nash. The auditorium is by Peach (1905) who completely replaced the Phipps interior of 1879-80. Subsequent sympathetic alterations to bars, etc. from 1939, mainly by John Murray.

The Haymarket is of great importance in theatre history. The first theatre to defy the monopoly of the Patent houses, the Little Theatre in the Haymarket (adjoining the present site) was built 1720; gained a limited patent itself 1766-77 and was afterwards granted a special licence. Rebuilt on present site 1821. A much studied theatre, the subject of many books and papers, but there is no detailed architectural account. The **Survey of London** (vol. XX) is, for once, quite inadequate. The building itself is nevertheless of outstanding architectural interest and great townscape value. It is one of the few substantial pre-1880 theatre buildings in London and shares with Drury Lane and the Lyceum the distinction of being entirely pre-Victorian in external appearance. Nash's hexastyle portico was sited a little to the south of the earlier theatre to close the vista from St. James's Square. The back elevation to Suffolk Street is designed as a stuccoed house front, domestic in conception apart from its tall scene door.

The 1904 drawings (kept in manager's office) show that Peach's works were limited to the auditorium, with only minor improvements backstage. Beyond this, little seems to be later than the mid-nineteenth century. Peach's auditorium is architecturally one of the most distinguished and best preserved of its period in London. Such alterations as have occured have been made with discretion, to preserve the integrity of the original design. The decorations are well preserved. Two balconies, the upper one extending back into a benched gallery of great interest and small comfort.

Proscenium 27ft. wide. Raked stage 42ft. deep. Although altered and improved in recent years (e.g. fly floors repositioned) most of the backstage is of considerable age and despite the introduction of counterweights in 1970, the stage remains partly hemp-worked. Some disused Victorian machinery (three bridges and sliders) remains in the deep cellar. Main roof and stage loft lit by dormers, but the property rooms, paint room, etc. formerly in the roof space have been removed. Capacity is 904 including 131 in the un-numbered gallery.

Listed Grade I. J.E.

Her Majesty's

★ ★ ★

Haymarket, S.W.1.
City of Westminster.
(Originally Queen's Theatre, then variously King's Theatre, Her Majesty's and His Majesty's; also known as Italian Opera House until 1847).
1704-5, first building by Sir John Vanbrugh.
1778, interior remodelled by possibly Robert Adam.
1782, remodelled by Michael Novosielski.
1790-1, rebuilt after fire by Novosielski.
1793, concert room added by Novosielski.
1796, altered by Marinari.
1816-18, new facades built and Royal Opera Arcade added by John Nash and George Repton.
1846, renovated and redecorated by John Johnson.
1860-3, auditorium altered and proscenium boxes removed.
1868-9, rebuilt within shell (following fire) by Charles Lee.
1897, all demolished with the exception of Nash's Royal Opera Arcade.
and rebuilt by C. J. Phipps with int. decs. by Romaine Walker. Theatre.

The Phipps theatre is a magnificent pile in French Renaissance style, robbed of part of its original impact by the demolition of its companion building, the Carlton Hotel (by Phipps, Isaacs and Florence), conceived as part of the same architecturally unified scheme but now replaced by the unsympathetic bulk of New Zealand House. The theatre, nevertheless, remains an important building in the street scene, with its open loggia and imposing dome and it makes an instructive contrast with Nash's Haymarket theatre, nearly opposite. The older Royal Opera Arcade (at the rear) is an important work in its own right and of great townscape value. The auditorium of this, 'one of the best planned theatres in London' (**Survey of London**) is opulent. Architecturally, a two-balcony design (the gallery being a backward extension of the upper tier) with details adapted from Gabriel's Opéra at Versailles. Scagliola proscenium frame with three tiers of boxes on either side framed by Corinthian columns with rich entablatures, carrying the deep, elliptical, coffered arch. Blind-arcaded side walls; deep, enriched cove carrying ceiling and saucer dome. Paintings in eighteenth century manner.

Proscenium 34ft. 6in wide; flat stage (reputedly the first flat stage to be built in Britain) 47ft. 6ins deep. Very important and complete complex of wooden stage machinery in excellent state of preservation, including four substage

Her Majesty's GLC

bridges, sloats, grave trap, four post trap, cellar drums, winches, thunder run, grid drums, etc. The sub-stage machinery is archaeologically the most important survival of its kind recorded in London and it appears to be restorable. Capacity of theatre is 1,134. It is impossible to give a short account of this oustandingly important theatre without significant omissions. **Survey of London** vol. XXIX contains a comprehensive (28 page) account of the architecture but adds that 'the history of the theatre has still to be satisfactorily elucidated'. Only the Drury Lane theatre site has a longer record of continuous theatrical use. Handel, Haydn, Vanbrugh, Congreve, Sheridan and Jenny Lind all associated with earlier buildings. Beerbohm Tree, who commissioned Phipps to design the present theatre, had a suite and his 'acting academy' in the dome over the present structure.
Listed Grade II.   J.E.

Hoxton Hall

★ ★ ★

128a (formerly 64b) Hoxton Street, Hoxton.
Hackney.
(Formerly Mortimer's Hall 1863; MacDonald's Music Hall 1866-1872).
1863, James Mortimer.
1867, reconstructed, architect unknown.
1880, converted to mission hall.
1977/1979, music hall restored by Lidbetter and Betham (Richard Betham).
1981, facade restored by Lidbetter & Betham (Adrian Betham).
Community Theatre and Neighbourhood Centre.
This building is unique in Greater London and one of the most important survivals of an early music hall building to be seen anywhere (cf. Wilton's, (Royal) Clarence, Glasgow Britannia and Cardiff Philharmonic). An unusually early example of a purpose-built music hall **not** attached to a pre-existing public house. Lost its licence 1871. Purchased by Blue Ribbon Temperance Mission 1879; taken over by Bedford Institute (Quaker) 1893 and incorporated into new buildings in 1910. Excellently restored and in regular theatrical use today as part of a busy Quaker neighbourhood centre.
For a more detailed historical account, see J. Goodfellow; **Hoxton Hall: a short history,** Hoxton Hall and Hackney BC. 1977.
No elevation to Hoxton Street. Entered through a narrow corridor beside a shop. A simple pedimented stucco facade to a side street, Wilks Place, with Mortimer's monogram and date 1863.
The auditorium is a remarkable room of great archaeological importance. Originally a pilastered hall with a single balcony facing the stage, supported on two wooden columns. Fireplaces on either side. In 1867 it was raised to accommodate two tiers of balconies around three sides of the hall, supported on iron columns and with ornamental *bombé* iron fronts. No pro-

scenium. A typical pre-1880's music hall stage arrangement with a high platform and doors at the back (original architectural treatment not known). The balconies extend over the stage to the back wall. Width between balcony fronts about 16ft.
Small two-balconied halls were probably always rare. This hall had suffered some makeshift alterations and war damage but the 1977 works restored it to a form close to what must have existed after the 1867 enlargement. The ceiling is all of 1977. Necessary modifications (e.g. raised guard rails to lower balcony front) have been made discreetly. It is now licensed for an audience of 140 in the body of hall and lower balcony, the upper balcony remaining disused except for private performances. DH. 393.
Listed Grade II ★.   J.E.

Inverness Court Hotel Theatre

★ disused

Inverness Terrace, Bayswater.
City of Westminster.
c.1905, Mewès & Davis.
Bar.
This was originally a private theatre formed within the ground floor of a large house which subsequently became an hotel. The house itself was probably built in the late 1850's and was later radically altered and enriched. Mr Louis Spitzel, a merchant banker, took a 99 year lease in 1905 and the theatre was probably made for him. He died in 1906.
The house has panelled and painted rooms in opulent taste at ground and first floor levels. The theatre is a spectacular plaything, contrasting with Normansfield q.v., which was clearly intended to work for its living. After alteration to its present form as a bar, it consists of two rooms divided by a 'pro-

Islington Palace   *G.L.C.*

scenium' arch. Much of the original Rococo plaster ornament is intact. The 'auditorium' is flat-floored, domed, mirror lined and has (displaced) *bombé* balustrades enclosing the seating area. Nothing in the way of stage equipment. Further research is needed. No evidence has been found to support the supposed association with Lillie Langtry.
Listed Grade II.   J.E.

Islington Palace

★ disused

Upper Street, Islington.
Islington.
(Formerly St. Mary's Hall; Mohawk's Hall from 1870's; later known as Blue Hall and Gaumont Cinema).
c.1869, architect unknown, but presumably F. Peck.
Derelict.
Islington Palace forms part of the Royal Agricultural Hall complex, all now disused and in the ownership of Islington Borough Council. The Palace is sometimes confused with Berner's Hall

Inverness Court Hotel Theatre   *GLC*

(a room of no theatrical pretensions in the same complex) and with Islington Empire (facade survived until 1981).

The Royal Agricultural Hall was built 1861-2 to the designs of Frederick Peck of Maidstone. The St. Mary's Hall, later the Palace, was in existence by c.1869 and was licensed to hold 3,000. Altered in c.1900 for cinema use. Last used for bingo.

The entrance from Upper Street is independent of the main R.A.H. entrance, but makes little impact in its own right. A rectangular hall with very restrained plaster ornament. Single balcony, originally extending round three sides but now at back only. Essentially a large concert room and more suitable for variety than drama. It was an ideal hall for the famous Mohawk Minstrel troupe, who occupied it continuously for 24 years from 1876. Particularly interesting, even in its altered condition, as the only surviving large minstrel hall in London.

A thoroughly useful building which ought to be returned to some form of public use. Its future is, however, bound up with the intractable problems of the entire R.A.H. complex. Its condition (excellent in 1974) is now poor and deteriorating rapidly. D.H. 401.
Listed Grade II.   J.E.

Kings Cross Theatre (Royal Clarence)
pre-1914 fragment only.
Birkenhead Street, Kings Cross.
Camden.
1830, architect unknown.
Offices.
The Survey of London vol. XXIV states that a stuccoed facade on the west side of Birkenhead Street, just south of Euston Road is that of the former Royal Clarence Theatre. It was not licenced after 1879. The present facade has clearly been much altered, but is certainly that of the theatre. The internal structure however (1980) shows no trace of its theatrical origin. See also D.H. 434.   J.E.

Kingston Empire
pre-1914 fragment only
Richmond Road.
Kingston-upon-Thames.
1910, architect unknown.
Shop/offices.
A large supermarket has been constructed within the auditorium, with ancillary offices above. Some upper sections of the gallery and roof still survive

but are inaccessible. The main foyer and stage have been completely ripped out. The upper part of the heavily impressive red brick Baroque facade and most of the body of the building (whose side wall still boldly proclaims the name Kingston Empire) survive.   D.C.

London Coliseum
★ ★ ★
St. Martin's Lane.
City of Westminster.
(Known as Coliseum Theatre 1931-1968).
1904, Frank Matcham; several later alterations; partly restored by Martin Carr 1968 etc.
Theatre.
Arguably Matcham's most important single work. Built for Oswald Stoll and conceived as a magnificent and elaborately equipped variety theatre with splendidly appointed public rooms. Vast auditorium. Present seating, for 2,358, exceeds capacity of both Drury Lane and Covent Garden.

The Coliseum dominates the southern end of St. Martin's Lane and its bold silhouette is important in the view from Trafalgar Square, where it is seen behind and beyond St. Martin-in-the-Fields.

Coliseum   *Victor Glasstone*

147

Terracotta (now painted). Original convex roofs removed. Facade in free Italian Renaissance style, chanelled, with lavish ornament. Pedimented and balconied windows set in loggia at second floor level. Entrance bay, off-centre and slightly advanced, rises as a chanelled square tower with an altered iron-stayed canopy set in a giant two-storey archway. Balconied Venetian window at second floor level, above which the tower rises high over the facade, and is crowned by an elaborate cornice and a finely modelled Borrominesque spire derived from Wren's west towers of St. Paul's but incorporating four lions, since removed, and terminating in a great glass globe, originally revolving but now fixed. Flank wall to May's Court with name of theatre in gigantic Art Nouveau letters. Auditorium richly ornamented. At the back of the stalls there is a ring of stall boxes which originally had at its centre Britain's only permanent central Royal Box. The Grand Circle rises over and behind these boxes, there being no overhang at all. Over the Grand Circle there are two further 'cantilever' balconies with pairs of two-tier boxes with domed canopies on either side and, between these boxes and the proscenium, elaborate niches originally for an auditorium choir, but subsequently converted to stage boxes on two levels. Fine domed ceiling.
Very large stage. Proscenium width originally 55ft., now narrowed to 49ft. The unique triple revolve was removed in 1976-77.
This theatre is of outstanding importance and demands more description than can be given here. See Victor Glasstone **London Coliseum** (text and slide pack, Chadwyck-Healey 1980).
Listed Grade II.   J.E./I.M.

Palladium   GLC

(London) Palladium
★ ★ ★
Argyll Street, W.1.
City of Westminster.
(London Palladium since 1934).
1910, Frank Matcham, but incorporating parts of the fabric of the Corinthian Bazaar (1868 by Owen Lewis) & Hengler's Grand Cirque (1871 by J. T. Robinson, reconstructed 1884 by C. J. Phipps).
Theatre.
Built as a variety theatre to rival the Hippodrome and Coliseum. The facade, modified and with sculpture added by Matcham, is a striking relic of the Corinthian Bazaar which preceded the Palladium. Painted stone classical temple front with Corinthian columns on tall pedestals.
Separate booking hall, as big as a branch post office. Generous foyers and bars with most original ornament intact, even where obscured by modern, uncharacteristic 'screw-on' décor.
Big (but remarkably intimate) richly ornamented auditorium, one of the most magnificent creations of the variety palace boom. Elaborate ceiling with laterally elongated dome; two deep balconies with unsupported spans; boxes at three levels in paired arched niches. Fine proscenium arch. The style is described as 'French Rococo' but the ornaments are variously derived and freely used in a piece of bold Matcham mannerism.
Proscenium 47ft. 6ins. wide. Flat stage 40ft. deep. Capacity is 2,298. The **Survey of London** account of the building is authoritative.
Listed Grade II.   J.E.

London Pavilion
★ facade only
Piccadilly Circus.
City of Westminster.
1885, Saunders & Worley.
1900, Wylson & Long, reconstructed interior.
1918, interior reconstructed, architect unknown.
1934, F. G. M. Chancellor of Matcham & Co. (gutted for cinema conversion).
Cinema.

Occupies a triangular site with main elevations to Piccadilly Circus and Shaftesbury Avenue and should perhaps be regarded as the key building in the Circus group. The quality of Worley's elevations has recently been revealed by the removal of a clutter of advertisements and illuminated signs. Painted Portland & Bath stone, classical facades.
The existing auditorium (a radical recasting which left no trace of Wylson & Long's auditorium of 1900) has two balconies in the manner of a theatre but quite plain and with no boxes. Fragmentary remains of stage machinery.
There is a proposal (1978) to gut the building and insert shops, tourist funtraps and two cinemas, one above the other, partly housed in a 'conservatory' roof storey (by Chapman Taylor Associates).
The **Survey of London** vol. XXXI account of the building is full and authoritative.
Listed Grade II.   J.E.

Lyceum
★ ★ ★ disused
Wellington Street, Strand.
City of Westminster.
1834, Samuel Beazley (present portico and part of shell).
1904, Bertie Crewe (present interior including auditorium).
1919, minor alterations by Edward Jones.
1950-1, altered by Matthews & Sons, for Mecca.
Ballroom.
The history of the Lyceum(s) is complex. A public building of this name stood on an adjoining site (now covered by Wellington Street) in 1772, then a theatre from 1794 until Wellington Street was formed, when a new theatre was built on the present site. This opened 1834. It was for long managed by Sir Henry Irving and was famous for its association with him and Ellen Terry (their last performance 1902). The Crewe interior is post-Irving and was intended to be a variety house but soon reverted to drama. Purchased by LCC in 1939 for demolition in connection with a road improvement since abandoned. Now owned by GLC and leased to Mecca, who use it principally as a ballroom. Samuel Beazley's 1834 portico is a rare and valuable survival of its kind and date. It stands over the public footway (cf. Haymarket) and is a striking incident in the view up Wellington Street from the Strand. The modern signs are unsympathetic (1979).
Magnificent entrance foyer and grand staircase leading to Crewe's richly ornamented variety house interior, perhaps the most flamboyant in Britain. The auditorium has undergone some alteration to suit it for its present use, principally the insertion of a flat floor at or about stage level, uniting stage and former stalls areas. Bars have been inserted and staircases to left and right break through lower box fronts. Crewe's auditorium is, however, otherwise intact above the present floor; at higher levels, old discoloured decorations and ceiling paintings can be seen. Proscenium 42ft. 8ins. wide. Stage 80ft.

Palladium   GLC

× 55ft. deep. No old machinery survives. Original capacity about 3,000 seated, likely to be 2,000 (approximately) if re-seated to modern standards.

Despite alterations, this is an outstandingly important and fundamentally well-preserved building, rich in theatrical atmosphere. It could and should be restored to a more appropriate use.

Listed Grade II (probably originally listed on account of its classical portico, but the Crewe auditorium alone is worthy of a higher grading).   J.E.

Lyric Theatre Hammersmith

★ ★

**King Street, London W.6.
Hammersmith.
1979, (adaptation of 1895 Matcham design) Borough Architects of Hammersmith - with Theatre Projects Consultants.
Theatre.**

As now seen the auditorium is a re-creation of a Frank Matchams' 1895 design, modified by the Borough Council of Hammersmith, 1978-9. The original theatre was demolished in 1972 but, following a public inquiry, the plasterwork of the auditorium was partly removed and stored and partly recorded in cast moulds, to enable it to be reproduced in a new building. The auditorium has now been reconstructed by the Borough Council within a modern block.

The old building in Bradmore Grove (Lyric Hall, 1888, by Isaac Martin, altered 1890 by F. H. Francis and virtually rebuilt by Matcham, retaining the original facade) was externally of no architectural consequence. The new building is a typical town-centre block of the 1970's, unexceptional inside and out. The discovery of a late Victorian Rococo theatre auditorium embedded

within it, two storeys above the ground, is one of the most bizarre architectural experiences that London has to offer. The old auditorium was a beautiful invention, intimate, with excellent acoustics and "one of the best examples of the *fin-de-siecle* theatre interior in Greater London - one designed by a master of the art of theatre building" (Ashley Barker, giving the GLC's evidence at the Public Enquiry in 1969).

The new auditorium is still essentially Matcham's 1895 design, although modified in dimensions. The widening of the proscenium by approximately 4ft. created difficulties with the proscenium arch (which is semi-circular) and necessitated changes to the overall height of the auditorium and the dimensions of the ceiling. The problems have been cleverly overcome by stretching Matcham's design without obviously interfering with the proportions of the parts or introducing any ornamental element not present in the original theatre. The decision to place stage lighting and ventilation inlets above the ceiling has necessitated one radical alteration, **viz.** the introduction of a mesh in place of the flat plaster ceiling bed, the paintings on which had been lost in the nineteen twenties. While some will object to the mesh it must equally be said that the introduction of a full modern stage lighting layout has been most sympathetically handled. A splendid interior with a wealth of lively Rococo ornament. Two balconies. A round-arched proscenium enriched with leaf scrolls in the architrave and lined by a fantastic openwork valence or pelmet made of repeating scrolly ornaments. Boldly coved ceiling. The new width of the proscenium is 27ft. 7ins., stage depth is 27ft. The capacity is 541. There is now a forestage elevator the three positions of which - forestage, additional seating or orchestra pit - are carefully planned into the old plasterwork details.

Formerly listed Grade II.   J.E./I.M.

Lyric Shaftesbury Avenue   *GLC*

Lyric

★ ★

**Shaftesbury Avenue.
City of Westminster.
1888, C. J. Phipps.
1932, extensively redecorated by Michel Rosenauer.
Theatre.**

Considered in isolation, the exterior is unexciting, but it forms the westernmost element in an outstandingly valuable group of theatre facades comprising the Lyric, Apollo, Globe and Queen's Theatres. Brick and stone facade to Shaftesbury Avenue; three storeys plus lucernes and gables, with weakly accented bays variously treated in Renaissance style with somewhat hesitant Franco-Flemish details. Entrance with glazed canopy at right hand end. Left hand gable with name of theatre.

The facade to Great Windmill Street is of unusual interest. This was formerly the house (No. 16) built in 1767 by Dr. William Hunter, anatomist, as his home, anatomical theatre and museum. Now much remodelled internally to form a stack of dressing rooms in the backstage area, it is still recognisable for what it once was, notwithstanding the painting of the brickwork.

Despite some alteration the auditorium is one of the most pleasing in London and rich in theatrical atmosphere. Three balconies partly cantilevered from set back columns. The straight sides of the dress circle are divided into three boxes. Above this the balconies are of circular plan and all three terminate against the superimposed boxes on either side of the stage. The top balcony front continues as a notional entablature to the pedestalled giant Corinthian columns which frame the boxes and carry the deep elliptical arch over the proscenium. The circular ceiling centre follows the line of the upper balcony. Pretty plasterwork, alabaster and wood panelled finishes.

The extensive redecoration by Michel

Lyric Hammersmith   *S. Stephens*

Lyric   GLC

Rosenauer in 1932 affected entrance vestibule, crush room and stalls bar. It is fortunate that Phipps's interior (although altered) was not then completely devastated for the sake of fashion.
Proscenium 29ft. 6ins. wide. Stage 39ft. 10ins. deep. Still partly hemp worked. Small revolve.
See **Survey of London** vols. XXXI and XXXII.
Listed Grade II.   J.E.

Myddelton Hall
Almeida Street.
Islington
c.1878, architect unknown.
Workshop.
The professional status of this hall is uncertain, but some well-known 'pros' seem to have appeared here. In 1892 the published LCC list shows it as licenced for music with a seating capacity of 600. It remained licenced until at least 1912 when it was said to be used for 'theatrical performances, concerts and dances' (Stage Yearbook). It is now a shopfitter's joinery workshop. Despite this, the brick street elevation (more or less facing the Almeida, the old Islington Literary Institute) is recognisably that of a public hall. The hall is now divided in its height by a workshop floor which cuts through the proscenium about half way up. The proscenium arch, however, can still be seen, complete with its plaster ornamentation.
The Myddleton is probably **not** the same as Wellington Hall (D.H. 850) and it must be distinguished from the Almeida which was not built as a theatre.   J.E.

Normansfield Hospital Amusement Hall
★ ★
Teddington.
Richmond-upon-Thames.
1879, Rowland Plumbe.
Entertainment Hall.
Not a public theatre, but included here because of its extreme rarity and vulnerability. A complete and unaltered survival of the 1870's.

Normansfield was founded in 1868, as an institution for the mentally afflicted, by Dr. John Haydon Langdon-Down, who gave his name to Down's Syndrome. The patients were (unusually for the time) given training and encouraged in remedial activities. This, together with Mrs Langdon-Down's great love of the theatre, led to the building of the Amusement Hall, so called.
Externally it is unimpressive; like a large chapel, attached to one wing of the much extended original house. It makes no impact from any public viewpoint. The auditorium, situated above what was originally the 'kindersaal' is, by contrast, almost spectacular.
Flat floor with open pine-trussed roof, fair-faced brick walls and tall windows, like an assembly hall. Iron fronted balcony across the end and a complete, well-preserved sun-burner in the roof. Richly modelled, coloured and gilded proscenium with pairs of doors (one practical, one dummy) on either side, giving on to a shallow forestage and steps with iron balustrades. The whole of the original decoration to the proscenium, including figure-paintings, seems to have survived intact.
The stage is particularly interesting as a miniature version of a regular theatre of the period. It has a simple groove system, still workable, with very old, possibly original wing pieces. Some early borders, a creed and Lord's prayer

drop and a painted cloth, etc. also still in position.
Understage, a basement and cellar level, but these are simply rooms and never had machinery. A scene designer's model can be seen in the basement. On the balcony are some old figure paintings for a production of **Ruddigore** but these seem to have been made for a full-size professional stage.
Used as a cinema, chapel, place of assembly, entertainment hall, etc. by staff and inmates. In excellent condition, but the future of the institution itself has seemed insecure in recent years.
Unique in London. Of architectural, historical and archaeological interest. This building should be meticulously recorded and preserved.
Proscenium about 18ft. wide. Stage about 21ft. deep. Would probably seat over 300 in reasonable comfort if seated to modern concert hall standards.   J.E.

Old Assembly Rooms
pre-1914 fragment only.
between Friars Way and Old Friars, Richmond Green.
Richmond-upon-Thames.
Architect unknown.
Part of a house.

Normansfield Hospital Amusement Hall   GLC

The eighteenth century assembly rooms on Richmond Green were reputedly in regular theatrical use (but *distinguish* from the Georgian theatre in Richmond Green, demolished in 1884). The old brick facade remains, with altered ground floor to accommodate a vehicle entrance. Listed Grade II. J.E.

Old Vic

★ ★ ★

New Cut, S.E.1. Lambeth.
(Formerly: Royal Coburg Theatre, Royal Victoria Theatre, Victoria Theatre, New Victoria Palace, Royal Victoria Hall Coffee Tavern. Its popular name 'the Old Vic' has now become its official title.)
1818, Rudolph Cabanel.
1871, interior entirely reconstructed by J. T. Robinson.
1879, minor alterations by Elijah Hoole.
1928, minor alterations by Frank Matcham & Co. F.G.M. Chancellor.
1930's, proscenium altered by Wells Coates.
1950, proscenium altered by Douglas Rowntree and Pierre Sonrel.
1963, proscenium altered by Sean Kenny. Theatre.
Occupies an important site at the crossing of Waterloo Road, New Cut and Lower Marsh. Mid-Victorian stone and stucco classical facade with early nineteenth century brick flanks relieved by an arcaded treatment of tall, round-arched recesses, as seen in the earliest engravings of the theatre.
Th roof and the exterior brick shell (with the exception of the entrance facade), are largely of the first period of building. The entrance facade and auditorium are mainly the work of Robinson (whose other major surviving work is the Theatre Royal Margate q.v.) with later alterations. Despite a succession of unsympathetic modifications the auditorium with its two lyre shaped enfolding balconies with raised plaster decoration on their *bombé* section, retains most of its 1871 appearance with a ceiling which is probably older. The proscenium has suffered the most radical modernisation attacks and the boxes have been removed. The architectural quality and pleasing theatrical atmosphere of this auditorium will not be fully recognised and appreciated until it is more or less restored to its Robinson form. Such a restoration, which as well as satisfying the architectural and theatrical historian could also reflect the current mood of re-establishing close contact between performers and audience, should not be prohibitively difficult. Historically, as well as architecturally, the Vic is one of London's most precious theatrical possessions. Its present grading in the Statutory List does not reflect the outstanding interest of the building. Built as a 'minor' for melodrama and pantomime, it was always important in the history and development of the popular theatre. An attempt to convert it to a coffee music hall in 1870 (architect: Rowley) was abortive, but it was subsequently converted by the Coffee Palace Association and reopened as the Royal Victoria Coffee Music Hall under Emma Cons in 1880. Became world famous under Cons and Lilian Baylis.
The management of the Vic and the history of its productions have formed the subject of innumerable books and papers, but there is no authoritative architectural and architectural study. The **Survey of London** vol. XXIII provides only a sketch outline. The permanent proscenium, now sheathed in Sean Kenny's 1963 shuttered plaster, is 30ft. wide; the stage depth is 32ft. 3ins. and the present fore stage 17ft. deep. The capacity is now 878.
Listed Grade II. J.E./I.M.

Palace of Varieties

pre-1914 fragment only
Stonebridge Park, Willesden.
Brent.
1907, M. T. Saunders.
Shop.
At the side of and originally an amenity of the Coach and Horses P.H. which also survives. The pub and its Music Hall (originally so called) were designed in a kind of Old English style, brick, render and half timber. The music hall is now much altered but recognizable by its fly tower. The first design shows a room like a tiny theatre, with balcony, raked stage, tall fly tower and grid. As built, it had no balcony, a basket-arched plain proscenium and low tower. The stage had a two-part safety curtain and scene doors in the back wall. Held about 400. Small (auditorium 36ft. × 26ft.) but still surprisingly theatrical for its date, kind and location (cf. Park, Ealing).
By 1909 it was a picture palace but was still listed in **Stage Yearbook** under its old name a year later and shown as retaining its stage plays and music and dancing licences. J.E.

Old Vic

Palace Theatre

★ ★ ★

Cambridge Circus.
City of Westminster.
(Formerly the Royal English Opera House and the Palace Theatre of Varieties).
1891, T. E. Colcutt and G. H. Holloway.
Theatre.

An oustandingly important High Victorian monument designed for D'Oyly Carte as home for English grand opera. Now much defaced but worthy of careful restoration. Architecturally unlike any other London theatre. Elevation in a free early Renaissance manner, related to the style of the same architect's Imperial Institute. Octagonal shafts divide the red brick and buff terracotta banded facades into bays with many small arched windows linked vertically and horizontally into varied groupings, all with terracotta balconettes and floridly ornamented friezes. The shafts and octagonal corner towers rise above the parapet like minarets and are crowned by domes. A broad, banded gable rises behind the main facade facing the Circus. Entrance canopy extended and altered to its detriment. Much of the richly moulded facade ornament was shaved off in the late 1960's.

Opulent but now seedy-looking auditorium with three balconies, the marble and onyx linings mostly painted over. One of the saddest sights in London, this auditorium is in need of thoroughgoing restoration. Proscenium 33ft. 9ins. wide. Stage 31ft. deep. Cellar 20ft. deep.
The relics of machinery above and below stage are unique in London and of considerable archaeological significance. It was an extraordinarily elaborate wood and iron installation designed (for opera) by Dando. All moving parts now removed but what remains is a forest of framed timber with traps, chariot slots, etc. The capacity is 1,095 plus a gallery holding 350.
Listed Grade II. J.E.

Palaseum

226 Commercial Road, Stepney.
Tower Hamlets.
1912, George Billings, Wright & Co.
Cinema.

Opened in March 1912 as a theatre and opera house (the Temple of Art), reputedly the only one in the U.K. specifically built as a Jewish theatre. First productions were **King Ahab** (a Yiddish opera) and **Rigoletto**, but it became a cinema within six months under the name Palaseum. Known by

1960 as the Essoldo but has since reverted to Palaseum.
The exterior is of little distinction, but it makes an interesting incident in the wreckage of Commercial Road. Main body looks like a windowless chapel; stock brick and slated roof with a low fly tower in unmatching brick. Facade in machine-made brick with minimal stone trim all now painted. Central domed feature set back over entrance, flanked by little square towers, now with flat tops (originally domed). Some Moorish arches.
Sometimes confused with the Grand Palais, q.v. J.E.

Park Hall,

Park Hotel, Greenford Avenue, Hanwell.
Ealing.
c.1890, architect unknown.
Public Hall.

Built as a hall attached to a substantial corner pub, but uncommonly large (capacity given as 500 in 1912, but by modern standards probably 300 at most) and unusually theatrical in character for its location and period. cf. Palace of Varieties, Stonebridge Park for a less well preserved example of such a hall.
The red brick and stone pub, with little bartisans and conical pinnacles, is of

Palace

no great architectural quality but has some environmental value at this point in Greenford Avenue, where there is a triangular green at a road junction. Hall is integral with pub but declares itself in the view across the adjoining car park by its long, plain flank wall with escape doors, two chimney stacks and unmistakable fly tower and lantern. The auditorium has a flat floor; six bays divided by piers, whose moulded caps form the corbels for thin wooden trusses, the upper parts of which are concealed above the coved ceiling. Two chimney breasts on one side. Plaster ornamental proscenium. Proscenium 22ft. wide and stage 18ft. deep (**Stage Yearbook** 1910). Raked with good headroom in basement (no substage machinery); sunk orchestra now lacking its balustrade and concealed by a fussy modern staircase. The grid and fly floor (on PS) are concealed by a false ceiling, but still accessible via an external staircase. Remains of stage gas intake and old electric lighting control panel; 38 sets of hemp lines. Dressing rooms backstage converted to lavatories.

An interesting and unusual building of uncertain status which should be fully researched. A superficial investigation shows that it was well established with m. & d. licence by 1913 and applied successfully for a stage plays licence. Us-ed as a cinema from c.1914. At the time of inspection (1978) it was well preserved and restorable in all its parts, but a proposal to divide into squash courts and insert a sauna into the stage area was under consideration.   J.E.

Players' Theatre

173 and 174 Hungerford Arches, Villiers Street, W.C.2.
City of Westminster.
(Formerly: The Arches P.H.; Gatti's Arches or Charing Cross Music Hall from 1867; Arena cinema 1910-23; Forum cinema 1928 to World War II; Players' from 1946).
1867, converted from railway arches, architect unknown.
Club Theatre/Music Hall.

The exterior makes no visual impact, being no more than the sparsely detailed filling of two railway arches. Set back from the general shop-frontage line in Villiers Street behind a vestigial garden.

Although the auditorium is apparently in the same position as the Gatti's Hall, it has clearly been much modified. Floor rakes sharply to the 'shelf' (so called; an upper flat-floored level of seating) with a bar behind. Small buffet on prompt side flank. There is no gallery. The tunnel roof is concealed by a striped velarium. The proscenium is an architectural mishap. Supper room adjoins entrance foyer. Proscenium 18ft. wide. No flying. All scenery got in through auditorium. The capacity now is 300.

Playhouse

★ ★ ★ disused

Northumberland Avenue, W.C.2.
City of Westminster.
(Formerly: Royal Avenue Theatre 1882-1912).
1882, F. H. Fowler and Hill.
1905, interior remodelled by Blow & Billerey.
1907, Blow & Billerey (rebuilt internally after part of Charing Cross Station collapsed on building during previous reconstruction) with Mortimer Menpes advising on interior decoration.
Closed.

On an important site at the bottom of Craven Street, alongside the railway bridge and visible from the Embankment. The external elevations in Portland stone, curving round the corner of Villiers Street, are those of the 1882 theatre, but now lacking the figure sculpture above the parapet. Marie Tempest's name is stil just legible on the brick flank facing Platform 6, Charing Cross Station.

Excellent foyers, etc. lead to a magnificently uninhibited auditorium in French taste, a design of flowing curves with fine plasterwork and painting. Deep proscenium whose splayed architectural frame embraces two tiers of boxes with spirited female terms carrying the upper tier. The proscenium jambs sweep into a depressed basket arch. The curving walls of the auditorium similarly sweep up into pendentives carrying a dome. The dome, pendentive-roundels and large elliptical-headed wall panels are all painted. Serpentine balcony fronts in two tiers with slender balustraded upper box fronts, the upper balcony terminating abruptly against the wall paintings. Extensive basement accommodation with good headroom below auditorium. (This is the result of raising the 1905/7 auditorium by about 5ft. above the level of the 1882 auditorium. Proscenium 26ft. 6ins. wide. Stage depth 26ft. Capacity approximately 620. There is a splendidly preserved complex of sub-stage machinery, second in importance in London only to Her Majesty's, with grave, bridges, thunderrun, etc. all more or less intact.

This outstanding theatre should be restored to public use as quickly as possible with minimum disturbance to its architectural character. In 1981 restoration properties were submitted (architects M.A.P. with Theatre Projects Constultants Limited).
Listed Grade II.   J.E.

Queen's Theatre

★

Shaftesbury Avenue, W.1.
City of Westminster.
1908, W. G. R. Sprague.
1959, reconstructed by Bryan Westwood with (Sir) Hugh Casson.
Theatre.

Playhouse   GLC

153

Designed with the Globe as part of a single compostion, originally with closely similar architectural treatment to the two corners of the block, but now, since thre partial rebuilding of the Queen's after war damage, startlingly contrasting.

No doubt in 1957 the restoration of the facade to its original appearance seemed impractical and the substitution of a glass curtain wall, revealing the foyers and bars to the passer-by (and the passer-by to the foyers and bars), was seen as exciting and new. Now it looks outdated, un-theatre-like and even heartless. Flank and rear elevations original; red brick with repetitive stone trim.

The Sprague auditorium has been remodelled but much of the original design and detail has survived. Two 'cantilevered' balconies, altered boxes, square proscenium with coved sounding board and domed ceiling, all with good plaster ornament.

Proscenium 30ft. wide. Stage depth is 35ft. Capacity is now 983.

Listed Grade II.   J.E.

Queen's   *GLC*

Railway Tavern

Plumstead Road, S.E.18.
Greenwich.
probably 1867 and possibly by J. O. Cook Sr.
Derelict 1980 and demolition probably imminent.

Professional status uncertain. Capacity 140 in 1892. Archtecturally unelaborate concert room, irregular in shape with flat floor, simple stage, rooflight, fireplace. Entered through a bar.

D.H. 641.   J.E.

Richmond Theatre
★ ★ ★

Little Green.
(Richmond upon Thames).
(Formerly: Royal Hippodrome, Prince of Wales Theatre, Theatre Royal and Opera House).
1899, Frank Matcham.
Theatre.

Of outstanding importance as the most completely preserved Matcham theatre

Richmond Theatre

Victor Glasstone

in Greater London and one of his most satisfying interiors.

Symmetrical red brick and terracotta facade; twin towers with cupolas; Baroque centre piece with arched entrance below a scrolled pediment. The only architectural mishap is the self-conscious tented entrance canopy of the 1950's. It should be removed to the accompaniment of dancing in the streets. Magnificent auditorium with rich plasterwork in 'Elizabethan' style; two balconies; marble proscenium arch with massive key panel; proscenium flanked by elaborately draped truncated columns carrying figures of Tragedy and Comedy; fine domed ceiling wth relief plaster ornament of scenes from Shakespeare plays.

Well cared for. The entrance vestibule has recently been restored to a form close to its original appearance.

Proscenium width 26ft. 9ins. Stage depth is 31ft. Present capacity is 919.

Listed Grade II ★   J.E.

(Royal) Brunswick Theatre

Wellclose Square, E.
(actually in Ensign St.) Tower Hamlets.
1828, Stedman Whitwell.
Bollards only.

The theatre fell down during rehearsals immediately after the completion of the structure, but a row of iron bollards, each bearing the monogram RBT remains in Ensign Street to define the precise position of the theatre frontage. It is included here because the bollards are listed.

Listed Grade II.   J.E.

Royal Clarence Music Hall

★ disused

College Approach,
Greenwich.
1830's, architect unknown.
1875, altered, architect unknown.
Recording/Film Studio.

Formerly attached to the Admiral Hardy public house, adjoining to the east. The concert room was formed c.1839 within the existing building (part of the Greenwich Market complex of 1829-36 by J. Kay). It is a large room at first floor level over the north entrance to the market. It is possible that it was improved in the

Royal Clarence   *GLC*

mid-1840's and it was certainly completely refurbished in 1875. By 1888 it was 'principally used for dancing but occasionally as a music hall'. Finally closed 1890 and subsequently divided from the public house.

A rectangular room approached by a staircase from the street. There is a balcony at one end. Much overlaid by acoustic linings, etc. but it is said that the shallow tunnel-vaulted ceiling and plaster *bombé* balcony front are still more or less intact, although concealed. A report of 1875 refers to a 'new stage. . .proscenium. . .balcony and private boxes'. It appears that the boxes were under the balcony. The doorway on the landing formerly linking the hall with the pub is still visible.

Probably unique in London and an extremely rare survival of an 1830's/40's concert room. It should be thoroughly investigated with a view to possible restoration to 1875 form. Capacity would probably be around 150 to modern seating standards.

Listed Grade II (as part of the Market Complex) D.H. 678.   J.E.

Royal Court

★

Sloane Square, S.W.1.
Royal Borough of Kensington and Chelsea.
1888, Walter Emden and Bertie Crewe.
1952, interior reconstructed by R. Cromie. 1956, altered.
1980, altered by Rod Ham.
Theatre.

Built to replace the earlier Court Theatre (DH 181; this is D.H. 679) the present building was used as a cinema 1935-40 and closed (after bombing) 1940-52. The fine red brick, moulded brick and stone facade in a free Italianate style, facing Sloane Square, was undamaged although there have been alterations around the entrance. The auditorium is unremarkable, but it has a pleasing and intimate atmosphere which made it a very suitable venue for the success of the English Stage Company.

Proscenium width is 21ft. Stage depth is approximately 24ft. 6ins.

Capacity now 442.

Listed Grade II.   J.E./I.M./V.G.

Royal Opera House

★ ★ ★

Bow Street, W.C.2.
City of Westminster.
Previously known as Theatre Royal.
Covent Garden and the Royal Italian Opera (from 1847) with variations from time to time.
1731-2, Edward Shepherd.
1782, auditorium remodelled by John Inigo Richards.
1792, extensively reconstructed by Henry Holland.
1809, entirely new theatre built by Sir Robert Smirke.
1847, auditorium entirely rebuilt by Benedict Albano.
1858, entirely new theatre built by E. M. Barry.
1899 & 1902, stage entirely reconstructed and minor alterations to

auditorium by Edwin O. Sachs.
1964, amphitheatre altered by Peter Moro.
1981, major addition by Gollins, Melvin and Ward.
Opera House.

The present building is essentially that designed by Edward M Barry in 1857 and opened in 1858 (together with the adjoining Floral Hall, opened 1860) but with some sculptural work salvaged from Smirke's theatre. A full and authoritative architectural account is contained in **Survey of London** vol. XXXV.

The Opera House is an imposing monument in E. M. Barry's Roman Renaissance manner. Although it has always been seen (until recent demolitions around Covent Garden Market) from narrow streets in foreshortened views, its impact is considerable. On the Bow Street front a tall hexastyle Corinthian portico is raised on a rusticated base, formed by the enclosure of the original *porte cochére*. The facade incorporates two magnificent bas reliefs by Flaxman and statues by Rossi from the 1809 theatre. The upper level of the portico now contains a glazed conservatory, extending the crush bar.

The interior is superb. 'Few would dissent from the view that the Royal Opera House has the most beautiful auditorium in Great Britain . . .' (**Survey of London** 1970).

It was designed (as were many earlier theatres) to be readily convertible to ballroom, assembly hall and exhibition hall use. The well of the auditorium (originally pit and pit stalls) is enclosed by the lowest box tier, above which there are three horseshoe tiers of balconies cantilevered forward from their supporting iron columns, plus an amphitheatre-gallery. Nearly all the old box-divisions, with their twisted gilt shafts, have now been removed and the benched amphitheatre slips and gallery have been rearranged (1964) as a single, spaciously-seated tier extending back from the top balcony. The horseshoe curve of the main balcony fronts is governed by a semicircle of the same radius as the circular saucer-domed ceiling, which is supported on four elliptical arches and pendentives, the arch on the west side enclosing a parabolic sounding board above the stage, which formerly had an apron of the same depth as the recess so formed.

The plaster ornament is rich and robust. The proscenium has a coved frame with gilt twisted shafts on either side, which were originally designed to move, thereby widening the scenic opening. The sounding board carries a modelled relief of symbolic figures. The tier fronts are of *bombé* section, enriched with trellis and foliage and divided into bays by winged female terms. The saucer dome has a wide margin band and panelled sectors with a central oculus.

Barry's splendid grand staircase and entrance hall, crush bar and Royal suite have been altered but, as with the auditorium, the original design has not been seriously damaged.

The 1858 theatre completely abandon- the old scene groove system, all back scenes being flown. The stage was completely reconstructed between 1899 and 1902 by Edwin O. Sachs with a flat stage surface and with elaborate metal machinery. It is the most extensive system of sub-stage machinery of the kind existing in London. Extensive counterweight system installed in 1902 and still working satisfactory in 1981. In 1972 there could also be seen the remains of old wooden machinery, including drums and shafts on the grid and traces of a thunder run (GLC Survey).

Proscenium 44ft. 3ins wide, 76ft. 9ins deep. Capacity is 2,158.

On the departure of the Covent Garden market in the 1970's the entire site enclosed by James Street, Bow Street, Russell Street and the Piazza was acquired on behalf of the R.O.H. Sketch plans included a second auditorium to the south, the reabilitation of the Floral Hall and the building of a new Royal Ballet School. Finally, it was decided that Phase One, at a cost of £8 million, should be an elongation of Barry's building in similar style (architects Gollins, Melvin and Ward) to James Street. This will accommodate new rehearsal facilities as well as new dressing rooms to replace those built in 1933. Opening date is 1982.

No brief summary can do justice to this building. Covent Garden occupies a key position in the history of the theatre and the opera in England. The theatre shares with Drury Lane the distinction of not being subject to either the Lord Chamberlain's or the Greater London Council's Licencing control. Its right to present theatrical entertainment derives from the Royal Patent conferred by Charles II on Davenant in 1662. This patent, after many vicissitudes, came to rest on the present site. The document itself seems to have been lost, but the fact that Gye re-opened his opera house in 1858 without a licence is evidence that the Lord Chamberlain accepted that the authority of the patent attached to this site.

The exterior is later in date than Drury Lane, the Haymarket, the Lyceum and the main shell of the Old Vic, but the Royal Opera House is the oldest complete theatre building executed to a single design now standing more or less intact in London. Its architectural importance cannot be overrated.
Listed Grade I.   J.E./I.M.

Royal Victor Music Hall

Old Ford Road, Bethnal Green.
Tower Hamlets.
1867, architect unknown.
1890, reconstructed, architect unknown.
Disused.

A large (and long disused) brick and stucco Italianate pub at the bend of the Old Ford Road, and immediately alongside the Regent's Canal.
The first concert room occupied the greater part of an upper floor. Later (c.1890) a small plain music hall, rectangular, with a rooflight, was added at the rear. This still exists. Closed 1903.
See D.H. 697.   J.E.

Ruby

Clapham.
Wandsworth.
(Formerly Imperial Cinema and said to have been built as the Grand Hall of Varieties or Muntz's Music Hall).
Date and authorship unknown.
Cinema (now closed).

A plain rectangular room of 'cinévariety' form, with pilastered walls and ceiling divided by corniced beams; single plain-fronted balcony. Intention to redevelop site announced late 1978.
                    J.E.

Sadlers Wells

pre-1914 fragment only
Rosebery Avenue, E.C.1.
Islington.
1683, (a wooden Music House.)
1765, rebuilt in stone by Thomas Rosoman, builder.
1879, interior remodelled by C. J. Phipps.
1901, partly remodelled by Bertie Crewe.
1931, rebuilt, F. G. M. Chancellor (of Matcham & Co.).
1959, proscenium and other alterations by Martin Card and Hope Bagenal.
Theatre & Opera House.

Royal Opera House   *Victor Glasstone*

The present theatre is, to all appearances, essentially Chancellor's cheerless 1931 design and therefore not eligible for this survey, but some parts of the earlier theatres were incorporated and a detailed examination of the lowest parts of the internal structure would be worth undertaking. It seems to have been listed for its archaeology rather than its architecture. Listed Grade II. J.E.

St Martins
★ ★ ★
West Street, W.C.2.
Camden.
1916, W. G. R. Sprague.
Theatre.
Although post-1914 and therefore not strictly qualifying for inclusion here, the St. Martin's Theatre must be noted because it was planned before 1914 and should have been completed at the same time as the Ambassadors Theatre q.v. of 1913. The two theatres were separate ventures but they were designed as companion buildings and stand on either side of Tower Court. Further research is needed to establish whether the executed design was modified in any way during the three years delay in building.
St Martin's has a rather more imposing facade than Ambassadors; ashlar faced in five bays with giant attached Ionic columns through the upper three storeys, supporting an entablature and parapet. Plain modern canopy over the entrance. Good foyer.
The prettiness of the Ambassadors auditorium gives no warning of the classical sobriety to come at the St. Martin's. Sprague's St. Martin's auditorium abandons completely the exuberant displays of fibrous plaster work which typified theatre design (including Sprague's own designs) in previous decades. The style was described as 'Georgian'. Much polished hardwood. Walnut dados. Flat side walls with imposing fluted Doric columns, rising from pedestals at first balcony level to carry a correct entablature with triglyphs and mutules, continuing over the rectangular proscenium. Two balconies, their fronts differently curved, both with turned hardwood balustrades. Glazed dome in ceiling.
Proscenium 26ft. wide. Stage depth is approximately 26ft. (raking back wall). At time of 1973 GLC survey the stage had a fine set of original wooden machinery, almost complete but marred by the insertion of a substage control room, obliterating trip levers and slider joists. Two single traps and grave trap. Two bridges in excellent condition. No

St. Martin's   GLC

sloats. Paddle levers on OP side. Timber winches between posts. Twenty eight sets of counterweights plus hemp lines. Capacity is now 550.
Listed Grade II. J.E.

Savoy Theatre
Strand, W.C.2.
City of Westminster.
1881, C. J. Phipps.
1903, altered by A. B. Jackson.
1929, auditorium and interior totally remodelled by Frank A Tugwell and Basil Ionides.
Theatre.
Although the 1929 reconstruction was total internally, much of the external shell remained from the original building and the character of Phipps's elevations can be seen at the rear (originally the entrance facade).
The present Art Déco interior is one of the most memorable of its period and attracted praise when it was opened.
Listed Grade II. J.E.

Shaftesbury Theatre
★ ★
Shaftesbury Avenue, Holborn
(near New Oxford Street).
Camden.
(Formerly: New Princes and Princes).
1911, Bertie Crewe.
Theatre.
The theatre occupies a prominent corner site and is viewed across a wide road junction. The elevations, however, are somewhat reticent in treatment and the corner tower makes a punctuation of unmonumental character.
Good foyers. Spacious auditorium with two cantilevered balconies, the fronts varied in both form and decoration. Uninhibited plaster decoration, robust rather than elegant, but producing a splendidly theatrical atmosphere. Rectangular ceiling with enriched cove and

St. Martin's   GLC

Shaftesbury *GLC*

cornice and circular flat-domed centre. Segmental proscenium arch with figure reliefs in spandrels over. Bow-fronted boxes paired in two tiers and magnificently framed by giant Ionic columns rising from heavy console

Shaftesbury

brackets and carrying an entablature, the whole composition crowned by a semi-circular arch. In the arch tympanum a sculptural group is set over each upper box.

Designed as a melodrama house this theatre has had a varied history and has been dogged by misfortune in recent years. After the run of 'Hair' (1968-1973) its survival appeared to be in doubt. A ceiling fall in the auditorium in 1973 necessitated closure and seemed likely to lead to the demolition of the theatre. It was then, however, added to the statutory list and the ceiling was eventually restored and the theatre reopened. The present colour scheme is a dull overall white. When the theatre was inspected in 1981 the auditorium was disfigured by temporary ventilation trunking serving a range of projectors. Proscenium 32ft. wide. Stage depth approximately 20ft. Capacity is now 1,305.

Listed Grade II *J.E./D.C.*

Shepherd's Bush Empire *GLC*

Shepherd's Bush Empire
★ ★ disused
Shepherds Bush.
Hammersmith.
1903, Frank Matcham.
B.B.C. Television Studio.

An unusual Matcham design. Roughcast elevations with terracotta dressings. Asymmetrical, the centre with four-bay arched entrance (now much obscured by a particularly insensitive B.B.C. sign); to right, a taller bay with segmental gable and beyond that a broad, splayed return; to left, a stocky tower with little windows and a lively baroque top stage, lantern and cupola, now lacking some ornament. Even in its present condition the facade to the Green is an interesting example of the Art Nouveau spirit in Matcham's work. The interior is altered and the auditorium has been overlaid and obscured, but the painted-out upper parts seem to be completely intact and show that it was a theatre of some magnificence and could be restored. It should probably be listed.

Proscenium approximately 30ft. wide. Capacity if reseated to modern standards approximately 1,000. D.H. 736.
J.E.

Strand
★ ★ ★
Aldwych, W.C.2.
City of Westminster.
(Formerly: The Waldorf (1905-9) and also known briefly as the Whitney (1911)).
1905, W. G. R. Sprague, auditorium decoration by Van Hooydonk.
Theatre.

Built as part of the Aldwych/Kingsway development and designed as a pair to the contemporary Aldwych Theatre. Elevations closely similar but not identical to its pair.

Auditorium with rich plaster ornament, described as 'in the Louis XIV style'. Circular ceiling with deep bracketed cove and allegorical paintings. Three balconies, the top two set back behind the flat curve of the lowest (dress circle) and the top one following the circular curve of the ceiling. Bold plaster relief with figures over square proscenium. Two boxes on either side (not level with balconies) framed by Ionic pilasters rising from huge console brackets. Boxes formerly at back of dress circle removed by 1930. Colour scheme modern and insipid, but the ceiling paintings give some idea of its original richness. Second balcony front disfigured with lights.
Proscenium 31ft. 6ins. wide. Flat Stage 33ft. 6ins. deep. Almost entirely hemp worked. Present capacity is 927.
Listed Grade II.   J.E.

Stratford Theatre Royal
★ ★

Angel Lane/Gerry Raffles Square, E.15.
Newham.
1884, J. G. Buckle.
1887 & 1891, additions, Buckle.
1902, minor alterations by Matcham.
Theatre.

The modern setting of the building suggests that it was grudgingly excluded from the massive clearances which preceded the Stratford town centre development, but there are welcome signs that it has now become an object of civic pride. In metropolitan terms it is a rare and precious survival and it is an excellent working theatre. Major restoration proposals in preparation 1979-80.
The Royal is the only London surburban theatre with a complete pre-cantilever (hence pillared) auditorium. Designed by the author of **Theatre Construction and Maintenance** (published in 1888, incorporating more extensive work done by Buckle and Woodrow for a series of articles in **Building and Engineering Times;** Woodrow later became Sachs's partner and collaborator in **Modern Opera Houses and Theatres**). Stratford Theatre Royal seems to be Buckle's on-

Strand   GLC

ly surviving work. Although designed as a suburban theatre, with a distinctly provincial character, it achieved national siginficance as the home of 'Theatre Workshop' from 1953 and was the birth-place of many Littlewood/Workshop 'originals'.
The external architectural treatment is offhand in the extreme and its weakness is emphasized by the fact that it now no longer forms part of a street but is left architecturally unsupported on the edge of a modern shopping precinct.

GLC

Stratford Theatre Royal

The auditorium, by contrast, is pleasing and efficient, with good sighting from all parts of the house. Shallow in depth. Two balconies supported on cast iron columns; delicate plaster ornament to balcony fronts and ceiling. Box fronts have arched heads with pendant centres. Enriched architrave to proscenium with scrolly cartouche and festooned frieze over.
The plan of the building reflects the manner in which the site was assembled and additions were made. The main vestibule extends along one side of the auditorium and leads to a long bar projecting to the right, alongside the stage - a mystifying but not displeasing arrangement.
Proscenium 23ft. wide. Large stage 42ft. deep. Raked. Hemp worked. Two-piece safety curtain. Capacity is now 499.
Listed Grade II ★   J.E.

Talk of the Town
★ facade only.

Cranbourne Street, W.1.
City of Westminster.
(Formerly: London Hippodrome).
1900, Frank Matcham.
1909, altered by Matcham.
1958, auditorium reconstructed.
Theatre.

Originally built for Edward Moss as a hippodrome for circuses and water spectacles. The 1909 works enlarged the stage and advanced the proscenium to suit if for variety and (from 1912) revue.

The building occupies an island site with principal elavations to Charing Cross Road and Cranbourne Street and contains, in addition to the theatre, ground floor shops on the main frontages, with Cranbourne Mansions in the upper storeys. Elevations in red sandstone in a free classical style, the bays divided by giant Ionic pilasters supported on elongated brackets which occupy the full height of the first floor, the pilasters rising through the second and third floors to carry a weakly accented fourth floor attic storey and a crowning balustrade. Most bays have canted windows rising from terms and linked by a balustrade at second floor level. The corner bay is framed by giant Ionic engaged columns carrying entablature blocks and an open pediment, above which rises a short but floridly detailed tower with a skeletal iron dome crowned by a lively sculptured group of a chariot with rearing horses. Giant letters with the name of the theatre on the Little Newport Street front. In 1958 its old iron and glass entrance canopy was replaced by one of no interest and the corner bay was obliterated by a gross illuminated sign.

Matcham's gorgeous auditorium has been mutilated beyond recall, but some traces of its original character can be seen above the 1958 suspended ceiling. Listed Grade II.   J.E.

Tottenham Palace   *GLC*

Tottenham Palace
★ ★
Tottenham High Road.
Haringey.
1908, Wylson & Long (Oswald Wylson).
Bingo.

A large theatre - capacity given as 3,000 (including standing) in 1912. Restrained symmetrical entrance facade in red brick and stone; a well-considered composition with Ionic pilasters and pediments. The Ionic theme is carried consistently through the foyer and auditorium.

Auditorium with 2 balconies; good plaster decoration with details of 18th century character; gilded figures of the Muses flanking the proscenium.

Proscenium c.30ft. wide. Stage when built 40ft. deep. Present capacity if reseated to modern standards likely to be 1,500 to 1,800.

The building looks cared for and the conversion to bingo (principally the introduction of a stepped level floor in the stalls) has been achieved with no significant architectural loss.

Now the only complete example in London of a theatre by the architects who rebuilt the Oxford Music Hall in 1893 (dem.), reconstructed the Blackpool Winter Garden auditorium, 1897, designed the Brixton Empress of 1898 (gutted) and reconstructed the interior of the London Pavilion 1900 (gutted). One of the few surviving big suburban variety palaces and one of London's most important unlisted theatres.

Twentieth Century Playhouse
Westbourne Grove, Notting Hill.
Kensington & Chelsea.
(Also known as Victoria Hall, Bijou Theatre).
1863, architect unknown.
1892, altered.
Warehouse and shop.

Entrance pedimented, in a stucco-fronted terrace. Foyers, etc. altered. Auditorium a rectangular room with pilastered walls and brackets supporting ribs to tunnel vaulted ceiling with roof light. Balcony across one end. Basket arched proscenium flanked by fluted Corinthian pilasters. See also D.H. 823.
Listed Grade II.   J.E.

Uxbridge Theatre Royal
pre-1914 fragment only
32 Chapel Street, Uxbridge.
Hillingdon.
(Formerly: Wildman's Theatre and with address sometimes given as Windsor Street).
1869, architect unknown.
Engineering Workshop.

Proposed in 1854 but probably not completed until 1868 (rated from 1869). It was built for Walter Edwin who also controlled a theatre in Northampton. It had a reputed capacity of 365, with balcony and 'gallery'. Not rated as a theatre after 1878 but said to have been

Talk of the Town   *Victor Glasstone*

Talk of the Town   *GLC*

used occasionally until World War 1. Mutilated beyond recognition. The remains of this building are now so fragmentary as to be indecipherable to any but the most inquiring investigator. Noted here because it seems to be the only surviving trace in Greater London of the very smallest kind of cheap purpose-built country-town theatre of the mid-Victorian period.   J.E.

Vaudeville

★ facade only

Strand, W.C.2.
City of Westminster.
1870, Phipps.
1887, altered by Phipps.
1891, rebuilt by Phipps.
1926, rebuilt by Robert Atkinson, (but the facade, at least, dates from the 1891 works.)
Theatre.

The stone facade to the Strand is four storeys in height, five windows wide, canopy over entrances, balustraded front to arcaded first floor loggia (recently glazed) and rather domestic-looking windows with thin Italianate detail above. Parapet originally had central panelled blocking crowned by pediment. Atkinson's Maiden Lane facade is built in yellow brick and stone with a big stone Venetian window with fan lunette, all contained under a brick arch.

The auditorium is rectangular, two balconies with neo-Adam ornament. Although largely Atkinson's work (1926), the cove and ceiling date from Phipps's 1891 building.

Proscenium 23ft. 9ins wide; stage about 29ft. 6ins deep. Some wooden machinery above and below stage, including grave and small bridge in restorable condition and thunder run stored on OP fly floor in 1972.

Capacity is now 657.

For a full account of building history of the site see **Survey of London,** Vol. XXXVI p. 243 *et seq.*
Listed Grade II.   J.E.

Vaudeville   *GLC*

Victoria Palace   *GLC*

Victoria Palace

★ ★ ★

Victoria Street.
City of Wesminster.
(Built to replace the old Royal Standard Music Hall).
1911, Frank Matcham.
Built as a variety theatre for Alfred Butt and used for variety and musical productions for almost all of its 70 years.

A distinctive building with a main entrance block faced with white patent stone. Symmetrical classical facade; the lower three storeys channelled with a modern canopy over the entrances and a central giant arch; above this is an open loggia with Ionic columns, flanked by festooned oval windows. The elevation is crowned by an entablature with a central pediment behind which rises a baroque tower with pedestalled Ionic columns and a dome, originally crowned by a figure of Pavlova.

Despite some alterations, the auditorium is splendid. Two balconies with heavily enriched cartouches and consoles and two tiers of three boxes on either side (the lower tier stepped). Architraved proscenium. Domed ceiling. The manner in which the junction is formed between the upper box fronts and the top balcony demonstrates that any architectural problem can be solved with confidence and fibrous plaster. Gloomy red colour scheme. Fine foyer. Proscenium 35ft. 3ins wide. Stage 31ft. deep. Capacity is 1,565.
Listed Grade II.   J.E.

Victoria Palace   *GLC*

Wilton's Music Hall

★ ★ ★ disused

Graces Alley, Wellclose Square, E.
Tower Hamlets.
(also known as Prince of Denmark PH
by 1830, the (old) Mahogany Bar
by c. 1839, Albion Saloon by 1843,
Wilton's (Grand) Music Hall by 1853
and Frederick's Royal Palace of
Varieties 1874).
1859, Jacob Maggs (replacing old concert room).
1878, reconstructed after fire probably
by J. Buckley Wilson.
Undergoing restoration 1981.

Originally concealed by surrounding
buildings and still attached to its
original, progressively enlarged, parent
pub. It has, therefore, no external elevations of any consequence. In this it is
typical of its kind and period.
Auditorium, entered through paved lobby (formerly yard of pub) is an
astonishing survival. Big rectangular
room with apse at back, simple arched
proscenium and high stage (which had
replaced an original apsidal platform by
the 1870's). Single balcony on three
sides, supported on extraordinary
helical-twisted cast iron columns;
balcony has *bombé* plaster front. Side
walls with paired arches above balcony
supported on alternating piers and ornamental brackets. Elliptical vaulted
ceiling with ornamental ribs and
skylight. An unelaborate but profoundly
evocative room.
This is the most important early music
hall building now extant in London and
the only surviving representative of the
big 'new generation' halls of the 1850's
modelled on the success of the second
Canterbury (1854), Evans's New (Supper
Room) Music Hall (1856) and Weston's
(1857).
It was for many years in mission hall
use and subsequently served as a rag

warehouse until it came into the
possession of the present owners, the
Greater London Council, in 1966. It has
stood disused since then and its condition gives cause for some concern, but
the GLC has agreed to lease it to a body
which will undertake its physical
restoration and return it to public use.
Its rarity is such that failure cannot be
contemplated. Archaeologically as well
as architecturally of outstanding interest.
Listed Grade II ★   J.E.

Wimbledon Theatre

★ ★

Wimbledon Broadway.
Merton.
1910, Cecil Masey & Roy Young
(perhaps following a 1908 design by
Frank H. Jones.).
Theatre.

On a prominent corner site. The brick
exterior is not of outstanding quality
but has some townscape value. The
winged figure which formerly surmounted the dome over the corner entrance is now lacking.
Good entrance foyer with Corinthian
columns. Well-preserved but somewhat
cavernous auditorium with eclectic
plaster ornament. Two balconies with
ornamental iron-balustraded fronts,
very unusual in Britain, but common in
Spain and Portugal. Segmental proscenium arch set in a deep recess with
an arched sounding board spanning
between boxes framed by Corinthian
columns carrying Baroque segmental
pediments.
Bodly modelled reclining figures in proscenium spandrels. Shallow, semi-
domed, ribbed ceiling.
Proscenium 34ft. wide. Stage 40ft.
deep. Present capacity is 1,700.
Listed Grade II.   J.E./V.G.

Wimbledon Theatre   GLC

Wood Green Empire

pre-1914 fragment only

Tottenham High Road.
Haringey.
1912, Frank Matcham.
Submerged in other buildings.

Largely demolished in 1970, but a
recognizable fragment of the facade remains, i.e. the top storey only of the
centre block, with its tall hipped near-
pyramidal roof with a dormer on the
front, but now lacking its crowning turret and cupola. On either side of this are
two three-storey two-bay wings, brick
with stone dressings, each crowned by
a little tower with ogee roof and finial.
                                          J.E.

Wyndham's

★ ★ ★

Charing Cross Road, W.1.
City of Westminster.
1899, W. G. R. Sprague.
Theatre.

Backs on to the later Albery Theatre q.v.
Principal elevation, stone in free
classical style with a distincly French
flavour. Three major bays; the wide centre bay with *oeil-de-boeuf* windows at
first floor and arched balconied windows with shell tympana to second
floor, set between pilasters carrying a
rich pediment contained in a sheer attic
with crowning balustrade; the outer
bays narrower, subdivided by piers carrying term figure sculpture at attic level.
The auditorum is one of Sprague's most
delightful inventions. Extravagantly
decorated in Louis XVI style. Two curving 'cantilever' balconies with prettily
painted panels. The gallery is the rearward extension of the upper tier. Boxes
with bowed fronts in three storeys (the
lowest at dress circle level) paired, with
semicircular arches at the two upper
level and set between pilasters carried

Wilton's Music Hall   GLC

on massive brackets. The proscenium was designed as a complete picture frame with an elegantly enriched architrave, above which is a composition of allegorical winged figures in the round, carrying festoons and supporting framed portraits. The elaborate festooned house curtain was replaced in the late 60's by a new curtain which faithfully reproduced the original design, a rare and costly gesture by the considerate Albery management whose forebears built the theatre. Magnificent circular ceiling painted in the manner of Boucher. The saloon and public foyers, etc. are in complementary style.

Proscenium 27ft. 3ins. wide. Stage 26ft. deep. Minor remains of old machinery. Capacity is now 759.

This is one of London's finest theatres, well preserved and cared for. The paintings have recently been restored. Listed Grade II. J.E./I.M.

Wyndham's   *Victor GLasstone*

Wyndham's   *Victor Glasstone*

Londonderry,
Northern Ireland

Artillery Lane Theatre
pre-1914 fragment only
1789, architect unknown.
Part of shell incorporated in Church of Ireland Diocesan office.

Long Eaton,
Derbyshire

Palace
Queen Street.
1897, architect unknown
Motor repair shop.

1897, architect unknown.
Motor repaire shop.
Opened as the Lyceum, name changed to Palace in 1906. Clad in corrugated iron sheeting and known locally as the "tin trunk". Interior gutted. C.B.

Longton,
Staffordshire

Empire Theatre
★ ★ ★ disused
Commerce Street.
1896, Frank Matcham.
Bingo.
A rebuilding of the Queen's Theatre (opened in 1887, architect John Taylor, and burnt in 1894). Renamed Empire in 1916. This theatre has a marvellous auditorium (capacity approx. 1,000 by present standards) one of the best, and least known, examples of Frank Matcham's surviving work. It is virtually intact apart from a hideous scheme of decoration and the trappings of bingo. There are three balconies with excellent sightlines - the first of six rows, the second of three rows, and a gallery above of nine rows (the front of which is in line with the rear of the second balcony). The balconies are set out on double curves and continue into short slips to meet superimposed stage boxes - two at first and one at second balcony level on either side, separated by short Corinthian pilasters with enriched shafts. The balcony and box fronts are encrusted with foliated scrolls, masks etc. The ceiling is rectangular with a slightly cambered border enriched by oval panels and masks, surrounding a circular centrepiece. The oval panels originally had paintings by Binns of Halifax, now obliterated. The proscenium (31ft. 6in. wide × 37ft. high) has a foliated frame, square-headed with rounded corners, and forms a splendidly imposing transition between auditorium and stage. The stage itself is unusually deep at 48ft., and retains its fly galleries and grid above a false ceiling.

The exterior is of little merit - in painted cast stone, the upper part and balustrade having been removed. The entrance is through an asymmetrically placed bay to the left, flanked by broad pilasters and surmounted by a flattened arch at third storey level. The conurbation of Stoke-on-Trent (population aporoximately 300,000), of which Longton is a part, is without a theatre capable of taking full size professional productions of opera, ballet, musicals, etc. The Empire, if refurbished, could readily satisfy this need, and a first class example of Victorian theatre architecture would be ensured of preservation.
Listed Grade II. C.B.

Loughborough,
Leicestershire

Sparrow Hill Theatre
pre-1914 fragment only
1822, architect unknown.
Shop.
In use until 1856. Plain exterior largely intact. Interior gone.

Lowestoft,
Suffolk
Hippodrome
★ facade only/disused
Battery Green Road.
1904, R. S. Cockrill.
1947, converted to theatre from circus by Brown & Marsh.
Bingo.
Elegant exterior with fine Art Nouveau terracotta panels and general detailing. The original interior held both a stage and a circus ring (in the French manner). The latter was removed during complete reconstruction as a very dull theatre in 1947. Remarkably, the very ornate original proscenium arch was retained.   E.G./D.F.C.

Marina Theatre
London Road North.
1897, R. F. Brett.
1901, reconstructed by E. Runtz.
1930, reconstructed as cinema.
Cinema.
Nothing recognizable remains of the old theatre following the extensive 1930 reconstruction.   C.B.

Sparrow's Nest Theatre
(Formerly: Sparrow's Nest Grand Pavilion).
1913.
Theatre.

Theatre Royal
Crown Street.
1827, architect unknown.
Community Centre.
In use as a theatre only until 1840. Interior completely altered, but the tall, elegant facade is largely original.
E.G./D.F.C.

Macclesfield,
Cheshire
Theatre Royal
Mill Street.
1811, architect unknown.
1875, largely rebuilt as Salvation Army Citadel.

Manchester
Greater
Manchester
Alhambra
Old Ashton Road, Openshaw.
1908, H. A. Turner.
Derelict.
Situated in a bleak suburb approximately 1½ miles from the city centre. Dull fan-shaped auditorium with one

balcony of 14 rows and one box at each side with pilasters and canopy over, sharply angled away from the proscenium. Flat ceiling. Fly tower with a shallow range of dressing rooms framed-up on three floors inside the rear wall. Brick exterior with terracotta dressings in a vaguely Tudor style. Theatre entrance through a narrow central pavilion originally surmounted by a square dome, of which only the metal framework survives. Flanking shops with straight gables and mullioned windows.   C.B.

Hulme Hippodrome
★ ★ ★ disused
1901, J. J. Alley.
Bingo.
Opened as the Grand Junction Theatre. Renamed the Hippodrome c.1905. A splendid music hall which has survived intact, despite being standed in a desolate landscape of concrete blocks of flats, approximately 1 mile from the city centre. Built immediately alongside the Hulme Playhouse (1902). They share the same completely plain brick elevations, although the Hippodrome is at present swathed in plastic-coated metal strip. It is an extraordinary experience to leave the world of concrete and tarmac, and to pass through this anonymous exterior into the riot of gilded Rococo plasterwork inside the magnificent auditorium (capacity approximately 1,200 by present standards). The basic design is very like the Playhouse next door, but apart from this and other, now demolished, theatres designed by Alley for the Broadhead circuit, the concept is quite unlike any other contemporary theatre or music hall. Unusually spacious foyer with delicate cast iron fretted balcony around four sides, the whole giving the effect of a mid-19th century concert room. In the auditorium there are two balconies -the upper one of eight straight rows spanning directly between the side walls, the lower one of nine straight rows in the centre, and side arms of four straight rows parallel with the side walls, diminishing to two. The ends are divided off to form a stage box on either side of the proscenium. Above each box is a further box, reached by a little staircase at the side of the balcony. The box and balcony fronts are very richly decorated with delicate Rococo plasterwork. The balconies are supported by iron columns with foliated capitals (some of them Gothic!). At the sides the columns are carried up from the balcony fronts to support the main ceiling which is coved and decorated with festoons at the sides and panelled in the centre. The proscenium (30ft.) is surprisingly formal, being flanked by giant fluted Ionic columns with an enriched straight entablature over, and a large central cartouche supported by *putti*. Stage depth 32ft., grid approximately 50ft. Bingo is probably the only viable use the theatre could have at present, and it seems entirely appropriate; providing an Aladdin's Cave into which the local people can retreat from their grim environment.
Listed Grade II.   C.B.

Hulme Playhouse
★ ★ disused
(Formerly: Hulme Hippodrome, Grand Junction Theatre).
1902, J. J. Alley.
B.B.C. Studio.
Opened as the Hippodrome. Renamed Junction Theatre c.1905, and Playhouse in 1951. Paired with the Hulme Hippodrome and, although smaller (approximately 900 seats), the design of the auditorium is very similar, with two straight balconies. As at the Hippodrome the first balcony (here six rows in centre), returns along the sides with four rows diminishing to two. Unlike the Hippodrome, however, the upper balcony also has slips (of one row) which run along the side walls directly to the proscenium. Again the balconies and their slips are supported by iron columns, although here, despite the fact that the rest of the plasterwork is Baroque, the capitals are all of stiff-leaf Gothic foliage with polygonal tops - there is even a Gothic frieze and cornice on the inner face of the underside of the second balcony! The ceiling is again divided by beams on the lines on the columns; each section decorated by a lozenge-shaped panel. The proscenium (32ft.) is framed by giant fluted Ionic demi-columns supporting a straight entablature with a trophy of arms above. Stage depth 39ft., grid approximately 50ft. The plasterwork, although rich, lacks the vibrancy of that at the Hippodrome. The balcony fronts are decorated with large shell motifs between trophies of musical instruments. Various temporary partitions have been inserted sealing off the upper balcony etc.
Listed Grade II.   C.B.

Opera House
★ ★ disused
Quay Street.
1912, Farquharson, Richardson & Gill.
Bingo.
Opened as the New Theatre. Renamed New Queen's Theatre in 1915, and Opera House in 1920. Until its closure in 1979 the Opera House had been for a long period the principal touring theatre

Manchester, Opera House
Victor Glasstone Collection

of Manchester. The large auditoruim (2,070 seats) has two very deep, slightly-curved cantilevered balconies of approximately 550 seats each, which overhang to an excessive degree, producing poor sight-lines at the rear and a feeling of oppressiveness. The space between the balcony fronts and the stage is architecturally impressive, and displays an assured handling of Neo-Classical motifs. Flanking each side is a stack of superimposed boxes between pairs of giant fluted Corinthian columns. The upper boxes are a later insertion, following the removal of heavily draped canopies over the dress-circle boxes. The balcony and box fronts are formed of enriched iron balustrading. Spanning between the entablatures over the giant columns is a deep, coffered segmental arch which forms a tympanum above the high rectangular proscenium, filled by a large circular medallion flanked by winged gryphons. The proscenium is 37ft. wide, stage depth 42ft. and grid 57ft. The immensely high main ceiling, covering the full width and depth of the auditorium, is in the form of a coffered segmental tunnel vault. The theatre is ingeniously planned to take maximum advantage of the site, with the stalls below street level and the main entrance foyer formed within the void of the first balcony - the rear wall of the auditorium thus forming the wall of the street facade. This explains its relative blankness, there be-

Manchester, Opera House

ing just one row of small windows, which in fact light the void below the second balcony. The stuccoed facade is an impressive essay in the Neo-Classical manner of C. R. Cockerell (q.v. the Theatre Royal). Above the ground floor are five bays of Ionic demi-columns in the centre, with three bays of pilasters on either side. Above the three middle bays is large relief of a horse-drawn chariot, framed within a semicircular arch. This rises into a very broad pedimental gable carried on curv-

ed brackets. The theatre is at present used for Bingo - a sad fate, but it is difficult to see how the Opera House is to be returned to theatre service because, except for its facade, it is theatrically and architecturally inferior to the Palace on which so much money has been lavished.
Listed Grade II. C.B.

Palace Theatre
★ ★ ★

Oxford Street.
1891, Alfred Darbyshire & F. B. Smith.
1913, auditorium reconstructed by Bertie Crewe.
1953, Exterior refaced.
1979-80, Major refurbishing and stage increased in depth by Smith and Way. Theatre.

Darbyshire's splendidly opulent facade was obliterated by unprepossessing faience tiles in 1953. In his reconstruction of the theatre in 1913 Bertie Crewe retained the stage and the basic outside shell of the 1891 building. Although the stalls of Darbyshire's theatre were already below street level it does nevertheless appear that Crewe may have been influenced by the Opera House, Manchester, in the design of his auditorium (2,180 seats). Again there are two very large, slightly curved balconies of about 16 rows each, with the entrance foyer partly formed within

Manchester, Palace Theatre *Norman Edwards Associates*

Manchester, Theatre Royal
Victor Glasstone

the void of the first balcony. It also appears that Crewe may have been influenced by the Graeco-Roman style of the Opera House. His London Opera House (dem.) and Shaftesbury Theatre of 1911 were both in an extremely opulent version of the French Renaissance style whereas the Palace and also his Golders Green Hippodrome, both of which opened in December 1913, are distinctly Graeco-Roman. But Crewe was no academic, as were Richardson and his partners. He was, however, a well practised theatre architect and a comparison between the design of the Palace, and the Opera House will clearly show this. Partly as a result of its more robust interpretation of the Neo-Classical repertoire, but also due to the more satisfactory overall proportions of the auditorium, the Palace is vastly superior theatrically. A major contributory factor is the way the wide, though not too deep, auditorium relates to the wide proscenium (42ft. 6in.). The side walls are impressively articulated by ranges of boxes under curved and draped canopies, separated by giant fluted Ionic columns. The high ceiling has a central, coffered saucer-dome. Following threats of closure to both the Palace and the Opera House in 1978, the Palace was chosen in early 1979 as Manchester's large touring theatre for the future. The initiative was taken by Mr. Raymond Slater who purchased the building from Moss Empires. The Manchester Palace Theatre Trust was formed and a major restoration scheme costing £3 million put in hand (John Wyckham Assocates, consultants). This included increasing the depth of the stage from 37ft. to 57ft., raising the height of the grid by 12ft. to 77ft., new orchestra pit, new dressing rooms, and the auditorium and front-of-house redecorated to splendid effect (by Clare Ferraby). The theatre is now able to house adequately the largest touring opera, ballet, musicals and drama productions. The Palace reopened successfully in March 1981 and in May 1981 The Royal Opera staged a 3½ week season - their first in Britain outside London for 17 years.
Listed Grade II.   C.B.

Theatre Royal

★ ★ disused
Peter Street.
1845, Irwin & Chester.
1875, interior reconstruction by E. Salomons.
1921, internally reconstructed as a cinema.
Bingo.
The principal home of drama and opera in Manchester throughout the second half of the 19th century. In 1921 the stage (originally 50ft. deep) was removed and the space absorbed into a completely remodelled auditorium, to reopen as a cinema. The auditorium now has two balconies connected to an elaborate proscenium arch by narrow slips. The ornate ceiling has deeply coved sides and basket work enrichment reminiscent of Covent Garden. The stuccoed exterior of 1846 is virtually intact, however, and the facade is one of the finest examples of theatre architecture in Britain to have survived from the first half of the 19th century. Its Neo-Classicism would appear to derive from the influence of C. R. Cockerell's Bank of England branch office in King Street, Manchester, and possibly also from the Liverpool branch; both which were built in 1845. The theatre shares with these two buildings a broad pedimental gable into which rises a semi-circular arch. The arch in this case is open and supported by two giant Corinthian columns in-antis, which are carried down to ground level. Above the entrance, in the centre of the recessed wall behind the columns, is a statue of Shakespeare in a niche. The facade of the Theatre Royal, as well as Cockerell's banks, were also clearly a source of inspiration for Richardson and his partners when designing the front of the Opera House. The two side-elevations of the Theatre Royal are articulated by tall blank arcading above ground floor level. The building could easily be restored to theatrical use, and could be a fine 'end-stage' complement to the 'arena stage' of the Royal Exchange Theatre.
Listed Grade II.   C.B.

Mansfield, Nottinghamshire

Civic Theatre
Leeming Street.
(Formerly - Palace Theatre).
1910, architect unknown.
Theatre.
Originally a cine-variety house with one shallow balcony at the rear, panelled side walls and a small stage with low grid. Undistinguished brick facade. Now operated by Local Authority as a largely amateur theatre with occasional professional tours. On acquisition in 1956 certain improvements were carried out to the front-of-house and backstage and the rake of the stalls floor was increased. Seating capacity now 480.   C.B.

Grand Theatre
Leeming Street.
1907, C. W. Woodhouse.
Cinemas.
Undistinguished exterior largely original, although facade altered. Interior completely gutted to form three small cinemas.   C.B.

Margate, Kent

Theatre Royal
★ ★ ★ disused
Hawley Street.
1787, architect unknown.
1874, reconstructed by J. T. Robinson.
Bingo.
The structure of the 1787 building partly remains, but Robinson drastically remodelled the theatre by removing the old auditorium and stage, increasing the width by demolishing one side-wall, and doing very odd things with the old roof trusses in order to extend their span. He also rebuilt the front-of-house and facade. This is in stucco, undistinguished and very restrained - of two storeys and four bays, defined by pilaster strips topped by a cornice and parapet. The two bays to the right curve around to the side street, with the entrance in the end bay on the corner. Robinson's auditorium (approximately 550 seats by present standards) is delightful, and rather like a smaller version of his earlier Old Vic auditorium of 1871 - two horseshoe balconies supported by slender iron columns along the line of their fronts, which are of pulvinated section and decorated by swags. The balconies curve around the sides to meet the elliptically-arched proscenium (22ft. wide), which rises directly to the underside of the saucer-domed ceiling. Audience-right boxes blocked in 1940's to form escape staircase. The stage is 21ft. deep and the grid 30ft. high. Although the owner is doing his best to maintain the building, a theatre of such major significance deserves to be fully refurbished and restored to use as a playhouse and possible chamber opera house for Margate and the surrounding area.
Listed Grade II ★   C.B.

Maryport, Cumbria

Empire Palace
Senhouse Street.
c.1911, architect unknown.
Closed.
A cine-variety house. Narrow auditorium with one balcony and plain side-walls. Proscenium altered for cinerama. Stage depth 23ft. Tall brick fly tower. Dull facade of banded brick and cast stone - two storeys and three bays, with curved pediment over tall first floor window, projecting above eaves line of pitched roof. Now closed and in derelict condition.   C.B.

Merthyr Tydfil,
Glamorgan
Theatre Royal
Pontmorlais.
1891, T. C. Wakeling.
Bingo.
The auditorium was completely rebuilt in the late 1920's and one large balcony inserted. Stage intact. The originally handsome stuccoed facade has been marred by the removal of the pediment over its three middle bays, and the replacement of the left-hand pair of the original seven arched doorways by a modern entrance.   C.B.

Methil,
Fife
Dunbeath Theatre of Varieties
Wellesley Road.
(Formerly: Gaiety Theatre).
1908,Swanston & Syme.
Bingo.
A small variety house. Auditorium completely altered. Plain and undistinguished exterior - three narrow bays and three storeys under a gable.   C.B.

Middlesbrough,
Cleveland
Empire
★ ★ ★ disused
Corporation Street.
1899, Ernest Runtz.
Bingo.
The exterior of the theatre, faced in terracotta, makes a significant contribution to the townscape of central Middlesbrough. Situated on an open site adjacent to the Town Hall, each corner of the building, as originally built, was marked by a square tower surmounted by a crested parapet and an octagonal cupola. Between the towers, in the upper storeys of the front and the two side elevations, are a series of closely-set arched windows divided by slender attached columns. The style was described in the opening souvenir brochure as being "Spanish Renaissance". The stage was bombed during the Second World War and the rebuilding omitted its flanking towers. The entrance foyer and principal saloon above, retain their original plasterwork. Fine and intimate auditorium (capacity approximately 1,100, if reseated to present standards) with two curved balconies of six rows each terminating in superimposed stage boxes; each framed within an arch and flanked by colonnettes with enriched shafts. Rectangular proscenium and circular ceiling incorporting six circular panels.The plasterwork on the balcony fronts, proscenium etc. is in a rich and delicate Renaissance style.

Proscenium 30ft., stage depth 35ft., grid 55ft.
The Empire is important as being the best of the only three surviving theatres designed by Runtz - the others being the New Theatre, Cardiff, and the Hippodrome, Hastings (of which only the exterior now survives). The change of use to Bingo was carried out with the minimum of alteration and the owners, Mecca Ltd., appear to be proud of the building and its history. The success of the nearby Forum Theatre, Billingham (1967) seating 630, shows that there is a revival of theatre on Teeside. It is, therefore, likely that the day will soon come when the Empire, with its fine auditorium and more acceptable seating capacity, will be able to stage touring opera, ballet and drama which cannot visit Teeside at present because of the limited size of the Forum.
Listed Grade II.   C.B.

Hippodrome
Wilson Street.
1906, G. F. Ward.
Bingo.
Interior completely altered and a new entrance formed through the rear wall of the stage. Exterior basically intact -brick with painted terracotta dressings. The axis of the auditorium and stage lies parallel to the main street with the former entrance at the left-hand end. This is between two square pavilions each with a steeply pitched roof. In the centre the upper storey has three rectangular openings with curved balustraded balcony fronts. The central bay is emphasized by coupled attached Ionic columns with a segmental pediment over.   C.B.

Minehead,
Somerset
Queen's Theatre
The Esplanade.
1914, architect unknown.
Amusements.

Small, plain auditorium - capacity approximately 700. Proscenium 28ft. Shallow stage and grid approximately 30ft. (no fly tower). Undistinguished brick facade with iron and glass canopy.   C.B.

Morecambe,
Lancashire
Alhambra
★ disused
Marine Road West.
1901, H. Howarth.
Disco.
Large, free-standing, stone building on seafront. Music-hall at first floor level above shops. The auditorium was long and narrow and had a balcony around three sides and a segmental barrel-vault ceiling. In 1970 a fire gutted the interior and destroyed the roof. The remodelling, as a disco, omitted the big fanciful gable on the seafront facade thus depriving the building of much of its character.   C.B.

Palace Theatre
Sandylands.
1910, architect unknown.
Seasonal theatre.
A cheaply constructed building with a segmentally-arched roof reflected internally in the form of the auditorium ceiling. One straight-fronted balcony and blank side walls. Seating capacity 997. Small stage without a fly tower. Completely plain, straight-fronted, rendered exterior with a simple canopy on iron columns.   C.B.

Winter Garden Theatre
★ ★ ★ disused
Marine Road Central.
1897, Mangnall & Littlewood.
Closed.
A large music-hall (approximately 2,000 seats). very wide auditorium (95ft.) with one balcony, returning along the side-

Morecambe, Alhambra   *James Dunbar-Nasmith*

Morecambe, Winter Garden Theatre *James Dunbar-Nasmith*

stalls and one balcony. The balcony has side arms which stop short of the proscenium with steps down to the stalls. The most notable feature of the auditorium is the elaborately fretted cast iron balcony front. Timber boarded ceiling with canted sides. Rectangular proscenium frame (27ft.) flanked by plasterwork panels. Potentially restorable to theatre use with ancillary functions in the institute rooms.

C.B.

walls with five rows, and an upper level of shallow slips above the side promenades. Elaborate composition of bow-fronted boxes flanking the stage -two at stalls level and two at balcony level on each side, with plasterwork canopies. Richly ornamented balcony and box fronts. Proscenium (32ft.) framed by coupled columns with garlands twisted around their shafts. The auditorium is dominated by a vast, segmental tunnel-vaulted ceiling. This covers the whole space, including the area over the tops of the boxes, and is divided into richly decorated plasterwork panels. The curve of the ceiling forms a huge tympanum above the proscenium and boxes, decorated at the sides by painted muses etc., and in the centre by elaborate plasterwork panels above the proscenium. The front of the theatre, prominently sited on the seafront and standing alongside the Winter Gardens Ballroom of 1878, is an ornate, symmetrical composition in painted brick and terracotta. A big central gable, with an elaborately scrolled outline, expresses the rear wall of the auditorium, and is flanked by projecting square towers with shaped gables to the front. Following its closure in the mid '70's the condition of the theatre and adjoining ballroom has gradually

deteriorated. An application to demolish the complex was refused and, in 1979, a further application to demolish only the ballroom was also refused. As a building of very considerable architectural character and the only large theatre in a wide area it is to be hoped that a means of its return to theatrical use can be found. The local Winter Gardens Action Group is fighting to achieve this.
Listed Grade II.   C.B.

Mountain Ash,
Rowe's New Theatre
★ disused
1898, architect unknown.
Bingo.
Opened as Nixon's Public Hall and Institute - a miner's institute and theatre (q.v. Aberaman Grand Theatre) and valuable as a completely preserved example of its type. The free-standing exterior resembles a large Non-Conformist chapel - a big, gabled facade in brick with three storeys and five bays articulated by superimposed pilasters. Tall, round-headed windows in the upper storey which continue along the rendered side elevations. Low fly tower of the stage rising behind. The auditorium is on the upper floor, above the institute rooms, and has approximately 800 seats on a slightly raked

Nelson, Grand Theatre *Victor Glasstone*

Nelson,
Lancashire
Grand Theatre
★ facade only
Market Street.
1888, T. Bell.
Cinema.
In 1923 the galleries of the old auditorium were removed and replaced by one large balcony. Exterior survives intact. Unusual facade - mixed Gothic and classical. Stone-faced of three storeys and seven bays divided by pilaster strips, all under one big pedimental gable. Closely spaced mullioned and transomed first floor windows with cusped heads, and a continuous series of small rectangular windows below the pediment.   C.B.

Palace Hippodrome
★ ★ disused
Leeds Road.
1909, Landless.
Bingo.
Exterior of little merit with only a small square tower above the corner entrance to make any impact. Auditorium (capacity approximately 1,400) with two deep, slightly-curved balconies, the fronts of which are both divided into panels decorated by cartouches. The

Mountain Ash, Rowe's New Theatre *Bill Slinn*

Morecambe, Winter Garden Theatre
John Champness

upper balcony directly abuts the side walls, with the decorative treatment of the front continued along the walls as panels. The first balcony has short slips which run into the principal visual feature of the auditorium - a single box on each side between giant Ionic columns supporting a broken segmental pediment. Rectangular proscenium (32ft.) with an enriched frame. Flat ceiling with a circular central panel. Although the level of the stalls floor has been altered and the stage has a false ceiling, the theatre could be relatively easily restored to use. Unfortunately, the entrance foyer and square tower are to be demolished for road widening.

C.B.

Newark,
Nottinghamshire
Theatre
Middlegate.
1773, architect unknown.
Electricity Board Showrooms.
In use until 1852.　　　　D.F.C.

New Brighton,
Merseyside
Winter Garden Theatre
Atherton Street.
1908, architect unknown.
1910, reconstructed, architect unknown.
1931, reconstructed.
Closed.
Basic structural shell of 1908. Stuccoed front largely of 1931, when the auditorium was completely reconstructed with one deep balcony.

C.B.

Newcastle-Upon-Tyne,
Tyne and Wear
Balmbra's Music Hall
Cloth Market.
1840.
1862, rebuilt.
1962, reconstructed.
Disco (since 1981).
The present facade dates from 1862. The interior was recreated as a pastiche in 1962 when it was reopened as a pub music hall after having been used as a billiard hall since the 1890's. It has the character of a small music hall of the concert room type - flat floor, small balcony at one end and a very small stage.　　　　D.W./C.B.

Gaiety Music Hall
★ facade only/disused
Nelson Street.
1838, architect unknown.
Opened as The Music Hall - a small concert hall at first floor level above a lec-

Nelson, Palace Hippodrome　　　　*Victor Glasstone*

ture room. Re-named New Tyne Concert Hall in 1879 and Gaiety Music Hall in 1884. Auditorium reconstructed at various times. All that now remains is the fine, classical, ashlar facade, articulated by pilasters at first floor level. Grade II.　　　　C.B.

Pavilion
★ facade only/disused
Westgate Road.
1903, Wyslon & Long
Closed.
Interior drastically altered in the 1960's when the ceiling collapsed. The proscenium was removed and everything

Pavilion Newcastle-on-Tyne
Christopher Brereton

at stalls and first balcony level was completely reconstructed. The old gallery and the stage grid still survive, however, above a false ceiling. The grid contains a large drum and shaft. The brick and stone facade remains largely intact (apart from an altered ground floor) - an enjoyable mish-mash of styles with three tall storeys of almost equal height and three wide bays divided by rusticated pilasters. Columned loggia at first floor level in the middle bay flanked by *oeil-de-bouef* windows. A large, arched and traceried window in the centre of the upper storey and a low attic above with three *oeil-de-bouef* windows under a broken segmental pediment.　　　　C.B./D.W.

Theatre Royal
★ ★ ★
Grey Street.
1837. J. & B. Green.
1901, interior reconstructed by Frank Matcham.
Theatre.
Outstandingly fine classical exterior of 1837, unusually monumental for an English theatre and playing a crucial part in the splendid sweep of Grey Street. A free-standing building in ashlar sandstone. The symmetrical facade is dominated by a portico of giant Corinthian columns projecting over the pavement. Flanking bays with giant Corinthian pilasters at the angles repeated around each corner. Restrained three-storeyed side elevations with an attic above the cornice. Following a fire in 1899, the auditorium was completely reconstructed in 1901 by Frank Matcham and is remarkably intimate for its

Newcastle-upon-Tyne, Theatre Royal
Newcastle Chronical & Journal

seating capacity of 1,500. There are three slightly-curved cantilevered balconies and two boxes on each side at first and second balcony levels, divided by pilasters. The line of the third balcony front continues above the upper boxes, first as an ornamental panel and then as a broken pediment above the stage box. Tall rectangular proscenium (31ft.) with an alabaster frame and a curved tympanum above, enclosing a frieze of plaster figures depicting music and drama etc. Flat main ceiling elaborately panelled and carried on triple arches above the gallery slips. Rich Rococo plasterwork on balcony and box fronts and ceiling. Stage depth 38ft. Grid 57ft. The theatre is owned by the Local Authority and is now the North East's major touring theatre.
Listed Grade II ★.   C.B.

Newcastle-upon-Tyne, Theatre Royal   *Victor Glasstone*

Tyne Theatre
★ ★ ★

Westgate Road.
1867, W. B. Parnell.
1893, minor alterations by Oliver and Leeson.
Theatre.

Interesting Italianate brick and stone facade of 1867. Three storeys and five bays with large round-arched Venetian Renaissance traceried windows in the upper storey. Bracketted cornice, with a pediment over the three central bays. Ground floor altered. Magnificent auditorium of 1867. Capacity potentially approximately 1,200 but gallery at pre-

Newcastle-upon-Tyne, Tyne Theatre   *Terence Rees*

sent only in partial use with built-up viewing platforms opening out from 'club' premises in gallery bar. Three horse-shoe balconies sweeping splendidly round to superimposed boxes which flank the imposing, richly-framed, elliptically-arched proscenium (28ft.). Extraordinary and very beautiful circular panelled ceiling, tilted upwards from the proscenium towards the gallery. Excellent plasterwork. This auditorium is undoubtedly one of the finest of its date in Britain. Stage depth 54ft., grid 65ft. The stage retains all its original machinery - due to the fact that the theatre was used as a cinema (called the Stoll Picture Theatre) from 1919 without alteration. This is a rare and valuable survival, now fully repaired and in working order - an achievement without parallel in the whole country. Following the closure of the cinema in 1974 a local group was formed called the New Tyne Theatre Trust and funds raised for the purchase of a lease. In 1980 the freehold was acquired. Much voluntary refurbishment work has been done and the theatre is now used for amateur productions of musicals, plays etc., as well as providing a superb base for lively local theatrical activities. Without doubt this is the most successful instance in Great Britain of a new life being given to an old theatre for which it would otherwise have been 'curtains'!

Listed Grade II. C.B./I.M.

The entrance front, in painted stone, is of extremely modest proportions - just wide enough for three closely-spaced bays defined by pilasters, with three arched doorways on the ground floor and three plain rectangular first floor windows. Pedimented attic with lunette above central bay, linked to ball finials above the end pilasters. Delightfully intimate auditorium (650 seats). Two horse-shoe balconies with rich and delicate plasterwork on their fronts. Single boxes on each side at first balcony level, between pairs of giant Corinthian columns. The entablature above the columns supports a deep elliptical arch in front of the enriched frame of the narrow (21ft.) but high proscenium. Stage depth 34ft., Grid 64ft. Phipps was not afraid of repeating himself and the theme of deep panelled coves above the gallery slips, rising up to a circular ceiling, may be seen in many of his theatres (Eastbourne, Wolverhampton, Glasgow Theatre Royal, Edinburgh Lyceum etc.) At Northampton the plain surface surrounding the Rococo plasterwork in the centre of the ceiling was repainted in the form of stylized clouds in 1960 by Osborne Robinson who added other murals elsewhere at the same time. The theatre possesses a rare painted act-drop of c.1897 with an oval Venetian scene surrounded by elaborate draperies. This is now in storage due to

Northampton, Theatre Royal
Keith Gibson

its fragile condition. The only other old painted act-drops known to survive and actually in use are at the Grand Theatre, Wolverhampton and the Gaiety Theatre, Douglas. An unusual feature of the theatre is that, due to the constricted site, the scenery store and paint room etc. had to be located on the other side of a narrow street to the rear, linked to the stage, which is below street level, by an underground passage. The theatre has been used as a repertory playhouse since 1927 and was purchas-

Newmarket, Suffolk

Theatre
pre-1914 fragment only
High Street.
1823, architect unknown.
Shop.
Originally on the Fisher circuit. In use until 1848. Only the much altered basic shell remains. E.G./D.F.C.

Newry, Northern Ireland

Theatre Royal
Hill Street.
1783, architect unknown.
Shops.

Northampton, Northamptonshire

Royal Theatre
★ ★ ★
Guildhall Road.
1884, C. J. Phipps.
1887, restored after fire by Phipps.
Theatre.
One of the smallest of Phipps' theatres - comparable in scale internally with the Royal Hippodrome in Eastbourne (q.v.).

Northampton, Theatre Royal
Keith Gibson

ed by the Local Authority in 1960. In mid 1980 it was decided to build a multi-purpose concert hall/theatre with a seating capacity of approximately 1,500, to the rear of the Royal Theatre adjacent to the old workshops. In a subsequent phase of building works it is proposed to modernise the back-stage areas of the Royal.
Listed Grade II.   C.B.

North Walsham,
Norfolk

Theatre
1828, David Fisher.
Furniture saleroom.
Used as a theatre until 1845, then a school until 1877, and a church hall un-til 1977. Externally a long, plain building. Internally completely altered.
D.F.C./E.G.

Nottingham,
Nottinghamshire

Bulwell Olympia
pre-1914 fragment only
Market Square.
1915, architect unknown.
Parts incorporated in new store on site, 1956.   D.F.C.

King's Theatre
pre-1914 fragment only.
Market Street.
(Formerly: Talbot Palace of Varieties, Gaiety Palace of Varieties).
1878, architect unknown (converted from skating rink of 1875).
1913, reconstructed as a cinema.
Cinema.
All that now remains from 1878 of this small music hall is the basic structural shell. The narrow, two-bay entrance front was also rebuilt in 1913.   C.B.

Malt Cross
No.14, St. James Street.
1877, E. Hall (converted to music hall from an older building).
Restaurant.
Following closure by the police just before the outbreak of the Great War - it had become a notorious haunt of pro-stitutes - it was used for many years as a wholesale drapers. It is now a restaurant - all theatrical fittings re-moved.   D.F.C.

Theatre Royal
★ ★ ★
Theatre Square.
1865, C. J. Phipps.
1897, reconstructed by Frank Matcham.
1978, reconstructed by Renton Howard Wood Levin.
Theatre.

Nottingham Theatre was Phipps' se-cond theatre commission and his splendid colonnade of giant Corinthian columns survives to terminate the vista up the steep gradient of Market Street. In 1897 Frank Matcham removed the three balconies and the boxes of Phipps' auditorium and replaced them with three new cantilevered balconies with improved sightlines and a new stack of boxes flanking the pro-scenium; the whole richly decorated with lively Rococo plasterwork. The result was an auditorium of remarkable intimacy and vibrantly theatrical at-mosphere. It now seems likely, on the evidence available that the proscenium, as it existed prior to the reconstruction of 1978, was the result of re-design by Phipps prior to 1897, and left intact by Matcham. It was certainly not Phipps' 1865 proscenium and was quite un-typical of Matcham. It did, however, have much in common with pro-sceniums designed by Phipps later in his career. Further evidence of a return visit by him were the small bulbous-based columns re-used by Matcham at the sides of the auditorium, again characteristically 'late Phipps' and to be seen at his Lyceum Theatre, Edin-burgh of 1883. In view of this it is most unfortunate that the old proscenium was unnecessarily demolished in 1977 and replaced by the present out of scale arrangement of giant Corinthian col-umns awkwardly surmounted by a curiously shaped arch. It is no less sad that Matcham's distinctive second balcony level boxes and their plaster-work canopies were removed in favour of the present top heavy upper boxes, badly related to the new proscenium and exposing areas of blank wall. These are bad points in what was otherwise a magnificent revitalisation of the old theatre. In the auditorium the part-pastiche colonnade encircling the stalls seating, the arcaded boxes at the rear of the dress circle (inspired by the arcade at the rear of the dress circle of Phipps' Edinburgh Lyceum), the reseating of the old gallery, and the green and gold colour scheme are all a success. (Theatre consultants were Theatre Projects Consultants Limited.) Equally welcome are the spacious new foyers and bars replacing the cramped wedge between the facade and the curved wall of the auditorium. Backstage everything has been transformed, with a heightened grid, side stage, scene dock, new dressing rooms, offices etc. Phipps' facade was improved by new return-bays, setting it off from the receding curves of the new building on each side, and by the restoration of balustrades and urns. It is ironic that this restoration of one of Britain's best theatrical facades should, within only three years, be disfigured by the addition of a twentieth century newscaster across the attic storey. The project was courageously financed by Nottingham Corporation at the time of economic austerity. The seating capaci-ty is now 1,138. Proscenium 30ft.; stage depth 45ft. plus rear stage of 20ft. and full wing stage, stage right; grid height 61ft. In 1980 work started on a new 2,500 seat concert hall to the rear of the Royal and connected to it both

Nottingham, Theatre Royal   *Victor Glasstone*

backstage and through the stalls bar to the right of the auditorium.
Listed Grade II. C.B.

Nuneaton,
Warwickshire

Empire Theatre
Leicester Road.
1909, C. F. Ward.
Warehouse.
Opened as the Empire Hall and skating rink. Became a music hall in 1910. Interior stripped out. Undistinguished red brick and terracotta facade of three storeys with a triangular pediment over three middle bays which encloses a subsidiary serpentine pediment. C.B.

Prince of Wales
pre-1914 fragment only
Bond Street.
1900, Owen & Ward.
Derelict.
Later renamed Hippodrome. Now a roofless shall with the exterior walls demolished down to second storey level. The remains of the entrance front, in red brick and terracotta, consist of four wide bricked-up openings at ground floor level with rusticated segmental arches, and Ionic pilasters with banded rustication defining the three middle bays at first floor level. Some remains of plasterwork in the shattered interior, e.g. on the lower half of the proscenium. C.B.

Scala Theatre
Abbey Street.
1914, architect unknown.
Closed.
A cine-variety house (approximately 700 seats). Auditorium with one balcony and panelled side walls. Shallow stage with fly tower. Three-storeyed pedimented street front of three main bays. Centre bay at first floor level has a large semi-circular arched window set within a deeply recessed rusticated surround. C.B.

Oldham,
Greater
Manchester

Empire Theatre
Waterloo Street.
1897, Sir Sidney Stott.
Derelict.
A large variety theatre with a wide and deep auditorium with one balcony, remodelled in 1930's for use as a cinema. (Capacity approximately 1,700). Proscenium 32ft., shallow stage, grid height 43ft. Stalls below street level, which explains the lowness of the entrance front - plain and rendered with ranges of narrow, arched windows. Small square tower above central bays. Derelict and vandalised. Threatened with demolition in 1981. C.B.

Palace
Union Street.
1908, Bertie Crewe.
Cinemas.
Interior gutted to form three cinemas. Exterior intact - long frontage to Union Street an axis of auditorium/stage. Very restrained in brick with terracotta dressings. Entrance at right-hand end with five bays of tall rectangular windows with heavy keystones at first floor level, separated by coupled pilasters. Attic storey above with a small pediment over the central bay flanked on either side by two *oeil-de-boeuf* windows. C.B.

New Grand Theatre &
Opera House
Union Street.
1908, Thomas Taylor.
Discotheque.
The brick and terracotta exterior was much altered, and the corner entrance rebuilt in 1936. At the same time the interior was rebuilt completely as a cinema. C.B.

Hippodrome
Union Street.
1868, architect unknown.
Closed.
Opened as the Adelphi Theatre, renamed Gaiety in 1879, and Hippodrome in 1913. Small music hall with interior much altered. Plain rendered facade with altered ground floor. C.B.

Oxford,
Oxfordshire

Oxford Hippodrome
Cowley Road.
(Formerly: East Oxford Theatre; Empire Music Hall).
1902, converted from a hall of 1890, by A. Ward.
Warehouses and offices.
Pitched roofed shell of auditorium and fly tower remains but completely gutted

Penzance, Theatre
Christopher Brereton

internally and large windows inserted in outside walls. Frontage to Cowley Road of domestic appearance - bay windows and gables. Theatre entrance, now altered, between shops with flats over. C.B.

Pembroke,
Dyfed

Queen's Theatre
Queen Street.
1905, architect unknown.
Warehouse.

Penrith,
Cumbria

Alhambra Theatre and
Palace of Varieties
Middlegate.
1906, architect unknown.
Bingo.
Plain stone exterior forms part of a row of shops with flats over, from which the theatre can be distinguished only by a modern canopy. The auditorium has one balcony, returned as slips along the side walls to meet the proscenium, which is flanked by pilasters. Flat, panelled ceiling. C.B.

Penzance,
Cornwall

Pavilion Theatre
Promenade.
1911, F. G. Drewitt.
Amusement arcade.
A typical seaside theatre of its date. Small rectangular auditorium with segmental tunnel-vaulted ceiling, lunette windows, panelled side walls, no balcony and flat floor. Segmentally-arched proscenium with Baroque plasterwork enrichment. Shallow stage without fly tower. Long low facade to Promenade in Cornish granite. A five-bay Tuscan colonnade between two squat, square towers, each with an *oeil-de-boeuf* window in the upper stage. Large doorways with open segmental pediments carried by atlantes. The interior is now full of amusement machines. C.B.

Theatre
★ disused
Chapel Street.
1787, architect unknown.
Furniture store.
Situated at the rear of the Union Hotel, but a separate structure, constructed of rubble with a slated pitched roof and gabled ends. Overall external dimensions 61ft. × 31ft. The ground level slopes steeply away along one long-side and the space under the theatre was used as part of the hotel stables. It

now houses cars rather than horses, and wide openings have been formed in the side wall. The theatre was entered through a gabled elevation facing a narrow alley. Simply framed double doors in the centre, and a single door to the right. Although much altered and subdivided internally there are still vestiges of the original use. e.g. remains of a gallery now encased, possibly a refixed proscenium door etc. Closed as a theatre in 1831 and dismantled in 1839. Further investigation is necessary to discover whether or not sufficient evidence exists for a complete restoration of this Georgian playhouse, an increasingly rare type of theatre following demolitions in the last 15 years at Dorchester and Newbury.
Listed Grade II.   C.B.

Perth,
Perthshire

Perth Theatre

Facade only
Atholl Street.
1820, architect unknown.
Theatre demolished but restrained ashlar facade remains; not readily distinguishable from the other frontages of this wide and dignified street.
Listed Grade B.   C.B.

Perth Theatre & Opera House

★ ★

High Street.
(Formerly: Royal Theatre).
1900, W. Alexander.
Theatre.
Superseded the theatre in Atholl Street as the town's theatre. Exterior even more difficult to identify - in fact very nearly invisible, being a single arched doorway sandwiched between shop fronts on the ground floor of a four-storeyed block of stone tenements. A narrow foyer links the entrance with the brick auditorium and stage block at the rear of the tenements. Good intimate auditoruim of approximately 800 seats (including the second balcony not at present in use). The first balcony front is richly decorated with foliated scrolls and consoles at intervals, and the upper balcony front has repeated delicately-modelled festoons. Each balcony curves around into slips to meet a tall, narrow stack of superimposed boxes framed by pilasters flanking each side of the proscenium. The pilasters have enriched shafts and the upper box is surmounted by a blank-arched panel; a motif which is continued along the top of the square-headed proscenium (24ft. wide, stage depth 32ft.). Plain, flat, circular centrepiece to the ceiling with coved edges. The auditorium has been to some degree marred by the erection of a partition to form a corridor on each side behind the first balcony slips, in line with the front of the gallery slips. The theatre houses a repertory company and also takes occasional tours including Scottish National Opera. In 1981 plans were prepared to modernise the front-of-house and backstage areas.
Listed Grade B.   C.B.

Plymouth,
Devon

The Globe Theatre

Stonehouse Royal Marine Barracks.
1864, converted to theatre from racquets court; architect unknown.
1887, altered; architect unknown.
Amateur Theatre.
A former racquets court of 1788, permanently converted into a theatre in 1864, and enlarged in 1887. The auditorium is Neo-Classical in character suggesting the Regency rather than the mid-Victorian period. There is a single horseshoe gallery supported on slender iron columns, which continue up to the ceiling. On each side of the well-proportioned rectangular proscenium are false proscenium arch doors, set between engaged square

Plymouth, Palace Theatre
Christopher Brereton

Tuscan columns, reminiscent of the theatres of William Wilkins (q.v. Bury St. Edmunds). In 1928 new exits were introduced which reduced the seating capacity to 250. (In the 1880's it had been 600-700). The building was overhauled and re-decorated in 1971. Now used by Marines and local amateur groups.   I.M.

Palace Theatre

★ ★

Union Street.
1898, Wimperis & Arber.
Theatre.
A large variety theatre built on a corner site together with an hotel. Elaborate Flemish Renaissance style facade in terracotta - three main bays and three storeys with steeply pitched tiled roofs. Wide central entrance bay surmounted by a big Flemish gable with two statues of Spanish soliders standing against the front face on projecting brackets. Small, closely-spaced, arched windows in the upper storey. Three large arched windows between Ionic demi-columns in the *piano noble*, flanked in the end bays by semi-circular panels of coloured tiles depicting scenes of the Spanish Armada. The ground floor has seven bays of Tuscan columns supporting a continuous entablature. The elevational treatment of the front is continued for one main bay around the corner and the angle is surmounted by

Perth Theatre & Opera House   *James Dunbar-Nasmith*

Plymouth, Palace Theatre   *M. Rogers*

an octagonal turret with cupola and projecting balcony; probably intended to resemble the top of a lighthouse. Much Art Nouveau decorative detail, e.g. on the frieze above the first floor windows, and in the panels below the windows. The facade is at present marred by a crude modern canopy projecting from half-way up the height of the columns. A wide, balustraded staircase leads from the entrance foyer to an unusually spacious saloon lit by the three large first floor windows. The elaboration of the exterior is not, unfortunately, fully matched in the auditorium - it was originally, but a serious fire occured eight months after the opening and presumably funds were not available for a complete restoration. The fronts of the two deep balconies are, however, decorated with plasterwork incorporating military motifs, and the large boxes flanking each side of the proscenium at dress circle level have canopies with two projecting ships lanterns. Plain, domed ceiling. The present seating capacity is 1,200. Proscenium 30ft. 6ins., stage depth only 22ft. (could be extended on land to rear), grid 55ft.. After a period of use for bingo the theatre was courageously reopened as a private commercial venture in 1978, despite the proposal of Local Authority to build a large new theatre (to be opened in 1982) - perhaps a rather suprising decision in view of the existence and potential of the Palace. The owner of the Palace intends to perservere in building up an audience and still hopes to deepen the stage in order to improve facilities for touring opera and ballet etc
Listed Grade II.   C.B.

Portsmouth, Hampshire

Globe Theatre
Eastney Royal Marine Barracks.
c.1899.
Disused.
Externally a brick and corrugated iron building of no distinction. Internally it has the air and grace of a theatre even if the finishes are utility. In use as a theatre until 1973. The seats have since been removed but the capacity is approximately 450. Raked stalls, one balcony supported by cast iron columns, and slips at the sides. Wood finish to front of balcony, and ceiling painted in panels with some open ironwork. Proscenium 21ft., stage (raked) 30ft. deep. No fly tower. Under threat of demolition.   M.S.

King's Theatre
★ ★ ★
Albert Road, Southsea.
1907, Frank Matcham.
Theatre.
Sited between two converging roads with the entrance at the apex, dominated by a big hexagonal tower with a steeply pitched roof surmounted by a cupola. The auditorium has three

well curved balconies and is intimate for its large capacity of 1,780 (this includes the gallery). The first and second balconies abut two superimposed stage boxes on each side. The lower boxes have arched canopies which also form the fronts of the boxes above. These are framed by squat Ionic columns and are backed by shell-hooded niches. The gallery front curves directly into the side walls and is separated from the stage boxes on each side by a further large shell-hooded niche (a favourite Matcham decorative motif). The ceiling is in two sections - a flat lower part spanning between the stage boxes, and a large oval saucer-dome at a higher level, decorated with six painted panels. The proscenium is segmentally-arched with an enriched plaster out frame and an inner frame of alabaster. Proscenium 30ft., stage 45ft. (including 10ft. under rear paint frame), grid height 54ft. That the King's is 'late Matcham' is apparent in the heavy modelling of the Baroque plasterwork when compared with, for example, his Gaiety, Douglas (1893) or Grand, Blackpool (1894), and also in a relative clumsiness in the handling of some of the forms, e.g the composition of the boxes, and the over emphaisised proscenium frame. When considered in an overall context, however, the King's is an important and complete example of Edwardian theatre architecture.
Listed Grade II.   C.B.

Theatre Royal
★ ★ ★ disused
Guildhall Walk.
1856, converted to theatre from Landport Hall of 1856, architect unknown.
1884, rebuilt by C. J. Phipps.
1900, reconstructed by F. Matcham.
Closed.

Phipps' restrained but handsome pedimented classical facade of 1884 survived the 1900 reconstruction. Matcham did, however, make an addition which completely transformed the appearance of the theatre - a remarkable projecting enclosed balcony of enriched iron and glass, supported by an arcade of slender coupled colonnettes. Matcham built a new stage (65ft. deep) and enlarged Phipps' auditorium by absorbing part of the old stage (36ft. deep) within it, and building a range of four bow-fronted boxes on each side between the ends of the balconies and the new proscenium (30ft. wide). He also partly reconstructed the balconies themselves, although making use of Phipps' supporting iron columns. The lyre-shaped first balcony of six rows is pure Matcham and is cantilevered out from a line of columns which rise up to support the fronts of the two Phippsian horseshoe balconies above. The sides of the upper balconies were altered to improve sight-lines. The overall decora-

Portsmouth, King's Theatre Southsea   *Victor Glasstone*

175

tions (by De Jong) are of an incredible richness. The boxes are framed by giant polygonal columns and each upper box has an arched canopy which bellies forward with a scolled top above an oval panel. Linking the capitals of the columns on each side is a wide semi-circular arch, originally framing a bust. The proscenium is flanked by niches, originally with statues. Surmounting the opening is a large flared painted panel with trumpeting tritons in plasterwork at its base. The whole is held together by a scheme of extremely detailed plasterwork with a predominantly nautical theme. The first tier panels are decorated with naval symbols - mermaids, dolphins, anchors and shells. The second tier honours the army; laurel wreathed lions spouted forth electric globes while between are draped guidons and colours. The third has continuous deeply moulded Rococo acanthus motifs which gently emphasise its earlier form. Most of the panel painting was lost in a 1948 redecoration although there does survive the excellent large panel over the proscenium showing Thespis and boys at play. In 1959 the Theatre Royal became a bingo hall. In 1971 an application for listed building consent to demolish was refused. The stage was destroyed by fire in 1972 and the building was closed. Following this members of the Theatre Royal Society worked at weekends to protect the building from decay and vandalism. The New Theatre Royal Trustees (Portsmouth) Ltd. was formed and in 1980, sufficient funds were raised to buy the freehold. At the time of writing a scheme was being evolved for the rebuilding of the stage and for the reopening of the theatre. (Consultants: Theatre Project Consultants Limited). Much will depend on the total strategy for theatre in Portsmouth and Southampton areas as to whether it will be possible to realise the full potential of the Theatre Royal. The site to the rear would allow as extensive a stage, wings or rear-stage and backstage accommodation as any company could wish. The sightlines from the balconies are very good and would allow a forestage to be built forward of the proscenium which would enable the splendid auditorium to function as a most exciting setting for drama. The comparatively large volume, which does not detract at all from the intimacy of the theatre, and the unusual sloping angle of the ceiling, suggests a superb acoustic for opera and music theatre, as well as for speech. The gallery has its original padded benches, admittedly uncomfortable by present standards, but if retained could provide acceptable cheap seating for young people when the demand was there. A factor which will determine whether or not the City backs the project whole-heartedly will be the Council's resolve to complete the Esher plan. A reopened Theatre Royal would inject life into the City centre where it is at present lacking. Listed Grade II.   C.B./I.M.

Ramsey,
Isle of Man
Palace Theatre
Waterloo Road.
c.1905, architect unknown.
All purpose hall.
Little is known about this theatre. It is listed in the 1907 Green Room Book and in subsequent directories. Later it became a cinema. It is still extant and is used for various activities. In 1981 there were proposals to redevelop the site.
V.G.

Ramsgate,
Kent
Royal Palace Theatre
pre-1914 fragment only
High Street.
1908, converted to theatre from amphitheatre of 1883, architect unknown.
All of this impressive theatre, the adjoining hotel, and a shop were demolished 1960. Remainder of block, comprising four shops, and the covered access to the pit, remain.   D.F.C.

Royal Victoria Pavilion Theatre
1904, S. D. Adshead.
Casino.
The external structure - in the "French Academic style", remains virtually intact, but the interior, based on J. A. Gabriel's theatre at Versailles (1770), has been altered considerably at various times, and in 1976 was completely gutted to house the Club Tiberius.   D.F.C.

Redditch,
Hereford and
Worcester
Palace Theatre
★
Alcester Street.
1913, Bertie Crewe.
Theatre.
A small theatre (now 400 seats); indeed diminutive when compared with other jobs which Crewe was handling at about the same time (e.g. Palace Theatre, Manchester, q.v.). Stuccoed facade alongside the auditorium/stage in a rather hamfisted Neo-Classical manner - three storeys and nine bays; the five middle bays with a rusticated ground floor supporting panelled Ionic pilasters in the first and second storeys. Straight entablature and parapet. Intimate and quite pleasing auditorium with restrained Neo-Classical plasterwork. One balcony on

Redditch, Palace Theatre
Gordon Brittain

a shallow curve, linked to one large box on either side, framed by Ionic pilasters with pediment over. Rectangular proscenium with reed-moulded frame. Proscenium width 22ft., stage depth 22ft. Flat ceiling with central circular rose. After a period of use for bingo the theatre was purchased by the Local Authority in 1971, refurbished and a three-storeyed extension built to the right of the original front, with a new entrance around the corner. It is mainly used by amateurs with occasional professional tours.   C.B.

Rhyl,
Clwyd
Gaiety Theatre
★ ★
Promenade.
c.1908, architect unknown.
Concert party theatre.
This is possibly the only surviving pre-1914 concert party theatre in Great Britain. The resident concert party from 1927 to 1964, 'The Quaintesques', were some say the inspiration for J. B. Priestley's 'The Good Companions'. The theatre has no proscenium, only a semi-circular thrust stage approximately 32ft. across and 16ft. deep. The auditorium holds 800 in a single raked 90 degree arc interrupted only by a line of columns supporting the roof. Both the roof and the facade facing the front have been altered, the walls rendered; however, on the shore side, originally facing the pier the plain brickwork of the amphitheatre is stolidly impressive. The building appears in the Stage Guide of 1912 as 'The Pier Amphitheatre' with a Music and Dancing and Kinematographic license, Electric Light but no Kinema projection box. The owners were then, as now, the Rhyl Council. The word 'Pier' was dropped at some time the theatre being known as 'The Amphitheatre' until 1959 when the name was changed to 'The Gaiety'. There is still some confusion about theatre history in Rhyl. The Pier Amphitheatre stood on the site of 'The Grand Pavilion (1890-1901) and is not to be confused with either The Pier Pavilion or The Bijou Pavilion, both of which were on the now vanished pier, or

'The Pavilion' which was built later further down the promenade, closed in 1972 and demolised in 1974 after being found unsafe.

The slightly seedy atmosphere of The Gaiety, which is till used in the old tradition intensively by the present licensee Aubrey Phillips, is unique and will be relished by anybody interested in the survival of traditional seaside entertainment.   I.M.

Lyric Hall
Market Street.
(Formerly: Operetta House).
1890, architect unknown.
Store.
A small music hall above shops. Interior completely altered. Simple brick exterior with pitched roof. Shop fronts on ground floor and plain sash windows above.   C.B.

Queen's Theatre
Promenade.
(Fomerly: Queen's Palace Theatre).
1902, architect unknown.
1908, reconstructed after fire, architect unknown.
Discotheque/amusement arcade.
Facade with large domed pavilion destroyed by fire in 1907 and rebuilt, without the pavilion, in a similar manner to the adjacent hotel - brick with oriel bay-windows and a tiled pitched roof. Auditorium reconstructed in 1926. C.B.

Richmond, North Yorkshire

The (Georgian) Theatre
★ ★ ★
1788, architect unknown.
1963, restored by Richard Leacroft and Richard Southern.
Museum with occasional stage performances.
From the outside this tall almost windowless building, which measures only 28ft. by 81ft. in plan, looks like any stone barn of the Yorkshire dales. All exterior indications that it is a theatre date from the restoration of the 1960's, but inside almost everything, from paybox to proscenium arch doors is authentically Georgian. Nowhere else in England is the earthy immediacy of the 18th Century playhouse evoked so strongly. The proscenium is tiny (18ft. wide by 20ft. high) but well proportioned. This sense of scale within so small a building allows at once for big acting as well as a remarkably intimate actor-audience relationship. The auditorium itself is one three levels; an 18ft. square benched pit reached by pit passages running underneath the side boxes; an enfolding level of 11 boxes, four on each side and three facing the stage with a playwright's name over each box (the lettering over the centre box,

SHAKESPEARE, is original as is the Richmond Borough coat of arms on the front of the stage box on the actors' left); and above the rectangular gallery supported by 11 Tuscan columns which are not taken up to the ceiling. The auditorium is decorated in a range of carefully recreated Georgian green, relieved by red *trompe d'oeil* swagged curtains on canvas at the back of the boxes. The attempt to create a period lighting effect is only half successful -the miniature bulbs on the simulated candle candelabra providing too steady a light, while there has been no attempt to provide the oil 'rings' over the stage. Unfortunately late 19th Century gilt ballroom chairs are often substituted for the correct backless benches in the boxes but elsewhere the seating is original or a faithful copy of the 'knife edge' benches, not quite so closely spaced as they once were. The licensed capacity is now 238 while records show that the Theatre held approximately 450 during its first life from 1788 to 1841. Then the theatre closed and became first an auction room and later a wine store. Moves to restore the theatre started in 1943 and were not completed until 1963, under the supervision of Dr. Richard Southern and Richard Leacroft. The chief problem was that at some time in the late 19th Century brick built vaults had been inserted into the length of the building immediately below stage level. Thus the dressing rooms and trap room under the stage, like the

Richmond Theatre, North Yorkshire

pit and orchestra pit, are reconstructions. On the stage itself, which measures 28ft. wide and 24ft. deep, no trace either of the original grooves or of any 19th century suspension system survive. Since the reopening further dressing rooms, bars, the necessary escape stairs and a scene dock have been added, all sympathetically finished in the local stone. In an adjoining building in Friar's Wynd there is a small museum which is open in conjunction with the theatre itself.
Listed Grade I.   I.M.

Ripon,
North Yorkshire
Victoria Opera House
Low Skellgate.
1886, architect unknown.
Furniture showroom.
Exterior only survives. Built as the Victoria Hall - a flat-floored hall at first floor level, of modest dimensions with a proscenium and stage (20ft. deep) at one end. Interior now completely altered. Simple, painted-brick exterior with slated roof. Altered ground floor and a series of five tall sash windows above, along the side-wall of the former auditorium.   C.B.

Rochdale,
Greater Manchester
Empire
Town Hall Square.
1909, architect unknown.
Bingo.
Only the stone, gabled facade survives from 1909. Originally built as a small music hall with one balcony and a shallow stage. In 1930 the interior was completely gutted, the stage removed and the whole rebuilt as a cinema with a straight-fronted balcony.   C.B.

Rochester,
Kent
Lyceum Theatre
pre-1914 fragment only
Star Hill.
(Formerly: Victoria Hill, Theatre Royal).
1791, architect unknown.
Theatre demolished in 1884 and replaced by the present Conservative Club building. The original manager's house remains, although its portico was removed in 1972.
Listed Grade II.   D.F.C.

Rotherham,
South Yorkshire
Empire
Westgate.
1913, Chadwick & Watson.
Two Cinemas.
The free-classical exterior in white faience is largely original. Interior completely altered to form two cinemas, although the stage and fly tower remain.   C.B.

Rugby,
Warwickshire
Prince of Wales Theatre
Railway Terrace.
(Formerly: Palace Theatre 1910-1913; Hippodrome 1913-1924).
1910, Franklin and Newman.
Furniture Store.
Stuccoed facade in free-classical style. Wide central bay of two storeys with a large lunette window surrounded by decorative stucco work. Flanking pavilions of 2½ storeys with straight cornice and parapet. Auditorium (capacity approximately 700) with two balconies and single boxes either side of the proscenium. Restrained plasterwork. Proscenium 26ft., stage depth 36ft., grid 46ft. Altered for use as Regal cinema in 1933 and again for present purpose.   C.B.

Runcorn,
Cheshire
Palace Theatre
High Street.
1897, W. S. Snell.
Bingo.

Rushden,
Northamptonshire
Palace Theatre
High Street.
1910.
Shops/car showroom.
Built as a cine-variety house, showing films only from the late 1920's.

Royal Variety Theatre
1911.
Derelict.
Also built for cine-variety with films only from the early '20s. Converted to a car saleroom approximately 17 years ago. Recently gutted by fire and now a shell.

St. Helens,
Merseyside
HIPPODROME
Corporation Street.
1902, J. A. Brown.
1930's, interior remodelled.
Bingo.
Auditorium completely remodelled for cinema use with one deep balcony in 1930's. Stage with fly tower remains (depth 38ft.). Exterior largely original -tall brick walls with ornamental surrounds to windows etc. in terracotta.   C.B.

Pilkington Theatre
Corportion Street.
(Formerly: Theatre Royal & Opera House).
1889, F. Matcham.
1901, reconstruced after fire by Matcham.
1964, reconstructed by Westwood, Piet & Partners.
Theatre.
The present name dates from 1964 when the theatre was acquired by the Pilkington Glass Company. The auditorium front-of-house and facade were then completely rebuilt. Matcham's stage (depth 40ft.) is all that is left of the 1889 or 1901 building. The theatre is used for both professional drama and music as well as for events connected with Pilkingtons.   C.B.

Theatre Royal
Milk Street/Waterloo Street.
1861, A. Beattie.
Salvation Army.
A small, pitched-roofed gabled building on a corner site. Interior completely altered following change of use to Salvation Army in 1889. Stuccoed exterior with tiers of arched windows in front and along side elevation.   C.B.

Salford,
Greater Manchester
Victoria Theatre
★ ★ ★ disused
Great Clowes Street, Broughton.
1899, Bertie Crewe.
Closed.
Terracotta facade - two storeys and five main bays with Ionic pilasters separating pairs of tall first floor windows. Pedimented central bay surmounted by small tower with a square dome. Straight-sided pavilion roofs over end bays. Excellent intimate auditorium with two balconies (approximately 1,000 seats by present standards). First balcony has a raised rear section behind a balustraded parapet. Superimposed stage boxes - two at each side. Lower boxes flanked by squat Corinthian columns, and upper boxes by terms which support arches framing

Salford, Victoria Theatre
Victor Glasstone

richly scrolled plasterwork. The balcony and box fronts are divided into panels which contain gilded plasterwork. Spanning the auditorium betweeen the tops of the boxes is a deep elliptical arch which frames a tympanum above the rectangular proscenium (width 36ft. stage depth 48ft.). In the entrance foyer is a marble plaque commemorating the opening of the theatre in October: 1899, by Sir Henry Irving. Repertory was tried from 1963 but bingo took over in 1973. Even this failed, however, and the theatre stands forlornly surrounded by empty ground destined for new council housing (1980). This is a fine theatre, designed by an important theatre architect. Hopefully a suitable use will be found for it before it becomes too seriously damaged by decay and vandalism.
Listed Grade II.   C.B.

Scarborough,
North Yorkshire

Alexandra Music Hall

★ facade only
(Formerly: St. George's Hall, Old Spa Music Hall).
1859, architect unknown.
Partly shops.
Built as a music hall adjoining the Old Spa Vaults. The hall was on the first floor with bars etc. below. It had a flat main floor and a gallery around three sides. Closed in the late 1870's to become an auctioneers, and more recently a restaurant. Brick exterior largely intact apart from shop fronts on ground floor. Very tall first floor arched windows with stone surrounds - one in each end bay and three grouped in the centre. Low attic storey above the main cornice.
Important as a fairly substantial survival of an early music hall.   C.B.

Floral Hall Theatre
Alexandra Gardens, Peasholme Road.
1910, architect unknown.
Seasonal Theatre.
A large, rambling, iron and glass, conservatory-like structure of no par-

ticular interest. 1,600 seats on a flat floor. Proscenium 30ft., stage depth 19ft., grid height 30ft.   C.B.

Royal Opera House
★ ★
St. Thomas Street.
1876, built as circus.
1900, converted to theatre, architect unknown.
1908, reconstructed by Frank Tugwell. Theatre.
Originally built, in 1876, as Prince of Wales Circus. In 1900'converted to a theatre and renamed Zalva's Hippodrome. Reconstructed in 1908 and reopend as New Hippodrome. Renamed Opera House in 1910. Delightful, intimate auditorium (970 seats). Lower balcony of six rows which curves around into an unusual arrangement of boxes on each side. There are two boxes at lower balcony level, bow-fronted with lattice decoration. The front of the stage box also forms a curved cowl over a box just above stalls level. The upper balcony has a serpentine front and straight arms returned to the proscenium. The balcony fronts have gilded plasterwork scrolls, festoons, masks etc. Imposing segmentally-arched proscenium with

Scarborough, Royal Opera House
Keith Gibson

deep reveal richly decorated with scrolls, groups of cherubs, and a central cartouche. Flat ceiling, simply panelled. Proscenium width 31ft. 6ins. Stage depth 30ft., grid, 44ft. The exterior is very plain - merely part of a three-storeyed terrace of shops with flats above. Painted brick with gabled dormers. Arched first floor windows and a wide, arched entrance. The theatre was threatened with demolition

Scarborough, Royal Opera House   *Keith Gibson*

Scarborough, Spa Theatre

following closure in 1971. It was listed, however, in 1972, and a locally formed preservation society raised funds, negotiated a lease and reopened the theatre in 1976 after a thorough restoration. It now takes tours as well as presenting summer shows, occasional repertory and large scale amateur productions.
Listed Grade II. C.B.

Spa Theatre

The Spa.
1879, Hunt & Verity.
Theatre.
An addition to the Spa Complex originally designed by Paxton c.1860. Unusual auditorium (639 seats) with the character of a seaside pavilion theatre. One straight-fronted balcony of ten rows at the rear, and side balconies at right angles, each divided into two equal bays by square columns which support a line of clerestory windows above. Flanking the proscenium were originally shallow niches framed by pilasters. The proscenium is straight-headed with rounded corners and decorated with cable ornament. Above the proscenium there was originally a frieze depicting the muses and other figures but this has since been painted out. Plain, slightly-curved ceiling. Proscenium 20ft., stage depth 24ft., grid 23ft. In season use for summer shows. Listed Grade II (as part of Spa Buildings). C.B.

Scunthorpe,
Lincolnshire
Palace Theatre
Cole Street.
1912, architect unknown.
Supermarket.
As originally built the stuccoed facade had a high arched opening in the centre under a curved gable, flanked by small square towers with ogee domes. In 1938 this was altered and the interior completely rebuilt as a cinema (Savoy). In 1978 the building was gutted to form a supermarket. C.B.

Seacombe,
Merseyside
King's Theatre
Victoria Road.
(Formerly: Irving Theatre; Hippodrome).
1899, architect unknown.
1908, reconstructed after fire, architect unknown.
1930's, interior rebuilt.
Bingo.
Auditorium completely rebuilt with one large balcony in the 1930's for cinema use (Embassy). Stuccoed exterior basically intact apart from altered ground floor. Nine tall, rectangular first floor windows surmounted by a continuous frieze of festoons and scrolls. Smaller second floor windows with the two left-hand bays carried up above the cornice as a blank attic. An interesting facade which makes a significant contribution to the streetscape. C.B.

Shanklin,
Isle of Wight
Shanklin Pier Theatre
Esplanade.
(Formerly: Casino Theatre, Pier Pavilion).
1891, architect unknown.
1927, reconstructed after a fire.
Grade II (Pier). D.F.C.

Sheerness,
Kent
Criterion Music Hall
High Street, Blue Town.
(Formerly: Royal Oxford Music Hall; New Music Hall).
c.1851, architect unknown.
Store/Workshop.
Used as a cinema from 1920. Closed and gutted in 1951. The undistinguished shell now houses a store and workshop. D.F.C.

Sheffield,
South Yorkshire
Britannia Music Hall
★ disused
West Bar.
(Formerly: Tankard Tavern Music Hall).
c.1860, architect unknown.
Disused warehouse.
A small music hall situated at the rear of the former Old Tankard public house. Exterior hidden from view and just a plain brick shell with a pitched roof. The auditorium was entered through the pub and consisted of stalls (37ft. × 40ft.) and a gallery of five rows. Proscenium 19ft. wide and stage 10ft. deep. The hall and the pub were closed

Sheffield, Lyceum Theatre *Victor Glasstone*

Sheffield, Lyceum Theatre
Architectural Review

in c.1896, and used as a warehouse. The hall was altered by the insertion of an intermediate floor and the proscenium wall was boxed-in. Disused since 1978. Pub music-halls are now very rare and the Britannia, although altered, is important as a substantially surviving example. C.B.

Lyceum Theatre
★ ★ ★ disused
Talbot Street.
1897, W. G. R. Sprague.
Pop concerts.

Sprague was responsible for some of the most beautiful theatres in London (q.v. Wyndham's, The Albery, The Globe, The Strand, etc.). The Lyceum is his only remaining work in the provinces. Built on the site of the City Theatre (1893). A free-standing building with plain brick side elevations and a restrained four-storeyed stuccoed front to Tudor Street. Corner entrance under a domed tower - a feature in common with some of Sprague's London theatres. Very fine auditorium, especially notable for its superb Rococo plasterwork. Two slightly-curved cantilevered balconies - the upper one with tightly packed gallery seating. Unusual treatment of the side walls which are articulated by broad pilasters at each level, forming bays containing bow fronted boxes. All the surfaces are enlivened by delicate plasterwork and at dress circle level the pilasters have attached coupled columns. The proscenium has a rectangular moulded frame which encloses a riotous Rococo openwork plaster valance - along the

top, in the corners and spreading halfway down the sides. Coved and panelled ceiling with fine plasterwork. If reseated to today's standards the capacity of the theatre would be approximately 1,000. The proscenium is 28ft. 6ins. wide, stage depth 31ft., and grid height 56ft. The Lyceum closed as a theatre in the mid 1960's and became a bingo hall. This failed in 1972 and the owners made an application for consent to demolish which was refused on appeal. Since this time the building has remined closed and neglected. The Lyceym Theatre Trust was formed to campaign for reopening of the theatre. The City Council, however, which built the immediately adjacent thrust stage Crucible in 1971, has consistently declined to give support. In 1981 permission was granted to a new owner for the theatre to be used as a venue for pop concerts. Although this is preferable to the building standing empty it is incredible that the country's sixth largest city should have allowed this to happen to its only remaining theatre capable of housing opera, ballet and other musical productions. On must also ask whether, with present increases in the cost of travel, the citizens of Sheffield will long continue to be prepared to travel 30 miles to the Grand Theatre, Leeds, (q.v.) to see the range of theatre at present denied to Sheffield.
Listed Grade II. C.B.

Shildon,
County Durham
Hippodrome
Byerley Road.
c.1911, architect unknown.
Bingo.

Built as a cine-variety house. A freestanding building with a big slated pitched roof and fly tower. Stuccoed facade of no merit - two gabled end bays flanking a recessed centre. A little projecting oriel on the upper floor for the projection room. Dull auditorium - approximately 1,000 seats on one level with the rear seats slightly raised up behind a boarded parapet. Plain side walls and plain ceiling. Simple elliptically-arched proscenium 28ft. wide, stage depth 30ft., grid 46ft. C.B.

Shotton,
County Durham
Theatre Royal
1834, architect unknown.
Bingo.

Now called "The Royal Tombola Social Club". Plain, brick facade, probably added in the 1930's. The remainder of the structure may be original. Small auditorium with one balcony (capacity approximately 350) - much altered and of not interest. Stage intact - proscenium 25ft., depth 20ft. D.W.

Shrewsbury,
Shropshire
Theatre Royal
Shoplatch.
1835, architect unknown.
Furniture store.

Became a cinema early in this century. Damaged by fire in 1945 after which the interior was completely rebuilt as a furniture shop. The stuccoed exterior, although altered, is basically recognizable as the original design of 1834. As the facade lay parallel to the axis of the auditorium and stage it is of considerable length - over 100ft. It is also high, as the theatre itself was above a rusticated base containing shops with a mezzanine housing dressing rooms and the manager's flat. This has now been opened up for display windows etc. The upper part of the facade consisted of 2½ storeys with a straight entablature above, four bays in the centre and two-bay wings, slightly advanced between giant Tuscan pilasters. The original windows have been replaced by very tall ones embracing both storeys. Above the entablature a blank attic storey was added - probably early this century, judging by the festoons decorating the end bays. The roof of the stage, with haystack lantern, is still visible above the left-hand bay. The building is wedge-shaped on plan, tapering to a width of only 30ft. at the stage end. C.B.

Skegness,
Lincolnshire
Arcadia Theatre
Drummond Road.
1914.
Theatre.

Altered 1933 when balcony added. Now split into two auditoria of 560 and 200 seats each. M.G.

Pier Theatre
1881.
Closed.

Pier swept away in 1978 and theatre now marooned in the sea. Stripped out and derelict. M.G.

Smethwick,
West Midlands
Empire Theatre
St. Paul's Road.
1910, G. Bardon.
Shop.

Auditorium completely redone in the 1930's-one deep balcony. Shallow stage (25 ft.) with fly tower, original. Undistinguished painted brick facade intact-symmetrical in free-classical style. Giant Ionic pilasters defining end bays with curved pediments, and central bay with steep triangular pediment enclosing a lunette window. C.B.

Southborough, Kent

Broomhill House Theatre

Spelhurst.
c.1890.
Part of Hospital.
Private theatre of Sir David Salomons. Listed Grade II.

Royal Victoria Hall

★

1900, William Harmer.
Theatre.
The 1912 Stage Guide lists this as a hall and does not mention that it has a full-scale fly tower, and proscenium arch. The auditorium has permanent seating in a straight-across gallery, while on the main floor seats are erected on stepped platforms (part of the hall's original equipment) as occasion demands. Between 1977 and 1979 the foyer and bars were remodelled to provide a new box-office and a large bar running the full-length of the hall. The original chapel-like facade was also 'modernized' by the removal of a fine cast-iron canopy and the rendering over of the formerly pleasant red brick with a particularly noxiously-coloured ochre cement. The building was erected by Sir David Salomons (of Broomhill House, q.v.), for the Urban District Council to celebrate Queen Victoria's Golden Jubilee in 1897, licensed to use Royal Coat of Arms in 1899 and opened in 1900. It has always been run by the Local Authority. All the renovations have been undertaken by volunteers. The theatre is used by both amateurs and professionals. Stage 40' × 25', proscenium 28' × 14½'; capacity 450.   D.F.C.

Southend, Essex

Kursaal Palace

1901, architect unknown.
Closed.
Large flat-floored music hall/ballroom with stage and dressing rooms within Kursaal complex. Last used in the mid 1970's for pop concerts, but since then all fixtures and fittings have been removed and the whole edifice is in a poor state of repair.   D.F.C.

Palace Theatre

★ ★

London Road, Westcliff-on-Sea.
(Formerly: Raymond's New Palace).
1912, architect unknown.
Theatre.
Jolly facade characteristic of its date, in red brick and stucco. Broad centrepiece, with a high-level panel, originally bearing the name of the theatre in bold lettering (now removed), topped by a curved moulding enclosing an *oeil-de-boeuf* window. Above is a straight, balustrated parapet linked by scrolls to symmetrical flanking towers with curly parapets and two stages of closely-spaced pilasters. The former pit and gallery entrances, at the base of each tower, have bold semi-circular pediments enclosing cartouches supported by mermaids. The towers were originally capped by small domes but these have unfortunately been removed. In the 1960's the main entrance doors and windows were completely altered. The design of the auditorium is an interesting example of the tail-end of the Victorian/Edwardian tradition; clearly showing the influence of the cine-variety type. Although the present seating capacity is only approximately 700 (including a gallery with original benched seating) the impression is of a much bigger auditorium. This is largely due to height and depth rather than width - which is only 43ft. The first balcony has 10 rows then a gangway, but beyond this is a narrower rear section with a further 6 rows, the last of which is 75ft. from the stage - a considerable distance. Both balconies directly abut the side walls but are linked decoratively to concave plasterwork panels to the most impressive features of the auditorium - pairs of boxes on either side of the proscenium at 1st balcony level, surmounted by rather splendid, onion-domed, plasterwork canopies. The proscenium is rectangular (26ft. wide) and has a curved sounding-board above it. Set in front of this, however, on a line midway between the domes of the boxes, is an unusual feature - a flattened, pointed arch which spans the full width of the

Southend, Palace Theatre Westcliff-on-Sea   *Victor Glasstone*

auditorium. Above this is the main ceiling which is flat and geometrically subdivided by fruit and flower mouldings. The auditorium still has its original brass light fittings. On either side of the proscenium are decoratively framed panels which were used to indicate the programme number of variety acts - two such panels now survive. The fly tower is very shallow - stage right depth 18ft.

Southend, Palace Theatre Westcliff-on-Sea   *Victor Glasstone*

6in., stage left depth 16ft. To supplement this a permanent apron stage was put in at an early date - 9ft. 6in. deep. Grid height is 51ft. In 1980 it was proposed to reseat and widen the row spacing of the balcony (losing 2 of the 10 rows in the main section) and to use the old seats to reseat the gallery. This will reduce the seating capacity to approximately 520. Further proposals include a new foyer, bar and studio theatre to the right of the present building. At present the theatre is used for both repertory and touring shows.

C.B.

Southport,
Merseyside
Vaudeville Theatre
Portland Street.
(Formerly: Royal Music Hall).
1874, converted from a music hall of 1863, architect unknown.
Store.
After ceasing to be used as a theatre it was first adapted as an office building, and in 1890 became a house and store.

D.F.C.

South Shields
Tyne and Wear
Empire Palace Theatre
King Street.
1899, rebuilt by Frank Matcham with W. & T. R. Milburn.
1930's, interior rebuilt as a cinema.
Bingo.
A rebuilding of the old Thornton's Varieties. The layout of the bulding is most unusual - the entrance foyer on King Street is separated from the auditorium and stage block by a narrow street with the stalls reached by a tunnel and the first balcony by a bridge. The gallery had direct access by means of a staircase from the rear street. The auditorium and stage were completely remodelled as a cinema in the 1930's with only parts of the external wall retained. Matcham's narrow, stone-faced entrance front on King Street survives largely intact however, apart from an altered ground floor. It is of only one wide bay with a large semi-circular-arched window occupying the full width at first floor level. Above this are two small arched windows separated by a shallow niche which rises up into a tall gable consisting of five stages linked by scrolls.

C.B.

Theatre Royal
★ facade only
King Street.
1866, by T. H. Clemence, interior by C. J. Phipps.
Shop.
Situated immediately alongside the Empire Theatre. Only Clemence's three-storeyed stuccoed facade remains.

Although the ground floor has been opened up as a shop-front it is otherwise intact. It is of three bays defined by giant Corinthian pilasters - single at the ends and coupled either side of the centre. Straight entablature above with well modelled cornice. Three tall pedimented windows at first floor level.

C.B.

Tivoli Palace
Laygate Lane.
1902, architect unknown.
Shop.
Built as a small music hall situated at first floor level above a row of shops. Originally with a flat main floor, one balcony with boxes at the sides, and shallow stage without fly tower. Closed in 1934. Became part of a department store in 1946. Subsequently the interior was completely altered and an intermediate floor inserted at the former balcony level.

C.B.

Stamford,
Lincolnshire
Theatre
★ facade
St. Mary's Street.
1768, architect unknown.
1978, interior rebuilt.
Theatre.
In 1871 the whole of the interior of the theatre was stripped out and sold. The original shell and ashlar facade, however, remain. Although somewhat countrified in design the facade is a rare and valuable surviving example of the front of a Georgian playhouse. It is of two storeys and five bays under a continuous bracketted cornice and straight parapet. There is a large pedimented central doorway with an arched window over, and two small side doorways. In 1978 the building was internally rebuilt as a theatre for amateur use with occasional professional tours (170 seats). Repeated pleas for an authentic reconstruction were rejected on the assumption that insufficient evidence remained. The present interior bears no resemblance whatsoever to a Georgian playhouse. However the evidence still extant in the 1970's and the lesson learnt at Richmond (Yorks) and King's Lynn would have made restoration possible.
Listed Grade II.

C.B./I.M.

Stirling,
Central Scotland
Alhambra Music Hall
(Formerly: Arcade Theatre).
1882, John McLean.
Closed as fire risk but parts of building remain - including side balconies.D.F.C.

Stockton-on-Tees,
Cleveland
Hippodrome
Dovecote Street.
1905, William Hope.
Cinemas.
Interior rebuilt after a fire in 1932. More recently subdivided to form separate cinemas. Exterior intact but entirely lacking in interest - a big, plain, brick building on a corner site with the entrance and dressing rooms etc. contained in a low range running parallel with the main auditorium/stage block. C.B.

Theatre in Green Dragon Yard
pre-1914 fragment only
1766, architect unknown.
Warehouse.
Only the completely plain shell remains. Originally built in the late 16th century by the Bishop of Durham as a tithe-barn. In 1766 it was converted into a theatre by Thomas Bates - the sandstone walls being increased in height with brickwork. The auditorium had a pit and one gallery. Boxes were added in 1819. In 1874 it was taken over by the Salvation Army as a meeting hall. The stage and gallery were removed and the present balcony installed.
Listed Grade II. C.B.

Stoke-on-Trent
see
Hanley
Longton
Tunstall

Stratford-upon-Avon,
Warwickshire
Shakespeare Memorial Theatre
pre-1914 fragment only
1879, Dogdshun and Unsworth.
Conference room (part of present theatre complex).
Only the semi-circular brick shell of the auditorium remains of Dogdshun and Unsworth's delightful Gothic theatre following the fire of 1926. The associated museum, which had been linked to the theatre by a galleried bridge, survived the fire. A conference room was formed within the old auditorium shell which is now to the rear of the stage of the 1929/32 theatre. In 1980 proposals were announced to build a 400 seat open stage theatre in the conference room. C.B.

Sunderland, Empire Theatre
Keith Gibson

Sunderland, Empire Theatre   *Keith Gibson*

Sunderland,
Tyne and Wear

Empire Theatre

★ ★

High Street.
1907, W. & T. R. Milburn.
Theatre.

Built as a large variety theatre (present capacity 1,574). Intact inside and out. Wide auditorium with two slightly-curved, deep balconies. An unusual feature is the provision of staircases down to stalls level from the ends of the first balcony. Even more unusual are the extraordinary boxes bulging out on either side of the proscenium at second balcony level and surmounted by elaborately tiered cupolas. It seems almost as though they were designed with the object of distracting attention away from the stage! At each side of the first balcony is a little six-bay arcade with four of the bays made into boxes. Rectangular proscenium with a large, flat tablet above the centre. The ceiling has very high coves over the proscenium and at the sides, divided into panels by strips of moulding. Heavily modelled and sparsely applied Baroque plasterwork. Proscenium 34ft. 6ins., stage depth 42ft., grid 55ft. The exterior is mostly hidden behind the frontages of the main street, but above the corner entrance is a big, circular, domed tower with a bodly projecting cornice and *oeil-de-boeuf* dormers. Beyond the tower, along the side, is an unexpectedly charming series of Arts and Crafts bow windows in the upper floor. The Empire was purchased by Sunderland Corporation in 1960 - one of the first local authorities to take the initiative of giving a new lease of life to an ailing com-

mercial touring theatre. W. & T. R. Milburn went on to design several very large, and generally rather dull, variety theatres in the 1920's e.g.; The Empires in Edinburgh, Liverpool and Southampton (now the Gaumont).
Listed Grade II.   C.B.

Star Music Hall

Upper Sans Street.
1885, converted to music hall, architect unknown.
Garage.

Following use as a Salvation Army Barracks (1893-1914), and a cinema (1914-1925), the building stood empty from 1925-1933. It is now a garage.
D.F.C.

Theatre Royal

Bedford Street.
1855, Middlemiss.
Bingo.

Auditorium competely rebuilt in 1933 within the original shell. The stuccoed classical facade survives from 1855, although altered in detail. Three wide bays defined by giant pilasters on pedestals, embracing the first and second storeys. Rusticated ground floor with a central arched doorway (now blocked) with a bust of Shakespeare on the keystone and flanked by Ionic pilasters. A single tall rectangular window in each bay at first floor level - the central one framed by pilasters in line with the doorway below. Above the entablature the middle bay is surmounted by a pediment set against a low attic storey. Unfortunately the appearance of this interesting facade has been marred by the removal of the mouldings on the pediment and the detail of the capitals of the pilasters. The entrance foyer is housed in a three-storeyed addition to the left of the original building, with a 1930's frontage.   C.B.

Swaffham,
Norfolk

Theatre

pre-1914 fragment only

1822, David Fisher (owner and designer).
Garage.

Most of the building was destroyed by fire in 1928, but two walls are incorporated in the garage now on the site.
E.G./D.F.C.

Swansea,
West Glamorgan

Grand Theatre

★ ★ ★

Singleton Street.
1897, William Hope.
Theatre.

A fine theatre, fully intact inside and out. Excellent auditorium (1,100 seats) -very intimate with two, well curved balconies and two superimposed bow-fronted boxes on each side, framed by pilasters. Proscenium flanked by fluted colonnettes standing on extremely elongated pedestals. The head of the proscenium reaches directly to the underside of the ceiling which has concentric circular mouldings contained within an overall rectangular frame. Rich and lively plasterwork on balcony and box fronts, proscenium and ceiling -recently picked out, to splendid effect, in gold against an ivory background. The balconies are supported by iron columns with remarkable Art Nouveau capitals. Proscenium 29ft., stage depth

Swansea, Grand Theatre *Christopher Brereton*

30ft., grid 55ft. The theatre is built on a corner site and has a good stuccoed facade with a rusticated ground floor and 2½ storeys above. On the corner is a two-bay pavilion flanked by pilasters, a pediment to the front and a steeply-pitched roof with ironwork cresting around the top. A matching pavilion occurs beyond the two bays to the right, but this is asymmetrically placed facade continues with a further two bays. Below the parapet linking the pavilions is the name "Grand Theatre" in large *Art Nouveau* style lettering in relief. The theatre is owned by Swansea Corporation and successfully operates a programme of mixed touring productions, including the Welsh National Opera. The Grand is the only remaining complete theatre by William Hope - his Blythe Theatre Royal is in a badly neglected condition and threatened with demolition.
Listed Grade II. C.B.

Palace Theatre

★ ★ disused
High Street.
1888, Bucknall and Jennings.
Closed.

Opened in 1888 as Swansea Pavilion. Name changed to Empire in 1892. Renamed Palace Theatre in 1900. Dramatic exterior on triangular site, in brick with ample stone dressings. Circular tower at the apex (stage end) originally domed, and a square tower at each of the other two corners with curved pavilion roofs. The base of the triangle (rear wall of the auditorium) faces a narrow street and is in plain brickwork. The other two facades, however, flank major streets, and on approaching the theatre from the High Street both fronts can be seen simultaneously as they splay outwards from the corner. The elevational treat-

ment of the two fronts is similar - the ground floor with banded rustication and a series of semi-circular arched doorways and windows, and the two upper floors embraced by giant Tuscan pilasters. These form an interesting rhythm of bays - alternately blank and with windows; vertically linked by panels containing busts and pedimented in the upper storey. Above the pilasters is a deep entablature, carried continuously around both fronts. The auditorium is at first floor level, in order to provide space below for the necessary ancillary accommodation on the tight site. It is very intimate with two steeply-raked balconies which curve around close to the proscenium without stage boxes. The upper balcony has its original gallery seating (Total capacity if re-seated to modern standards approximately 1,000) Balcony fronts in the form of open ironwork balustrades. As the stage is at the narrow end of the site it is consequently rather small and wedge-shaped; proscenium 32ft., stage depth 35ft., grid 50f.
Listed Grade II. C.B.

Taunton,
Somerset
Lyceum Theatre
Station Road.
1913, architect unknown.
Cinemas.

Built as a cine-variety theatre. Auditorium completely altered to form two cinemas. Exterior basically intact. Prominently situated on a corner site. Undistinguished brick facade with plain pilasters. Small fly tower at rear of long, low auditorium block. C.B.

Thetford,
Norfolk
Theatre
pre-1914 fragment only
1819, David Fisher (owner and designer).
House.

Swansea, Palace Theatre
Christopher Brereton

185

Todmorden, Empire Theatre   *Victor Glasstone*

Todmorden, West Yorkshire

Empire Theatre
★

(Formerly: Hippodrome, New Todmorden Hippodrome).
1908, architect unknown.
Amateur theatre.
Street front on axis of auditorium/stage - rather blank, in brick relieved only by fanciful gable at the stage end. Auditorium long and narrow with one deep balcony with Baroque plasterwork on its front. Plain segmental barrel-vault ceiling. Balcony slips continue along side walls to proscenium which has an enriched rectangular frame (22ft. wide). Stage depth 20ft. Present seating capacity 400 (a large bar has been formed in the former rear stalls area under the balcony). The theatre is operated by a lively amateur group.   C.B.

Tonypandy, Mid-Glamorgan

Hippodrome
Dunraven Street.
1912, architect unknown.
Bingo.
Built as a cine-variety theatre. Simple auditorium with one balcony. Shallow stage (approximately 20ft.) with low fly tower. The entrance is through the ground floor of a terrace of shops with flats over - domestic in character; brick

with series of bay windows projecting at first floor level. The ground rises steeply behind with the utilitarian auditorium/stage block at a higher level.   C.B.

Torquay, Devon

Pavilion Theatre
1912.
Roller skating.
Suitably festive seaside theatre on the edge of the harbour. The whole of the outside is clad in white faience tiles and at each of the four corners is an octagonal projection surmounted by an open-sided domed kiosk with cast iron column supports. Auditorium in music hall manner (capacity approximately 1,200) - balcony around three sides with a cast iron balustrade, and a domed lantern light in the centre of the ceiling. Now used for roller skating with a café on the balcony.   C.B.

Scala Theatre
★ facade only
Torwood Street.
1914, Richardson, Gill & Moore.
Shops and Garage.
Designed by Richardson and Gill, who had recently built the Opera House, Manchester, and by the local architect F. G. Moore. This was to have been a large and important theatre but it was never completed beyond the main

structural walls. Imposing French classical style, ashlar-faced elevations. The main entrance is on a splayed corner and has four giant Ionic columns above the ground floor, surmounted by a pediment with a relief of Neptune in the tympanum. The monumental treatment is continued along the frontage to Torwood Street. The ground floor has shops fronts between rusticated piers. In the end bays, at first floor level, are very large round-arched windows with console keystones and sculptural groups set above the deep entablature and parapet. The five middle bays break forward from the ends and have giant Ionic columns above the ground floor dividing wide, rectangular windows. Straight entablature and parapet.
Listed Grade II.   C.B.

Theatre Royal & Opera House
Abbey Road.
(Formerly: Winter Gardens of 1878).
1888, reconstructed as a theatre, by C. J. Phipps.
c.1920, reconstructed as a cinema.
Cinemas.
Interior completely rebuilt as a cinema in c.1920, and more recently as two small cinemas. Only the basic structural shell with slated pitched roof survives from 1888. The entrance front is on Abbey Road, parallel to the axis of the auditorium/stage. The ground floor with three arched doorways under a modern canopy is largely original. Above this, however, the facade was altered in c.1920 with a three-bay, columned loggia. Behind the Abbey Road front the ground level falls away steeply so that from the entrance one descended to the stalls. The tall rear elevation, fronting a narrow street, shows the original stone rubble walling, patched up with later brickwork, and a serpentine-headed frontispiece to a lower entrance of c.1920.   C.B.

Totnes, Devon

Prince of Wales Theatre
Seymour Hotel.
c.1856, architect unknown.
Hotel ballroom.
The theatre was a flat-floored room added to the original building in c.1856, linked to the hotel but also with separate side entrance. Intended as an assembly room/theatre it was provided with a proper stage, 15ft. deep, proscenium 16ft. wide. In 1912 the seating capacity was 300. The room was completely altered and a new scheme of decoration introduced after theatrical use ceased in c.1920. The proscenium was removed and the stage walled off as a separate space.
Listed Grade II (as part of hotel building).   C.B.

Totnes, Theatre   *Evelyn Kearns*

Theatre

★ facade only
High Street.
1707, architect unknown.
Shop.

This is probably the oldest surviving theatre building in the country (apart from the Banqueting House, Whitehall, London q.v.) of which anything substantial now remains. The shell of the tiny auditorium and stage survives but has been stripped of all features pertaining to its theatrical use. The facade survives virtually intact, however, above the ground floor shop window and fascia. In appearance it is a fine early 18th Century house - stuccoed with three rectangular windows in the first and second floors and a moulded cornice with a gable above. The upper windows have retained their sashes and have decorative scrolls in stucco at the sides. The first floor windows now have 1930's casements. The walls at this level have channelled rustication with large keystones over the windows. It is these which display the only external evidence remaining that the building was a theatre - delightfully naive masks of 'Tragedy' and 'Comedy' above the side windows and a female head in the centre. The adjacent house to the left is contemporary and has giant pilasters in the upper two storeys, and a smaller cornice and gable as on the theatre.
Listed Grade II.   C.B.

Treharris,
Mid-Glamorgan
Palace Theatre
The Square.
c.1850, architect unknown.
Bingo.

Originally built as Temperance Public Hall at first floor level above institute rooms etc. Became a theatre with the addition of a small stage in the early years of the century. Flat main floor with one balcony, curved in the centre and straight arms at the sides. Undecorated, boarded front. Plain flat ceiling. Simple elliptically-arched proscenium - width 27ft., stage depth 18ft., low grid. Big, plain gabled front dominating the centre of the small town.   C.B.

Truro,
Cornwall
Theatre Royal

★ facade only.
High Cross.
1772, Charles Ebden.
Offices.

Only the exceptionally fine, ashlar facade remains, situated close to the towering west front of the cathedral. Two storeys and three bays, surmounted by a pediment. Wide, arched doorway with fan-light in the centre of the ground floor, flanked by single, arched doorways with straight-headed surrounds. Three tall sash windows at first floor level with finely carved reliefs over - two gryphons supporting a tripod within a rectangular frame over the central window, flanked by profile busts of Shakespeare and Garrick in circular frames. The tympanum of the pediment contains a circular plaque with a draped

---

female figure holding a mask and a mirror. Used as a seasonal theatre and assembly room until 1869, when replaced by new Public Rooms. Although the interior survived for some time afterwards, it has since been completely rebuilt behind the facade, and is now used for offices. A thorough restoration of the facade which received a European Architectural Heritage Year Award was carried out in 1975.
Listed Grade II ★   C.B.

Tunbridge Wells
Kent

Opera House
★ ★ ★ disused
Mount Pleasant Road.
1902, John Briggs.
Bingo.

This is a fine theatre with a medium-sized auditorium, still intact apart from minor modifications for bingo. The grandiose design of the exterior is quite misleading as it gives the impression of being the front of a major theatre with 2,000 rather than only approximately 750 seats (to present seating standards). The style is a mixture of Edwardian Baroque and Neo-Georgian, carried out in brick with ample stone dressings. The theatre entrance is, in fact, only the centrepiece of a 23-bay, symmetrically composed block housing shops with two storeys of offices above. It is in the form of a single, wide bay, flanked by coupled pilasters above

Tunbridge Wells, Opera House   *Victor Glasstone*

187

the ground floor carrying a broken pediment and framing a deep niche with a projecting balcony. Set back above the pediment and dominating the facade is a big Baroque dome. Flanking this centrepiece, on either side, are three plain bays with ground floor shop fronts, and then giant coupled pilasters surmounted by steep pediments. Beyond these, on each side, are two further groups of three plain bays, defined by rusticated pilasters, before the curved ends of the facade which are emphasized by subsidary domes. After all this bombast it comes as a surprise to enter the small foyer and intimate auditorium. The auditorium has two, slightly-curved balconies of six and eight rows each with straight slips running to ranges of superimposed boxes -four on each side. The upper boxes have gryphons at the head of each subdividing pilaster. The proscenium is rectangular with elaborately scrolled brackets in the corners and a curved pedimental tablet above the centre. The main ceiling is in the form of a panelled saucer-dome set within a richly moulded rectangular frame. Unfortunately the plasterwork on the balcony and box fronts, proscenium and ceiling has been given an overall stipple treatment which obscures the fine detail. Proscenium width 28ft., stage depth 32ft. The theatre could be readily restored to use and would make an excellent home for a repertory company with occasional touring opera, ballet etc.
Listed Grade II.   C.B.

The Theatre
pre-1914 fragment only
The Pantiles.
1802, architect unknown.
Only the portico and facade of Sarah Baker's second theatre on this site are said to have been retained when it was replaced by a Corn Exchange. A curious fact about this theatre was that its auditorium was in Kent, and its stage in Sussex.   D.F.C.

Wallsend, Borough Theatre &
Hippodrome   *James Dunbar-Nasmith*

Tunstall,
Staffordshire
Theatre Royal
Ladywell Street.
(Formerly: Prince of Wales Theatre).
1863.
Salvation Army.
Closed in 1880 to become a Salvation Army hall. A small, pitched-roofed building in brick with a rendered, gabled facade with arched windows · probably altered post 1880. Interior completely remodelled for present use. C.B.

Tynemouth,
Northumberland
Palace-by-Sea
1878, J. Norton & P. E. Macy.
Dancing/Cabaret.
A very large beach pavilion on six floors in the French Baroque style · brickwork, with moulded brickwork to window pediments, string courses, rustication etc. Big auditorium with flat main floor, now much altered. Stage originally 40ft. deep.   J.D.N.

Wakefield
West Yorkshrie
Opera House
★ ★ ★ disused
Westgate.
1894, Frank Matcham.
Bingo.
This theatre has a most delightful auditorium, typical of Matcham's earlier style and similar in scale to his Lyric, Hammmersmith. It is virtually intact and deserves to be restored to use as a playhouse - capacity if re-seated by present standards would be approximately 600. There are no stage boxes but the two balconies (five and ten rows) curve around the sides, separated from the proscenium only by elaboarate plasterwork panels - as at Hammersmith. There are boxes, however, behind the seating in the first balcony - one on each side half-way round. The upper balcony retains its original gallery seating in the form of padded risers. The balcony fronts have frothy Rococo plasterwork, but the panels on the first balcony have lost their original painted decoration. Flat, circular ceiling with circular panels surrounded by Rococo scrollwork. Segmentally-arched proscenium with richly-banded frame and a big central mask. A floor has been inserted above the stage, half-way up the proscenium opening, but this could be removed. Proscenium width 26ft., stage depth 30ft. The lower part of the facade has unfortunately been altered. Originally in brick with cast stone dressings it has been crudely rendered and the windows mostly blocked. The upper level, however, has five circular windows with arched surrounds, each

separated by a projecting bust of a composer in a circular frame with a scrolled top. The keystones of the window arches continue up, in the form of pilaster-strips, into the wide gable which surmounts the facade. A lower, two-storeyed section to the left has a small copper dome above the curved corner.
Listed Grade II.   C.B.

Wallsend,
Tyne and Wear
Borough Theatre &
Hippodrome
★ ★ disused
High Street East.
1909, Davidson & James.
Bingo.
Good auditorium, completely intact, but at present with a suspended ceiling cutting off the upper balcony. Total seating capacity approximately 1,100. The two balconies, of about eight rows each and slightly curved, come well forward towards the stage and end in a single, semi-circular box on each side. The lower boxes have plaster canopies supported by slender Ionic columns. Between the boxes and the stage, on either side, are two levels of niches holding female figures, all contained within a giant enriched Ionic order standing on pedestals at stalls level. The lower balcony front is decorated with heavy, paired consoles forming panels filled with cartouches. Oval ceiling with central gas burner. Proscenium 30ft. wide, stage depth 30ft. Apart from the alterations to the entrance the exterior is also intact but of little merit. The main front is slightly concave with brick walls and plain, painted stone pilasters with crudely detailed tops. The building is in good condition and could be restored to use relatively easily.
                                    J.D-N/C.B.

Walsall,
West Midlands
Imperial Theatre

Darwell Street.
1860's, architect unknown.
1915, interior rebuilt.
Bingo.
Opened at the Agricultural Hall, but provided with a stage and also used for theatrical performances. Renovated in 1887 and reopened as St. George's Hall and Theatre. Further "extensive renovation" in 1889. In 1900 renamed the Imperial Theatre, but in 1902 called Imperial Hall. In 1915 internally reconstructed as a cinema with a characteristic segmental barrel-vault ceiling and single balcony. The simple brick facade with arched windows and surmounting gable is basically that of the original Agrcultural Hall.   C.B.

Walton-on-Naze, Essex

King's Theatre
Mill Lane.
1900, architect unknown.
Factory/Warehouse.

Warrington, Cheshire

New Theatre Royal
Scotland Road.
1818, architect unknown.
1884, rebuilt by Pierpoint & Adams.
1950's, auditorium reconstructed.
Bingo.

Opened as the New Theatre; renamed Theatre Royal 1846; New Theatre Royal in 1884, and Royal Theatre of Varieties in 1907. Only the altered facade and the basic structural shell remain of the 1884 building. The auditorium was completely altered for bingo in the 1950's with an additional level inserted above, and forward of, the former stage area. The form of the single balcony may be of 1884 but all decorative plasterwork etc. has gone. The lower half of the facade was rendered and re-done in c.1921 but the brick upper part dates from 1884 and is divided irregularly into five bays with tall windows in four of them - three straight-headed and one pedimented. Continuous bracketted cornice and balustraded parapet. Next to the theatre is a pub called the Theatre Tavern.   C.B.

Palace Theatre
★
Friars Green.
1907, G. F. Ward.
Bingo.

Opened as the New Palace Theatre and Hippodrome. The auditorium, never particularly attractive, was mutilated in the 1960's by the removal of the boxes and

Warrington, Palace Theatre
Victor Glasstone

Waterford, Theatre Royal
Liam Murphey

of the plasterwork from the fronts of the two balconies. It is otherwise intact, however, and could be restored without too much difficulty. The capacity would be approximately 1,100 when re-seated. The balconies have eight rows each and curve around slightly to meet the splayed walls where the boxes originally were. There was one box on either side with pilasters and a pediment, similar to the arrangement at the Civic Theatre, Darlington (q.v.), by the same architect. The panelled ceiling and rectangular proscenium retain their Baroque plasterwork. Proscenium width 30ft., stage depth 30ft. The exterior is little altered, apart from the ground floor and entrance canopy. The main front, in brick with stone dressings, is an asymmetrical composition in a not very appealing mixture of Edwardian Baroque and Arts and Crafts. To the left, on the corner, is a four-storeyed square tower with rusticated base and quoins and a pavilion roof surmounted by a cupola. To the right is a three-storeyed 'tower' with a low dome. The entrance, in the middle, is marked by two narrow, slightly projecting turrets with little domes, flanking a wide central bay with a curved parapet and a broad, elliptically-arched window at first floor level. Plain brick side elevation, relieved only by blank arcading.
                                          C.B.

Waterford, Eire

Theatre Royal
★ ★
1778, John Roberts, as Assembly Rooms.
1876, interior reconstructed as a theatre, architect unknown.
Theatre.

The former Assembly Room building of 1778 has a fine facade of 2 tall storeys

and 9 bays with a 3 bay centre piece articulated by engaged Ionic columns at *piano nobile* level. The theatre occupies the portion defined by the 3 left hand bays - the remainder is now the Town Hall.
It was fitted up within the existing shell in 1876 and has a most delightful auditorium (present capacity 650) with 2 horseshoe balconies which run directly up to the tall, narrow proscenium arch. The balconies are supported along their front edges by iron columns which continue up to support a ring of arches below the circular ceiling. These arches are pointed - a Gothic touch which is also taken up in the clustered shafts framing the proscenium. Painted canvas panels depicting cupids etc. in the tympanum of the proscenium arch and framed by the ceiling arches on either side. Fine new Waterford Glass chandelier suspended from the ceiling. Waterford has so much in common with the design of the old Shakespeare Memorial Theatre, Stratford-on-Avon (q.v.), of very nearly the same date (1877 - 2 horseshoe balconies with plain, panelled fronts, Gothic arches supporting the ceiling, and Gothic clustered shafts on the tall, narrow proscenium arch), that one is tempted to attribute it to the same architects Dogshun and Unsworth.   C.B.

Watford, Hertfordshire

Palace Theatre
★ ★
Clarendon Road.
1908, H. M. Theobold.
1910, front extended and facade built.
Theatre.

Free-standing red brick building, its facade flanked by two squat towers with lead cupolas. A small foyer (seemingly consisting mostly of steps) leads to a spacious, yet intimate, auditorium -capacity 490 plus a gallery rarely used.

Watford, Palace Theatre

189

Seating is on three levels. Sightlines are good from all parts, proscenium width 27ft., stage depth is shallow - 20 -20ft with splayed back wall. A removable apron stage was constructed in 1978. The back-stage facilities, like the front-of-house, are in need of improvement - this might be possible if the adjacent cinema and vacant lot could be acquired. The cinema (Carlton) is a rotunda, and was built in 1919 as a skating rink. Owned by Local Authority since 1960's and operated as a repertory playhouse. In 1981 the auditorium was renovated and redecorated to a very elegant scheme by Clare Ferraby.
Listed Grade II.   D.F.C.

Wellingborough,
Northamptonshire
Palace Theatre
1911, architect unknown.
Cinemas.
Built as a cine-variety theatre on the site of the Empire Music Hall; a wooden building erected in 1909 and destroyed by fire in 1910. Auditorium originally had one balcony. Proscenium was 31ft., stage depth 32ft. In 1969/70 a new entrance front was put on and more recently the interior was converted into three small cinemas.   C.B./D.W.

Wells,
Norfolk
Theatre
pre-1914 fragment only
1812.
Cottages
                                    D.F.C.

Wells,
Somerset
Palace
Priory Road.
c.1914, architect unknown.
Shop/Warehouse.
Opened as the Electric Picture Palace and Variety Hall - a small cine-variety theatre. Interior completely altered. Simple two-storeyed, stone exterior. Ground floor altered for shop front but retains original iron and glass canopy.
                                    C.B.

Westcliff-on-Sea,
Essex
see
Southend.

Weston- Super-Mare,
Avon
Grand Pier Pavilion

1904, P. Munroe.
Amusement Arcade.
An ambitious example of its type - a big, rectangular building on the pier with a domed, octagonal tower at each corner and a cupola in the middle of the roof. Open promenade around the sides at first floor level, supported by slender iron columns. Auditorium originally with one balcony around three sides and flat main floor. Proscenium with florid rectangular frame and a big cartouche over the top. Ceiling originally with canted sides and a flat centre, painted with elaborately shaped panels. Proscenium width 28ft., stage depth 33ft., grid 32ft. Although the basic form is still there, many subsequent alterations have taken place.   C.B.

Knightstone Pavilion and Opera House

1901, J. S. Stewart.
Seasonal theatre.
A good example of a typical seaside all-purpose hall/theatre of the date. Situated on a tongue of land jutting out into the sea. A long, low pitched-roofed hall, partly stone and partly rendered. On the entrance side the gable of the hall is flanked by square Italianate towers with low pyramid roofs. Projecting forward from each of these is a two-storeyed gable-ended wing with a low entrance foyer fitted between - now altered. At the stage end of the hall roof (there is no fly-tower) are smaller square towers with depressed domes. Stretching between these and the bigger towers at the front are low colonnades of coupled Tuscan columns with balustraded parapets. These form open promenades at the sides of the auditorium, reached by means of wide, segmentally-arched windows. The auditorium (650 seats) is a long, rectangular hall with a segmental barrel-vaulted ceiling. The main floor was originally flat but a rake was provided in 1958. At the rear is a straight balcony which continues along the sides where it is supported at the front edge by square piers in five bays. These rise above the level of the balcony and are linked by segmental arches below the ceiling. Very restrained plasterwork. Proscenium 24ft., stage depth 28ft. No flying.   C.B.

Wexford,
Eire
Theatre Royal
High Street.
1832, architect unknown.

1942, reconstructed.
1961, stage rebuilt.
Cinema/Theatre/Festival Opera.
The theatre of 1832 had two balconies, a small stage and a narrow auditorium. It was reconstructed as a cinema in 1942. The old balconies were removed and a single, deep balcony formed. (200 in balcony, 225 in stalls). The stage and dressing rooms were retained. In 1951 the Wexford Festival Opera was inaugurated - a short season at the end of the summer devoted to performances of rarely heard operas. In 1961 the old stage was removed and the space absorbed into the auditorium for extra seating and an orchestra pit. The fomer rear wall of the old stage became the line of the new proscenium and a new stage was erected beyond. In 1972 the front-of-house was extended, following the acquisition of two houses in the High Street.   C.B.

Weymouth,
Dorset
Theatre Royal
pre-1914 fragment only
West Street.
1884, converted to theatre from chapel of 1864, architect Samuel Johnson.
Demolished in 1968 with the exception of part of the entrance front.   D.F.C.

Whitby,
North Yorkshire
Spa Theatre
1870, J. O. Mayhew & E. H. Smales.
Seasonal and amateur theatre.
Originally called the West Cliff Saloon -a flat-floored hall with a rear balcony of nine rows continuing into narrow side balconies. Total seating capacity 513. Plain ceiling and proscenium - width 26ft., stage depth 27ft., no fly tower. The building is of stone and situated on a levelled-off piece of ground dug out of the side of a steep slope down to the sea from the Royal Crescent. It is 'E' shaped in plan facing the sea with the low, pitched-roofed auditorium placed lengthwise between projecting two-storeyed wings with Dutch gables and finials. The theatre is used for summer shows and amateur performances. C.B.

Whitley Bay,
Tyne and Wear
Empire
Whitley Street.
1898, architect unknown.
1920's, reconstructed.
Ballroom.
Largely rebuilt in the 1920's as a cinema (Gaumont), only part of the basic structure being retained. The present neo-

Adam stuccoed facade dates from the rebuilding. Interior completely gutted for present use.   J.D.N./C.B.

Playhouse

Park Road.
(Formerly: Kursaal).
1911, architect unknown.
1920's, reconstructed.
Theatre & cinema.

Opened as the Kursaal. Burnt out in the 1920's and largely rebuilt as a cine-variety theatre with a shallow stage and fly tower. Completely plain exterior. Plain, remodelled interior with 850 seats on one level. Owned by County Council and used for theatre, cinema, concerts, etc.   J.D.N./C.B.

Spanish City Theatre

Esplanade.
c.1910, architect unknown.
Bingo.

Typical seaside pavilion - a large flat-floored hall with a shallow stage and no fly tower. One deep balcony at the rear with straight rows, continued into narrow arms at the sides. The proscenium is set back within a very deep, segmental arched splay. The whole space is dominated by a huge, coffered, barrel-vaulted ceiling. White stuccoed exterior - a wide front with a central arched entrance and nine bays of Tuscan columns at first floor level under a straight parapet. Slim, square towers at the ends, now lacking their original cupolas. Set back behind the facade is a big, bulbous dome with *oeil-de-boeuf* windows.   J.D.N/C.B.

Whitstable, Kent

Theatre

Horsebridge.
1868, architect unknown.
Bingo/shop.

This unprepossessing building was damaged by a bomb in 1940 and remained derelict until converted for use as a bingo hall (upstairs) and shop (downstairs) c.1960.   D.F.C.

Widnes, Cheshire

Alexandra Theatre

Alexandra Street.
1887, architect unknown.
Derelict factory.

Burnt out but adapted to use as a factory, which closed in 1978.   D.F.C.

Wigan, Greater Manchester

Hippodrome

pre-1914 fragment only
King Street.
(Formerly: Grand Hippodrome).
1904, Owen & Ward.
1909, reconstructed by J. & W. Thornley.

Burnt out in 1956 and rebuilt as a supermarket in 1959. All that remains of the theatre is a chimney with the letters "HIP" vertically on the side!   C.B.

Royal Court Theatre

★ facade only/disused
King Street.
1886, R. T. Johnson.
1899, remodelled by J. P. Briggs.
1930, interior reconstructed.
Closed.

Externally the theatre is little altered. Internally however, the auditorium was

rebuilt as a cinema in 1930 and some of the stage area was incorporated within its volume. The interesting brick facade is of two dates - the upper storey, with round-arched windows and surmounting gable with the name "Royal Court Theatre", dates from 1886. The two-storeyed lower part, projecting one bay forward from the original building, dates from 1899. At first floor level, above a canopy of 1930, are five bays of large windows lighting the principal saloon, divided by fluted Ionic pilasters. The central bay has a rectangular window with a broken segmental pediment and an *oeil-de-boeuf* window above. The bays on either side are pierced by very wide, elliptically-arched windows with leaded lights.   C.B.

Winchester, Hampshire

New Theatre Royal

★
Jewry Street.
1914, Chancellor.
Theatre.

An excellent example of small cine-variety theatre which has survived in an almost unaltered state. The auditorium (capacity 419) has a typical segmental barrel-vaulted ceiling spanning the full width, and a single, slightly-curved balcony. In this case, however, something rather more positive than usual was retained of the theatre/music-hall tradition, in that the balcony has side arms which become two-bow-fronted boxes at each end, flanking the proscenium (23ft.). Florid Baroque plasterwork on balcony and box fronts. Typically shallow stage (20ft.) and low fly tower. Pleasing stuccoed facade which incorporates part of the facade of the hotel which occupied the site prior to 1914. It ties in well with

Wigan, Royal Court Theatre
Iain Mackintosh

Winchester, Theatre Royal   *Christopher Brereton*

the adjoining terrace. The first floor has four wide bays defined by coupled Ionic pilasters. Each bay has a single rectangular window with an ornamented surround and three festoons above. Straight bracketted cornice and a low attic storey above the centre. Almost always used as a cinema. Following its closure in 1974 the Winchester Theatre Fund was formed in 1977 and money raised to purchase the building with the object of restoring it and re-opening as a theatre. It is now run as a touring theatre while funds are raised for more extensive improvements.
Listed Grade II.   C.B.

Windsor,
Berkshire
Theatre Royal
★ ★

Thames Street.
1902, William Shipley.
1912, interior reconstructed after a fire by F. T. Verity.
Theatre.
Situated (literally) in the shadow of the castle. Tall, narrow, stone facade with big mullioned and transomed window. This dates from 1902. Frank Verity's auditorium has one deep balcony and boxes on either side linking it to the proscenium which is flanked by engaged columns. The rear part of the stalls is raised-up behind a curved parapet and has a good rake. French Neo-Classical style plasterwork on ceiling, proscenium etc. In 1965 Verity's open iron-work balustrades to the balcony and boxes were replaced by solid fronts, ornamented with plasterwork in a style sympathetic with the remainder but perhaps to be regretted - ironwork balustrades are rare generally in theatre architecture but a few appeared around this period; Verity's own Scala Theatre, 1905 (demolished), Wimbledon Theatre, 1910 (q.v.), and The Opera House, Manchester 1912 (q.v.). Seating capacity 620. Proscenium 28ft., stage depth 30ft., grid 54ft. Workshops at rear of stage. The theatre is privately owned and run as a repertory playhouse.
Listed Grade II.   C.B.

Wisbech,
Cambridgeshire
Angles Theatre
★

Alexandra Road.
1793, architect unknown.
Amateur theatre.
A country town theatre, first on the Lincoln and later (from 1847) on the Norwich circuit. In 1897 it became part of a school and was considerably altered internally. In 1977, however, Mr. Richard Leacroft made a careful survey of the building and discovered sufficient evidence to enable him to produce an account of its internal arrangement

(*Theatre Notebook Vol. XXXII (2)*). The basic structural shell survives - a plain brick rectangle measuring 60ft. × 26ft. inside the walls, with a pitched roof. Internally it now consists of a hall with a timber floor and a room partitioned off at one end, and a basement below. Under the floor Mr. Leacroft discovered a beam which had formerly supported the front edge of the stage and also beams which had supported the front edges of the side boxes and front boxes. These beams revealed a rectangular arrangement of boxes similar to Richmond Theatre, Yorkshire (q.v.). He also found, part-way up the height of the partition dividing the hall from the smaller rooms, beams which had supported the front edge of the gallery, and two cast iron columns which rose from the basement to support these beams. The line of the auditorium ceiling is also original - flat over the pit area and sloping upward over the gallery area. Thanks to this careful research it has been possible to add considerably to our knowledge of the design of a typical Georgian country playhouse. In 1978 an amateur theatre/cinema with 120 seats was opened in the building, which was renamed the Angles Theatre.   C.B.

Wolverhampton,
West Midlands
Grand Theatre
★ ★ ★

Lichfield Street.
1894, C. J. Phipps.
Theatre.
This is among the most important of Phipps' remaining theatres and he himself regarded it as one of this most successful designs. The auditorium has a remarkable degree of intimacy for its 1,400 seats. This is achieved largely by two means: First; the width (68ft.) is greater than the maximum depth (50ft. horizontal distance from the back rows of the stalls and first balcony to the curtain line, and 65ft. horizontal distance from the back of the second balcony to curtain line). Secondly; the rows of the balconies, especially the first one, are very fully curved and come around close to the stage to the detriment, it must be admitted, of sight-lines at the extreme sides. This drawback, however, is a small price to pay for the superbly vibrant atmosphere which this auditorium possesses. The balconies are partly cantilevered and partly supported on iron columns, and have plasterwork of early Renaissance character. The ends of the balconies are separated from the stage by a single box on each side at dress circle level. These are framed by fluted Corinthian columns which carry curly broken pediments. The design of the beautiful ceiling follows a pattern frequently used by Phipps - a large, flat, circular centre, divided into richly decorated radiating panels, supported at the sides, above the upper balcony slips, by

Wolverhampton, Grand Theatre
Victor Glasstone

high, panelled coves. The proscenium is well related in width (35ft.) to the scale of the auditorium. The design of its reticent rectangular frame, decorated with filigree plasterwork and surmounted by a pedimental tablet, has much in common with the proscenium which existed at Nottingham Theatre Royal (q.v.) prior to its unecessary removal in 1978. There is a splendid contemporay painted act drop, still in everyday use - one of only two of the period in the country to be so (q.v. The Gaiety Theatre, Douglas). It depicts a classical landscape with dancing nymphs, hung about with elaborately swagged and tasselled draperies. Stage depth 42ft., grid 54ft. The facade to Lichfield Street is of considerable width - approximately 100ft. It is in brick with painted stone dressings and the design is very French in character. In the centre is a tall, arcaded loggia, set in front of the first and second floor saloons. This is flanked at either end of the facade by two-bay pavilions with steep mansard roofs. Following a threat of closure in 1969 the theatre was promptly acquired by Wolverhampton Corporation. Since then although technical improvements have been carried out, there have also been some unfortunate alterations to

Wolverhampton, Theatre Royal
Victor Glasstone

the interior. During an amateur redecoration of the auditorium the delicate arabesques on the coves below the ceiling were obliterated. A grossly unsympathetic 'acoustic tile' false ceiling has been installed in the well proportioned dress circle saloon, and the panelled doors covered over. A theatre of this importance deserves a thorough refurbishing under the direction of an experienced theatre architect or theatre consultant.

Listed Grade II.   C.B.

Theatre Royal

★ ★ disused
Bilston Street.
1865, architect unknown.
1914, reconstructed after fire, architect unknown.
Closed.
Opened in 1865 as the Star Theatre. In 1903 renamed Prince of Wales, in 1907 the Hippodrome, and in 1908 the Theatre Royal. Gutted by fire in 1913 and reopened in 1914, after reconstruction, as the New Theatre Royal. The stuccoed facade is basically intact from 1865 and quite handsome, in spite of alterations to the pedimental gable which was given a stepped profile probably in 1933 when building became a cinema. The ground floor is treated as a podium on which stand five bays of giant Corinthian pilasters with a straight entablature above. The end bays have decorative stucco panels and curved pediments. The three central

bays have arched windows, now partly blocked, and projecting busts in circular frames. The auditorium dates from 1914 but has suffered alterations to the boxes and proscenium. There are two balconies of eight rows each, slightly curved in the centre with reverse curves at the ends. Their fronts have the same decorative treatment -consoles at intervals forming panels decorated by extremely florid cartouches. Two boxes on either side at first balcony level separated by square Ionic columns supporting gallery slips above. They now have plain, panelled fronts. The lower half of the rectangular proscenium frame has also lost its mouldings. The side walls at upper balcony level have blank arcades with flattened arches. Flat, panelled ceiling over the whole space, with coved edges. The seating capacity is approximately 1,000, proscenium 28ft., stage depth 30ft. The building is now in poor condition, and has been threatened with demolition.

Not listed.   C.B.

Woodbridge, Suffolk

Theatre
pre-1914 fragment only
1814.
Auction rooms on site incorporate a few remains of Fisher's Theatre. Theatrical use ceased in 1860.   D.F.C.

Wolverhampton, Theatre Royal
Victor Glasstone

Worcester, Hereford and Worcester

Prince of Wales Theatre
Lowesmoor Wharf.
1869, architect unknown.
Salvation Army.

Wolverhampton, Grand Theatre   *Christopher Brereton*

Long utilitarian frontage of 2 storeys with wide windows between pilasters buttresses. There is nothing theatrical about it and it appears to have been re-done by the Salvation Army. Interior also completely rebuilt for non-theatrical use. C.B.

Workington, Cumbria

New Opera House
Pow Street.
1888, architect unknown.
1897, reconstructed after explosion, architect unknown.
1927, reconstructed after fire.
Bingo.
Originally opened as the Queen's Jubilee Hall and Opera House - a small theatre with two balconies. Gutted by fire in 1927 and rebuilt completely as a cine-theatre except for part of the structural walls on one side. It now has a wide auditorium with one deep balcony and approximately 1,200 seats. Proscenium 36ft., stage depth 30ft., grid 44ft. In 1963 the narrow street front was re-built in aluminium and glass.
C.B.

Theatre Royal
Washington Street.
1866, architect unknown.
1879, altered, architect unknown.
1888, altered, architect unknown.
1912, reconstructed, architect unknown.
Amateur Theatre.
Of the original building all that now remains is the basic structural shell and the stage. The 1866 auditorium had a horseshoe balcony with arms to the proscenium and a gallery above. In 1912 the balconies and side arms where removed and a single balcony constructed with ten straight rows. Completely plain side walls and ceiling. In its overall proportions the auditorium is long and narrow. The rear seats of the balcony appear particularly remote from the stage, although the actual distance is not great - the present capacity is 270. The proscenium was also re-designed in 1912 as a rectangular moulded frame with a central cartouche. Proscenium 22ft., stage depth 23ft. (on centre-line of sloping rear wall), grid approximately 35ft. The narrow, stuccoed facade forms part of the general street frontage and in overall appearance and detail dates from 1912 - three storeys of unequally disposed windows under a steep gable.
C.B.

Worksop, Nottinghamshire

Gaiety Theatre
Bridge Street.
1875, architect unknown.
1908, converted to theatre, architect unknown.
Closed.

Originally built as the Criterion Hall. Stage added and other alterations carried out in 1908 and re-opened as Gaiety Theatre. Long narrow auditorium - approximately 80ft. long × 30ft. wide; quite hopeless theatrically. Capacity approximately 600. The stage is the same width as the auditorium 30ft., proscenium 20ft., grid 38ft. Two-storeyed stuccoed facade with shops either side the central entrance doors, and five tall casement windows above at first floor level, topped by a balustraded parapet. In 1979 planning permission was granted for re-development as shops.
C.B.

Wrexham, Clwyd

Wrexham Hippodrome
Hope Street.
1907, architect unknown.
Cinema.
Built on the site of the Public Hall which was destroyed by fire. Plain, two-storeyed brick front. Interesting lozenge-shaped auditorium (approximately 800 seats); One curved balcony with Baroque plasterwork on its front. No boxes. Tiny triangular stage in one corner of the lozenge. Proscenium at present obscured by curtains surrounding the cinema screen. Used as a cinema since 1930. C.B.

York, North Yorkshire

Empire Theatre
★ ★ disused
Clifford Street.
1902, J. P. Briggs.
Bingo.
Originally a corn exchange and warehouse of 1868, reconstructed as a theatre in 1902 and opened as The Grand Opera House. Renamed the Grand Opera House and Empire in 1903. The elevation to King Street, which is the rear wall of the auditorium, is basically that of the warehouse, with four storeys of narrow, segmentally-arched windows. The rear wall of the stage on Cumberland Street still has the semi-circular arched windows of the corn exchange hall, and it is possible to make out the shape of the original gable in the brickwork - later heightened for the fly tower. The theatre does not have a show-front of its own - the main entrance being through a wide arch in the ground floor of a three-storeyed row of shops with offices over; also part of a corn exchange development. The style is vaguely Italian Gothic with closely-spaced arched windows at first floor level, separated by stone shafts. The entrance foyer is long and narrow with a

York, Theatre Royal   *Henk Snoek*

194

good plaster ceiling. The interior is completely intact apart from the lowering of the stage floor to stalls level. The auditorium is very intimate and would seat approximately 1,000, by present standards. Unfortunately it has recently been re-decorated in gloss paint to a hideously garish colour scheme. There are two balconies - the first, of nine rows, has a serpentine front decorated with an unusual repeated arched panel motif. The sight-line to the stage in the vertical plane from the rear of this balcony is severly cut by the extremely low overhang of the upper balcony. The upper balcony, however, has unusually good sight-lines in the vertical plane; its front being set well below the edge of the main ceiling. There are two bow-fronted boxes at the level of each balcony on either side, tied together as a composition of giant Corinthian columns linked at the top by arches. The main ceiling is in the form of a saucer dome, decorated by a plaster 'sunburst' radiating from the centre. Rectangular, moulded proscenium frame with cartouche over the top. Proscenium width 29ft., stage depth 34ft., grid 42ft. The building is not listed but should be. C.B.

York, Theatre Royal   *Henk Snoek*

Theatre Royal

St. Leonards Place.
1765, architect unknown.
1820's, reconstructed, architect unknown.
1835, Gothic 'piazza' added by John Harper.
1880, new facade by George Styan.
1902, new auditorium and stage by Frank Tugwell.
1967, new foyer by Patrick Gwynne (consultant Victor Glasstone).
Theatre.

A theatre was first built on the present site in 1765, and a Royal patent was acquired in 1769. The building was often reconstructed. The present facade dates from 1880, and the present auditorium and stage from a major rebuilding of 1902. The stone facade is in a gutsy Victorian Gothic style - three storeys under a wide gable flanked by corbelled turrets, and crowned by crocketted niche containing a statue. A big oriel window projects from the centre of the first floor and at ground level there is an open arcade of five pointed arches. In 1967 the stonework was cleaned, ugly accretions removed and the arcade opened up. The auditorium is superbly intimate, yet also has a feel-

ing of noble spaciousness. This is partly due to the overall proporions (60ft. wide × 55ft. stage to rear rows), and partly to the sweeping curves of the closely-spaced shallow balconies (six rows each). Sight-lines are excellent, even from the sides of the steeply-raked upper balcony. Flanking the stage are ranges of superimposed, bow-fronted boxes - two on each side at the levels of the first and second balconies and a single, wide box at the top. The boxes are framed by tall, panelled pilasters, linked just below the ceiling by a wide elliptical arch. The proscenium has a segmentally-arched top and a deep curving sounding-board. Although some of the plasterwork is conventional Baroque, e.g. the balusters on the fronts of the lower boxes, the majority is in an imaginative and fluid version of the *Art Nouveau* - possibly the only example of the full-blooded use of this style in British theatre design. In 1967 the stalls were re-seated with continuous rows and the rear part partitioned off to form a new cloak-room and exhibition space. The seating capacity was reduced from 1,300 to 950 - unfortunately, at the same time reducing the theatre's viability for touring opera and ballet etc. The pro-

scenium width is 30ft., and stage depth 27ft. stage right, and 30ft. stage left, grid 47ft.. Also in 1967 a new entrance foyer, restaurant and bars were added to the left of the theatre. These were housed in an elegant glass-walled pavilion consisting of a cluster of hexagonal concrete 'mushrooms' sprouting from slender tapered columns. The lightness of the new work forms a pleasing contrast with the Gothic solidity of the old. It is infinitely more successful than the similarly briefed, and near contemporary addition at Liverpool Playhouse (q.v.). Access to all levels is now gained by a single, sinuous staircase set alongside the exposed stonework of the flanking elevation of the old building. As part of the same project, the dressing rooms, offices, workshops etc. were modernised and partly rebuilt. The auditorium was also re-decorated in a rather dull scheme using 12 shades of green. Fortunately in 1979 this was changed to a warmer, more attractive scheme using brown, cream and gold. The theatre is owned by the City Council and has a resident repertory company and also takes occasional tours.
Listed Grade II.   C.B.

1867 tier fronts of Newcastle's recently restored Tyne Theatre

Iain Mackintosh

Historical Profile
Iain Mackintosh

Prepared by Iain Mackintosh, based on the work of Christopher Brereton and John Earl

"**The Theatric Tourist:** being a genuine collection of correct views, with brief and authentic historical accounts of all the Principal Provincial Theatres in the United Kingdom. Replete with useful and necessary information to theatrical professors, whereby they may learn to choose and regulate their county engagements; and with numerous anecdotes to amuse the reader. By a Theatric Amateur. . ."

Thus the introduction to James Winston's **Theatric Tourist**, a part work, the first part of which was published in 1804, but which petered out the following year after featuring only 24 of the proposed 90 principal out-of-London theatres. But this was not all: there still survive various diaries, notebooks and even watercolours in Harvard, Birmingham and Sydney with notes prepared between 1800 and 1904 of nearly 350 theatres. The **Curtains!!!** committee sympathizes with Winston; there were moments when this project seemed as likely to fail. But the committee also admires Winston's solo achievement as this was as formidable as the facts he gathered. (It is worth remembering that between 1682 and 1694 there had been only one theatre in London plus a handful of strolling players in the rest of Britain). Sadly, of Winston's 300 theatres which were the fruit of Britain's first great theatre building boom in the Provinces (a phrase then including Philadelphia and Baltimore as well as Ireland and the Islands) only 4 theatres remain in anything like restorable state — and none of these date from before 1766.

Of course one very early theatrical building does still stand; the Banqueting House in Whitehall. Here the tantalising possibility of recreating Inigo Jones's multi-level fit up structure for audience and stage need not for ever be a dream. But that is a special case; the hard truth is that we have no Elizabethan theatres, no Jacobean theatres and no Restoration theatres. Our oldest theatre is the Theatre Royal, Bristol (1766), some say modelled to the same size as contemporary Drury Lane, Wren's building of 1663 in its penultimate state prior to the extensive redecoration of 1775 by Robert Adam. But here must be entered a caveat: the Bristol Theatre Royal was much altered between 1800 and 1830, a gallery inserted and mouldings added on the circle fronts and elsewhere which in certain respects makes Bristol later in atmosphere than the only theatre in Britain that really does evoke the eighteenth century playhouse, the unique, and possibly most exciting theatre of them all, the restored Georgian Theatre, Richmond, of 1788.

The hope survives that such a restoration might be possible elsewhere. More confident scholarship and the experience of Richmond would allow as much authenticity to be recreated from less evidence. But the opportunity was, sadly, lost at Stamford, Lincolnshire, where behind a fine 1768 facade will be found a new unimaginative cinema-type auditorium. The shell of the Newbury Theatre Royal, with its interior largely unresearched and its miniature town square of cottages in front still standing, was wantonly destroyed in the mid 1970s. A few years earlier, the more rudimentary yet restorable first floor theatre in Dorchester had been lost. Now only Penzance and Wisbech seem to retain enough to permit a plausible reconstruction although in these pages will be found records of other fragmentary remnants, for the most part scattered through East Anglia. This means we have lost well over 250 theatres which were thriving 175 years ago. But generally these are not twentieth century losses: most of these theatres vanished within 30 or 40 years of being built.

From the 1820s to the 1840s theatre in Britain declined; the closures and consequent unemployment were on a scale worse than that which followed later disasters of the sort which seem to overtake us at twenty five year intervals: the arrival of moving pictures, of talkies, of television and now, of government cut-backs. A **Times** leader in 1825 reported: "the state of theatrical property in England is wretched beyond description. Many of the large towns which supported a theatre three or four months in the year do not now encourage a week's acting and in many places where the theatres are open, the performers are starving." The aftermath of war, economic decline (especially in the country towns), the rise of sectarianism in an increasingly God fearing society, the melodramatic style of acting encouraged by the building of elephantine auditoriums in the major London houses, even the spread of railways, which resulted in fewer but larger provincial centres and which took the fashionable audience to London, all contributed to the decline of theatre-going and of theatre building. Few theatres were built from 1820 to 1850 and hence few survive.

Today we have but three theatres from the first half of the nineteenth century. The only one in use was built a year or two before the slump, the magnificent Theatre Royal, Bury St. Edmunds of 1819 designed by William Wilkins, best known today as the architect of the National Gallery, London and Downing College, Cambridge; best known then as lessee of the entire East Anglian circuit based in Norwich, the theatres of which were all built or rebuilt by Wilkins father and son. The second is another Wilkins theatre now a scenic workshop: the Barnwell Theatre at Cambridge, known as the Festival since 1926 when its stage but not its auditorium was rebuilt by Terence Gray. The third is the little 'Court Theatre' of the Devonshires at Chatsworth, modest but charming.

During the next period, 1856 to 1875, many new theatres were built in the great cities. However, nearly all were replaced at the end of the century when even greater magnificence and seating capacity were demanded. Hence what little remains is extremely valuable. The Royal Opera House, Covent Garden of 1858 is, of course, pre-eminent and is our only auditorium to rival the metropolitan magnificence of Europe's nineteenth century national or municipal houses. Brighton's Royal (1866) lost much of its moulding and most of its character in the improvements of 1927. But six support theatres of a scale appropriate to today's drama, to chamber opera and to ballet, survive, having suffered little or no 'improvement'. These six consist of Phipps' oldest theatres, the Theatre Royal, Bath (1863), and the Gaiety Dublin of 1871, the unique Tyne Theatre built in 1867 in Newcastle, which is one of Britain's most beautiful theatres and is complete with a uniquely complete set of original stage machinery and the two surviving examples of the work of Robinson, the architect who trained Matcham himself: the Theatre Royal, Margate, the auditorium of which dates from 1874, and the Old Vic, London, of 1871. The latter, were the ravages to the proscenium zone of 1928 and 1963 to be repaired, could once again become one of Europe's most perfectly balanced playhouses. Lastly note must be taken of three fine music halls: in Leeds (City of Varieties), London (Hoxton) and Glasgow (Britannia). In London there are three curious oddities, The Royal Clarence within the Greenwich Market Building, the Islington Palace within the Agricultural Hall and the Alexandra Palace Theatre within Ally Pally.

The legacy of the years of 1876 to 1895 is a mix of theatres that in a sense belong to an earlier age and of those which presage the Boom Years to come from 1896 to 1910. Looking back, so to speak, are two major small music halls, the Philharmonic, Cardiff (1877) and the famous Wilton's of London (1878), Verity's unusual and underground Criterium of 1884, plus a clutch of Phipps' theatres: the Lyceum, Edinburgh and Royal Hippodrome of Eastbourne (both 1883), the Northampton Royal (1887), the Lyric, Shaftesbury Avenue, (1888 but worked over in 1932), the Garrick (1889) and lastly his two finest surviving provincial auditoriums, the Grand, Wolverhampton of 1894 and the new home of Scottish Opera, the Theatre Royal, Glasgow of 1895. Looking forward are the early Matcham houses, the recently restored theatres at Belfast (1895), Blackpool (1894) and Hammersmith (1895), and the yet-to-be reborn but charming Opera House, Wakefield of 1894. This leaves first a few good theatres by minor architects, second two private theatres, rare in Britain, one instigated by a world famous soprano in Wales, the other by a Doctor's wife in an asylum in the Home Counties, and third one exceptional work by a man who built only one theatre in his life, the incomparable Grand Theatre, Leeds, completed in 1878. Despite the loss of some irreplacable stage machinery the Grand, with its introduction of Gothic grandeur, proclaims all the might and self confidence that built an Empire, a Greater Britain, and some would say, an even greater Yorkshire.

This brings us to the Boom Years of 1896 to 1910, 15 years when the greater part of our surviving old theatres and auditoriums were built. Of the 86 that still exist, 43 are working theatres while 8 fall into categories of circus, flat floorhall, Kursaal or concert party house (3 still in use). This leaves 31 which are 'resting' and no longer welcome a new company each Monday morning. All these are in fact rescuable, especially those in Aberdeen, Aberystwyth, Barnsley, Brighton, Colchester, Doncaster, Longton (Stoke-on-Trent), Middlesbrough, Sheffield and York. The opportunities presented by these theatres is dealt with elsewhere in this book in an article entitled **Sleeping Beauties.**

At the turn of the century theatre architects, led by Frank Matcham who built more theatres than any other Englishman in any age, were confident and competent. The theatre business was extremely profitable, capital outlay being often recovered in under five years. However, Edwin O. Sachs, who in 1896 wrote the definitive three volume **Modern Opera Houses and Theatres,** which deal with theatre architecture across the whole of Europe was dismissive: "In the work of C. J. Phipps and Frank Matcham there is no architectural feeling in the treatment either of exterior or of interior, architectural grouping or even careful detail is a thing unknown." Grudgingly he noted Matcham's cost, cost control and rapidity of execution. Sachs, whose most enduring work is the present stage of the Royal Opera House, preferred the grander theatres of Europe built by Princes and Governments to stand on spacious sites.

And yet it was the commercial pressure in Britain to pack as many people as possible on to a small city centre site that resulted in theatre auditoriums which by sheer concentration of humanity can raise the theatrical temperature to a point unrealisable in the vaster less densely populated theatres of a later age, for all their perfect sightlines and their so called functional efficiency. The years 1896 to 1910 gave us Wyndhams, the Richmond Theatre, the Buxton

Opera House, Newcastle Royal, the present Haymarket auditorium, and the York Theatre Royal, all of which attract performers as much as they delight theatregoers. There are many more, both in use and usable, which suggests that this period is the only one for which the legacy is of reasonable proportion. And there can be no doubt that the finest Edwardian theatres, which incidentally form the stock of our present West End, represent some of the finest theatres ever built by man.

Move past 1910 and the auditoriums that remain of the relatively few that were built generally have a heaviness which makes them less attractive than the auditoriums of earlier theatres. These auditoriums were larger, mostly as a direct consequence of the greed of successful entrepreneurs. But somehow the same amount of plasterwork seems to have been spread thinner. The Greek or Roman styles, more appropriate to the head office of a bank or the outposts of an Empire, were introduced in a way that reduces the actors to pygmies in a dictator's triumph. Occasionally these larger auditoriums convince as does the Manchester Palace of 1913 (Bertie Crewe), but even here a straight play is likely to fail unless tricked out with big budget scenery. There are a few surprises such as the fact that one of the later of these auditoriums, the Drury Lane interior of 1922, appears to be the exception to the general rule that no decent theatres were built in Britain between 1920 and 1950. Generally only the smallest of the auditoriums from the twilight years can be said to make fine theatres regardless of age. Two such are the St. Martin's London (1916) and the 1920 remodelling of the Opera House, Dunfermline. Their rarity makes them all the more significant.

Our profile ends at the beginning of the twenties. Omitted from the scope of this book are the movie palaces of the late twenties, such as the Playhouse, Edinburgh or the later Empires and other large variety houses, mostly built by Milburn for the Stoll and Moss circuits. Such late theatres have their admirers, especially in towns such as Birmingham which has managed to lose all of its earlier and finer theatres. Yet however much money is spent on paintwork or orchestra pits one can not but help feeling in these later auditoriums that things have got out of hand — the architects working to a set of rules that failed to distinguish live performance from cinema, the managers anxious to wring every last penny from as many theatregoers as possible who could only be drawn by the few stars able to project in these over-large houses.

In these later auditoriums the prosceniums are hardened and the circles no longer break into waves of boxes and plasterwork to engulf the actor. Had not the First World War been followed by more than a partial recovery in theatrical fortunes, then in Britain, as in America, many more of the good theatre auditoriums from earlier years 1895 — 1910 would have been 'improved' or replaced entirely by inferior and larger constructions. Thus, there is no difficulty in putting an end to the **Curtains!!! Gazeteer** at 1914 and in allowing only a few to slip through after and only for special reasons. And if there are those who question this judgment then one can only invite them first to savour the distinct pleasures of the Georgian Playhouse, of the mid-Victorian Opera House or Playhouse, and of the finer Edwardian theatres and then to experience the Empires or Hippodromes of the late twenties. Only the partisan who prefers, say, the Cambridge to Her Majesty's, or those who, out of London, have nothing better in their cities in which to stage the drama, variety, ballet or opera would advance the claims of the movie palace or over-large variety theatre of the twenties against those of the pre-1914 theatres. No apology, therefore, is needed for taking the First World War as the date for ringing down a curtain on this 155 year profile of Britain's old theatres.

From Georgian to mid Victorian · 1766 to 1855

Bristol, Royal
Richmond, Georgian

—1800   1801—1805

Penzance, Theatre
Wisbech, Theatre (Angles)

Key

The historical profile on this and the following nine pages places all the surviving theatres of quality (★ ★ ★, ★ ★ or ★) on a line divided into 5 year sections from pre-1800 to post-1916.

The position on the line of each theatre is determined by the date of its surviving auditorium. Hence the Theatre Royal in the Haymarket, London, is placed in the span 1901-1905 because its auditorium was built in 1905 although the portico dates from 1821. Theatres altered for their auditoriums e.g. the Old Vic is seen as 1871 when Robinson put in the present auditorium, not 1819 the date of the building nor 1928 or 1963 when the proscenium zone was successively remodelled, the Theatre Royal, Brighton 1866 not 1927 etc.

The theatres above the line printed in **bold** are in theatrical use, those below the line in light are disused but restorable.

As elsewhere in the Gazetteer and in the maps Roman type is used both above and below the line for conventional theatres with attributes appropriate to their age, e.g. flytower, proscenium arch, raked stalls and one or more balconies while *Italic* type is used for all other auditoriums: music halls, circus theatres, private theatres occasionally used by professionals, pier theatres, Kursaals and other flat floor theatres.   I.M.

| 1806—1810 | 1811—1815 | 1816—1820 |

Cambridge, Festival

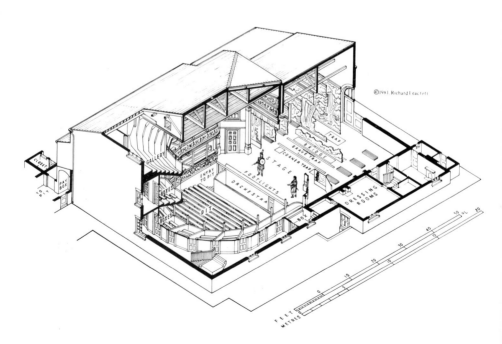

©1981 Richard Leacroft

The Festival Theatre Cambridge as it was when first built by William Wilkins   cutaway drawing Richard Leacroft

Chatsworth, Theatre

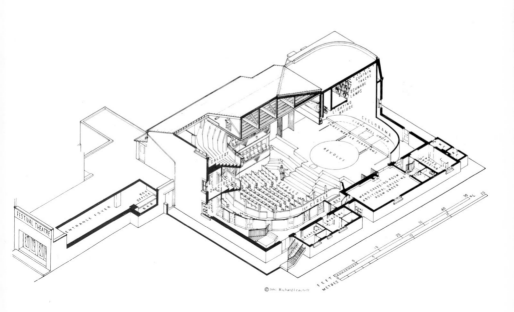

The Festival Theatre Cambridge as it was in 1926 after remodelling by Gordon Craig   cutaway drawing by Richard Leacroft

| 1836—1840 | 1841—1845 | 1846—1850 |

Mid Victorian · 1856 to 1875

	London, Royal Opera House	Bath, Royal Leeds, City Varieties
1851—1855	**1856—1860**	**1861—1865**
	Glasgow, Britannia	Birkenhead, Music Hall

Bath Theatre Royal Auditorium, 1863, by
C. J. Phipps   *copyright N.M.R.*

Brighton, Royal *London, Hoxton* **Newcastle, Tyne**	Dublin, Gaiety London, Old Vic	Glasgow, Citizens Leeds, Grand *Scarborough, Spa* Waterford, Royal
1866—1870	**1871—1875**	**1876—1880**
London, Islington Palace	*London, Alexandra Palace* *London, Royal Clarence Geenwich* Margate, Royal	*Cardiff, Philharmonic* *London, Normansfield* *London, Wilton's*

Newcastle Tyne Theatre Iain Mackintosh

· 1876 to 1895

		Belfast, Grand Opera
		Blackpool, Grand
		Blackpool, Tower Circus
		Cheltenham, Everyman
		Craig-y-Nos, Patti's
		Glasgow, Athenaeum
Eastbourne, Royal Hippodrome	London, Garrick	Glasgow, Royal
Edinburgh, Lyceum	London, Lyric	London, Duke of York's
London, Comedy	London, Royal Court	London, Lyric Hammersmith
London, Criterion	Northampton, Royal	London, Palace
London, Stratford East	Plymouth, Globe	Wolverhampton, Grand

1881—1885   1886—1890   1891—1895

	Swansea, Palace	Bournemouth, Boscombe, Hippodrome
		Wakefield, Opera House

London Duke of York's

London Coliseum

Boom Years 1896 to 1910

Ayr, Gaiety
Buxton, Opera House
Eastbourne, Devonshire Park
Glasgow, Pavilion
Glasgow, King's

Blackpool, Tower Ballroom
Douglas, Gaiety
Dublin, Olympia
Harrogate, Opera House
Llandudno, Grand
London, Her Majesty's
London, Richmond
London, Wyndhams
Nottingham, Royal
Perth, Theatre
Plymouth, Palace
Southborough, Royal Victoria
Swansea, Grand

Great Yarmouth, Hippodrome
Halifax, Civic
Harrogate, Royal Hall
London, Albery
London, Aldwych
London, Apollo
London, Coliseum
London, Haymarket
London, Strand
Newcastle, Royal
York, Royal
Weston-Super-Mare,
Knightstone Pavilion

Aberdeen, His Majesty's
Cardiff, New
Darlington, Civic
Edinburgh, King's
Folkestone, Leas Pavilion
Lancaster, Grand
Lincoln, Royal
London, Globe
London, Palladium
London, Queens
London, Wimbledon
Portsmouth, King's Southsea
Scarborough, Opera House
Sunderland, Empire
Rhyl, Gaiety
Watford, Palace

1896—1900 | 1901—1905 | 1906—1910

Barnsley, Royal
Blackpool, Winter Gardens
Blyth, Royal
Brighton, Hippodrome
Chatham, Royal
Doncaster, Grand
London, Coronet
London, Dalston
London, Grand Clapham Junction
Longton, Empire
Middlesborough, Empire
Morecambe, Winter Garden
Mountain Ash, Rowe's New
Portsmouth, Royal
Salford, Victoria
Sheffield, Lyceum
Wallsend, Borough

Aberystwyth, Coliseum
Brighton, Palace Pier
Colchester, Hippodrome
Hyde, Royal
Liverpool, Olympia
Liverpool, Royal Hippodrome
London, Camden
London, Hackney Empire
London, Inverness Court Hotel
London, Shepherds Bush Empire
London, Lyceum
Manchester, Hulme Hippodrome
Manchester, Hulme Playhouse
Tunbridge Wells, Opera House
York, Empire

Aberdeen, Tivoli
Aberaman, Grand
Bishop Auckland, Hippodrome
Glasgow, New Metropole
Liverpool, Pavilion
Nelson, Palace Hippodrome
London, Tottenham Palace
London, Playhouse

Twilight · after 1911

Birmingham, Old Rep
Bradford, Alhambra
Bristol, Hippodrome
Crewe, Lyceum
Liverpool, Playhouse
London, Ambassadors
London, Shaftesbury
London, Victoria Palace
Manchester, Palace
Southend, Palace
Winchester, Royal
Windsor, Royal

Jersey, Opera House
London, Drury Lane
London, St. Martin's

1911—1915

1916—

Ayr, Pavilion
Bangor, County
Barnsley, Alhambra
Burnley, Empire
Consett, Globe Music Hall
Derby, Hippodrome
London, Golders Green
Manchester, Opera House
Redditch, Palace
Wolverhampton, Royal

Cardiff, Prince of Wales
Dunfermline, Opera House
Manchester, Royal

The Principal Architects

Biographical notes by Victor Glasstone
The work of the architects collated by David F. Cheshire, John Earl and Michael Sell

This section introduces the work of the most prolific of British theatre architects. For reasons of space the list of theatres relating to each architect has been compressed to provide the following information:

the date the theatre opened

the name given is the final name by which the theatre is known

a theatre name, not immediately followed by a town, indicates that the buiding is in the London area

those theatres appearing in bold type are buildings which are still in existence

★ indicates that the architect undertook alterations, renovations or a major rebuild of an existing theatre

Some theatres which appear in bold may retain little of the work of the architect under whom they appear because a later and major rebuild has obliterated most of their work e.g. Darbyshire, Palace Manchester; Matcham, Theatre Royal St. Helen's.

BEAZLEY, Samuel: 1786-1851

The son of the army accoutrements maker of Westminster: received his architectural training in the office of his uncle, Charles Beazley: fought in the Peninsular War: became the leading theatre architect of his day, and a fashionable man about town: was the author of over a hundred operas, farces and plays, many of which he directed himself: besides theatres, designed many important country houses, castles, hotels and railway stations.

Although Beazley used a variety of styles in his general architecture, his theatres were all neo-classical and Grecian: the most impressive and important being the Lyceum - the splendid portico of which survives, with a later interior by Bertie Crewe, marvellously opulent and vulgar, but sadly now wasted as a dance hall. His 1822 alterations to the auditorium of the Theatre Royal, Drury Lane, introduced to London the Continental fashion of stage boxes framed by giant Corinthian order. This interior has twice been rebuilt, but Beazley's 1831 Ionic colonnade in Little Russell Street is still intact. These two important and irreplacable fragments are all that remain of his many theatres. The others were on a less monumental scale, but were nonetheless well integrated and intimate Regency/early Victorian commercial theatres; those in the provinces being a great advance on the little homemade Georgian playhouses of his predecessors. He also designed theatres erected in South America, Belgium and India, but little is known about them.

1816: Lyceum*; 1820: Theatre Royal, Birmingham*; 1821: Theatre Royal, Dublin; 1822: **Theatre Royal, Drury Lane*** auditorium; 1831: **Theatre Royal, Drury Lane*** colonnade; 1834: **Lyceum***; 1836: St. James's Theatre, Leicester; 1837: Royal Soho, City of London; 1841: Adelphi.

BRIGGS, John (Priestly), FRIBA: 1869-1944

Articled to Middleton, Prothero and Philpott, architects of Cheltenham: was sometime clerk-of works to Frank Matcham: in private practice in London, 1897-1939: besides theatres, architect to Lloyds Banks (Provincial) and Teddington Memorial Hospital, etc.

Briggs's theatre work neatly spans the boom period: mostly alterations of existing buildings. His stylistic variation in external treatment of new theatres varies enormously: Grand, Doncaster, a delicate 1890s interpretation of Regency; Grand Opera House, Harrogate, a severe Arts and Crafts creation, and Opera House, Tunbridge Wells, an imposing and very early use of neo-Georgian. Internally, the theatres bear a closer family resemblance. Both Harrogate and Tunbridge Wells have almost square proscenium openings with decorative infill to top corners; decorated friezes support the ceilings; and there is a nice compactness and busyness, quirky with spiked decoration surmounting the somewhat standard treatment of box and balcony fronts.

1897: **Palace, Gloucester**; Royal Opera House, St. Leonard's*; 1898: Theatre Royal, Preston; 1899: **Grand Doncaster** (with J. W. Chapman); **Royal Court, Wigan***; 1900: **Grand Opera House, Harrogate**; Royal, Peterborough; 1901: Royal, Colchester*; Royal, Preston*; 1902: **Opera House, Tunbridge Wells; Empire, York.** 1908: Central, Northwich.

CREWE, Bertie: d. 1937

Architectural education in the office of Clement Dowling, London, and at the Atelier Laloux, Paris, a firm that did the Gare d'Orsay, etc. Matcham claimed that Crewe and Sprague worked at one time for him, something never admitted at either. From Crewe's practice sprang four theatre architects who gained fame in the post-boom period: Robert Cromie, J. C. Derham, Edward Jones and Cecil Masey.

Crewe specialized entirely in theatres and, subsequently, cinemas. One of the most dynamic architects of the 1890s - 1900s, with a florid, at times almost wild splendour, coloured by a mannerist Baroque, probably the influence of his time in Paris. His early work with Sprague was tepid by comparison with his later extravagance (Lyceum; Palace, Glasgow; Shaftesbury). Crewe's work is typified by horizontal balconies tied to ranges of stage boxes set in a frame, the whole making a gorgeous and elaborate frontispiece. His decorative features are inevitably completely three-dimensional, stunning caryatids, giant elephant heads, seated Gods -an envigorating atmosphere for the music halls and melodrama houses which his theatres invariably were. With the Stoll, he designed an opera house, more dignified than his music halls, but exuberantly magnificent in the best Continental mode, with borrowings from American giantism. Unlike Matcham, whom in many ways he resembles, Crewe could produce really competent facades which were convincing in both theatrical and architectural terms. After the Great War he went on to design many cinemas, and a few theatres, but his manner became tame, and he dwindled into the rounded banalities of the Odeon style.

1888: **Royal Court, Sloane Square (with W. Emden)**; 1889: Shoreditch Olympia (with W. G. R. Sprague)*; 1890: Olympic (with W. G. R. Sprague); c.1890: Alhambra, Brussels; 1893: **Theatre Royal, Lincoln** (with W. G. R. Sprague); 1894: Camberwell Empire (with W. G. R. Sprague); 1898: Queen's, Poplar*; 1899: Bedford*; 1900: **Victoria, Salford;** Euston Palace (with Wylson and Long); Woolwich Hippodrome; 1901: Salder's Wells*; 1902: Hippodrome, Glasgow; **Royal Hippodrome, Liverpool*** (with A. Shelmerdine); 1904: Palace, Glasgow; Queen's, Poplar*; **Pavilion, Glasgow; Lyceum; Alhambra, Paris;** 1906: Theatre Royal, Bury St. Edmund's*; **Royal Hippodrome, Belfast;** Tivoli Palace, Liverpool; Hippodrome, Coventry; 1907: Hippodrome, Sheffield; 1908: Hippodrome, Devonport; Hippodrome, Portsmouth; Royal Hippodrome, Nottingham; **Palace, Oldham;** Hippodrome, Accrington; 1909: Variety Theatre, Hoxton*; Hippodrome, Southend; Theatre Royal, Blackburn*; 1911: Stoll, Shaftesbury; Bedminster Hippodrome, Bristol; 1913: **Palace, Manchester*; Palace, Redditch; Hippodrome, Golders Green;** 1922: Tivoli Cinema (with Ganton & Ganton); 1928: **Piccadilly** (with Stone); 1930: **Phoenix** (with Scott & Macey); 1931: **Saville** (with Bennett & Sons).
He also designed many cinemas including: Kinema, Londonderry; Electric, Fore Street, Devonport; Roxy Kinema, Blackheath; Globe Kinema, Clapham; Odeon, Southgate; Royal, Belfast.

DARBYSHIRE, Alfred, FSA, FRIBA: 1839-1908

Born in Salford, Lancs. of a Quaker family: educated at Friends' School, Ackworth, and at Alderley: articled to J. J. Alley, who designed a few theatres: set up in practice in Manchester 1862: travelled on the Continent 1864: Vice-President of the RIBA 1902-5: President of the Manchester Society of Architects 1901-3: President of the Building Construction and Equipment section of the International Fire Congress held in London in 1903. Ran a successful general practice with F. Bennett Smith FRIBA (Darbyshire & Bennett Smith), but was much interested in theatre design and wrote **The Irving-Darbyshire Safety Plan** 1884, **An Architect's Experiences: Professional, Artistic and Theatrical** 1897, and **The Art of the Victorian Stage** 1907. The first work advocated the use of an asbestos safety curtain between stage and auditorium; its general principles were subsequently incorporated into his rebuilding of the Exeter theatre after the disastrous fire of 1887, which nearly wrecked Phipps's career. The Safety Plan also advocated the elimination of overhanging balconies and stage boxes, and the provision behind the seating of ample colonnades connected directly with the exits. Darbyshire's theatres were characterized by an overall neatness and professionalism: a breadth of vision with no overstatement. Both internally and externally there was a strong flavour of French and German theatres of the 1830s, with echoes of Victor Louis. His most important, the Palace, Manchester, (the structure of which remains within Crewe's rebuilding of 1913), was clearly influenced by W. H. Ward's Grand, Birmingham, 1883, with its arcading and dome over the facade, The Palace probably influenced Phipps' final masterpiece, Her Majesty's, 1897.

1869: Prince's, Manchester*; 1884: Gaiety, Manchester; 1887: Lyceum, Crewe; 1889: Royal, Exeter; 1891: **Palace, Manchester;** 1892: Royal Court, Warrington (with John Bland); 1898: Grand, Rawtenstall; 1901: Prince's, Manchester.

EMDEN, Walter: 1847-1913

Born in London: second son of William S. Emden, sometime proprietor of the Olympic Theatre: studied mechanical engineering in the workshops of Maudsley, Sons & Field, Lambeth, and was a civil engineer in the firm of Thomas Brassey: became an architectural pupil of Kelly & Lawes FFRIBA 1870: was for a long period a member Strand District Board of Works, and for seven years their Chairman. In 1890 he was elected a member of London City Council 1900, becoming Mayor in 1903. Retired 1906, presenting his practice to his four principal assistants, S. H. Egan, W. S. Emden, A. J. Croughton and T. C. Ovenstone, who carried on as Emden, Egan & Co. Besides theatres, was the architect of many hotels, restaurants and similar buildings.
Emden exemplified the mid-Victorian laissez-faire attitude to theatre architecture: In his 1870 reconstruction of the Globe (done in his first year of "studying" architecture) he was already calling himself "architect". His lack of formal training shows in his early work: until he started collaborating with Crewe and Phipps, his was the epitome of charming architectural illiteracy. The exterior of Terry's was a typical pub of the period, and the famous Tivoli a glorified fun palace, quite different in manner to the stately colonnade of the Garrick, which clearly indicates the hand of Phipps. Internally too, he graduated from simple, delicately decorated balconies supported on slender columns -curtained at the proscenium ends to form stage boxes -to the firm elaborate style (still with low-relief ornament) of the Garrick or the Duke of York's, excellent examples of late 1880s-early 1890s Phipps. There is a well-behaved, precise quality to Emden's later work which properly reflects his social achievements in the world of affairs.

1870: Globe, Newcastle St.*; New Chelsea (later Royal Court), Lower George St.*; 1871: Belgravia (Royal Court), Lower George St.*; 1887: Terry's; 1888: **Royal Court** (with B. Crewe); 1889: **Garrick,** (with C. J. Phipps); 1890: Tivoli; 1891: Tivoli*; Lyceum, Ipswich; 1892: **Duke of York's;** 1893: City, Sheffield (with Holmes); 1895: Royalty, Dean St.*; **Theatre Royal, Newcastle** (with W. L. Newcombe); 1897: Palace of Varieties, Southampton; 1898: Imperial, Westminster*; Lyceum, Ipswich*; **Theatre Royal, Barnsley** (with H. Crawshaw); 1899: Theatre, Ealing; 1900: Empire, Swansea.

FINCH HILL & PARAIRE:
Finch Hill, W.: dates unknown
Paraire, Edward Lewis: 1826-1882

Nothing is known of Finch Hill's background; was in partnership with Paraire (who came of a French family naturalized in Britain) from c.1856-c.1867 when he either died or retired, the practice continuing in their joint names: were famous pub architects; Paraire later also designed churches and banks: besides their few straight commercial theatres are the main link in the pub-into-music hall development.
The early music halls were typical of the time: rectangular rooms with a single narrow balcony and a raised platform-stage at the long end set within a high alcove. "Finch Hill was a master of the opulent but never licentious classism of the 1850s. Audiences knocked back their beer in sumptuous settings designed by an architect who knew the churches of Gibbs, Archer and Hawksmoor" (Mark Girouard). Later theatres were charming and simple: double balconies running round to the proscenium arch, with boxes formed just by curtaining at the ends. The lighting decoration had a crisp fresh quality so different from the three-dimensional voluptuousness of the later 1870s and

1880s. Being built before the days of building regulations, the theatres had almost no street facade, merely
thin almost domestic slithers being presented to the
street.

1855: Evans's Music and Supper Rooms (Finch Hill only). 1857: Holborn Empire; 1858: Britannia, Hoxton. 1860
Islington Empire; 1861: Oxford Music Hall; 1864: Cambridge Music Hall; 1866: Theatre Royal, Holborn; 1869:
Oxford Music Hall*; 1870: Islington Empire*; 1873: Oxford Music Hall*; 1874: Islington Empire*.

HOPE, William: dates unknown; later in partnership with MAXWELL, J. C.: dates unknown.

Of Newcastle: other than the theatres, nothing is as yet
known of Hope, or of the subsequent practice of Hope
& Maxwell, which first appears in 1898. Neither were
members of the RIBA, nor received obituaries in the
technical press. Further research is needed in local
newspapers and archives.
Clearly amateur provincials (the Metropole, Glasgow,
alone has the sense of being by a trained architect), this
couple were nevertheless highly competent creators of
theatrical atmosphere, somewhat run-of-the-mill
without a strong personal flavour, but lavish in the context of the boom period. Although opulent in the style
of Matcham, there was none of his concern for integrated design or good sightlines: balconies run up
square to boxes which were merely decorated alcoves
at the proscenium, rich with plaster ornament and
heavy drapery. Usually on corner sites, the exterior
treatment of their buildings was almost ludicrous, the
architecture of entertainment run riot, with one elevation different from the other, and motivs from every architectural period muddled together quite in-
descriminately.

1894: Royalty Theatre, Wallsend. 1896: Metropole,
Gateshead; Theatre, South Sheilds; Grand (Byker),
Newcastle; Hippodrome, Margate (with J. C. Maxwell).
1897: **Grand, Swansea.** 1898: Grand, Southampton;
Metropole, Glasgow (with J. C. Maxwell). 1899: Queen's
Palace, Leeds (with J. C. Maxwell). 1900: **Theatre Royal,
Blyth** (with J. C. Maxwell); Theatre Royal, Mid-
dlesborough (with J. C. Maxwell)*. 1901: Central Palace
of Varieties, North Shields (with J. C. Maxwell). 1903:
Grand Opera House Middlesborough (with J. C. Max-
well). 1905: **Hippodrome, Stockton;** Her Majesty's
Theatre, Carlisle (with Bendle)*; 1907: Kings, Sunderland.

MATCHAM, Frank: 1854-1920

Born in Newton Abbot, Devon, the son of a brewery
manager who moved to Torquay after his birth: attend-
ed Babbacombe school there: 1868 apprenticed to a
local architect and surveyor, George Sondon
Bridgeman: mid-1870s joined the London practice of
Jethro T. Robinson, consulting theatre architect to the
Lord Chamberlain, marrying his daughter in 1877, and
taking over his work when he died the following year.
1878 was also important in being the year when the first
regulations regarding theatres were enacted - incorporating advice sought from Robinson.
Henceforth Matcham's success was unbounded, and
he went on to become the most prolific theatre architect of all time. His work completely spans the boom
period, and beyond. Despite his enormous output, he
developed a very personal style, instantly recognizable;
even his poor and often shoddy external treatment
always bears his stamp: yet no two buildings are ever
identical. He was the supreme example of the

unacademic architect who became a master of his
craft, and who could always be relied upon to deliver a
lively sensuous interior, inexpensively constructed, but
acutely aware of the technical difficulties of sightlines,
acoustics, and construction. Both he and his resident
engineer, Robert Alexander Briggs, took out patents for
cantilevers, lifts, etc. Matcham was at his best and
most fanciful in the 1890s, with a remarkable grasp of
the three-dimensional possibilities of auditorium
design, using every trick to achieve maximum effect:
dipping balconies, stage boxes stepping down, and set
forwards, and backwards to better the sightline; the
whole composition awash with a cornucopia of drapery
and decoration, often architecturally illiterate, but completely convincing and of a piece. After the turn of the
century, his style became more restrained, although
still brilliantly efficient and thoroughly under control.
His phenomenal success and popularity both with the
public and the great theatrical entrepeneurs was never
appreciated by the architectural critics of the day, who,
while praising his technical facility "marked by good
seating accommodation, economy on space and cost,
and rapidity in execution", damned his aesthetic sense
as "undistinguished". It is only in recent years that his
astonishing theatrical flair has been recognised as
near genius. He is the first Victorian theatre architect to
receive the accolade of book devoted to his life and
work.
1875: Oldway House Theatre, Paignton (?). 1879:
Elephant & Castle Theatre (completing J. T. Robinson's
work). Royalty Theatre, Glasgow* (with Eadie). 1880:
Gaiety Music Hall, Glasgow*. 1883: Islington Empire*;
Astley's; Elephant & Castle*. 1884: Canterbury, Lon-
don*; Mile End Empire*. 1885: Hengler's Grand Cirque.
Royalty, Glasgow. 1886: Theatre Royal, Blackburn*;
Grand, Brighton; Theatre Royal, Bolton; Theatre Royal,
Hanley* (with C. J. Phipps); Theatre Royal, Stockport;
1888**Grand, Douglas**. Alhambra, Brighton; Islington
Empire* (with C. Bell); Opera House, Blackpool;
Prince's, Bristol*; Theatre Royal & Opera House,
Rochdale*; **Theatre Royal, Bury;** Grand, Halifax; **Theatre
Royal, St. Helen's. Grand, Colchester*;** Alhambra,
Newcastle; Royal, Middlesborough; Grand, Woolwich;
1890: Empire, Liverpool*; Canterbury, London*. 1891:
Theatre Royal, Ashton-under-Lyne; **Everyman Theatre,
Cheltenham;** Theatre Royal, Hanley*; Opera House,
Southport. 1892: Empire Palace, Edinburgh; Eden,
Bishop Auckland*; Victoria Palace, Llandudno;
Prince's, Portsmouth; Theatre Royal, Great Yarmouth*.
1893: **Grand, Hull.** 1894: **Grand Opera House, Belfast;**
Empire Palace, Birmingham; **Grand, Blackpool;** Grand,
Bolton; Shoreditch Empire*; **Royal Opera House,
Wakefield; Comedy, Manchester*.** 1895: **Lyric Opera
House, Hammersmith*;** Royal County, Reading*;
Regent, Salford*; Empire, Sheffield; Princes, Bristol*
1896: Brixton, Borough; Empire, Cardiff; Empire, Liver-
pool*; **Theatre Royal, Hanley; Empire, Longton.** 1897:
Alexandra, Stoke Newington; **Crouch End Opera
House;** Theatre Royal, Dublin*; Victoria, Chatham; Em-
pire Palace, Hull; **Theatre Royal, Nottingham*; Tivoli,
Aberdeen*;** Empire, Glasgow; Metropolitan; Grand,
Lancaster*. Hengler's Grand Cirque, Glasgow*. 1898:
Alhambra, Birmingham; Theatre Royal, Great Yar-
mouth*; Empire Palace, Leeds; Royalty, Morecambe;
Grand, Hanley; Empire Palace, Nottingham; Princes,
Portsmouth*; Granville, Walham Green. 1899: Empire,
New Cross; Empire Palace, Newport; **Richmond
Theatre;** Broadway Theatre, Salford; **Lyric, Ham-
mersmith*; Empire Theatre, South Shields** (with
Milburn, W. & T.R.). 1900: Woolwich Empire*; **Talk of the
Town;** Queen's, Keighley*; **Palace, Manchester; Theatre
Royal, Portsmouth; Grand Theatre, Derby;** Islington Em-
pire*; **Gaiety, Douglas*;** Empire Palace, Cardiff*. 1901:
Hackney Empire; Holloway Empire; **Hippodrome,
Brighton*;** Palace, Leicester; **Theatre Royal (Grey**

Street), Newcastle*; Theatre Royal, St. Helen's; Theatre Royal (Tudor Street), Sheffield*; Grand Theatre, Birmingham (with Essex, Nicol & Goodman). 1902: Prince's, Bristol*; Empire Palace, Hull; Empire, Newcastle*; Olympia, Newcastle*; **Theatre Royal, Stratford.** 1903: **Opera House, Buxton; Devonshire Park Theatre, Eastbourne*;** Empire, Glasgow*; Marlborough; **Shepherd's Bush Empire; Royal Hall, Harrogate** (with R. J. Beale) 1904: **King's, Glasgow;** Ardwick Empire, Manchester; Hippodrome, Manchester, **London Coliseum.**1905: **His Majesty's, Aberdeen; Coliseum, Glasgow; Hippodrome, Ipswich;** Olympia, Liverpool; Empire, Leicester Square*; Holborn Empire*; Terry's Theatre*. 1906: Holborn Empire*. 1907: Hippodrome, Willesden; **King's, Southsea; Grand, Birmingham*;** 1908: Gaiety, Manchester*; Metropolitan*; 1909: Ilford Hippodrome; **Talk of the Town*; Tivoli, Aberdeen; Devonshire Park Theatre, Eastbourne*.** 1910: **Olympia, Glasgow;** Hippodrome, Keighley*; Finsbury Park Empire; Hammersmith Palace of Varieties*; **London Palladium.** 1911: Prince of Wales, Birmingham*; His Majesty's Opera House, Blackpool*; Alhambra Opera House, Brighton; Theatre Royal, Castleford*; Empire, Edinburgh*; Lewisham Hippodrome; Winter Gardens Theatre; **Victoria Palace.** 1912: Empire, Chatham; Empire, Edinburgh*; Alhambra*; Chiswick Empire; **Wood Green Empire; Hippodrome, St. Augustine's Parade, Bristol** (with B. Crewe); Palace, Leicester*; Karsino; Royal, Castleford*, 1913
He was also architect to a number of projects which did not reach function and designed cinemas in the period after 1912.

W. & T. R. MILBURN:
William, FRIBA, FRPS, MBE: 1858-1935
Thomas Ridley, FRIBA, JP: 1861-1943.
William (Jnr.), FRIBA, FRICS: 1885-1953

William (Snr.) and T. R., born in Sunderland, were the sons of Capt. William Milburn, who commanded Wear ships of both sail and steam: trained at School of Art, Fawcett Street, Sunderland: William (Snr.) served his articles with J. & T. Tillman FFRIBA, Sunderland. Up to 1897 the brothers carried on separate practices, but then joined forces to become W. & T. R. Milburn, one of the largest architectural practices in the North. William (Jnr.) - the son of William (Snr.) - was a Saxon Snell prizeman of the RIBA 1908, and two years later won the Institute's Godwin Bursary. He subsequently joined the family practice and later became its principal. All three Milburns were sometime Presidents of the Northern Architectural Association.
This Sunderland family were highly trained architects, who, on the evidence of their later work at least, had no feel whatsoever for the theatre. The remarkable towers of their Sunderland Empire (one at the corner entrance to the building; others flanking the proscenium) are in themselves splendid Mannerist conceits, owing much to Wren and Hawksmoor, but within the auditorium do nothing but distract the audience from the stage. The Milburn's Cardiff Empire (which replaced an excellent Matcham music hall) is a landmark in the transition from theatre to cinema, with over refined decoration, sparsely attached to boxes that face the audience and

not the stage, and a flat floor useless for watching actors, but eminently suitable for observing the flickerings from the "biograf-box" prominently situated at the back of the auditorium. The work of the Milburns supports the theory that only theatre specialists, no matter how "architecturally" innocent, are capable of producing a satisfactory theatrical atmosphere. Like Matcham, their theatres were principally for Moss Empires, and they made alterations to many of his buildings. Their auditoria in the 1920s were glorified cinemas, typified by the vast Dominion, Tottenham Court Road, built at a time when theatre design was nearly at its lowest ebb.

1882: Avenue, Sunderland; 1894: Avenue, Sunderland*; 1899: **Empire, South Shields** (with F. Matcham); 1901: Theatre Royal, Seaham*; Palace, Sunderland*; 1907: **Empire, Sunderland;** 1909: Empire, West Hartlepool; 1905: Empire Palace, Cardiff*; 1925: **Empire, Liverpool;** 1928: **Empire, Southampton; Empire, Edinburgh*;** 1929: **Dominion.**

OWEN & WARD:
Owen, ?: dates unknown.
Ward, W. H.: dates unknown.
Ward, Geo. F.: dates unknown.

A successful Birmingham practice who built many theatres, but about whom too little is as yet known. It would appear that W. H. Ward took in Owen and G. F. Ward about 1895 to make the firm of Owen & Ward. Only one of their auditoria, the Darlington Hippodrome (now Civic), remains in anything like its original form. Even early photographs are scarce; again only one, of Her Majesty's, Walsall, has so far come to light. Pronouncements on their architectural style are therefore only tentative. Both these interiors, however, have a neat and competent, unflamboyant quality: horizontal balconies running round to one, or two, stage boxes, topped by flattened arches,with bulbous fronts flanked by trim pilasters; The whole composition trimly adjacent to well considered proscenium openings. Externally, judgements are easier to make. The buildings range from W. H. Ward's splendid Birmingham Grand, 1883, the "Drury Lane of the Midlands", one of the most impressive British theatres of the late nineteenth century, to the gingerbread paste-on look of G. F. Ward's Gordon, Stoke-on-Trent, 1900, or Palace, Warrington, 1907. The Civic, Darlington, is in the same idiom, riotous and wonderfully busy - a solified fairground of shapes and motivs which proudly advertised the building's function as a hippodrome-music hall. These late Owen & Ward theatres are to be compared, internally, with Phipps, externally with Matcham. In fact, they use many of Matcham's themes, arched windows, turrets, broken pediments, and onion domes, yet executed with far more verve and conviction.

1878: Theatre Royal, Wolverhampton (W. H. Ward only); 1883: Grand, Birmingham (W. H. Ward only); 1893: Theatre Royal, Aston, Birmingham (W. H. Ward only); 1896: Theatre Royal, West Bromwich*; 1897: Theatre Royal, Smethwick; 1898: Empire, Wolverhampton; 1899: Grand, Walsall*; Imperial Palace, Bordesley, Birmingham; 1900: Her Majesty's, Walsall; **Prince of Wales, Nuneaton; Gordon, Stoke-on-Trent;** 1901: **Alexandra, Birmingham;** 1904: Palace, Grimsby; Hippodrome, Wigan. 1905: Poplar Hippodrome. 1906: Palace, Carlisle; 1907: **Palace, Warrington; Civic, Darlington;** 1908: King's, Birkenhead; Hippodrome, Middlesbrough; 1909: Empire, Nuneaton; 1911: Palace, Doncaster; 1913: Variety, Hoxton*.

PHIPPS, Charles John, FSA, FRIBA: 1835-1897

Son of John Rashleigh Phipps of Lansdowne near Bath: born Lansdowne: articled to Wilcox & Fuller, architects, of Bath, till June 1857: after a year's travel commenced on his own at Bath 1858, at Cornhill, London 1863-7 and at Mecklenburgh Sq. 1867 to death. FSA 19 June 1862: FRIBA 1866, member of Council 1875-6: advising architect to Theatre Royal, Drury Lane 15 years: exhibited 7 designs at R.A. 1863-97: besides theatres designed various business premises, blocks of flats, the Devonshire club, St. James's St., and the Carlton Hotel, part of the same design as Her Majety's Theatre, which was carried out and modified after his death by his partner and son-in-law, A. Blomfield Jackson (1868-1951), who continued the practice. Phipps's early designs for buildings and furniture were Gothic and ecclesiastical in the style of Godwin and Burges, but after his first theatre he adopted "a more appropriate classic manner".

The first of the great Victorian theatre specialists, Phipps was for over thirty years the acknowledged doyen in the field; the only theatre architect of the period to be found in the DNB, and one of the few in the standard biographical dictionaries of architects. Fortunately, many of this theatres remain more or less as he designed them. Phipps's most prolific years preceeded the flowering of the music hall in the 1890s, and his were primarily straight theatres. Stylistically, his work was much influenced by the great Continental (particularly, French) theatres of the eighteenth and mid-nineteenth centuries, with a solemn, seemingly solid dignity, quite different from the slender gimcrack feel of earlier English theatre interiors. The line of his balconies runs horizontally through to stage boxes, which often themselves form the proscenium opening, without the intrusion of an elaborate frame surrounding the stage. Decoration in a Phipps theatre is always applied in low relief, and restrained, unlike the integrated high key rumbustiousness of the later Matcham or Crewe theatres at their vibrant best. Externally, too, Phipps had an assured dignified touch, using the customary motivs of classic architecture with confidence; producing civic buildings with undeniable theatrical character which made an important contribution to the Victorian street scene. Those that remain, such as the Theatres Royal, Nottingham and Glasgow; Lyceun, Edinburgh and Her Majesty's, still retain thier viability in often very altered circumstances.

1863: **Theatre Royal, Bath***; 1865: **Theatre Royal, Nottingham***; **Theatre Royal, South Shields** (with T. M. Clemence); 1866: **Theatre Royal, Brighton***; 1867: Prince's, Bristol; Royal, Swansea; Queen's, Long Acre*; 1868: Gaiety; 1869: Variety, Hoxton; 1870: Vaudeville; 1871: **Gaiety, Dublin**; 1872: **Tivoli, Aberdeen** (with J. M. Matthews); 1873: Theatre Royal, Edinburgh; 1874: **Theatre Royal, Portsmouth***; 1875: Theatre Royal, Worcester*; 1876: **Theatre Royal, Dumfries***; Theatre Royal, Dunfermline*; 1877: Opera House, Cork; Opera House, Leicester; Royal Opera House, Londonderry; 1878: Theatre Royal, Worcester*; Rotunda, Liverpool (with E. Davis & Sons); 1879: **Sadler's Wells***. 1880: **Theatre Royal, Haymarket***; **Theatre Royal, Glasgow;** Princess's Theatre*; 1881: **Savoy;** Theatre Royal, Belfast; 1882: **Gaiety, Hastings** (with Cross and Wells); Strand*; **Theatre Royal, Leamington** (with Osborne and Reading); 1883: **Lyceym, Edinburgh; Hippodrome, Eastbourne;** Olympic*; 1884: Theatre Royal, Edinburgh*; **Theatre Royal, Northampton; Theatre Royal, Portsmouth***; Prince of Wales; London Palladium*; 1885: **Lyceum***; Theatre Royal, Exeter; 1887: **Vaudeville***; Theatre Royal, Darlington; **Theatre Royal, Northampton***; 1888: **Theatre Royal, Torquay***; **Lyric;** Shaftesbury Theatre; 1889: **Garrick** (with W. Emden);

1890: Empire, Devonport; **Theatre Royal, Glasgow***; Toole's*; **Vaudeville***; 1893: Daly's (with Chadwick); 1894: **Grand, Wolverhampton;** Pavilion, Whitechapel (with E. Runtz). 1895: **Theatre Royal, Glasow***. 1897: **Her Majesty's;** Royal Hippodrome, Dover; Royal County, Kingston* (with Bourne); 1898: Opera House, Coventry*; 1899: Holloway Empire.

ROBINSON, Jethro T.: d. 1878.

Constulting theatre architect to the Lord Chamberlain and, Frank Matcham's father-in-law.

Robinson's interiors make a nice comparison with Phipps's of the same period. Where the latter's were straightforward, and sensibly worthy, the former's were fanciful and delicate, with bulbous balcony fronts supported on slender cast iron columns: all somewhat reminiscent of the 1850s, but running through to jolly little boxes, very much of the '70s. Robinson's lighthearted touch made him eminently suitable as a designer of circuses and music halls, of which he built quite a few. In the nature of such ephemeral buildings, these have all disappeared, but we are lucky in still possessing two fine auditoria: the, as yet, quite intact Theatre Royal, Margate, and the Old Vic, emasculated of its boxes, but retaining its Robinson balconies, with their charming decoration.

1871: Hengler's Grand Cirque*, Argyll St.; **'Old Vic'***; 1872: Hackney Theatre; Astley's*; 1873: Park, Camden Town; 1874: **Theatre Royal, Margate***; Pavilion Theatre*; 1876: Grecian, Shoreditch*; **Hengler's Grand Cirque, Liverpool;** 1878: Elephant an Castle; Royal Cambridge Music Hall*.

RUNTZ, Ernest, FRIBA: 1859-1912

Sixth son of John Runtz of Stoke Newington, and brother of Sir John Runtz: after leaving school articled to Samuel Walker, Auctioneer, Valuer and Estate Agent, subsequently his partner: nearly 30 before commencing a study of architecture at University College, London, obtaining a Donaldson Silver Medal for Fine Art, and, with Frederick T. Farrow FRIBA, took qualifying examination for RIBA, but was not admitted as Associate because of partnership with Walker: dissolved same 1897, and took as partners A. C. Breden ARIBA and George McLean Ford FRIBA under the style of Ernest Runtz & Co.; on Breden's death the firm became Ernest Runtz & Ford 1903-09: thereafter Ernest Runtz & Son. In 1909 the RIBA relented, and he was invited in as a Fellow. His practice also designed many non-theatrical buildings.

Runtz was a curious figure! Extravagantly praised in his day, particularly by Sachs in **Modern Opera Houses and Theatres** (to the detriment of Phipps and Matcham), he appears now to have been only as good as his current partners, and a decidedly lesser figure. Sachs admired Runtz for his facades, which introduced a new Continental civic pomp to the British scene, and because his interiors lacked the vulgar theatrical qualities which we now esteem. In fact, he was always better outside than in! The Empire, Middlesborough, and the designs for the Opera House, Norwich, (later slightly adapted and built by Sprague), could be Central European Stadtheatres; the Gaiety was Edwardian London at its most impressive and grandiose: but then there the facades were designed by R. Norman Shaw, acting as consultant. In the New, Cardiff, the steep balconies (flanked by stark side walls) are completely divorced from the stage boxes, themselves clumsy and heavy. The building is an important step in the decline of the Victorian and Edwardian tradition.

1894: Pavilion, Whitechapel*; 1896: New, Cambridge; 1897: Holborn Empire*; 1898: Peckham Hippodrome; 1899: **Hippodrome, Hastings; Empire, Middlesborough;** 1901: **Marina, Lowestoft;** Adelphi Theatre*; 1902: Palace, Halifax; 1903: Gaiety (with Norman Shaw); 1904: Theatre Royal, Birmingham*. 1906: **New, Cardiff;** 1908: Holland, Hove.

SPRAGUE, W. G. R.: 1865-1933

Born in Australia, the son of W. A. Sprague, and Dolores Drummond, an English actress who gained fame after her return to London in 1874: at 16 became articled to Frank Matcham for 4 years; then with Walter Emden another 3.

Thereafter, well trained in the practicalities of theatre architecture, but uninhibited by the pedantries of an academic education, Sprague set up on his own and designed a large number of theatres, many of which fortunately remain as the most elegant smaller houses of the West End. His more extravagant music halls have all disappeared. Unlike his mentors whose knowledge of "correct" architectural precedent was haphazard (ignorance which they used to great advantage), Sprague gained, through reading and observation, a fine vocabulary of architectural form and detail/which he interpreted with a magnificent flair for theatrical atmosphere. As he himself observed, for his "frontages" he "liked the Italian Renascence", but modified and took liberties "that no architect would ever demur to do so as to get the best effects". Although his range was less extensive than Matcham's, and less dramatically imaginative - both spatially and decoratively - his control was invariably surer. His integration of balconies, boxes and proscenium arch is always masterly, and complete. Unlike Matcham, his facades were "at one" with his auditoria, and, although instantly recognizable as those of a theatre, never obtrude, or clash with adjacent buildings, but add a dramatic and well mannered feature to the urban landscape.

1890: Olympic Theatre (with Crewe); 1893: King's, Hammersmith (with Crewe); **Theatre Royal, Lincoln** (with Crewe); 1894: Camberwell Empire (with Crewe); 1896: Shakespeare, Battersea; 1897: Grand, Fulham; Grand, Coventry*; **Lyceum, Sheffield** (with E. Holmes)*; Broadway Theatre; Lyceum, Newport; 1898: **Coronet, Notting Hill Gate;** 1899: **Wyndham's;** Rotherhithe Hippodrome; Holloway Empire; Kennington Theatre; Stratford Empire; Theatre, Bolton; **Empire, Bradford;** 1901: **Camden Theatre;** 1902: King's, Hammersmith*; Balham Hippodrome; 1903: Hippodrome, Norwich; **Albery;** 1904: Royalty, Dean Street; Royal Artillery, Woolwich; 1905: **Aldwych; Strand Theatre;** 1906: **Globe;** 1907: **Queen's;** Palace, Reading; 1908: Hippodrome, Norwich*; **New, Oxford; Kilburn Empire; Edourd VII, Paris; 1910: Kilburn Empire*;** 1912: New, Northampton; 1913: **Ambassador's;** 1915: Penge Empire; 1916: **St. Martin's.**

VERITY, Thomas, FRIBA: 1837-1891

Articled to an architect: employed in the War Office, later in the architectural office at South Kensington assisting Captain Fowke in erection of South Kensington Museum, and principal assistant to Major-General Scott in erection of Royal Albert Hall 1867-70, doing all the detailing: won competition for Criterion Restaurant and Theatre 1870: FRIBA 1878: consulting architect to Lord Chamberlain 1878 to death. First in

partnership with G. H. Hunt, then in later years with his son, F. T. Also designed many non-theatrical buildings.

VERITY, Francis Thomas, FRIBA: d.1937

Born in London: educated at Cranleigh: articled to his father, also a pupil of R. Phené Spiers: studied at Royal College of Art, South Kensington: at University College; the A. A. and R. A. Schools, and in Paris. Gained the RIBA Tite Prize 1889, in which year elected ARIBA, becoming Fellow 1896. Continued his father's practice, subsequently rebuilding various theatres, and later, innumerable cinemas in London, the provinces and Paris: was European advisor to Paramount, and the Union Cinema Company. Many architects later to become famous, worked in his large and flourishing practice: in his last years was in partnership with son-in-law, S. Beverley FRIBA.

The Veritys were enthusiastic Francophiles, and introduced first, authentic French Empire, and later the grand Beaux Arts tradition to British theatre architecture. Thomas was the more successful in creating a satisfactory theatrical atmosphere, designing interiors which were sensible, warm and intimate: amongst the best of the late-Victorian. The Criterion and Comedy survive from this period. Frank, whilst reacting against the plush-and-gilt of the Matcham school, launched a theatrical severity of "correct" classical detailing and feature which gradually declined, via Lillie Langtry's Imperial, and the Scala, into the cinema style of the great balcony and the intimidating side wall. His own cinemas, however, were mostly built in the 1920s, pre-Modernistic therefore, and retaining the trappings of classical decoration, sparsely applied.

Thomas

1874: **Criterion;** 1879: St. James's*; 1880: **Spa, Scarborough*;** 1881: **Comedy;** 1882: Novelty; 1883: Royalty*; 1884: **Criterion*; Empire, Leicester Sq.;** 1887: Knightsbridge Hall.

Francis Thomas

1893: **Empire*, Leicester Sq.;** 1901: Imperial*; 1902: **Theatre Royal, Bath*;** 1904: **Empire, Leicester Sq.*;** 1905: Scala*.

Cinemas: 1912: New Gallery, Regent St; 1914: Pavilion, Marble Arch; 1923: Odeon, Shepherd's Bush; Paramounts in Tottenham Court Rd., Birmingham, Glasgow, Leeds, Liverpool, Manchester, Newcastle; 1926: Plaza, Lower Regent St.; Astoria, Charing Cross Rd.; 1928: Carlton, Haymarket. Also, dates unknown: Palace, Bristol, Gaumont, Peckham; Regal, Southampton; Ritz, Aldershot, Bexhill, Nottingham, Richmond; Vaudeville, Paramount, Paris, etc. Some survive; others do not.

WYLSON & LONG:
Wylson, Oswald Cane, FRIBA: c1858-1925.
Long, Charles, ARIBA: d.1906

Wylson was the son of James Wylson, an architect who had worked in the office of Charles Barry before becoming surveyor to various land societies: studied at R. A. Schools: served apprenticeship with Arthur Cates, architect to the Crown Estate. Nothing is as yet known of the background of Long: partnership first appears in the directories in 1883 when Wylson was 25: continued as Wylson & Long after death of Long.

An underrated firm, none of whose best theatres survives intact. Primarily designers of large music halls and pubs, Wylson & Long were the antithesis of

Sprague and the Veritys; their style more akin to Matcham, but lacking in their auditoria his three-dimensional virtuousity and fantasy. Sachs considered their style more akin to Matcham, but lacking in their auditoria his three-dimensional virtuousity and fantasy. Sachs considered their Empire, Bristol, and rebuilding the Oxford Music Hall, worthy of inclusion in **Modern Opera Houses and Theatres.** Their most important work was done at Blackpool, 1897-99, in the building on the Promenade comprising a variety theatre, (Alhambra, later Palace), a circus, restaurant, ballroom etc. at a cost of £89,000. Their facades, such as those of the Chelsea and Euston Palaces, and the Newcastle Pavilion, were spendid piles, pompous and showy, with a medley of classical motifs thrown together with a proper music hall disregard for architectural propriety or historical "correctness". Internally, the idiosyncratic vein continues, but in the Dalston Theatre and Tottenham Palace there is a wideness, highness and spaciousness which is unappealing: Dalston, surprisingly so, for its early date. The balcony is simply too far off the ground for symphathetic comfort; neverthess the much later Tottenham Palace has nobility, but more that of an impressive concert room, rather than a music hall.

1893: Empire, Bristol; Oxford Music Hall*, London; South London Music Hall*; 1895: **Palace, Bath;** 1897: **Winter Gardens Theatre, Blackpool*;** 1898: **Empress Music Hall, Brixton; Dalston*;** 1899: Palace, Ballroom and Circus, etc., Blackpool; Kilburn Palace, (with Palgrave & Son); 1900: **London Pavilion*;** 1901: Euston Palace (with B. Crewe); 1902: Canterbury Music Hall*; 1903: Chelsea Palace; Variety, Hoxton*; Walthamstow Palace; **Pavilion, Newcastle-upon-Tyne;** 1906: East Ham Palace; Euston Palace*; 1908: **Tottenham Palace.**

The Theatre, Bury St. Edmunds 1734, reconstructed by Robert Adam in 1794. Closed as a theatre in 1818 in preparation for the opening of Bury's other theatre, the Theatre Royal of 1819 which is still in theatrical use today while this building serves as a municipal art gallery.

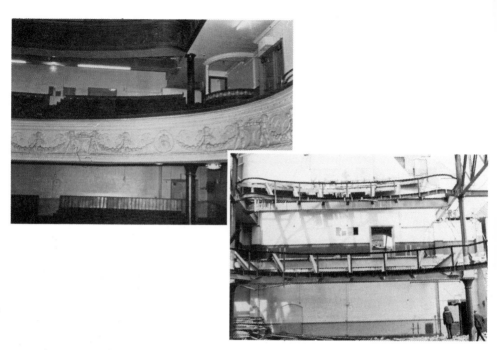

One of the 800 theatres, unremarkable and remarkable, which has been lost to future generations.

List of Demolished Theatres

Collated by David F. Cheshire with John Earl and Michael Sell

This section is arranged in exactly the same sequence of towns as the main Gazetteer. For reasons of space the entries have been compressed to provide the following information:

- the most recent name of the theatre in bold type
- the span of the theatrical life of that theatre building
- the name of the architect of the building followed, where the theatre has received major alterations which affected its character by a second, third or fourth etc., date and subsequent architect
- the eventual fate and date, where known, of the building

The List of Demolished Theatres is restricted to theatres in use at some time between 1900 and 1914 while the main Gazetteer includes a few theatres which closed long before 1900.

ABERDEEN, Grampian
Coachies Playhouse, c.1780 - ?/**Palace**, 1888 - ?/**Scott's Theatre**, c.1700 - ?/**Theatre**, Marischal Street, 1795 - ?/**Theatre Royal**, 1789 - 1877, ? dem. 1877.

ABERTILLERY, Gwent
Pavilion Theatre, 1900 - c.1927,?, dem. c.1927.

ACCRINGTON, Lancashire
Grand Theatre, 1882 - 1964, Turner, fire 1964/**Hippodrome**, 1903 - 1908, ?, fire 1908/**New Hippodrome**, 1908 - 1954, Crewe, dem. 1954.

ALDERSHOT, Hampshire
Cavalry Theatre, c.1880 - 1960, ?, dem. 1960/**Hippodrome**, 1913 - 1952, ?, dem. 1962/**Royal Opera House**, 1891 - 1953, ?, fire 1956 - dem. 1959.

ALTRINCHAM, Greater Manchester
Central Theatre, 1906 - c.1964, ?, dem.

ASHFORD, Kent
Corn Exchange Theatre, 1862 - 1966, ?, dem. 1966.

ASHTON-UNDER-LYNE, Greater Manchester
Theatre Royal, 1891 - 1953, Matcham, dem. 1972.

BANBURY, Oxfordshire
Palace Theatre, 1857 - 1916, dem. 1979.

BARNSLEY, South Yorkshire
New Empire Palace, 1909 - 1955, ?, fire 1955.

BARNSTAPLE, Devon
Theatre Royal, c.1830 - 1930, ? - 1895 Petter, dem. 1930.

BARROW-IN-FURNESS, Cumbria
Coliseum, 1907 - ?, dem. c.1970/**Gaiety**, 1914 - ?, ?, ?/**Her Majesty's Theatre**, 1864 - 1967, ?, dem. 1967/**Royal Theatre**, 1872 - 1937, ?, 1894 Mackintosh, dem. 1937.

BARRY DOCK, South Glamorgan
Royal Theatre, 1906 - 1909, ?, dem. 1909.

BEDLINGTON, Northumberland
Palace Theatre, c.1896 - c.1927, ?, fire c.1927/**Prince of Wales Theatre**, c.1890 -c.1918, ?, dem. c.1918.

BELFAST, Northern Ireland
Alhambra, 1873 - 1907, ?, 1887 Stevenson, fire 1959/**Coliseum**, 1909 - 1911, Swanston & Syme, dem. 1959/**Empire**, 1894 - 1961, Farrall, dem. c.1961/**Theatre Royal** (Arthur Street), 1881 - 1915, Phipps, dem. 1915.

BEVERLEY, Humberside
Thespian Theatre, 1904 - ?.

BEXHILL-ON-SEA, East Sussex
Pavilion Theatre, 1896 - 1935, ?, dem. 1936.

BIDEFORD, Devon
Palace Theatre, 1871 - 1961, Gould & Sons, dem. 1971.

BIRKENHEAD, Merseyside
Argyle Theatre, 1868 -1940, ?, bombed 1940 - dem. 1969/**Hippodrome**, 1893 -1940, Hesketh, bombed 1940/**New Theatre Royal**, 1905 - 1919, ?, dem. c.1935.

BIRMINGHAM, West Midlands
Aston Hippodrome, 1908 - 1939, Lister, Lea & Sons, dem. 1981/**Bordesley Palace**, 1899 -1929, Ramsell, dem. 1959/**Carlton Theatre**, 1900 - 1941, Guest, bombed, 1941/**Empire Palace**, 1894 - 1940, Matcham, bombed 1940/**Gaiety Music Hall**, 1846 - 1930, dem. 1930/**Grand Theatre**, 1883 -1933, Ward -1901 Matcham and Nicol & Goodman, dem. 1963/**Metropole**, 1899 - ?, dem. 1951/**Oldbury Palace**, 1899 - c.1927, Ramsell, dem. 1978/**Theatre Royal** (Aston Road), 1893 -1955, Ward, dem. 1970/**Theatre Royal** (New Street),

1774 - 1956, Saul - 1780 W.S. Wyatt -1792 Saunders - 1820 Beazley - 1904 Runtz, dem. 1956.

BIRTLEY, Tyne & Wear
Theatre Royal (Orchard Crescent), 1867 -1958, ?, dem. 1968.

BISHOP AUCKLAND, County Durham
Eden Theatre, 1892 - 1966, ? - 1902 Livesey, dem. 1966.

BLACKBURN, Lancashire
Grand Theatre, 1880 - 1956, Trevanson, dem. 1958/**Lyceum Music Hall**, 1880 -1902, Culshaw, dem. c.1902/**Theatre Royal**, 1818 -1931, ? - 1886 Matcham -1909 Crewe, dem. 1967.

BLACKPOOL, Lancashire
Alhambra, 1899 - 1961, Wylson & Long, dem. 1961/**North Pier Pavilion**, 1863 - ?, ?, dem./**Opera House**, 1889 - 1911, 1886 Matcham, 1902 Mangall & Littlewood, fire 1911/**Opera House**, 1911 - 1938, fire 1938/**Queen's Theatre**, 1877 -1972, ?, dem. 1972/**Rainbow Theatre**, 1892 - 1958, ?, fire 1958/**South Pier Pavilion**, 1892 - ?.

BLYTH, Northumberland
Gaiety, 1906 - ?, ?, dem./**Hippodrome**, ?, ?, dem. c.1927.

BOGNOR REGIS, West Sussex
Theatre Royal, 1911 - 1941, Barlow, dem. 1976/**Victoria Hall Theatre**, 1897 - 1903, ?, dem.

BOLTON, Greater Manchester
Grand Theatre, 1894 - 1963, Matcham, dem. 1963/**Hippodrome**, 1908 - 1961, ?, dem. 1961/**Theatre Royal**, 1888 - 1928, Matcham dem. 1963/**Victoria Theatre**, 1832 - c.1905, ?, dem.

BRADFORD, West Yorkshire
Palace, 1876 - 1938, ?, dem. 1964/**Prince's Theatre**, 1876 - 1959, ? -1900 Langley, dem. 1964/**Star Theatre**, 1875 - 1938, Jackson & Langley, dem. 1938

BRIDLINGTON, Humberside
Grand Pavilion, 1906 - 1936, ?, dem.
1936 (replaced)/New Spa Theatre, 1899 -
1906, Mangnall & Littlewood, fire
1906/Opera House, 1907 - 1932, ?, fire
1932/Victoria Theatre, ? - 1933, ?, fire
1933.

BRIGHTON, East Sussex
Alhambra, 1888 - 1914, Matcham, dem.
1956/Court Theatre, 1854 - 1964, ?, dem.
1970/Grand Theatre, 1887 - 1955, Matcham, fire 1955.

BRISTOL, Avon
Bedminster Hippodrome, 1911 - 1914,
Crewe, bombed 1941/Empire Theatre,
1893 - 1954, Wylson & Long, dem.
1963/Forester's Music Hall, 1870 - 1901,
?, dem./Prince's Theatre, 1867 - 1940,
Phipps - 1889 Matcham - 1902 Matcham,
bombed 1940/Tivoli Theatre, 1870 -1901,
? - 1895 Hancock, dem.

BROMLEY, Kent
New Theatre, 1889 - 1912 & 1946 - 1971,
W. A. Williams, fire 1971.

BURNLEY, Lancashire
Gaiety Theatre, 1880 - 1916, ?,
dem./Princess Alexandra Music Hall,
1870 - 1978, ?, dem. 1978.

BURY,
Greater Manchester
Hippodrome, 1875 - 1956, ?, fire 1966.

CADOXTON,
South Glamorgan
Theatre Royal, 1891 - 1910, Richards &
Gethin, dem. 1964.

CAMBRIDGE,
Cambridgeshire
New Theatre, 1896 - 1956, Runtz, dem.
1961.

CANTERBURY, Kent
Empire, 1861 - 1926, ?, dem.
1926/Theatre Royal, 1861 - 1926, ?, dem.
1926.

CARDIFF, South Glamorgan
Empire Palace, 1900 - 1961, Matcham
-1915 Milburn, dem. 1962.

CARLISLE, Cumbria
Her Majesty's Theatre, 1875 - 1963, ?
-1905 Bendle & Hope, dem. 1980.

CASTLEFORD,
West Yorkshire
Theatre Royal (Albion Street), 1873
-1958, ? - 1911 Matcham, dem. 1964.

CHATHAM, Kent
Barnard's Palace, 1886 - 1934, Nash, fire
1934/Empire, 1912 - 1960, Matcham,
dem. 1962/Gaiety, 1890 - 1911, Geo
Friend, dem. 1911/Globe Theatre, 1879
-1971, Bernays, dem. 1971.

CHELMSFORD, Essex
New Empire, 1912 - 1961, ?, dem.

CHELTENHAM,
Gloucestershire
Theatre of Varieties, 1886 - 1914, ?,
dem./Winter Gardens Theatre, 1878
-1942, Robson, dem.

CHESTERFIELD, Derbyshire
Theatre Royal, 1896 - 1955, Rollinson &
Sons, dem. 1961.

CHESTER-LE-STREET,
Durham
Empire, 1911 - 1971, ?, dem. 1971.

CHORLEY, Lancashire
Grand Theatre, ? - 1914, ?, fire
1914/Theatre Royal, 1911 - 1960. ?, dem.
1960.

CLACTON-ON-SEA, Essex
Pier Theatre, 1892 - 1977, ?, damaged by
storm 1977, dem. 1978/West Cliff
Theatre, 1894 - 1928, ?, dem. 1928.

CLYDEBANK, Strathclyde
Gaiety Theatre, 1904 - 1929, ?, dem.
c.1960.

COATBRIDGE, Strathclyde
Adelphi, 1909 - 1960, Robertson & Dobbie, dem. 1960.

COLCHESTER, Essex
Theatre Royal, 1812 - 1918, Wilkins
-1901 Briggs, fire 1918/Vaudeville Empire, 1911 - 1959, ?, dem. 1971.

COLNE, Lancashire
Kings Theatre, 1881 - 1936, Lindley
-1893 Rell, dem. 1944.

COLWYN BAY, Clwyd
Victoria Pier Pavilion, 1899 - 1922, ?, fire
1922.

CORK, County Cork
Opera House, 1855 - 1955, Benson -1877
Phipps, fire 1955.

COVENTRY, West Midlands
Empire Theatre, 1906 - 1931, ?, dem.
1973/Grand Opera House, 1882 - 1928,
Essex & Nicol - 1898 Phipps, dem.
1928/Hippodrome, 1880 - 1937, Turner, -
1906, Hattrell, dem. 1937.

COWES, Isle of Wight
Pavilion, 1902 - 1951, ?, dem.

DARWEN, Lancashire
Theatre Royal, 1877 - 1960, ?, dem. 1960.

DEAL, Kent
Marina Theatre, 1794 - 1910, ?,
dem./Playhouse, 1798 - 1910, ?, dem.
c.1912.

DEWSBURY,
West Yorkshire
Empire, 1909 - 1955, Chadwick & Watson, dem. 1960/Hippodrome, 1896
-1919, ? - 1909 Chadwick & Watson,
dem. 1950/Theatre Royal, 1865 - 1931, ?,
dem.

DONCASTER,
South Yorkshire
Palace, 1911 - 1970, Ward & Ball, dem.
1952/Theatre Royal, 1776 - 1900, ?, 1819
Lyndley, dem.

DOUGLAS, Isle of Man
Coliseum, 1912 - ?.

DOVER, Kent
Empire Palace, c.1880 - 1927, shelled
1944/Pier Pavilion, 1899 - 1926, Adcock,
dem./Royal Hippodrome, 1858 - 1944, ?
-1807 Phipps, shelled 1944 - dem. 1951.

DOVERCOURT, Essex
Empire, 1913 - 1940, ?, dem. 1962.

DUBLIN, Eire
Abbey Theatre, 1880 - 1951, ? - 1904
Holloway, fire 1951 - dem.
1961/Coliseum, 1913 - 1915, ?, fired dur-
ing Easter rising 1916/Hardwick Street
Theatre, 1913 - 1920, ?, dem./Queen's
Theatre, 1829 - 1966, dem./Theatre
Royal (Hawkins Street), 1897 - 1934,
Matcham, dem. 1934.

DUDLEY, West Midlands
Opera House, 1899 - 1936, Ramsell, fire
1936.

DUMFRIES,
Dumfries & Galloway
Lyceum, 1912 - 1936, Boswell, dem.
1936.

DUNDEE, Tayside
Dundee Theatre, 1800 - 1846/Her Majesty's Theatre, 1885 - 1919, Alexander,
dem. c.1960.

DUNFERMLINE, Fife
La Scala Music Hall, 1852 - 1924, Clerk,
dem.

DUNOON, Strathclyde
Pavilion Theatre, 1905 - 1949, ?, fire
1949.

DURHAM, County Durham
Palace Music Hall, 1909 - 1964, ?, dem.
1964.

EAST GRINSTEAD,
West Sussex
Whitehall Theatre, 1910 - 1936, ?, bomb-
ed 1943.

EBBW VALE, Gwent
Palace of Varieties, 1908 - ?, ?, dem.

EDINBURGH, Lothian
Alhambra Theatre (Leith Walk), 1914
-1958, ?, dem. 1974/Empire Palace, 1892
-1928, Matcham - 1910 Matcham - 1911
Matcham, dem. 1928/Gaiety Theatre
(Old Kirkgate), 1886 - 1956, ?, dem.
1963/Operetta House, 1875 - 1939, ?,
dem. 1950/Pier Theatre (Portobello),
1871 -1917, ?, dem. 1917/Theatre Royal,
1884 -1946, Phipps, fire 1946 - dem.
1960s.

ELLESMERE PORT, Cheshire
Hippodrome, 1904 - 1963, ?, fire 1963.

EXETER, Devonshire
Hippodrome 1908 - 1942, bombed/Theatre Royal, 1889 - 1962, Darbyshire, dem. 1962.

FALKIRK, Central Scotland
Grand Opera House, 1903 - 1929, Cullen, dem. 1934/Hippodrome, 1909 - ?, Robertson & Dobbie, dem.

FELIXSTOWE, Suffolk
Playhouse Theatre, 1912 - ?, Hooper, dem./Spa Pavilion, 1909 - 1941, ?, bombed 1941.

FLEETWOOD, Lancashire
Empire, 1909 - 1915, Winstanley, dem. 1960/Queen's Theatre, 1909 - 1937, ?, dem. 1976/Victoria Pier Theatre, 1911 -1953, ?, fire 1953.

FOLKESTONE, Kent
Pleasure Gardens Theatre, 1888 - 1964, ?, dem. 1964/Victoria Pier Pavilion, 1887 - 1945, ?, fire 1945 - dem. 1954.

GARSTON, Lancashire
Theatre Royal, 1892 - 1900, ?, dem.

GATESHEAD, Tyne & Wear
Alhambra, 1906 - 1967, Mould, dem. 1967/Metropole Theatre, 1896 - 1956, Hope, dem. 1960/Webb's Theatre, 1896 -1906, ?, dem. 1968.

GILLINGHAM, Kent
Grand Theatre, 1911 - 1959, ?, dem. 1960.

GLASGOW, Strathclyde
Alhambra, 1912 - 1969, Burnet, dem. 1970/Cambridge Music Hall, 1909 - ?, Robertson & Dobbie, dem./Casino, 1911 - ?, ?, dem./Empire Palace, 1897 - 1963, Matcham, dem. 1963/Gaiety Music Hall, 1896 - 1960s, ?, dem. 1960s/Grand Theatre, 1867 - 1915, Spence - 1903 Davidson, fire 1918/Hippodrome, 1902 -?, Crewe, dem. 1978/Lyceum Theatre, 1898 -1940s, Barclay, dem./Metropole, 1862 -1961, ? - 1874 Sellars 1897 Hope & Maxwell, fire 1961/Palace, 1870 - 1919, ? -1904 Crewe, dem./Queen's Theatre (Watson Street), 1870 - 1919, ? - 1904 Crewe, dem./Queen's Theatre (Watson Street), 1870 - 1952, ?, fire 1952, dem. 1972/Royalty Theatre, c.1870 - 1953, Thompson - 1879 Matcham and Eadie, dem. 1960/Savoy Theatre, 1912 - ?, Miller, dem. 1973.

GLOUCESTER, Gloucestershire
King's Theatre, 1766 - 1966, ?, dem. 1966.

GOLDTHORPE, South Yorkshire
Hippodrome, ? - 1914, ?, fire 1914.

GOOLE, Humberside
Palace of Varieties, 1909 - 1916, ?, dem.

GRANTHAM, Lincolnshire
Empire Theatre, 1874 - 1952, ?, dem. 1954.

GRAVESEND, Kent
Grand Theatre, 1894 - 1932, ?, dem. 1955.

GREAT YARMOUTH, Norfolk
Theatre Royal, 1892 - 1934, dem.

GREENOCK, Strathclyde
Alexandra Theatre, 1904 - 1973, Boston Menzies Morton & Cullen, dem. 1973/Empire Theatre, c.1906 - c.1970, ?, dem. c.1970/Hippodrome, 1858 - c.1930, ?, dem. c.1930.

GRIMSBY, Humberside
Empire Theatre, 1893 - 1906, ?, dem./Hippodrome, 1895 - 1905, ?, fire 1922/Palace Theatre, 1904 - 1931, Owen & Ward, dem. 1979/Prince of Wales, 1886 - 1936, Farebrother, dem. 1936/Theatre Royal, 1865 - 1904, ?, dem.

GUERNSEY, Channel Islands
Theatre Royal, Theatre Royal, 1792 -1900, ?, condemned & dem.

HALIFAX, West Yorkshire
Grand Theatre, 1889 - 1924, Matcham, dem. 1958/Palace Theatre, 1903 - 1958, Runtz and Ford - 1905 Horsfall & Sons, dem. 1959/People's Palace, 1900 - 1959, ?, dem. 1963.

HAMILTON, Strathclyde
Hippodrome, 1907 - 1946, ?, fire 1946.

HARTLEPOOL, Cleveland
Empire, 1909 - 1933, Milburn, dem. 1974.

HARWICH, Essex
Cliff Pavilion, c.1910 - 1973, ?, dem. 1973.

HASTINGS, East Sussex
Pier Pavilion (St. Leonard's) 1981 - 1939, Humphreys, fire 1939 - enemy action 1940 - storm 1941 - dem. 1951/Royal Opera House (St. Leonard's) 1879 -1921, ? - 1897 Briggs, bombed 1942.

HEBBURN-ON-TYNE, South Tyneside
Grand Theatre, 1897 - 1913, Simpson, dem.

HEREFORD, Hereford & Worcester
Kemble Theatre, 1911 - 1961, Stanton (as Corn Exchange 1857) - 1911 Jackson, dem. 1963.

HERNE BAY, Kent
Pier Pavilion Theatre, 1910 - 1928, ?, fire 1928/Town Hall Theatre, 1859 - 1925, Welby, fire 1925.

HIGH WYCOMBE, Buckinghamshire
Palace, 1902 - 1909, ?, fire 1909.

HORSHAM, West Sussex
Cornmarket Theatre, 1866 - c.1966, Burstow, dem. 1966/King's Head Music Hall, 1869 - 1978, ?, dismantled 1978.

HUDDERSFIELD, West Yorkshire
Empire, 1881 - 1904, ?, dem./Palace Theatre, 1909 - 1936, Horsfall & Sons, fire 1936/Theatre Royal, 1881 -1961, Entwistle, dem.

HULL, Humberside
Alexandra Theatre, 1902 - 1941, Guest, bombed 1941/Empire Palace, 1897 -1939, Matcham, bombed 1939/Hippodrome, c.1895 - 1913, ?, bombed 1941/Tivoli Theatre, 1871 - 1943, Smith, dem. 1959.

HUNSTANTON, Norfolk
Pier Pavilion, 1871 - 1939, Wilson, fire 1939.

IPSWICH, Suffolk
Lyceum Theatre, 1891 - 1936, Emden, dem. 1936.

JARROW, Tyne and Wear
Empire, 1912 - 1977, ?, dem. 1977/Palace of Varieties, 1895 - 1911, ?, fire 1911.

KEIGHLEY, West Yorkshire
Queen's Theatre, 1889 - 1956, Bailey -1910 Matcham, dem. 1961.

KETTERING, Northamptonshire
Avenue Theatre, 1903 - 1937, Payne, fire 1937/Victoria Theatre, 1888 - 1936, Gotch & Sanders, dem. 1970.

KIDDERMINSTER, Hereford & Worcester
Playhouse, 1903 - 1968, ?, dem. 1968.

KING'S LYNN, Norfolk
Theatre Royal, c.1814 - 1936, Newham, fire 1936.

LANCASTER, Lancashire
Palace of Varieties, 1896 - 1907, fire 1907.

LEEDS, West Yorkshire
Empire Palace, 1898 - 1961, Matcham dem. 1961/Hippodrome, 1864 - 1933, ? -1906 Winn, dem./Queen's Theatre, 1899 - 1923, Hope & Maxwell, dem./Theatre Royal, 1876 - 1957, Moore & Sons, dem. 1957.

LEICESTER, Leicestershire
Athenaeum, ? - 1908, ?, fire 1908/Palace, 1901 - 1959, Matcham - 1913 Matcham, dem. 1960/Pavilion Music Hall, 1890 -1929, ?, dem. 1929/Royal Opera House, 1877 ... 1960, Phipps, dem. 1960/Theatre Royal, 1836 - 1958, Beazley, - 1888 Barradale, dem. 1958.

LIMERICK, Eire
Theatre Royal, 1841 - 1922, ?, fire 1922.

LINCOLN, Lincolnshire
Palace, 1877 - 1930, Watkins (1872 as Masonic Hall) - 1901 Mortimer & Sons, bombed 1943 - dem. 1953.

LIVERPOOL, Merseyside
Adelphi Theatre, ? - 1921, ?, dem.

1921/**Bijou Opera House,** 1851 - 1891 or 1882 - 1937, ?, dem. 1937/**Coliseum,** 1909 - 1941, Sutton, bombed 1941/**Empire,** 1866 - 1923, Solomons and Phipps -1890 Matcham - 1896 Matcham, dem. 1923 (replaced)/**Gaiety Varieties,** 1867 -1900, ?, dem./**Haymarket Theatre,** 1882 -1910, ?, dem./**Lyric Theatre,** 1897 - 1932, ?, dem. 1974/**Metropole** (Bootle), 1911 -1941, ? bombed 1941/**New Parthenon,** 1880 - 1907, ?, dem. /**Pembroke Music Hall,** 1874 - 1907, ?, dem./**Prince of Wales Theatre,** 1860 - 1920s, Solomons, dem. 1920s/**Rotunda Theatre,** 1860 - 1930, ? -1878 Phipps and Davis & Sons, bombed 1941/**Royal Court Theatre,** 1881 - 1933, Sumners -1891 Kirby, fire 1933 (replaced)/**Sefton Theatre,** 1875 - 1902, ?, dem./**Shakespeare Theatre,** 1886 -1976, Sutton, fire 1976/**Stanhope Theatre,** 1894 - 1906, ?, dem./**Tivoli Palace,** 1847 - 1910, ? - 1906, Crewe, dem. 1978/**Theatre Royal** (Breck Road), 1888 -?, ?, dem./**Theatre Royal** (Williamson Square), 1772 - ?, Chambers - 1802 Foster, dem. 1965.

LONDON

Alexandra (Stoke Newington), 1897 -1950, Matcham, dem. c.1960/**Alhambra Palace,** 1854 (Panopticon) - 1936, Hayter Lewis - 1858 (conv), Lewis - 1864?, Rowley & Lewis - 1866, Rowley 1881, Perry & Reed - 1883, Perry & Reed - 1888, Clark - 1892, Clark & Pollard - 1897, Brutton - 1912, Matcham, dem. 1936 (replaced, cinema)/**Balham Empire,** 1900 - 1909, Hancock (conv.), dem. 1974/**Balham Hippodrome,** 1899 - 1939, Sprague, dem. 1960s/**Battersea Palace,** 1886 -1924, ?, - 1889 Newton, dem./**Bedford Theatre,** before 1840 - 1959, ? - 1861, Clark - C.1880, Clark - 1898 Crewe, dem. 1969/**Bow Palace,** 1892 - 1923, ?, dem. 1960/**Britannia Theatre,** 1841 - 1923, (?, Lane) - 1850, Warton - 1858, Hill & Paraire -bombed 1940/**Brixton Theatre,** 1896 -1940, Matcham, bombed 1940/**Broadway Theatre,** 1897 - 1911, Sprague, dem. c.1960/**Camberwell Empire,** 1894 - 1924, Crewe & Sprague, dem. 1937/**Camberwell Palace,** 1899 -1950s, Woodrow - 1908 Sharpe, dem. c.1955/**Canterbury,** 1852 -1942, Field -1854, Field - 1858, Field - 1876, Bridgman - 1884, Matcham - 1890 Matcham - 1902, Wylson & Long, bombed 1942, dem. c. 1955/**Chelsea Palace,** 1903 - 1957, Wylson & Long, dem. 1957/**Chiswick Empire,** 1912 - 1959, Matcham, dem. 1959/**Cottrell's Palace,** Brent, c.1905 -1908, ?, dem. 1911 (replaced, cinema)/**Croydon Grand,** 1896 - 1959, Brough, dem. 1959/**Crystal Palace Theatre,** c.1890 -1900, ?, fire 1936/**Daly's Theatre,** 1893 -1937, Chadwick & Phipps, dem. 1937 (replaced, cinema)/**Ealing Hippodrome,** 1899 -1958, ?, dem. 1958/**East Ham Palace,** 1906 - ?, Wylson & Long, dem./**Edmon-**ton Empire, 1908 - 1933, ?, dem. 1970/**Edmonton New Theatre,** ? - 1910, ?, dem. 1947/**Elephant & Castle Theatre,** 1872 -1928, Dean & Matthews - 1879, Robinson & Matcham - 1882 Matcham, dem. 1928 (replaced, cinema)/**Finsbury Park Empire,** 1910 - 1960, Matcham, dem. 1965/**Foresters' Music Hall,** before 1870 - 1917, ? - 1870, ? - 1889, Clark, dem. c.1964/**Fulham Grand,** 1897 -c.1950, Sprague, dem. 1958/**Gaiety Theatre (I),** 1864 - 1903, Bassett Keeling (Strand MH) - 1868 Phipps, dem. 1903/**Gaiety Theatre (II),** 1903 - 1939, Runtz & Ford with Shaw, dem. 1957/**Gatti's Palace,** 1865 -1924, ?, - 1883 Bolton, bombed c. 1943 -dem. 1950/**Granville Theatre of Varieties,** 1898 - 1956, Matcham, 1971/**Greenwich Theatre Royal,** 1864 -1910, Noble, dem. 1937/**Hammersmith Palace,** 1880-1944, ? - 1898, Brutton 1910, Matcham, dem./**Holborn Empire,** 1857 - 1941, Hill & Paraire - 1887, Lander & Bedells - 1897, Runtz - 1906, Matcham, bombed 1941 -dem. 1961/**Holloway Empire,** 1899 -1924, Sprague, dem. c.1976/**Hounslow Empire,** 1912 - 1954, ?, dem. 1954/**Ilford Hippodrome,** 1909 -1941, Matcham, bombed 1941, dem./**Imperial Theatre,** Canning Town, (before 1906 in Westminster), 1909 (re-erected) - 1931, Verity, burnt down 1931/**Islington Empire,** 1860 -1932, Hill & Paraire - 1870, Hill & Paraire -1874, Hill & Paraire - 1883, Matcham -1888, Matcham - 1901 Matcham, dem. c.1962 (aud.) and 1981 (facade)/**Karsino,** 1913 - 1928, Matcham, dem. 1971/**Kennington Theatre,** 1898 -1949, Sprague, dem. 1949/**Kilburn Palace,** 1886 - 1909, ? - 1895 Fayer, 1899 Palgrave & Co. with Wylson & Long, dem./**King's Theatre** (Hammersmith), 1902 - 1955, Sprague, dem. 1963/**Kingsway Theatre,** 1882 -, T. Verity - 1900 Murray & Foster - 1907, Walker & Foster, bombed 1941 - dem. 1959/**Lewisham Hippodrome,** 1911 -c.1950, Matcham, dem. 1961/**Little Theatre,** 1910 - 1941, Hayward & Maynard - 1912 Hayward & Maynard -1920 Hayward & Maynard, bombed 1941 - dem. 1949/**Marlborough Theatre,** 1903 -1919, Matcham, dem. 1962/**Marylebone Music Hall,** 1903 - 1919, Matcham, dem. 1962/**Metropolitan Music Hall,** 1836 - 1962, ? - 1862, ? Clark - 1880s, Emden - 1897, Matcham - 1908, dem. 1963/**Mile End Empire,** before 1850 - 1933, ? - 1885, Matcham, dem. 1937/**New Cross Empire,** 1899 -c.1950, Matcham, dem. late 1950s/**Oxford Music Hall,** 1861 - 1926, Hill & Paraire -1873, Paraire - 1893, Wylson & Long, dem. 1926/**Parkhurst Theatre,** 1890 -1909, Driver & Perfect, dem./**Pavilion, Whitechapel** 1828 - 193/ ? - 1856, Simmonds - 1874 Robinso ₍ -1894 Runtz (? & Phipps), bombed, dem. 1962/**Peckham Hippodrome,** 1898 -1912, Runtz, dem. 1930s (replaced, cinema)/**Princess's Theatre,** 1840 -1902, Nelson/Duncan -1880, Phipps, ? 1883, ? Buckle, 1897 Johnson & Moore, closed 1902, dem. 1931/**Putney Hippodrome,** 1906 - 1924, Hingston, dem. 1975//-**Queen's Theatre** (Poplar), 1856 - c.1958, ? - 1898 Crewe -1904 Crewe, dem. 1964/**Regent, Euston,** 1900 - c.1932, Sprague, dem./**Rotunda,** c.1826 (conv.) -1883, ? - dem. 1950s/**Royal Artillery Theatre,** Woolwich, 1863 (conv.) -c.1906, Noble (conv. hall by T.H. Wyatt), 1904, Sprague, closed 1956, dem./**Royal Cambridge Music Hall,** 1864 - c.1924, Finch Hill - 1878, Robinson - 1885. Clarke -1898, Percival, dem. 1936/**Royal County Theatre,** Kingston, 1897 - 1912, ?, fire 1940/**Royal Hotel Theatre,** 1888 -c.1914, Woodrow, dem./**Royalty Theatre,** 1840 -1938, Beazley - 1861 Bulot -1883 T Verity - 1895 Emden -1906 Smee & Cobay -1911, Gissing, closed 1938, dem. 1953/**St. George's Hall,** 1867 - 1940, Taylor - 1881, Tasker - 1905 ? -bombed 1941, dem./**St. James's Theatre,** 1835 -1957, Beazley - 1869, Macintosh - 1880, T. Verity - 1900 Jackson & Emblin -Walker with Macquoid, dem. 1957/**Savoy Theatre** (Uxbridge) 1873 -1921, ?, dem. (replaced, cinema)/**Scala Theatre,** 1810 (conv.) -1969, ? - 1831, ? -1865, ? -1904, F.T. Verity, dem. 1969/**Sebright Music Hall,** 1865 - 1910, ? - 1885, Buckle, dem. 1938/**Shakespeare Theatre** (Battersea), 1896 - 1923, Sprague, dem. 1956/**Shoreditch Empire,** (the London), 1856 - 1934, ? - 1894 Matcham, dem. 1935/**Shoreditch Olympia,** (Standard), 1837 - 1926, ? - 1867, ? - 1876, ? - 1888, Crewe, bombed 1940, dem./**South London Palace,** 1860 (conv.) - 1941, ? - 1869, Paice - 1893, Wylson & Long, bombed 1941 - dem. 1955/**Star, Bermondsey,** 1867 -1919, ? - 1883 Snooke & Stock, dem. 1963/**Stoll Theatre,** 1911 - 1957, Crewe dem. 1957, (replaced)/**Strand Theatre,** 1832 (Long) -1905, Broad - 1858 Reynolds - 1865 Ellis, 1882 Phipps, dem. 1905/**Streatham Grand,** 1888 -1940, Hollands, dem. 1973/**Surrey Theatre,** 1782 - 1920, ? - ? -1805 Cabanel - 1809, ? - 1810, ? -1852, Archer -1865 Ellis - 1904, Kirk & Kirk, dem. 1934/**Swallow Street Music Hall,** before 1860 - 1903, ?, dem. 1919/**Terry's Theatre,** 1887 - 1910, Emden, 1905 Matcham, dem. 1923/**Tivoli,** 1890 - 1914, Emden -1891, Matcham - 1900, Emden -1910, Emden, dem. 1957/**Variety Theatre,** Hoxton, 1870 -1910, Phipps -1882, Buckle -1887, Buckle - 1902, Wylson & Long, 1909 Crewe - 1913, Ward & Ward, dem. 1981/**Walthamstow Palace,** 1903 -1954, Wylson & Long, dem. 1960/**West London Theatre,** 1832 -1932, ?, bombed 1941 - dem. 1974/**Willesden Hippodrome,** 1907 -1927, Matcham, bombed 1940 - dem. 1957/**Winter Garden Theatre,** 1841 (Saloon) - 1960, ? - 1847, ? - 1872, ? -1880, Wright - 1891, ? - 1911, Matcham dem. 1965 (replaced)/**Wonderland,** (East London) 1834 - 1897, ? - 1846, Palmer -1852, Hudson - 1855, Lucas -1867, Hudson -1880, ? - dem./**Woolwich Empire,** 1835 - 1960, ? -1880s, J. O. Cook - 1895, Clark -1900, Matcham, dem. 1960/**Woolwich Hippodrome,** 1900 - 1923, Crewe, dem. 1939, (replaced, cinema).

LONG EATON, Derbyshire
Palace Theatre, 1907 - 1936, Ross, dem.

LOUGHBOROUGH, Leicestershire
New Theatre Royal, 1904 - 1930, King, dem. 1978.

LUTON, Bedfordshire
Alexandra Theatre, 1880 - c.1900, ?, dem. 1935/Grand Theatre, 1898 - 1957, Stoppe, dem. 1959.

MACCLESFIELD, Cheshire
Theatre Royal, 1882 - 1931, ?, fire 1931.

MAIDSTONE, Kent
Hippodrome, 1900 - 1908, ?, fire 1908/Palace Theatre, 1908 - 1914, ?, dem. 1957.

MANCHESTER, Greater Manchester
Ardwick Empire, 1904 - 1930, Matcham, dem. 1964/Chorlton Pavilion, 1904 -1916, ?, dem./Gaiety Theatre, 1884 -1922, Darbyshire - 1908 Matcham, dem. 1959/Grand Theatre, c.1883 - 1916, ?, dem./Hippodrome, 1904 - 1935, Matcham, dem. 1935/King's Theatre, 1905 -1933, Alley, dem./Metropole Theatre, 1898 - 1938, Alley, dem./Midland Hotel Theatre, 1903 - 1914, ?, dismantled 1914/Queen's Theatre, 1891 - 1911, ?, dem./Prince's Theatre, 1864 - 1940, Solomons - 1901 Darbyshire & Smith, dem./Queen's Park Hippodrome, 1904 -1965, Alley, dem. 1965/Tivoli Theatre, 1845 - 1921, ? - 1897 Percival, fire 1921 -dem. 1937.

MANSFIELD, Nottinghamshire
Empire Theatre, 1914 - 1960, ?, dem. 1973/Hippodrome, 1906 - ?, dem. 1979.

MARGATE, Kent
Grand Hall-By-The-Sea, 1874 - 1932, Clark, fire 1932/Hippodrome, 1896 -1958, Hope & Maxwell, dem. 1974/Pier Pavilion, 1893 - 1970, ?, storm damage 1970.

MEXBROUGH, South Yorkshire
Hippodrome, 1893 - 1939, ?, dem.

MIDDLESBROUGH, Cleveland
Grand Opera House, 1903 - 1930, Hope & Maxwell, dem. 1964/Oxford Palace, 1867 - 1907, ?, bombed 1941/Theatre Royal, 1866 - 1930, Blessley - 1900 Hope & Maxwell, dem. 1978.

MORECAMBE, Lancashire
Central Pier Pavilion, 1897 - 1933, ?, fire 1933/Royalty Theatre, 1898 - 1957, Matcham dem. 1957/Tower Pavilion, 1902 -1939, ?, dem./West End Pier Theatre, 1893 - 1917, ?, fire 1917.

MORLEY, West Yorkshire
New Pavilion Theatre, 1911 - 1913, ?, fire 1913.

MOTHERWELL, Strathclyde
New Century Theatre, 1902 - 1934, Cullen, dem. 1934/Olympia Theatre, 1902 - 1938, ?, dem.

NELSON, Lancashire
Majestic Theatre, 1910 - 1925, ?, dem. 1962/.

NEW BRIGHTON
Palace Theatre, 1881 - 1916, ?, dem./Tivoli Theatre, 1914 - 1978, ?, dem. 1978/Tower Grand Theatre, 1898 - 1925, ?, fire 1945.

NEWCASTLE-UNDER-LYME, Staffordshire
Theatre Royal, 1787 - 1910, dem. 1960's.

NEWCASTLE-UPON-TYNE, Tyne & Wear
Empire Palace, 1890 - 1963, Oliver & Leeson - 1903 Matcham, dem. 1963/Grand Theatre, 1908 - 1964, ?, dem./Grand Theatre (Byker) 1896 - 1954, Hope, dem./Hippodrome, 1912 - ?, ?, dem./Olympia, 1893 - 1903, ?, 1903 Matcham, dem. 1971/Queen's Theatre, 1913 - ?, ?, dem./Theatre Royal, Nelson Place, 1787 - 1910, Pepper, dem. 1960/Vaudeville Theatre, - 1900, ?, fire 1900.

NORTHAMPTON, Northamptonshire
Grapho's Theatre, ? - 1914, ?, fire 1914/New Theatre, 1912 - 1958, Sprague, dem. 1960/Palace of Varieties, 1860 -1913, ?, dem. c.1950.

NORTH SHIELDS, Tyne and Wear
Borough Theatre, 1902 - 1920, ?, dem. 1910/Central Palace of Varieties, 1910 -1927, Hope & Maxwell, dem./Theatre Royal (Prudhoo Street), 1879 - 1932, ?, dem. 1939.

NORWICH, Norfolk
Hippodrome, 1903 ... 1960, Sprague, dem. 1966/Theatre Royal, 1826 - 1934, W. Wilkins, fire 1934. (replaced)

NOTTINGHAM, Nottinghamshire
Empire, 1898 - 1958, Matcham, dem. 1969/St. George's Music Hall, 1884 -1902, ?, dem.

OLDHAM, Greater Manchester
Royal Court Theatre, 1892 - 1906, ?, fire 1906/Royal Court Theatre, 1907 -1960, Turner, dem. 1966/Theatre Royal, 1888 -1954, Cook, dem. 1967.

OXFORD, Oxfordshire
New Theatre, 1886 Drinkwater - 1908 - 1933, Sprague, dem. 1933. (replaced)

PAIGNTON, Devon
Oldway House Theatre, 1873 - 1904, Bridgman & Matcham, dismantled 1904/Pier Pavilion, 1879 - 1919, ?, fire 1919.

PAISLEY, Strathclyde
Hippodrome, 1906 - 1916, ?, fire 1916/Paisley Theatre, 1890 - 1959, ?, dem. 1960s.

PETERBOROUGH, Cambridgeshire
Theatre Royal, 1899 - 1959, Pye & Hayward (as an skating rink 1872) - 1899 Briggs, dem. 1961.

PLYMOUTH, Devon
Empire Theatre, 1980 - 1941, Phipps, bombed 1941/Grand Theatre, 1889 -1910, Stoell, dem. 1963/Hippodrome, 1908 - 1941, Crewe, bombed 1941/Promenade Pier Pavilion, 1891 -1941?, bombed 1941/Theatre Royal, 1879 - 1937, ?, dem. 1939.

PONTYPRIDD, Mid-Glamorgan
County Theatre, 1911 - 1939, ?, dem. 1939 (replaced)/Royal Clarence Theatre, 1890 -1911, ?, dem. 1911.

PORTSMOUTH, Hampshire
Clarence Esplanade Pier Theatre, 1882 -1941, ?, bombed 1941/Empire Theatre, 1891 - 1958, ?, dem. 1958/Hippodrome, 1908 - 1941, Crewe, bombed 1941/Prince's Theatre, 1892 - 1940, Matcham, bombed 1941/South Parade Pier Theatre, 1878 - 1904, ?, fire 1904/South Parade Pier Theatre, 1908 - 1967, gutted by fire during filming. 1974/Vento's Temple of Varieties, 1875 - 1912, dem. 1979.

PRESTON, Lancashire
Empire Theatre, 1911 - 1930, Bush, Hope & Tasker, dem. 1976/Hippodrome, 1905 - 1957, ?, dem. 1957/New King's Palace, 1913 - 1955, ?, dem. 1964/Prince's Theatre, 1900 - 1930, Mumford, dem. 1964/Theatre Royal, 1901 - 1927, Briggs, dem. 1927.

RAMSGATE, Kent
Promenade Pier Pavilion 1879 - 1917, ?, damaged in collision 1917.

RAWENSTALL, Lancashire
Grand Theatre, 1898 - 1937, Darbyshire & Smith, dem. 1937.

READING, Berkshire
Palace Theatre, 1907 - 1959, Sprague, dem. 1961/Royal County Theatre, 1895 -1937, Matcham, fire 1937.

RHYL, Clwyd
Grand Pavilion, 1891 - 1901, ?, fire 1901/Pavilion, ? - 1972, ?, dem. 1974.

RINGWOOD, Hampshire
Manor House Theatre, ? - 1914, ?, fire 1914.

ROCHDALE, Greater Manchester
New Hippodrome, 1908 - 1930, Hardman, dem./Theatre Royal, 1895 - 1954, ?, fire 1954.

ROTHERHAM, South Yorkshire

New Hippodrome, 1908 - 1932, ?, dem. 1960/Theatre Royal, 1894 - 1929, Platts & Rawmarsh, dem. 1957.

RUNCORN, Cheshire

Theatre Royal, 1869 - 1906, ?, fire 1906.

RYDE, Isle of Wight

Theatre Royal, 1871 - 1961, ?, fire 1961.

ST. ANNES, Lancashire

Ashton Pavilion Theatre, ? - 1977, ?, fire 1977/Pavilion, 1904 - 1974, ?, fire 1974.

SALFORD, Greater Manchester

Hippodrome, 1906 - 1962, Alley, dem. 1962/Palace Theatre, 1895 - 1929, Matcham, fire 1952.

SANDGATE, Kent

Alhambra Theatre, 1858 - 1914, ?, dem. 1962.

SANDOWN, Isle of Wight

Pier Pavilion, ? - 1919, ?, fire 1919.

SCARBOROUGH, North Yorkshire

Londesborough Theatre, 1871 - 1914, ?, dem. 1914/Theatre Royal, c.1767 - 1924, ?, dem. 1928.

SEAHAM, County Durham

Theatre Royal, 1873 - 1901, ?, dem. 1901.

SEVENOAKS, Kent

Club Hall Theatre, c.1889 - 1940, ?, bombed 1940.

SHEERNESS, Kent

Hippodrome, 1851 ... 1955, ?, dem. 1970.

SHEFFIELD, South Yorkshire

Adelphi Theatre, 1823 - 1914, Hurst & Woodhead - 1865 Hadfield & Sons, dem. 1914/Empire Theatre, 1895 - 1959, Matcham, dem. 1959/Hippodrome, 1907 - ?, Crewe, dem. 1963/Theatre Royal (Tudor Street), ? - 1935, ? - 1901 Matcham, fire 1935.

SHIPLEY, West Yorkshire

Queen's Palace of Varieties, 1907 -1913, ?, dem.

SKEGNESS, Lincolnshire

King's Theatre, 1912 - 1932, Owen & Ward, dem. 1936.

SMETHWICK, West Midlands

Theatre Royal, 1897 - 1932, Owen & Ward, dem. 1936.

SOUTHAMPTON, Hampshire

Empire Theatre, 1850 - 1927, ? - 1877 Mitchell, dem. 1927 (replaced)/Grand Theatre, 1898 - 1959, ?, dem. 1960/Hippodrome, 1883 - 1939, ?, bombed 1940/Palace of Varieties, 1897 - 1940, Emden, bombed 1940.

SOUTHEND-ON-SEA, Essex

Hippodrome, 1909 - 1936, Crewe, dem. c.1960/Pier Pavilion, 1889 - 1959, Brunkes, fire 1959.

SOUTHPORT, Merseyside

Opera House, 1891 - 1931, Matcham, fire 1931/Pier Pavilion, 1902 - 1933, ?, fire 1933/Scala Theatre, 1877 - 1909, ?, dem. 1962.

SOUTH SHIELDS, Tyne and Wear

Queen's Theatre, 1913 - 1941, Gibson & Steinlet, bombed 1941.

SPENNYMOORE, County Durham

Hippodrome, - 1909, ?, fire 1909.

STOCKPORT, Greater Manchester

Grand Theatre, 1867 - 1904, ?, dem. 1904/Hippodrome, 1905 ... 1957, ?, fire 1960/Theatre Royal, 1888 - 1957, Matcham, dem. 1960.

STOCKTON-ON-TEES, Cleveland

Castle Theatre, 1908 - 1914, ?, dem. 1968/Grand Theatre, 1875 - 1936, ?, dem.

STOKE-ON-TRENT, Staffordshire

Alexandra Music Hall, 1880 - 1924, ?, dem. 1960s/Crown Theatre, - 1900, ?, dem. 1900/Grand Theatre, 1898 - 1932, Matcham, fire 1932/Garden Theatre 1900 -1929, Lynam & Beckett, dem. 1965/Hippodrome 1911 - 1940, ?, dem. 1949/Music Hall, 1914 - ?, dem. 1960s/Wedgwood Theatre, - 1911, ?, dem. 1911.

STOURBRIDGE, West Midlands

Alhambra, ? - 1929, ?, dem. c.1975.

STRATFORD-UPON-AVON, Warwickshire

Hippodrome, 1912 - 1932, Homes & Lucas, dem. 1975.

STROUD, Gloucestershire

Empire Theatre, 1913 - 1927, ?, dem.

SUNDERLAND, Tyne & Wear

Avenue Theatre, 1882 - 1933, ? - 1894 Milburn, dem./King's Theatre, 1906 -1943, Hope, bombed 1943 - dem. 1960/Palace Theatre, 1891 - 1956, Moore, dem. 1973/Victoria Hall, 1872 -1883 & 1906 - 1941, ?, bombed 1941 (183 children crushed to death)/Wear Music Hall, 1868 - 1902, ?, collapsed 1902.

SWANSEA, West Glamorgan

Empire, 1900 - 1957, Emden, dem. 1960/Star Theatre, 1902 - 1931, ?, dem. 1973.

SWINDON, Wiltshire

Queen's Theatre, 1898 - 1929, Milverton Drake & Pizey, dem. 1959.

TIPTON, West Midlands

Regal Music Hall, ? - 1958, ?, dem. 1960.

TONYPANDY, Mid-Glamorgan

Theatre Royal, - 1912, ?, dem.

TROWBRIDGE, Wiltshire

New Theatre, 1914 - 1936, ?, dem. 1936.

WAKEFIELD, West Yorkshire

Hippodrome, 1909 - 1916, ?, dem.

WALSALL, West Midlands

Grand Theatre, 1873 - 1931, ? - 1890 Arnell, fire 1939/Her Majesty's Theatre, 1900 - 1933, ?, dem. 1937.

WARRINGTON, Cheshire

Music Hall (Market Place), 1773 -?, dem. 1978/Royal Court Theatre, 1892 -1906, Bland, Darbyshire & Smith, fire 1906/Royal Court Theatre, 1907 - 1957, Smith, dem. 1960.

WELLINGBOROUGH, Northamptonshire

Empire Music Hall, 1909 - 1910, fire 1910.

WEST BROMWICH, West Midlands

Empire, 1914 - ?, ?, dem./New Hippodrome, 1906 - 1922, ?, dem. 1922/Theatre Royal, 1896 - 1940, Owen & Ward, dem. c.1967.

WEYMOUTH, Dorset

Jubilee Hall, 1887 - 1926, Crickmay & Sons, dem. 1926/Kursaal Theatre, 1905 -1963, ?, dem. 1963/Pavilion Theatre, 1908 - 1940, Mangnall & Littlewood, fire 1954.

WHITEHAVEN, Cumbria

Royal Standard Music Hall, 1870 - 1954, ?, dem. 1954/Theatre Royal, 1769 - 1930, ?, dem. 1976.

WIGAN, Greater Manchester

Hippodrome, 1904 - 1935, Owen & Ward - 1909 Thornley, fire 1956.

WOLVERHAMPTON, West Midlands

Empire, 1898 - 1956, Owen & Ward, fire 1956.

WORCESTER, Hereford & Worcester

Empire Music Hall, 1889 - 1914, ?, dem./Theatre Royal, 1875 - 1960, Phipps - 1878 Phipps - 1903 Rowe, dem. 1960.

WORTHING, West Sussex

Pier Pavilion, 1889 - 1926, Mansergh, dem. 1926/Theatre Royal, 1897 - 1929, Cooke, dem.

YORK, North Yorkshire

Rialto, 1910 - 1935, ?, fire 1935.

Maps

The maps show where the principal pre-1914 theatres are to be found. Only 140 theatres are shown, all those awarded ★ ★ ★ —'a very fine theatre or, music hall of the highest theatrical quality', or ★ ★ —'a fine theatre or music hall etc. which is an excellent example of its type'. Hence the maps do **not** show every surviving theatre, simply the good ones. If a theatre does not appear on the map please consult the Gazetteer. It should be apparent why it does not fall in the ★ ★ ★ or ★ ★ category.

The names of town and theatre are printed in **bold** if they are in theatrical use, in light type if disused but restorable.

As elsewhere in the Gazetteer and the Historical Profile Roman type is used for conventional theatres with attributes appropriate to their age, e.g. flytower, proscenium and, raked stalls and one or more balconies. *Italic* type is used for all other auditoriums: music halls, circus theatres, private theatres occasionally used by professionals, pier theatres, Kursaals and other flat floor theatres.

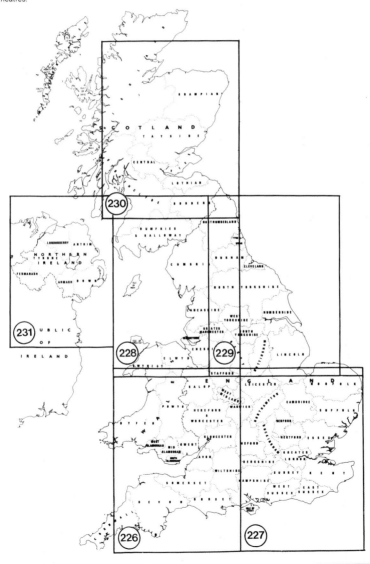

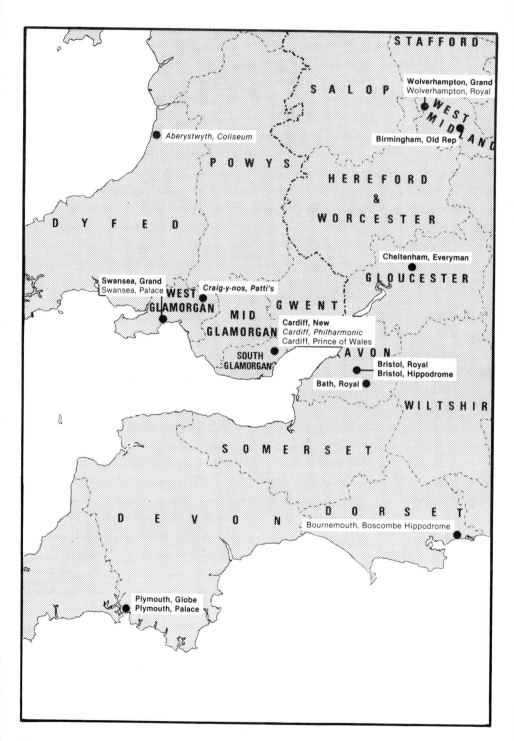

STAFFORD

SALOP

Wolverhampton, Grand
Wolverhampton, Royal

WEST MIDLAND

Aberystwyth, Coliseum

POWYS

Birmingham, Old Rep

HEREFORD
&
WORCESTER

DYFED

Cheltenham, Everyman

GLOUCESTER

Swansea, Grand
Swansea, Palace

Craig-y-nos, Patti's

WEST GLAMORGAN

GWENT

MID GLAMORGAN

Cardiff, New
Cardiff, Philharmonic
Cardiff, Prince of Wales

SOUTH GLAMORGAN

AVON

Bristol, Royal
Bristol, Hippodrome

Bath, Royal

WILTSHIR

SOMERSET

DEVON

DORSET

Bournemouth, Boscombe Hippodrome

Plymouth, Globe
Plymouth, Palace

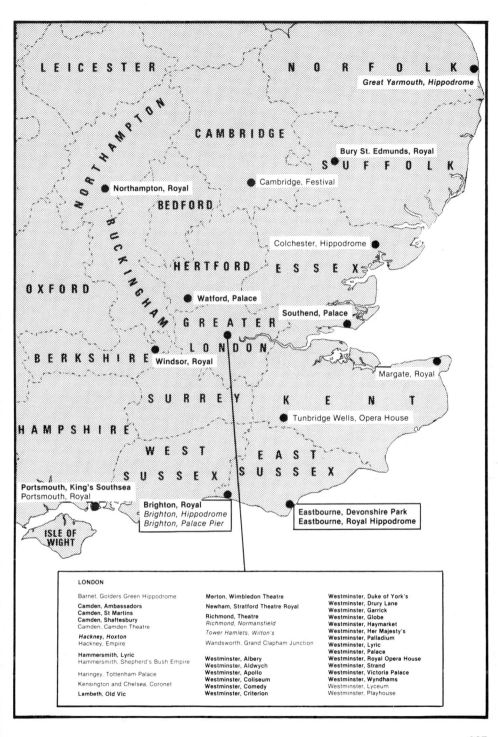

LEICESTER

NORFOLK

Great Yarmouth, Hippodrome

NORTHAMPTON

CAMBRIDGE

Bury St. Edmunds, Royal

SUFFOLK

Northampton, Royal

Cambridge, Festival

BEDFORD

BUCKINGHAM

Colchester, Hippodrome

HERTFORD ESSEX

OXFORD

Watford, Palace

Southend, Palace

BERKSHIRE GREATER LONDON

Windsor, Royal

Margate, Royal

SURREY KENT

HAMPSHIRE

Tunbridge Wells, Opera House

WEST SUSSEX EAST SUSSEX

Portsmouth, King's Southsea
Portsmouth, Royal

Brighton, Royal
Brighton, Hippodrome
Brighton, Palace Pier

Eastbourne, Devonshire Park
Eastbourne, Royal Hippodrome

ISLE OF WIGHT

LONDON

Barnet, Golders Green Hippodrome

Camden, Ambassadors
Camden, St Martins
Camden, Shaftesbury
Camden, Camden Theatre

Hackney, Hoxton
Hackney, Empire

Hammersmith, Lyric
Hammersmith, Shepherd's Bush Empire

Haringey, Tottenham Palace

Kensington and Chelsea, Coronet

Lambeth, Old Vic

Merton, Wimbledon Theatre

Newham, Stratford Theatre Royal

Richmond, Theatre
Richmond, Normansfield

Tower Hamlets, Wilton's

Wandsworth, Grand Clapham Junction

Westminster, Albery
Westminster, Aldwych
Westminster, Apollo
Westminster, Coliseum
Westminster, Comedy
Westminster, Criterion

Westminster, Duke of York's
Westminster, Drury Lane
Westminster, Garrick
Westminster, Globe
Westminster, Haymarket
Westminster, Her Majesty's
Westminster, Palladium
Westminster, Lyric
Westminster, Palace
Westminster, Royal Opera House
Westminster, Strand
Westminster, Victoria Palace
Westminster, Wyndhams
Westminster, Lyceum
Westminster, Playhouse

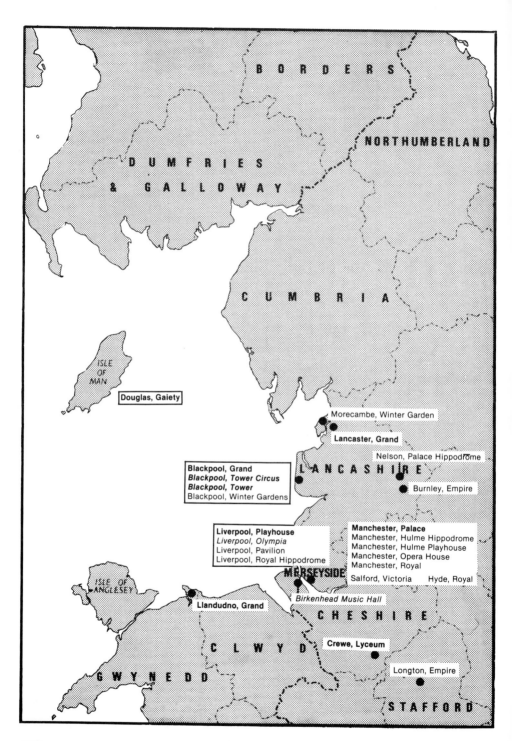

ISLE
OF
MAN

Douglas, Gaiety

Morecambe, Winter Garden

Lancaster, Grand

Nelson, Palace Hippodrome

LANCASHIRE

Blackpool, Grand
Blackpool, Tower Circus
Blackpool, Tower
Blackpool, Winter Gardens

Burnley, Empire

Liverpool, Playhouse
Liverpool, Olympia
Liverpool, Pavilion
Liverpool, Royal Hippodrome

Manchester, Palace
Manchester, Hulme Hippodrome
Manchester, Hulme Playhouse
Manchester, Opera House
Manchester, Royal

Salford, Victoria   Hyde, Royal

MERSEYSIDE

Birkenhead Music Hall

ISLE OF
ANGLESEY

Llandudno, Grand

CHESHIRE

CLWYD

Crewe, Lyceum

GWYNEDD

Longton, Empire

STAFFORD

BORDERS

NORTHUMBERLAND

DUMFRIES
& GALLOWAY

CUMBRIA

Blyth, Royal

Wallsend, Borough

TYNE
Newcastle, Tyne
Newcastle, Royal WEAR

Consett, Globe Music Hall

Sunderland, Empire

D U R H A M

Middlesbrough, Empire

Darlington, Civic CLEVELAND

Richmond, Georgian

Scarborough, Opera House

N O R T H   Y O R K S H I R E

Harrogate, Opera House
Harrogate, Royal Hall

York, Royal
York, Empire

Leeds, Grand
Leeds, City Varieties

Bradford, Alhambra

HUMBERSIDE

Halifax, Civic W E S T
Y O R K S H I R E

Wakefield, Opera House

Barnsley, Royal

S O U T H
Y O R K S H I R E

Doncaster, Grand

Sheffield, Lyceum

Buxton, Opera House

Lincoln, Royal

Chatsworth, Theatre

L I N C O L N

N O T T I N G H A M

Nottingham, Royal

S T A F F O R D

Derby, Hippodrome

229

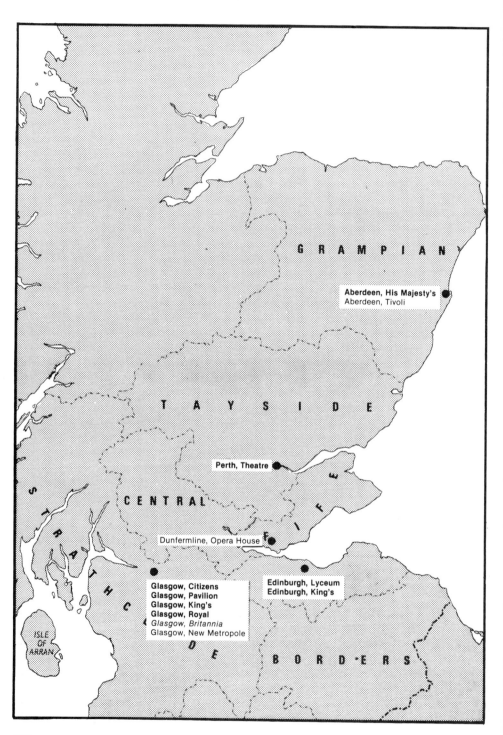

G R A M P I A N

Aberdeen, His Majesty's
Aberdeen, Tivoli

T A Y S I D E

Perth, Theatre

C E N T R A L

F I F E

Dunfermline, Opera House

S T R A T H C L Y D E

Glasgow, Citizens
Glasgow, Pavilion
Glasgow, King's
Glasgow, Royal
Glasgow, Britannia
Glasgow, New Metropole

Edinburgh, Lyceum
Edinburgh, King's

ISLE
OF
ARRAN

B O R D E R S

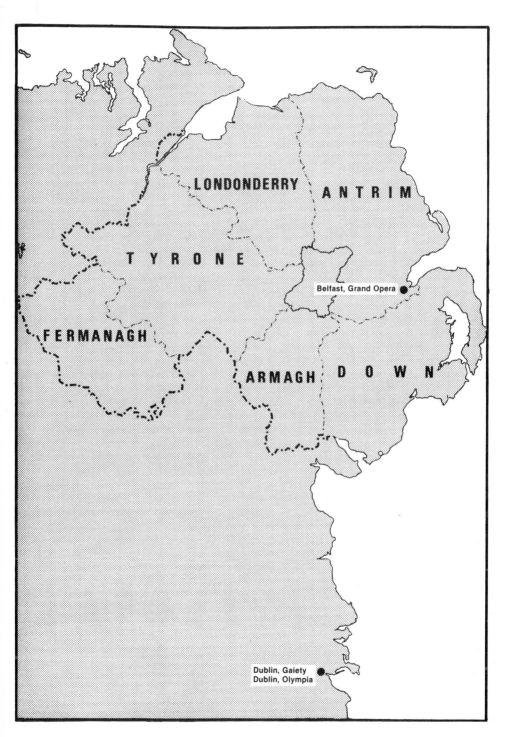

LONDONDERRY

ANTRIM

TYRONE

Belfast, Grand Opera ●

FERMANAGH

ARMAGH D O W N

Dublin, Gaiety
Dublin, Olympia ●

Summary

of starred theatres, excluding "★ Facade only"

	London	England & Islands	Scotland	Wales	Ireland	Total
★ ★ ★ in use	21	25	7	3	3	59
★ ★ ★ disused	3	17	2	2	-	24
★ ★ in use	7	17	1	1	-	26
★ ★ disused	8	18	2	2	-	30
Total ★ ★ ★ & ★ ★	39	77	12	8	3	139
★ in use	2	7	2	1	-	12
★ disused	5	6	1	3	-	15
Grand Totals	46	90	15	12	3	166

The key 139 theatres (★ ★ ★ and ★ ★) are divided into 85 in use and 54 disused and restorable. The 166 starred theatres of all categories divide into 97 in use and 69 disused and restorable.

The non starred entries and " ★ Facade only" entries in the main Gazetteer plus the whole of the Demolished List total over 800. About 65 of these refer to fragments of theatres that were closed long before 1900 leaving over 735 theatres which were in use 1900 to 1914 but which have not been either demolished or irreparably altered. Since there can be no doubt that there were some theatres which can not be traced at all, either as fragments or demolitions (especially in the *Italic* group) it can be said that Britain has lost approximately 840 of the 1000 theatres thought to be in operation between 1900 and 1914.

Acknowledgements

The **Curtains!!!** Committee is a completely independent ad-hoc group created solely to produce this Gazetteer and the associated travelling exhibition. Its members are unpaid but have had some of their expenses refunded from a fund set up to help pay for research costs common to both book and exhibition and to pay for the latter.

The principal benefactors have been the Arts Council of Great Britain, the Ernest Cook Trust and the Chase Charity. To these organisations and to their officers, chairmen and trustees the **Curtains!!!** Committee gives grateful thanks.

Equally important to the project has been the support and confidence of three groups of people: the publisher, John Offord, and his staff; the Museum of London which hosts the launching of the exhibition in March 1982 and the 'umbrella' organisation for **Curtains!!!**, SAVE Britain's Heritage, whose aims, approach and attitude it shares.

This book carries advertising, a device which ensures that the price is kept down to that acceptable for a Guide Book. To all the advertisers the **Curtains!!!** Committee extends its thanks and in particular to one, Bovis Construction Limited, who has made a special contribution to the project sufficient to pay for the 8 page colour section. Bovis have successfully renovated three important theatres in Bristol, Nottingham, and Buxton, using the Bovis Fee System Management Contract, a particular approach to building which, by reason of track record, is worth studying by any architect or client contemplating restoration of a pre-1914 theatre.

The two cut open isometric drawings of the Festival Theatre, Cambridge on pages 202 and 203 are taken from a new series of some 65 reconstructions illustrating the world wide development of theatre architecture from Ancient Greece to the present day in **Theatres and Playhouses,** drawn and written by Richard Leacroft, author of **The Development of the English Playhouse**. The **Curtains!!!** Committee are most grateful to Richard Leacroft for being allowed to be the first to reproduce these drawings.

In the introduction and key to the Gazetteer will be found explanation to the initials attached to entries. Here the Committee members would like to thank individuals who have given their time, knowledge and encouragement, some by contributing reports and others by helping setting up the project in the early stages: Colin Amery, Sophie Andreae, Geoffrey Ashton, David Atwell, Hendrik Baker, Marcus Binney, Ted Bottle, Harvey Crane, Mervyn Gould, Laurence Harbottle, Diana Howard, John Higgs, John Hutchinson, Elizabeth Grice, Mike Kilburn, James Dunbar-Nasmith, Graham Law, Peter Longman, Major Pare, Angus Stirling, Judith Strong, Bill Slinn and David Wilmore. To these names should be added those of librarians, planning officers and archivists throughout the country who patiently responded to demands for information.

The photographic credits are to found attached to each photograph. The Committee would like to thank all those who waived reproduction fees in particular the Architectural Review and the Greater London Council.

Lastly, the Committee would like to thank Theatre Projects for providing facilities for meetings and much photocopying and secretarial assistance through five long years.

I.M.

Short Biographical Notes

Principal Authors and Members of the Committee

CHRISTOPHER BRERETON is an architect at the Directorate of Ancient Monuments and Historic Buildings of the Department of the Environment and is therefore involved with a wide variety of historic buildings. Old theatres have long been a personal interest which led to his writing the seminal article **Act Now to Save Provincial Theatres** in the 1976 October issue of The Architectural Review. Part author of **Frank Matcham, Theatre Architect** (Blackstaff Press 1980). For **Curtains!!!** chief investigator, principal author and editor for the Gazetteer for Scotland, Wales and England outside of London.

DAVID F. CHESHIRE is the Faculty of Art & Design Librarian, Middlesex Polytechnic. He has compiled several extensive bibliographies on stage design and popular entertainment topics, the most recent being **British Music Hall 1840-1923** in collaboration with Laurence Senelick and Uri Schneider. His books include **Theatre: a reader's guide** and **Music Hall in Britain**. For **Curtains!!!** he has been principal archivist and initiator of the Demolitions and other check lists required for the progress of the project.

JOHN EARL is a building surveyor in the Greater London Council's Historic Buildings Division and has been professionally involved in various aspects of architectural conservation for over twenty five years. He was author of the London chapter of **Frank Matcham, Theatre Architect**. For **Curtains!!!** he was principal author and editor of the London section of the Gazetteer as well as being Honorary Treasurer.

VICTOR GLASSTONE is an architect, theatre consultant and historian who has been concerned exclusively with theatre architecture worldwide for over thirty years. His most recent theatre consultancies have been the Baxter Theatre, Cape Town and the Gaiety, Douglas Isle of Man. He has written extensively on theatre architecture for both specialist and national publications and has contributed to the theatrical encyclopaedias, **The Oxford Companion to the Theatre** and **Encyclopedia dello Spettacolo** and also to the recently published **Frank Matcham, Theatre Architect**. His books include **Victorian and Edwardian Theatres** (Thames and Hudson 1975) and **The London Coliseum**. Active committee member of The Society for Theatre Research, Theatres Advisory Council and the Housing the Arts Committee of the Arts Council of Great Britain. For **Curtains!!!** principal photographer and photographic editor as well as co-founder of the project.

IAIN MACKINTOSH started the Prospect Theatre Company in 1961 and in the next twelve years took Prospect on tour to twenty one countries to perform in one hundred and twenty five theatres, some new but mostly fine old theatres. Since 1973 he has put this experience to work and as a director of Theatre Projects Consultants has been as much concerned with planning for the future (his own design studies including the Cottesloe, the new South Hill Park Theatre, Bracknell and two major theatres in Canada) as restoring the past (old theatres in Nottingham, Buxton, Hammersmith and Bury St. Edmunds). Previous exhibitions devised include **The Georgian Playhouse 1730-1830** at the Hayward in 1975 and the Garrick exhibition **30 Different Likenesses** at Buxton in 1981. Begetter of the **Curtains!!!** project he has been its Chairman since 1976 which has meant fund raising, devising the exhibition and being general editor of this book.

MICHAEL SELL is Head of the General Studies Department at Chichester College of Technology and an author and lecturer whose work includes a chapter for **Frank Matcham, Theatre Architect** and numerous articles and reviews. He lives in Bognor Regis and in addition to his involvement in theatre has a particular interest in sport. For **Curtains!!!** he has been Honorary Secretary and co-ordinating editor of this book.

Guest Contributors to this book

KEN DODD, OBE is one of this country's foremost entertainers. Although known primarily for his work in his own laughter shows and pantomime, and as the creator of the Diddymen, he also played Malvolio in the Liverpool Playhouse Diamond Jubilee production of 'Twelfth Night'. A tireless worker for the theatre, his assistance to a number of theatre trusts has been most significant; he was awarded an O.B.E. in the 1982 New Year's Honours List as an "entertainer and for charitable services". His work in theatre preservation is significant.

CLARE FERRABY and NICHOLAS THOMPSON have frequently worked as a husband and wife team of architect (partner with Renton, Howard, Wood, Levin Partnership) and interior designer (Clare Ferraby Designs). Their shared projects include new theatres (the Crucible Theatre, Sheffield and the Warwick Arts Centre) and restorations (the Theatre Royal Nottingham and The Duke of York's London). Clare Ferraby has also been responsible recently for the interior scheme of restoration of the Palace Theatre, Manchester and the Palace Theatre, Watford.

FRANCIS REID recently spent two and a half years as Administrator and General Manager of the Theatre Royal, Bury St. Edmunds. Before and since he has continued his careers as a freelance lighting designer in the West End (a skill first practised as Lighting Director of Glyndebourne from 1959 to 1968) and as lecturer on lighting and stage management at RADA (since 1965) and on regular occasions at the Canadian National Theatre School in Montreal. His books, published in both London and New York, include **Stage Lighting Handbook** and **Staging Handbook**.

DEREK SUGDEN joined the engineering practice of Ove Arup & Partners in 1953, leaving them to become a partner of Arup Associates, a multi-disciplinary firm of engineers, architects and quantity surveyors, on its formation in 1963. He is now also a principal of the newly created specialist practice of Arup Acoustics. In recent years he has led teams from Arups Associates on a number of conversions and restorations for the performing arts: the Maltings Concert Hall, Snape; the Henry Wood Hall, Southwark; the Theatre Royal, Glasgow and the Opera House, Buxton.

DAVID WILMORE graduated from Newcastle University in 1978 and immediately became involved in the work of a charitable trust dedicated to restoring and running the Tyne Theatre, Newcastle. In the last three years he has been able to combine a research degree in Victorian Stage Machinery with the actual physical restoration of the entire below and above stage systems of the Tyne Theatre which are now uniquely in Britain, in full working order. Consequently he has been consulted by other organisations on partial rescue or complete conservation of nineteenth century machinery elsewhere, in particular the Theatre Royal, Bath; the Alexandra Palace Theatre, Haringey and the Playhouse Theatre, Charing Cross.

Bibliography

Diana HOWARD — **London Theatres and Music Halls 1850 - 1950 -** Library Association 1970.

Richard LEACROFT — **Development of English Playhouse** - Eyre Methuen 1973.

Iain MACKINTOSH — **Pit, Boxes and Gallery - The Story of the Theatre Royal Bury St. Edmunds** - The National Trust 1979.

Raymond MANDER & Joe MITCHENSON — **Lost Theatres of London** - Hart Davis 1961 and 1963; New English Library 1975.

Raymond MANDER & Joe MITCHENSON — **Theatres of London** - New English Library 1975.

Edwin O. SACHS & E. A. E. WOODROW — **Modern Opera Houses and Theatres - London 1896 - 1898** - Arno Press NJ 1968.

F. H. W. SHEPPARD (ed) — **The Survey of London** (principally vols XXIX to XXXVI)

Richard SOUTHERN — **The Georgian Playhouse** - Pleiades 1948.

Victor GLASSTONE — **Victorian and Edwardian Theatres** - Thames and Hudson 1975.

Victor GLASSTONE — **The London Coliseum** - Chadwyck Healy 1980.

Brian WALKER (ed) — **Frank Matcham - Theatre Architect** - Blackstaff Press 1980.

David F. CHESHIRE — **Music Hall** - David & Charles 1979.

ASHTON & MACKINTOSH — **Georgian Playhouses 1730 - 1830 - a catalogue** - Arts Council of Great Britain 1975.

Christopher BRERETON — **Act Now - Architectural Review** 160 No. 956 - pp 216 - 22.

The Stage Guide 1912,

THE ERA — **London 1875 - 1920.**

Articles relevant to theatre buildings may be found in a number of periodicals e.g. Tabs, Sightline, Architectural Review, Architectural Journal, Theatre Notebook 1945 to date, The Builder, Building News etc.

THE SOCIETY
FOR
THEATRE
RESEARCH

provides a meeting point for all those—scholars, research workers, actors, producers and theatregoers—who are interested in its history and technique. It encourages further research into these subjects and is especially concerned to link it to modern theatre practice. Founded in 1948, the Society now occupies an established and authoritative position in the United Kingdom, and its world-wide membership is able to act as a clearing house for historical and technical information.

An Annual Publication is sent free to all individual and corporate members and, in addition, from time to time, smaller works in pamphlet form. One additional copy of each publication may be purchased by individual and corporate members at prices lower than those charged to the general public.

Theatre Notebook, an illustrated journal devoted to the history of the British theatre edited by Sybil Rosenfeld, William A. Armstrong and Michael Booth, is sent to all individual and corporate members. In addition to full-length articles *Theatre Notebook* also includes book reviews, correspondence, notes and queries.

Monthly Meetings are held in London during the winter for members, their guests and the general public. Lectures are followed by discussions. An Annual Public Lecture is given, usually in May, following the Annual General Meeting.

ANNUAL SUBSCRIPTIONS

Individual Members: The annual subscription is UK £12 (USA $30; Elsewhere £14) This is reduced to UK £10.50 (USA $26.25: Elsewhere £12) for all new members on first joining and thereafter on renewal if the subscription is paid before the end of the calendar year. The Society's year begins on the 1st October.

Corporate and Institutional Members, such as Colleges and Drama Schools: The annual subscription is UK £16 (USA $40; Elsewhere £18.50). Such members receive two copies of **Theatre Notebook.**

Life Membership is open to individual members at a subscription of UK £100 (USA $250; Elsewhere £120)

All enquiries to

THE SOCIETY FOR THEATRE RESEARCH
77 KINNERTON STREET, LONDON SW1X 3ED

KING'S THEATRE EDINBURGH

75 Years And Still Going Strong

Enquiries to:
Peter Sloman, Head of Theatres & Halls,
King's Theatre, Leven Street, Edinburgh. Tel: 031-229 9687.

GAIETY THEATRE · AYR

The **LITTLE THEATRE** with the **BIG REPUTATION**

Open All Year Round

570 Seats

For details please contact:
**Bernard Cotton, Theatre Manager,
Gaiety Theatre, Carrick Street, Ayr
Tel: Ayr 264630**

Proprietors: Kyle & Carrick District Council

ALHAMBRA
THEATRE · BRADFORD
RON CUSSONS
Entertainment Manager
City of Bradford Metropolitan Council

The Bradford Alhambra was opened in 1914 by Francis Laidler, the man who started this theatre's famous tradition of pantomime. Today the Alhambra is still the leading home of pantomime in the North and a famous entertainment centre.

Halifax Civic Theatre

1600 Seats ★ Licence & Buffet Bars
Box Office ★ Full Stage Facilities

Some of the artists who have appeared recently:

ANDY WILLIAMS ★ GLEN CAMPBELL ★ MANHATTAN TRANSFER
BUDDY RICH ★ JOE LOSS ★ THE SHADOWS
THE SPINNERS ★ CLEO LAINE
TONY CHRISTIE ★ CILLA BLACK

Enquiries Welcome

**Manager Robbie Robinson,
Asst. Manager Les Milner,
HALIFAX (0422) 51156.**

Metropolitan Borough of Calderdale

THE NORTH EAST'S PREMIER THEATRE

THEATRE ROYAL
Newcastle upon Tyne

194 Years of Theatre Royal
on the same street

Box Office (0632) 322061

A Grand conference offers you all the facilities you need... in style!

Leeds Grand Theatre, the North of England's most beautiful, glittering Victorian Theatre is situated in the centre of Leeds at the crossroads of the M1 and M62 motorway together with superb British Rail access. Inspired by the Opera Houses of Italy the Grand is a fine example of a Victorian Theatre whose highly ornate auditorium with curved balconies, theatre boxes, vaulted ceiling and rich crimson and gold decor offers a conference organiser – style, in the true sense of the word.

so flexible too...

The typical theatre seating, tiered into different levels retains an intimate group "feel" with good contact between platform and audience. Smaller numbers never feel "lost" or larger numbers are never too removed from the speakers. The Grand is an ideal venue for conferences from 500 to 1,500 delegates.

The facilities offered are considerable and well worth a visit, but to whet your appetite, consider these:

- Excellent technical and catering both backstage and front of house
- Eight licensed bars and coffee lounges
- 1,554 seater auditorium
- Stage with full counter-weight flying system (approximately 5,000 sq. ft). Proscenium Opening 31 ft. wide and 40 ft. high
- Grand Hall accommodating 160 persons (approx. 1400 sq.ft)
- Board Room for 20 persons
- The Grand Suite for 300 persons (approx. 3,000 sq.ft)
- Q-File, 200 Way Lighting Control System
- Complete range of Audio/Visual Equipment

- Full time Staff provide complete back up service
- Home of English National Opera North and the best Live International Entertainment

Theatre & Opera House Leeds

Leeds Grand Theatre & Opera House Ltd.
46 New Briggate, Leeds LS1 6NZ
Telephone (0532) 456300 or 456014

For Full Details please contact:
Warren Smith,
General Manager,

GRAND OPERA HOUSE, BELFAST

Designed by Frank Matcham and opened on 23 December 1895 — four other Matcham theatres in Britain having already opened in the same year.

After long use as a cinema, the Grand Opera House was completely restored by its present owners, the Arts Council of Northern Ireland, to become once again one of the great theatres of the United Kingdom, with the original splendour of its exterior and auditorium combined with the latest technical facilities. The Grand Opera House reopened on 15 September 1980, and has since been fulfilling its original purpose as a leading No 1 touring theatre.

"The tastefully restrained foyers and staircases lead to the magnificently restored auditorium, which shows Matcham at his best. It is by far the most notable surviving example of his oriental manner, or, indeed, of any theatre in the United Kingdom decorated in this style . . . the sinuous curves of the balconies, the super-imposed boxes crowned by onion domes, the arches under the richly framed panels of the ceiling, and the overall intricacy of the Indian-style plasterwork, combine to produce exactly the right atmosphere". (Christopher Brereton, one of the distinguished contributors to **Frank Matcham, Theatre Architect,** Ed. Brian Walker, Blackstaff Press, 1980)

A compact exhibition on the life and work of Matcham was mounted for the Belfast Festival in 1980, and since then has been continuously touring theatres and galleries in the United Kingdom. Enquiries as to availability should be made to Mr Brian Ferran, Arts Council of Northern Ireland, 181a Stranmillis Road, Belfast BT9 5DU.

All other enquiries to Mr Michael Barnes, General Administrator and Artistic Director, Grand Opera House, Belfast, Telephone (0232) 667687.

One of the Finest Theatres in the Country—
well equipped and well maintained

* * * *

Presenting

BALLET OPERA PLAYS MUSICALS PANTOMIME FILMS

throughout the year

* * * *

Seating Capacity 1600

Also available for hire by Concert Promoters,
Conference and Trade Show organisers, and
indoor Sporting Event Promoters
(Darts, Snooker etc.,)

Restaurant, Theatre Bars, Coffee Bar

All Enquiries:
RUSSELL E. HILLS (Director),
Empire Theatre,
Sunderland.
Telephone: 0783 42517.

Theatre Royal
the home of
Scottish Opera

The Theatre Royal Glasgow, designed by Charles John Phipps, is one of the most beautiful Victorian theatres in existence today. Purchased and refurbished by Scottish Opera in 1974, the theatre reopened in 1975 as the home of Scottish Opera and Scotland's only opera house — a distinction which it still carries to the present day.

The theatre also hosts visits from the Scottish Ballet, The National Theatre, Sadlers Wells Royal Ballet, The Scottish Chamber Orchestra and many other national touring companies and artists.

For full details contact:

Box Office
041-331 1234
CREDIT CARDS
041-332 9000

Student standby and party concessions usually available.

Theatre Royal Hope Street
Glasgow G2 3QA

The Society of Theatre Consultants

The Society, which was founded in 1964, is a fully professional organisation, dedicated to the improvement of the design of all categories of buildings for entertainment.

The renovation of fine old theatres is one of the most challenging and enjoyable tasks undertaken by members of the Society. The following theatres were or are being renovated with consultancy services provided by members of the Society of Theatre Consultants:

> His Majesty's, Aberdeen
> Grand Theatre and Opera House, Belfast
> Theatre Royal, Bristol
> Theatre Royal, Bury St. Edmunds
> Opera House, Buxton
> Everyman Theatre, Cheltenham
> Leas Cliff Hall, Folkestone
> Theatre Royal Glasgow
> Albery Theatre, London
> Criterion Theatre, London
> London Coliseum, London
> Lyric Theatre, Hammersmith, London
> The Playhouse, Charing Cross, London
> Wyndham's Theatre, London
> Palace Theatre, Manchester
> Theatre Royal, Nottingham

In order to assist potential clients in the selection of the Consultant most likely to be suitable for a particular job, the Secretary will send, upon request, a list of all members of the Society, giving details of each individual's experience, qualifications and fields of speciality. The address and telephone number of the Secretary is:

THE SOCIETY OF THEATRE CONSULTANTS
4-7 Great Pulteney Street, London W1R 3DF. Tel: 01-434 3904.

CURTAINS!!!

A brief glance at this book will show that there are still many gaps in our knowledge, and particularly of those buildings which have been demolished.

It is our hope that many of these gaps and much additional information will be supplied by you, the reader, and we should be extremely grateful if you could forward further information or bring any errors to our attention.

Name of Theatre ....

Additional details ....

....

....

....

....

....

....

....

....

....

....

....

....

....

....

....

From ....

....

....

Please forward to:
The Secretary, "Curtains!!!", c/o John Offord Publications, P.O. Box 64, Eastbourne, East Sussex BN21 3LW.
(If you do not wish to cut this sheet from your book, simply photocopy).

Will it be **Curtains!!!**
or a new life
for this old theatre?